Bitter the Chastening Rod

Bitter the Chastening Rod

Africana Biblical Interpretation after *Stony the Road We Trod* in the Age of BLM, SayHerName, and MeToo

Edited by

Mitzi J. Smith
Angela N. Parker
Ericka S. Dunbar Hill

LEXINGTON BOOKS/FORTRESS ACADEMIC
Lanham • Boulder • New York • London

Published by Lexington Books/Fortress Academic
Lexington Books is an imprint of The Rowman & Littlefield Publishing Group, Inc.
4501 Forbes Boulevard, Suite 200, Lanham, Maryland 20706
www.rowman.com

86-90 Paul Street, London EC2A 4NE, United Kingdom

Copyright © 2022 by The Rowman & Littlefield Publishing Group, Inc.

All rights reserved. No part of this book may be reproduced in any form or by any electronic or mechanical means, including information storage and retrieval systems, without written permission from the publisher, except by a reviewer who may quote passages in a review.

British Library Cataloguing in Publication Information Available

Library of Congress Cataloging-in-Publication Data

Names: Smith, Mitzi J. (Mitzi Jane), editor. | Parker, Angela N., 1971– editor. | Hill, Erika, 1985– editor.
Title: Bitter the chastening rod : Africana Biblical interpretation after stony the road we trod in the age of BLM, Sayhername, and Metoo / edited by Mitzi J. Smith, Angela N. Parker, Ericka Dunbar Hill.
Description: Lanham : Lexington Books/Fortress Academic, [2022] | Includes bibliographical references and index. | Summary: "In this book, Africana biblical scholars argue that race, class, gender, and sexuality still matter for doing biblical interpretation/translation, centering the socio-political and cultural contexts of Africana peoples negotiating life, death, and hope in the age of #BLM, #SayHerName, #MeToo, and a global pandemic"—Provided by publisher.
Identifiers: LCCN 2021055287 (print) | LCCN 2021055288 (ebook) | ISBN 9781978712003 (cloth) | ISBN 9781978712010 (epub)
Subjects: LCSH: Bible—Criticism, interpretation, etc.—Africa.
Classification: LCC BS511.3 .B627 2022 (print) | LCC BS511.3 (ebook) | DDC 220.6—dc23/eng/20220107
LC record available at https://lccn.loc.gov/2021055287
LC ebook record available at https://lccn.loc.gov/2021055288

Contents

PART I: REMEMBERING THE PAST, LABORING IN THE PRESENT, AND SHAPING A HOPEFUL FUTURE   1

Chapter 1: "The Hill We Climb": Introduction   3
Mitzi J. Smith, Angela N. Parker, and Ericka S. Dunbar Hill

Chapter 2: A Eulogy for Cain Hope Felder   15
Brian K. Blount

Chapter 3: *Zoom*-ing in on a Watershed Moment in Biblical Interpretation   25
William H. Myers

PART II: GOD'S BLACK(ENED) PEOPLE IN THE WORLD—THUGS, SLAVES, AND CRIMINALS   37

Chapter 4: God's Only Begotten Thug   39
Allen Dwight Callahan

Chapter 5: Abolitionist Messiah: A Man Named Jesus Born of a *Doulē*   53
Mitzi J. Smith

Chapter 6: Reading with the Enslaved: Placing Human Bondage at the Center of the Early Christian Story   71
Emerson B. Powery

Chapter 7: "I am a Human": Racializing Assemblages and Criminalized Egyptianness in Acts 21:31–39   91
Jeremy L. Williams

Chapter 8: The Terror of White Hermeneutics: Black and Enslaved Bodies Interpreted in the Context of Whiteness 109
Marcus W. Shields

PART III: AFRICANA HERMENEUTICAL STRATEGIES, PEDAGOGY, TRANSLATION, AND #BLM 123

Chapter 9: Hoodoo Blues and the Formulation of Hermeneutical Strategies for Contemporary Africana Biblical Engagement 125
Hugh R. Page, Jr.

Chapter 10: Reflections on Teaching Biblical Interpretation through a Black Lives Matter Hermeneutic 139
Wil Gafney

Chapter 11: Revisiting the Caananites and Contemporary *Ites*: Pedagogical Insights into Cheering for the Wrong Team 157
Theodore W. Burgh

Chapter 12: Reading Romans in Greek: Translating and Commenting on it in Haitian Creole 171
Ronald Charles

PART IV: BLACK RAGE AND PROTEST IN TIMES OF #BLACKLIVESMATTER AND #METOO 189

Chapter 13: Rage, Riots, and Rhetoric: Psalm 137 and African American Responses to Violence 191
Stacy Davis

Chapter 14: Rethinking "God-breathed" in the Age of #BLM: A Womanist Reading of 2 Tim 3:10–17 211
Angela N. Parker

Chapter 15: Leah and Dinah in the Face of Abuse: What Do I Tell My Daughter? 229
Kamilah Hall Sharp

Chapter 16: Antichrist and Anti-Black: 1 John and "Black Lives Matter" 245
Dennis R. Edwards

PART V: RESPONSES 257

Chapter 17: John's Apocalypse and African American Interpretation 259
Thomas B. Slater

Chapter 18: Race Still Matters: Mapping the Afterlives of *Stony the Road We Trod* 267
Clarice J. Martin

Chapter 19: "To Think Better Than We Have Been Trained": Thirty Years Later 271
Renita J. Weems

Appendix 281

Editors and Contributors 285

PART I

Remembering the Past, Laboring in the Present, and Shaping a Hopeful Future

Chapter 1

"The Hill We Climb"

Introduction

Mitzi J. Smith, Angela N. Parker, and Ericka S. Dunbar Hill

> If we're to live up to our own time, then victory / Won't lie in the blade, / but in all the bridges we've made.
>
> —Amanda Gorman (2021, 19)

Last year, 2021, marked the thirtieth anniversary of the publication of *Stony the Road We Trod: African American Biblical Interpretation* (hereafter STR), a seminal text in the field of biblical studies and a collective hermeneutical memoir, road map, manifesto, and source of inspiration for Africana and other readers. The times have changed since the stressful, difficult, caesarian birth that brought STR to fruition. The project was not without its challenges and tensions, as Dr. William Myers shares in chapter three of this volume. Many of its original contributors lived through the victories and losses of the last decade of the twentieth century and the awakening of the twenty-first. They taught us, teach us, and write with us. Because of them, our path is not as stony or thorny. Under the guiding-light of their insights—a hermeneutical North Star—we do our work without groping in the utter darkness. Our experiences are different, similar, and overlapping. STR contributors lived in the violent pre–civil rights era and participated in the struggle for rights. Many contributors to this volume read about the struggle, having never felt intimately the terror of those days. We were quite young and our parents bore the brunt and shielded us from the violence, to the extent that they could. We did, however, most of us, across the testaments of STR and this volume,

Bitter the Chastening Rod (BTCR), vote for and celebrate, with all the jubilance we banked over the years, the election of Barack H. Obama, the first African American president of the United States of America; and we did so twice. We proudly supported the first Black First Lady, Michelle Obama. But together we felt the bitter rod of terror, as Black men, women, and children continued to be tried, convicted, and killed in the streets while doing the same mundane things white folks do (i.e., selling cigarettes, sitting in a car, walking), in our parents' neighborhoods, in automobiles with our children, in our homes, and in our churches. Some things remain the same. Cell phone video cameras placed us at the awful scenes and we witnessed Black men and women being wrestled like cattle until they were shot in the back while running away from the police. Those R+-rated clips provided irrefutable proof, so we thought, but justice still escapes the victims and our communities. The murder of Michael Brown ignited the Black Lives Matter Movement. We have been insisting for a long time that Black Lives Matter: Black Power! We are somebody! God is the God of the Oppressed! God is a Black man! God is a Black woman! Once again, we had to "say it loud." "Black lives matter!" chants reemerged within the matrix of Black precarity because of police brutality, racial disparities in employment and education, health care inequities, and erosion of voting and civil rights, all while battling a global pandemic.

Bitter the Chastening Rod (the second line, second verse of the Negro National Anthem *Lift Every Voice and Sing*)—a project and title that Dr. Randall Bailey, a contributor to STR, suggested we undertake—is a sequel to STR.[1] Dr. Cain Hope Felder (1943–2019), editor of the volume, wrote the following in the preface: "[s]lowly, but perceptibly, the world is changing—and in some respects the changes are not a cause for alarm or fear" (ibid., ix). We do write with some fears and rage, unapologetically, as a new and more contagious variant of the COVID-19 virus is sending many anti-vaxxers and others into hospital ICUs and as governments aggressively curtail access to the ballot, particularly impacting the poor and Black and brown peoples. We write in perilous times that dictate or impact the hermeneutic approaches and risks we take, the cultural resources we deploy, the subject matters we engage, and the questions we raise. Felder wrote, "any black interpretation of the Bible must take into very serious account the peculiarly intimate link between black biblical understanding and the vital life of the black church" (1991, 7). We also take seriously the vital life of Black communities in which our churches are embedded, and the ones too many Black churches and communities shun, like LGBTQ+ communities.

In STR, a *tour de force* (William H. Myers' description), Felder wrote, "African American interpretation is a fully grown tree near the dense forest of Eurocentric biblical exegesis and interpretation" (1991, 1). This statement remains true. Africana biblical scholars—scholars of African descent—are less than 10 percent of the Society of Biblical Literature's membership. Students of graduate (and undergraduate) theological education across race, ethnicity, and gender can earn their degrees and never sit in courses under the instruction of Africana biblical scholars. We continue to publish significant resources that can be utilized to create diverse theological educational experiences, despite our absence in many institutions.

Fifteen of the Africana hermeneuts, translators/interpreters, in this volume earned terminal degrees in biblical studies and three are PhD students or candidates. Different from STR, seven of the eighteen contributors to BTCR are Africana women biblical scholars, and two, Drs. Clarice Martin and Renita Weems—themselves pioneers and stepping stones to hermeneutical freedom—participated in the STR project. They mentored us through their publications, presence, and voices.[2] Black women's contributions in BTCR articulate, as Weems wrote in STR, African American women's ambivalent relationship to the Bible (1991, 59). How Africana women read the Bible has to do with their values and how or where the text corroborates those values, and equally impactful is "how the text arouses, manipulates, and harnesses African American women's deepest yearnings" (ibid.). We still refuse to read "(and respond) like a certain kind of man" (Weems 1991, 67). Because of STR, we do not have to make bricks from straw; we do not create *ex nihilo*. The chastening rod is bitter and the road still stony, but our hermeneutical shoes are better soled, and the journey is not quite as treacherous or as costly. Our work is important for birthing and equipping those (not yet) considering, wondering, imagining, and pursuing this rocky, often turbulent and hostile path.

Out of the past, we stand on change, the change forged by those who preceded us. Because of the ancestors, we can speak and think more often of climbing hills as opposed to mountains. In STR, Myers lamented that "the manner in which the African American approach developed and is presently utilized is . . . omitted in all major works on hermeneutical methodology" (1991, 47). We must and are creating our own methodological works (see Weems's essay, chapter 19, "To Think Better Than We Have Been Trained"). We find and fashion "space for maneuvering within confinement" as did Linda Brent, and other fugitives from captivity, journeying for/toward freedom (Snorton 2017, 68–69). In our hermeneutical maneuverings, we focus our lenses, our attention, unapologetically on the world in front of the text—Africana communities, churches, and the academy, where we negotiate our freedom. The church cannot lose sight of the community and the global neighborhood; neither should we. It is true, we still (struggle to) choose hope in the God of the Bible (mitigated by critical readings of problematic and violent portrayals of YHWH) and tempered by revelation from and the dynamic presence of the preexistent God prior to the Bible, in front of the Bible, and transcending it. God, we acknowledge, does not escape, even requires, translation. It matters who translates/interprets and who constructs theologies.

In STR, Thomas Hoyt, Jr., asserts, "the authority of Scripture is displayed not so much in the answers that are given but in the questions that are raised" (1991, 24). Questions are not raised in cultural vacuums. In the context of #BLM, #SayHerName, and #MeToo, we raise new questions and revisit old ones in our contexts and with diverse interdisciplinary approaches. Black interpretation has always been interdisciplinary, bringing together Africana culture, history, and traditions in conversation with biblical studies. We deploy critical race theory (CRT), sociology, anthropology, and the Black literary criticism, for example.

SUMMARY OF CONTENTS

We labor under a cloud of mighty witnesses, not all of whom were biblical scholars. In chapter 2, Brian Blount graciously revised the eulogy he presented at Cain Hope Felder's funeral at Howard University. Felder was Blount's friend, colleague, teacher, and mentor. Blount writes that Felder "troubled his mentors with this affinity for things and people African. He wandered off European and American scholarly shores onto the African plains and picked up the power of African peoples, African history, and African perspectives and brought that, too, to bear upon his brand of biblical research. Troubling. In those early days. When biblical scholars of African descent were so very few in number. Troubling for him and his future vocational prospects. Troubling for a biblical scholarship and its past, present, and future intentions—to keep biblical inquiry on an alleged objective, value-neutral, culture-free platform. Cain Hope Felder's work, in his scholarship, in his teaching, in his mentoring challenged such a notion from the start." At Howard University School of Divinity, Felder mentored and/or taught many who would become biblical scholars, including Rodney Sadler, Madeline McClenney, Teddy Burgh, Wil Gafney, and Mitzi Smith; three are contributors to this volume. All are "troublers of biblical waters" in their own way.

In his essay "*Zoom*-ing in on a Watershed Moment in Biblical Interpretation" (chapter 3), William H. Myers calls the roll and walks us through the trajectory and challenges of the STR project. In his essay he offers tributes to Cain Hope Felder and to Thomas Hoyt Jr. Myers writes, "I mentioned Hoyt and Felder, both deceased, in this tribute because they were key participants of the *Stony* project, one a convener, the other an editor, with whom I had a three-decade long friendship. Certainly, Charles Copher deserves honorable mention. He too is deceased since [STR] was completed. I did not know

Copher like I knew the other two. My association with him was limited to the time of the project and directly thereafter. Yet, he too was a vanguard in biblical studies before any of us and helped pave the way for us all." Ultimately, Myers stresses the priority that Africana scholars should give to building lasting relationships even as we engage and provide helpful critique of each other's work.

In part II, "God's Black(ened) People in the World: Thugs, Slaves, and Criminals," the contributors, Allen Dwight Callahan, Mitzi J. Smith, Emerson B. Powery, Jeremy L. Williams, and Marcus W. Shields, center the enslaved, the dehumanized, and the marginalized in this world and in the world the biblical texts create. They maintain that readers should not ignore the material realities of the oppressed and vulnerable. Thomas Hoyt wrote in STR that "[O]pressors and oppressed usually raise questions in light of their privilege or lack of it. For blacks, Jesus is human and identifies with the poor by suffering on their behalf" (Hoyt 1991, 29). Jesus not only suffered "on behalf" of the poor but Jesus suffered as one of the poor—as one of God's Black(ened) children. In "God's Only Begotten Thug" (chapter 4), Allen Callahan argues that all four Gospels agree, variously, that Jesus belongs to that "bottom half" of society: he is born without inheritance, lives without assets, and dies without bequest. Thus, Jesus is what the rap artist Tupac Shakur calls a "thug": "When I say thugs," explains Shakur, "I mean niggas who don't have anything." The Jesus of the four Gospels is one among the billions in the bottom half, one among the many of that cohort. Pauperized, marginalized, stigmatized, criminalized, "niggarized," he is God's Only-Begotten.

Mitzi Smith, building on the work of Clarice Martin and Winsome Munro, takes seriously Jesus's material reality as a Jewish man born to a *doulē* named Mary (chapter 5). She argues that Luke's Jesus, from birth to death, lived the life of an enslaved person. Of all the instances of the Greek word *doulos* in Luke's Gospel, translators interpret them all as "slave"—except in the birth narratives. A significant aspect of Luke's depiction of Jesus is lost in translation. How does Luke's Gospel read differently when we choose not to read *doulē* euphemistically and within the context of ancient enslavement? God's son is a Black(ened) Jewish man. Callahan and Smith place Jesus at (not near) the bottom of the social structure.

Emerson Powery and Marcus Shields visualize and challenge readers to examine biblical characters identified as slaves and the interpretative traditions of biblical texts where slaves are present. Like Smith, Powery's essay "Reading with the Enslaved: Placing Human Bondage at the Center of the Early Christian Story" (chapter 6) demonstrates that it matters who translates. A precursor to freedom is a consciousness of one's enslavement or oppressed status. We are becoming free. Powery argues "all writing toward Freedom is partial." He evinces the importance of reading the NT in the context of enslavement. The unspoken is as significant as the explicit. Examining Rhoda and Tertius (Acts 12; Rom 16), Powery explores the lived experience of the enslaved within the Jesus movement. Reading from the margins or bottom requires that we take the physical body seriously, and consider who benefits from a particular interpretation.

In Jeremy Williams' essay, "'I am a Human': Racializing Assemblages and Criminalized Egyptianness in Acts 21:31–49' (chapter 7), he employs Alexander Weheliye's concept of 'racialized assemblages," a combination of factors (an assemblage) ultimately meant to separate different human beings from full access to the category of the human. These frameworks assist Williams in contextualizing Acts 21, *and* provide tools for reading Josephus, Philo, and other Roman authors' elision of Egyptianness with criminality. Williams addresses how certain persons are criminalized in ways that others are not, which is linked to the question of who is considered fully human or worthy of the fullest protection under the law.

In the final chapter of part II, "The Terror of White Hermeneutics: Black and Slave Bodies Interpreted in the Context of Whiteness" (chapter 8), Marcus Shields examines interpretations of 1 Corinthians 7:21 and argues that there is inherent whiteness in the traditional interpretations of that verse. Shields asserts that "Just as black bodies are subject to violence due to the hermeneutic of whiteness so are enslaved bodies in the biblical text subject to violence because of whiteness in historical criticism. Whiteness in historical criticism is the failure to acknowledge existential dynamics of enslaved bodies in the biblical text. That is, interpretive concentration is geared toward literary design rendering enslaved bodies invisible." The hermeneutic of whiteness and historical criticism intersect as lenses of interpretation that impact Black and enslaved bodies. The former maintains stereotypes about Black bodies through the lens of whiteness.

In part III, "Africana Hermeneutical Strategies, Pedagogy, Translation, and #BLM," Hugh R. Page, Jr., and Ronald Charles demonstrate how culture can inform biblical interpretation and translation. Wil Gafney and Theodore W. Burgh address pedagogy in the context of Black Lives Matter. In chapter 9, "Hoodoo Blues and the Formulation of Hermeneutical Strategies for Contemporary Africana Biblical Engagement," Page advocates for a new paradigm, an intervention, for the interpretive engagement of the Bible based on Hoodoo Blues, a subgenre of American Blues music, that would enhance interdisciplinary dialogue between biblical studies and other fields like Africana and ethnic studies. Page asserts that "Textual Healing Algorithms for Africana biblical interpretation derived from Hoodoo Blues—i.e., flexible sets of procedures for bringing issues and cultural artifacts from either the African or African Diasporan *ethos* into more direct conversation with

Biblical texts, themes, and cruxes—are sorely needed as Africana Biblical Criticism continues to mature as a subfield."

Wil Gafney's essay "Reflections on Teaching Biblical Interpretation through a Black Lives Matter Hermeneutic" (chapter 10) reflects on the praxis of teaching a course on biblical interpretation at a mainline Protestant divinity school in light of the Black Lives Matter (BLM) movement. The course, offered in 2017 and 2021 at the Brite Divinity School in Fort Worth, Texas, examined the core claims and commitments of the BLM movement in light of the biblical text with an eye to preaching and teaching the scriptures in response to the extra-judicial killings of Black women, men, and children, and subsequent community responses to those killings. The participants developed and articulated BLM hermeneutic approaches to interpreting the scriptures, focusing on both the coming week's Revised Common Lectionary (RCL) texts and passages selected by participants reflecting both lectionary and non-lectionary congregational contexts. Gafney's essay shares and engages student writings and reflections as a model of academic study of the bible with congregational implications in response to emerging critical social, political, and theological issues.

In chapter 11, "Revisiting the Caananites and Contemporary *Ites:* Pedagogical Insights into Cheering for the Wrong Team," Theodore Burgh notes that the conquest of Canaan in the book of Joshua has been the subject of countless academic discussions, sermons, and hermeneutical treatments for some time. A general reading of Joshua presents a series of battles with an eventual victorious Israelite takeover of the land of Canaan—a geographical space claimed to have been promised to them by their god YHWH. Yet, the story raises a number of perplexing questions. For example, did the presence and activities of the inhabitants of Canaan warrant annihilation and destruction? If so, why, and who determined this was an appropriate measure of punishment? The Israelites, led by Joshua, the Moses protégé, institute a *cherem*, claiming YHWH commanded them to annihilate the Canaanites and other *Ites* (pronounced EYE-ts, a term that Burgh developed). *Ites* are the other groups occupying Canaan at the time. Exploring and considering the text from the perspective of the Canaanites and other *Ites*, encourages students to consider other questions, including how violated Black lives are modern-day *Ites*.

In chapter 12, "Reading Romans in Greek: Translating and Commenting on It in Haitian Creole," Ronald Charles reminds us that translation and the languages of peoples and groups that inhabit impoverished corners of the world also matter. In a project that is interested in biblical interpretation in the context of Black Lives Matter, a focus on non-Western languages, such as Haitian Creole, is also urgent. Haitian Creole matters because Haitians matter.

Charles channels his dreams through his scholarly work and social activism. He travels the long and arduous journey of reading Romans in Greek and translating it in English, the language of empire and the main linguistic instrument of today's (neo)colonization, while struggling to dust-off the debris of another colonizing linguistic element (French), before finally translating it and commenting on it in his Haitian Creole language.

In part IV, "Black Rage and Protest in Times of #BLM and #MeToo," the contributors value that which the dominant world and white supremacy devalues, namely Black anger/rage, Black Lives, and Black protest, in the context of anti-Blackness and Black survival, rights, and freedom. In "Rage, Riots, and Rhetoric: Psalm 137 and African American Responses to Violence" (chapter 13), Stacy Davis argues that rage is an appropriate and necessary response to the killing of unarmed Black people. While white rage and violence are justified and garner sympathy, Black anger or rage, peaceful demonstrations, and protests are regarded as unjustified and "inappropriate" and equated with mob violence or riots. In exposing the disparities, Davis explores Christian interpretations of Psalm 137, African American philosophical and theological works about anger, and media responses to African American and white rage.

Angela N. Parker's essay "Rethinking 'God-breathed' in the Age of #Black Lives Matter: A Womanist Reading of 2 Tim 3:10–17" (chapter 14) proposes a nuanced understanding of "God-breathed" that expands beyond a heroic view of Paul to engage womanist experiences. Specifically, Parker argues for womanist leadership and experiences through engagement with Eunice and Lois in 2 Timothy and what that means for understanding the creative breath of God that intermingles with womanist interpreters of 2 Timothy. Further, in the age of Black Lives Matter, Parker argues that the concept of "God–breathed" must be understood in the context of experiences, sufferings, and persecutions in a Black community that experiences racism, classism, death, and trauma in the age of Black Lives Matters protests.

In chapter 15, "Leah and Dinah in the Face of Abuse: What Do I Tell My Daughter?," Kamilah Hall Sharp addresses the dilemma she faces, as an African American mother, of explaining Dinah's rape in the Genesis narratives to her inquisitive teenage daughter as she begins reading the Bible for herself. Sharp argues that silence is not a viable option both while reading the biblical text and in the midst of contemporary silence and sexual violence. Reading through the lens of a womanist maternal thought hermeneutic, Sharp attempts to ascertain what happened to Dinah and Leah and how to engage honest conversations with girls about the implications. She raises contextual questions, unmutes silenced voices, and identifies issues in (or outside) the text that engender survival and wholeness.

In his essay "Antichrist and Anti-Black: 1 John and 'Black Lives Matter'" (chapter 16), Dennis R. Edwards proposes that 1 John supports the assertion that Black lives matter, despite opposition to the #BLM movement by some Christians. First John offers insights into the development of Christian division, resulting from multiple factors. Edwards asserts that "Doctrinal convictions are typically offered as the main reason for ecclesial separation, as if those convictions are distinct from cultural values. However, theological understandings and cultural codes of behavior are intertwined. For example, racism, sexism, and classism are built into some theological perspectives, exposing divisions within American Christianity." First John's message of perseverance can inform an appreciation of how the precarity of Black life requires perseverance.

In part V, "Responses," Thomas B. Slater's essay "John's Apocalypse and African American Interpretation" (chapter 17) reviews African American interpretations of Revelation, beginning with Thomas Hoyt's 1991 reading in STR. Slater's study examines the Revelation monographs of Brian Blount and Shanell Smith in comparison to Hoyt's essay. What one finds, Slater argues, is much of what Hoyt advocated three decades ago: They "stressed the importance of aligning the biblical story with the African American story and also the need for the study of the role of imagery and the use of imagination in biblical interpretation."

In "Race Still Matters: Mapping the Afterlives of *Stony the Road We Trod*" (chapter 18), Clarice J. Martin responds to earlier chapters in this volume. Martin extends Toni Morrison's invitation to view writing as map-making. She concludes that the essayists "deftly heighten and magnify the interface between their particular sociocultural histories and the present world we live in. We see this in . . . creative hermeneutical revisioning and enlivening of traditionalist interpretations of Hebrew Bible and Christian Testament traditions, and we see this in essays that foreground explicit dangers (and in Morrison's words, 'possible havens from dangers') to Black women, men, and children."

Renita Weems's essay, "'To Think Better Than We Have Been Trained': Thirty Years Later" (chapter 19), discusses the past and the present—what was, what is, and the overlap; what we learned and had to unlearn. Weems writes, "books like *Bitter the Chastening Rod* prove that there is no going back. We cannot unknow what we now know about police killings of black women and men, the rise of white supremacy, and so on. There is no return to a precritical period of reflecting on the discipline, the Bible, and its use in the hands of extremists. We have the responsibility to think and teach better than we have been trained. Even with thicker, more nuanced, and theoretically more sophisticated methodological tools at our disposal, we cannot avoid the need to be self-reflexive about our location and our training because while the

Bible may be neutral, and has no meaning beyond itself, readers and the act of reading itself are not so innocent." We cannot and will not step backwards.

CONCLUDING THOUGHTS

STR contained no contributions from LGBTQ+ communities. Of course, the Black church was quite homophobic in 1991. It is changing; we will continue to climb in and toward freedom. We invited self-identified Queer scholars to write, but in the end, they were not able to contribute to this work in this season. BTCR includes only one scholar beyond the USA context (although others were invited), namely, the Haitian scholar Ronald Charles, who lives and teaches in Toronto. We intentionally employ the word Africana as opposed to African American biblical interpretation in the title in recognition of and in solidarity with scholars of African descent located in the motherland (on the African continent) and in the African diasporas. There is still much collaborative engagement we must do in the areas of Bible translation, activist public scholarship across the continents, interdisciplinary work, and contextual biblical interpretation. There is always more conscientization (toward/for freedom) to do around poverty, privatization, economic injustice, ecological justice, the early criminalization of Black and brown children, liberative pedagogy, our missing children, homophobia in our churches, and so on. *Bitter the Chastening Rod* is an incisive step in that direction and lays the groundwork for future cutting-edge oppositional (to injustice) works and more collaborative projects. We are not going back; we will continue to labor in our liberty and toward greater freedom and wholeness.

NOTES

1. Fortress Press published an anniversary edition of STR in late 2021.
2. See the appendix for a list of Africana persons with earned terminal degrees in biblical studies. We are grateful to Ericka Dunbar for compiling this list in conversation with other scholars.

WORKS CITED

Felder, Cain Hope. 1991. *Stony the Road We Trod: African American Biblical Interpretation*. Minneapolis: Fortress.

Gorman, Amanda. 2021. *The Hill We Climb. An Inaugural Poem for the Country*. New York: Viking.

Snorton, C. Riley. 2017 *Black on Both Sides: A Racial History of Trans Identity*. Minneapolis: University of Minnesota Press.

Chapter 2

A Eulogy for Cain Hope Felder

Brian K. Blount

For those who knew him well, Cain Hope Felder was a disruptive force. The title of one of his earliest works, *Troubling Biblical Waters*, not only identified his approach to scriptural interpretation; it summarized his understanding of scriptural intent.

On the surface, the word *troubling* was a participle. It clarified Felder's hermeneutical engagement with the text. He was determined to reorient text study that interpreted through the lens of European and American interest and dominance. That reorientation was a first step in constructing a template for reading the Bible through the experience of those who have been oppressed and marginalized according to categories of race and class. He intended to trouble the way scholarship preferred to read from and alongside the perspective of the racially dominant and the socially preferred.

But *Troubling Biblical Waters* was more than a participle and an adjective modifying a highlighted noun. The title, in its entirety, was itself, in Felder's grip, a noun form. He wasn't just troubling biblical waters; according to his interpretative conclusions, scripture itself was a sea at storm, upsetting traditional life understandings, capsizing long standing social stratifications, flooding racial prerogatives, portending, even in its threat of dissolution, a new horizon filled with transformed opportunity. For Felder, every serious and honest engagement with scripture was an exciting foray into troubling biblical waters.

And so, I honored my teacher, mentor, and friend, on the occasion of celebrating his life at the end of his life, with a eulogy dedicated to the biblical spirit of disruption. The orienting text, the one about the troubling of biblical waters, of course, was the following:

> Now in Jerusalem by the Sheep Gate there is a pool, called in Hebrew Beth-zatha, which has five porticoes. In these lay many invalids—blind, lame, and paralyzed. One man was there who had been ill for thirty-eight years. When Jesus saw him lying there and knew that he had been there a long time, he said to him, "Do you want to be made well?" The sick man answered him, "Sir, I have no one to put me into the pool when the water is stirred up; and while I am making my way, someone else steps down ahead of me." Jesus said to him, "Stand up, take your mat and walk." At once the man was made well, and he took up his mat and began to walk. Now that day was a sabbath. (John 5:2–9, NRSV)

In 1978, Cain Hope Felder flowed in like a flood water onto the campus of Princeton Theological Seminary. As an entering student that year, I knew from the moment I met him that this man was going to be trouble. Princeton Theological Seminary in those days was a manifestly white space. I believe that there were three or four African Americans in an entering class of more than 130 Master of Divinity students. I was of the opinion that when you were that outnumbered, you kept your head down, moved about without attracting attention, and nodded agreement with the powers that be, even when you thought that what they were saying and doing was absurd. Cain was not of that opinion. And Cain was never one to keep his discomforting opinions to himself. If transforming a place meant troubling a place, Cain was in Princeton to oblige. He would lay claim to the troubling when, before faculty, staff, students, and anyone else who crossed his path, he penned and lectured his wonderfully complex, exegetical, engaging campus calls for better biblical literacy that simultaneously demanded a liberating biblical reading. He didn't just trouble biblical waters in the dissertation he was writing and the lectures he was giving; he was biblical trouble in real life, in real time.

The first African American, full-time biblical scholar to teach in the Bible Department on the faculty of Princeton Theological Seminary, even before he had concluded his PhD, he was a revelation. I know that many of my white student colleagues had never had an African American professor up to the point that they engaged Cain Hope Felder in the front of our New Testament Introduction class. Such was the world of higher, post-secondary education, that even for me, an African American, Cain was the first African American professor I had ever had. And from the moment he opened his trouble-making mouth in the public space of the lecture hall, I felt a pride hot and fierce. With his gift of intellect and his special brand of humor, he captured our classes. He was in command of the languages, ancient and modern, and he used those languages copiously on the blackboard and in the margins of our papers he was marking up to get us to see more than we thought we could possibly entertain. Greek and Hebrew coursed out of him, crackling like lightening, as if he had been born to the languages. He recalled bibliographic resources as though he'd just read the citations moments earlier. Volumes of text citations and scholarly notations spun off his lips as though he carried a full theological library around in his head. I remember at times looking around the large lecture hall at my mostly white colleague students and wondering what they were thinking. There were so few African American students in the room. We didn't have numbers, we didn't have strong representation, we didn't have a lot of folk like us in the bibliographies of the other course syllabi, we didn't have books by authors representing biblical and theological inquiry from a perspective like ours, but we did have Cain Hope Felder. And this man, this brilliant man, this powerful professor seemed like he was on a cause. To trouble the perception of what a biblical scholar looked like. To trouble the notion that the African American experience was not an appropriate experience to use as a lens for doing biblical and theological inquiry. Here was a man who knew all the languages. Knew all the classical biblical scholarship: German, Anglo Saxon, American. He carried the membership card of biblical studies that indicated he had sat at the feet of Eurocentric biblical scholars and that he had learned all their methods and appropriated all of their techniques.

But he troubled his mentors with this affinity for things and people African. He wandered off European and American scholarly shores onto the African plains and picked up the power of African peoples, African history, and African perspectives and brought that, too, to bear upon his brand of biblical research. Troubling. In those early days. When biblical scholars of African descent were so very few in number. Troubling for him and his future vocational prospects. Troubling for a biblical scholarship and its past, present, and future intentions—to keep biblical inquiry on an allegedly objective, value-neutral, culture-free platform. Cain Hope Felder's work, in his scholarship, in his teaching, in his mentoring, challenged such a notion from the start. He perceived that "value-neutral" was in reality value predisposed to European and American social and cultural perspective. He perceived that values African and African American were treated as invasive and troubling, not just because they represented a different cultural reading perspective, but because they did not represent the dominant Euro-American cultural reading perspective. He realized how much power played a role in interpretive agendas. And, having recognized it, he taught it, he researched it, he wrote it. And I was privileged to see it first hand, up close, from the beginning. This troubling of the water that would find its way ultimately into texts like *Troubling Biblical Waters* and *Stony the Road We Trod* and *The African Heritage Study Bible*. I was not surprised when these books rippled waves of interpretative consternation across the previous calm of biblical studies. I was there, basking in the glow of a pride I was too young and inexperienced at the time to appreciate properly, when Cain Hope Felder started stirring the waters in

Princeton on his way to fully troubling the waters through his stellar career at Howard.

In his first book, Cain echoed the biblical story of the troubling of the waters in the Gospel of John for a reason. The story's presentation of the infirm man and Jesus's question to him and action for him reveal something about how Cain understood the path upon which God had set him. You heard the story when I read the scripture. Cain would be annoyed if I left out the text. It is not all about us, I learned from him. It gets to us, but it starts with the text. With an ability to see the text in its language and time, through a clear and truthful lens of our place and time.

Cain would want me to give you a little archeological background so we could hear this text in its proper historical context. He'd want me to tell you that "Herod the Great was probably responsible for the porticoes which surrounded the two pools with another portico in between" (Sloyan 1988, 78–79). You want to know what a portico is? You can go look it up. Cain wasn't giving away answers you could research for yourself.

Still, so you can visualize what the text is narrating, it is helpful to know that "the pool was probably below street level . . . to catch the rain as a means of supplementing the underground [water] sources" that fed the pool (Sloyan 1988, 79). Archeological information gives us a good deal more information. "The pool with five porticoes corresponds to one excavated northeast of the temple grounds, near the Sheep Gate and in the Jerusalem vicinity called Betheza by [Jewish historian] Josephus" (Thompson 2015, 119–20). In actuality, there were two large pools there, trapezoidal in shape. These pools were covered by porch-like porticoes and surrounded by colonnades on each side and divided by a fifth colonnade. "Archaeologists suggest that it was a *miqveh*, a pool used for ritual immersion and purification in Jesus's day; later, under the Roman Emperor Hadrian (117–138 CE), it was dedicated to Asclepius, the god of healing, pointing to its reputation as a place of healing" (Thompson 2015, 120).

Yes, this is a story about a pool. By the Sheep Gate in Jerusalem. I tried as I prepared for this message to think of how Cain would teach this text, or teach a young scholar to write on this text. When he took your paper, he wrote more on it in the margins than you had yourself typed up on the page. When he reconstructed your argument for you, he supplied evidence and support that you had missed in your library forays. Scribbling in his astute asides, he often made your case better than you had made it yourself, even if he disagreed with your argument, because he could see all the sides even as he pressed his side.

In those early days under his tutelage, when I was that young student who would have been fussing over the name of the sheep gate, and the history of the name, and been preoccupied with the porticoes, identifying what they looked like, what they held up, and why people wanted them around in the first place, he would have been reading my paper impatiently, "yeah, yeah, but what about these broken people sitting all around the place? Don't you see them? Why do you wait so long to address them? Is the brick and mortar more important than the flesh and blood? Why are you giving me all these pages on porticoes? I want to see what you say God is going to do about these broken people."

For Cain, it was about the people. God's people in these texts who were struggling. Learning about them so we could learn to apply what we learned to God's people struggling in this world today. The powerful people behind this text put up picturesque porticoes. They cleaned the pool. They prepared a place beside the pool for the broken to huddle. But they didn't do anything to better their condition. They just contributed to the circumstance that limited their ability to do something about their condition.

The broken lie all around us. Unseen by some. Seen but unattended by others. Years and years pass by. We fix the porticoes but we leave broken the people. We, too, are preoccupied by porticoes. Church buildings. Political constructs. Academic agendas. Administrative minutiae. Legal maneuvering. Pompous prophesying. We have a way of tilling the texts and leaving fallow the people for whom the texts were written.

The scholars who crafted Euro-American biblical scholarship did something similar. They were preoccupied by perspective. Their own Euro-American cultural perspective which they seemed to think ought to be everybody's perspective. If you didn't operate from it, you weren't operating appropriately. Euro-American scholars crafted clean lines of scholarship, put up so-called objective methods of doing that scholarship, and addressed that scholarship to, from, and for their particular perspective. There was breaking and brokenness in this. In the introduction to *Stony the Road*, Cain observes: "The extent of uniformity in scholarly norms throughout the world is striking evidence of persisting Euro-American domination. Indeed, the worldwide uniformity itself reinforces the academic prejudice that the European way of doing things is 'objective' and somehow not culture bound" (Felder 1991, 6). It is an argument he had introduced already in *Troubling Biblical Waters*: "European/Euro-American biblical scholars have asked questions and shaped answers with the framework of the racial, cultural, and gender presuppositions they hold in common. This quiet consensus has undermined the self-understanding and place in history of other racial and ethnic groups" (Felder 1989, xi). The waters of biblical scholarship would remain calm, as long as the people doing biblical scholarship calmly swam in the appropriate Euro-American current.

A troubled Cain Hope Felder was having none of it. He wrote to address not the beautiful presentation of biblical studies, how tantalizingly seductive it was with its promise of finding the true objective meaning of text; he wrote to address how it refused to see the many others, particularly African American others, whose presence was not wanted in the interpretive pool. He makes his case right from the start in *Troubling Biblical Waters*. "The purpose of this book is to provide some sorely needed correctives regarding the Bible in relation to ancient Africa and Black people today. Despite the fact that the Bible has a favorable attitude about Blacks, post-biblical misconstruals of biblical traditions have created the impression that the Bible is primarily the foundational document of 'the White Man's religion.' The mistaken notion widely persists that the relation of Black people to the Bible is a post-biblical experience. Such historical distortions, created by Eurocentric scholars and missionaries to the detriment of Blacks, have long been one of my concerns. . . . Under the influence of Western culture and its by-product, racism, too many Blacks themselves believe that they are latecomers in the history of salvation. This book seeks to illuminate the Black story within The Story, so the ancient record of God's Word takes on new meaning for the Black Church today" (Felder 1989, xi).

This was the scripture according to Cain Hope Felder. A manifesto for ministry in scholarship. He walked up to the pools of academia, and started stirring up trouble. He saw that while the surface water was serene, the anguish of countless generations of believers of color churned in the depths, writhing and twisting, as they tried to break the surface calm, struggle up, and gasp for a biblical interpretation that included them and their stories, from their perspectives. Cain aimed to help them by lobbing his research, scholarship, and publications into the calm pool like a theological grenade, intended to shatter the surface, shake the depths, trouble the waters. "On the whole," he wrote, "the waters of Eurocentric Bible scholarship have been rather calm, with mostly polite disagreement" (Felder 1989, xi). Cain Hope Felder offered some decidedly discourteous disagreement. "My intent," he wrote, "in these chapters is to 'trouble' (more precisely 'divide': *schizō*) the waters of the biblical Sea of Reeds (LXX, Exo 14:21) and clear a new pathway that leads to the Bible as an indispensable tool for liberation—sociopolitical and economic, as well as spiritual" (Felder 1989, xiv).

Cain Hope Felder was particularly interested in reading the Bible as an indispensable tool for the liberation of African and African American folk. This is why he sought to illuminate the Black story with The Story, to see the Black story within The Story. It was his mission particularly to mentor African American scholars like me to pursue this vision and then share this vision with others. Only in this way, of teachers creating more teachers, could true healing, true *inclusive* biblical interpretation occur. People on the margins could not wait for people in the centers of academic, social, and political power to interpret the texts in ways that would be meaningful for them; they would have to learn to interpret the texts from their marginal spaces and experiences themselves. Cain Hope Felder was a leader in teaching from the margins of African American experience. Cain Hope Felder was a recruiter of students from the margins who could follow him in his work. Like Jesus in this story, Cain Hope Felder witnessed the struggle and sought to use his powers to change the circumstances of the struggle. By troubling both those on the margins and those who put them there.

Jesus, you will recall from the scripture, stirred up everyone, including the broken ones on the margin, by starting with a question to one of the ones on the margin. A particularly striking question. "Do you want to get well?" What kind of question is that? I often thought that about Cain's questions in the classroom and in his office when he was pressing me on a point I'd been trying to make. Hard questions that pressed me to think harder than I ever thought I could. "Do you want to be made well?" The man must have been thinking, "I've been lying here for thirty-eight years, waiting. Of course, I want to be made well." But you see what the question did, what Cain's hard questions often did—it allowed the man to explain his circumstance. He had no one to help him. No Cain Hope Felder to show him the way.

I suppose Jesus was really asking the man, "why are you just sitting here? Why not get up and get in the water when the angel troubles it?" That was the legend, of course. Some ancient texts proclaimed that an angel of the Lord went down on certain seasons into the pool and stirred up the water and whoever stepped in first after the stirring of the water was healed of whatever disease he had. Jesus asks the question so the man can publicly give the answer. No one will help him. There is no one willing to help a man who had been struggling every day for thirty-eight years.

Cain Hope Felder spent his life in the Jesus role with so many students in the classrooms at Howard, in lecture halls around the world, in church pulpits and church classrooms around the world, in his study writing his papers and books. Jesus knew the back story. Knew the angel story about the water. And, I suppose, he knew the man couldn't get up fast enough, given his condition. So, Jesus calls out his circumstance and his condition in light of his context in a way that all could hear, so that the gravity of the situation could be laid bare. Jesus wasn't mocking or challenging the man; he was identifying with him, loudly, so all could hear and see him identifying with him. Sure, the man wanted to be made well, but the circumstance prevented that possibility. In making the man's circumstance clear, Jesus made it clear to all who overheard his conversation with the man that they had allowed this deplorable circumstance to occur at the Bethesda pool. They had allowed it to be a free-for-all where the strongest among the weak were guaranteed better access to the divine health care. So, this man, weak as he was, though he had been there thirty-eight years, always saw someone stronger jump ahead of him and receive the healing power. Who was going to look out for this man?

Who was going to give power to this man? Clearly, not the authorities, not the other broken people—they were fighting each other for the power. Clearly, not even the angel. The angel stirred the water, the angel didn't dictate who got in the water first. You would have thought the angel could have at least made up a lottery or something. This man had no one, not even the angels, to fight for him in his weakness. Until Jesus came along.

I have felt that way about biblical studies from an African American perspective. Until someone like Cain Hope Felder came along, we did not have someone to fight the fight of reading and interpreting text from an African and African American perspective. He wasn't the only one. But he was a seminal one. We didn't have someone to help us see history from an African and African American perspective. Believe me, when you're sitting on the porticoes of biblical scholarship and theological relevancy, we are all broken people vying for the healing touch of knowledge. That knowledge represents power. White European and American biblical interpreters and theologians have known this for a long time. This is why they wanted us to read biblical texts from Euro-American male lenses, using methods developed by Euro-American male scholars with the understanding that such reading is objective reading, and that if you would read rightly you would be healed of the brokenness of paralyzing, culturally infected readings. Since such scholars not only controlled the reading process, but also controlled the scholar production pipeline, there was little hope that people wanting to read from their African American cultural perspective had a chance to frolic in the water.

I remember the first time I was encountering these ideas from Cain Hope Felder, as a twenty-one-year-old first-year Master of Divinity student. He was talking about Jesus's ethnicity and how his ethnicity had lost its African roots and Palestinian heritage. I was sitting broken by the pool side, shocked with this new revelation. I hadn't ever had a Black professor before. I was paralyzed by the idea of a Black Jesus. It was like Cain was looking down at me from the lecterns, asking, "Brian, do you want to be made well? Look, there's water here. Why don't you get in?"

"Well, because, Cain Hope Felder, if I'm going to graduate from this seminary, I've got to show them that I read like them, interpret like them, think like them."

"Brian, do you want to be made well?"

"Well, what's in the water, Cain?"

Oh, this is the stuff of exegesis, and hermeneutics, and history, and cultural interpretation. This is the water of biblical exploration. The water you have known is the water of Euro-American perspective. I know, that is the only water that has ever been made available to you. That's okay. Before you wade in there, I'm going to trouble it for you.

No, I'm worried no one is going to help you get in the water once I trouble it, so I tell you what, I'm going to walk you around the water so you can find the healing you need elsewhere. I'm not going to just trouble this water; I'm going to trouble the whole pool house. I'm going to make it possible for you to swim in God's word without having to get into their pool.

Look at the text again. The thing with the sick man in John's story is that the circumstance is just too overwhelming. He will never be able to get into the water when it is troubled because he will always be too powerless, too slow, because of his brokenness. Jesus, realizing this, gives up on the angel troubling the water and decides himself to trouble the entire situation. If people who make the rules won't operate the rules justly, Jesus decides he'll just ignore the rules and create his own rules. Forget about the stirred-up water. Let's stir up this whole situation. Forget waiting in line. Get up and go around the line. The time for portico preoccupation and pool side praying is over. Time to take up your mat and walk. Find your place by finding your way to me.

I think that is what Cain Hope Felder did. With Jesus in his sights, Cain Hope Felder stepped out of line, took up his biblical mat, and walked. And, then, as a scholar and professor, he encouraged his colleagues and his students to follow. Why? He knew that by opening opportunities for African and African American scholarship he could help widen the interpretative vista for all biblical scholarship. My friend and colleague Professor Rodney Sadler said it this way: "Perhaps the most significant moment for me was when he paused in his impromptu lecture and emphatically stated that the Bible was not a book for black folk or people of any particular color. 'The Bible is everybody's book!' he exclaimed. He proceeded to express his concern that some had missed this in his scholarship . . . for which he was sorry. He was not trying to solely center black people, but to ensure that we were included at the table with everyone else . . . that was the point of his corrective historiography."[1]

Cain said it himself quite succinctly this way in his introduction to *Stony the Road*: "black scholars must challenge the Eurocentric mindset not only for the sake of the black community but also for the health of *all* scholarship" (Felder 1991, 7). In the end, Cain Hope Felder wasn't just making trouble, he was trying to make a new way, an inclusive way of studying, interpreting, teaching, and preaching the biblical texts. He was, in his own way, by troubling us, trying to get us to take up our mats and follow.

I suspect that Cain is himself doing that just now. Bypassing the porticoes and the lines and striding purposefully behind Jesus on his way to resurrection relationship with God. In the end, all of us, in this human life, broken by the poolside, awaiting the stirring that will lift us into God's eternal embrace. Jesus's presence in this story is the promise of his presence in our lives after this life. To walk us around the brokenness of death and bring us into the healing of new life. This story in the gospel of John is a testimony that the water, stirred or not, in it or not, is not the route to that new life. Jesus is. I don't know anyone who was more stirred up about getting out of line, taking up his mat, and following Jesus into this kind of troubling newness than Cain Hope Felder.

NOTE

1. Social Media Posting by Rodney Sadler on the occasion of Cain Hope Felder's death.

WORKS CITED

Felder, Cain Hope. 1991. *Stony the Road We Trod: African American Biblical Interpretation.* Minneapolis: Fortress.
———. 1989. *Troubling Biblical Waters: Race, Class and Family.* Maryknoll, NY: Orbis.
Sloyan, Gerald. 1988. *John.* Atlanta: John Knox.
Thompson, Marianne Meyer. 2015. *John: A Commentary.* Louisville, KY: Westminster John Knox.

Chapter 3

Zoom-ing in on a Watershed Moment in Biblical Interpretation

William H. Myers

TRIBUTES

On Wednesday, November 6, 2013, I sat in Howard University's Cramton auditorium, between Vincent Wimbush and Cain Hope Felder at Tom Hoyt's funeral. Little did I know at the time that I would return to that same site in the same season, less than six years later for Cain's funeral. After the three of us greeted and consoled Hoyt's wife, Cain insisted that we sit near the front. So, we did. When I returned for Felder's funeral, I sat alone in the back. Life comes at us fast, weaving a tapestry of intersections that transform our lives, then leaves us just as quickly as it came. I pen here this small tribute to two dearly beloved friends: two giants in the faith and the struggle in the discipline we shared together for the liberation of our people, the church, and the guild that we all loved. Such tributes will not do justice to the totality of their lives and contributions. It will merely give a glimpse of the intersection of our lives in one long temporal and spatial moment. Hopefully, someone else will do a well-deserved festschrift at some point.

THOMAS HOYT, JR., THE CONVENER, THE ECUMENICAL PASTOR/SCHOLAR

I first met Hoyt in 1984 at the annual AAR/SBL Conference in Chicago. I believe he was at Hartford Seminary then. This tall, engaging, friendly scholar met me as if we had known each other all our lives. "New Testament scholar, huh? That's what we need," he said. He told me about a gathering he was trying to convene. He wanted to assemble the few biblical scholars in Collegeville, Minnesota, and invited me to come. I told him I would come. Across the remaining days at the annual SBL meeting we would talk a lot and attend numerous sessions together.

A number of things were self-evident about Hoyt. He knew many people across numerous denominational and faith lines, and was well received by all. That is, his ecumenical spirit was genuine. The same was true of his scholarship, and those who knew him in the guild. He introduced me to so many people. The biggest treat of all was meeting the Black biblical scholars I never knew existed. After all, Hoyt mused, this is a major reason we need to get together, so we can know each other.

Hoyt's big pastoral heart was what led him to go deep into the ecclesial levels of his denomination, the CME (Christian Methodist Episcopal) Church, as well as the ecumenical associations he maintained. Hoyt planted both feet in the academy and both feet in the church. Evelyn Parker, president of the Society for the Study of Black Religion (SSBR), a CME scholar in her own right, shared with me an interesting story. She said that as a young scholar, in her exuberance for scholarship, she tried to talk Hoyt out of becoming a bishop. She told him that they had enough bishops, but they needed more scholars who would write and publish. Nevertheless, Hoyt not only became a bishop in the CME church, he became the presiding bishop of the entire denomination. The truth is that though Hoyt was a scholar in his own right, having taught at Howard Divinity School, ITC (Interdenominational Theological Center, Atlanta), and Hartford Seminary, his pastoral heart and love for the church universal was too big to remain solely dedicated to the guild. He sponsored my membership into the SSBR, while also urging me to assume the mantle of the church when the founding pastor died.

The pastoral heart of Hoyt was clearly self-evident as he worked to pull the five-year *Stony the Road* project together. Yes, he was very interested in assembling all the biblical scholars at Collegeville, so that we might collaborate on our scholarship. However, it was just as important to Hoyt that we gathered to become acquainted with each other as brothers and sisters in the same, often lonely struggle. He wanted us to know each other—our hopes and hurts, our dreams and disasters—so that long after our meeting together and publications, our friendships and support of each other would matter the most. When we gathered at Hoyt's funeral, Wimbush told me that he had to be present for Tom. He said that Hoyt *always* showed up at every major event in his career. Such was Tom's pastoral heart. He was always there, not just as scholar, but as friend and pastor.

Tom's heart was also evident across the three years we met at Collegeville. At the outset, Hoyt was encouraging us to share the stories of our journey, in life and most especially in the academy. Those were some sobering revelations. Aspects of those appear in *Stony the Road*. However, the real depth and emotions of those disquieting "dangerous memories" (to use Walter Fluker's phrase) do not come close to capturing the moment. We debated vigorously over how much of our interactions we should publish in the book. Hoyt felt that it needed to be heard. We settled on a compromise to allow certain excerpts so as not to overshadow the critical work we were trying to produce.

Hoyt's pastoral heart was apparent as he always tried to intervene with a soothing touch as tensions arose throughout the years when we convened (see more under "Tensions" below). That spirit of pastoral leadership and genuine spirituality overflowed naturally. I recall one specific occasion when Patrick Henry invited us to his home for a cookout. Hoyt was driving the van we rode in. As he drove, he began singing and urged us to join in: "Lord drive this van, while I run this race. Drive this van, while I run this race, 'cause I don't want to run this race in vain." So, we sang together all the way to Henry's house. Hoyt did not run this race in vain. He impacted all who crossed his path. Your race is over, dear brother, leader and friend. I miss you to this very day, but I will see you again. But, not yet, not yet.

CAIN HOPE FELDER, THE TROUBLER OF BIBLICAL WATERS

After Hoyt's funeral, Cain, Vincent, and I went looking for somewhere to eat. We walked down the street until we found an upstairs place where we could dine. We sat and shared our memories of Tom for some time. Cain had a class to teach, so we parted. Vincent and I tried to wave down a cab; however, even with suits on we were still two Black men in the hood. So, instead of stopping, the cab driver almost ran us over. We caught the subway and parted for our respective hotels, both of us carrying the weight of a bygone friend, and stating how we needed to keep in touch because life is so short.

Indeed, less than six years later, on Saturday, October 19, 2019, I sat yet again in the same auditorium, for the same purpose. It seemed to me like I was in the movie *Groundhog Day*. Could this really be happening again? It seemed only yesterday that we were here together for Hoyt. Here was Brian Blount, giving a masterful eulogy for Felder. But, wait. I was just in Richmond merely a moment ago, when he did the same masterful job for Katie Cannon, and a mere three months earlier, I was in Harlem at Riverside for the funeral of James Cone. Marvin Gaye's song, "What's Going On," a half century ago resonated with me.

However, this time I sat in the back. There was no Wimbush or any of the gang of thirty years ago. It was just me, by myself, to ponder the brevity of life. So, I did not want to be up front, too close. There was no Cain to share this with, this time. For it was Cain who was up front, this time, but not sitting next to me. This death struck a more piercing blow. Maybe, it was because I was still reeling from Katie and Jim's deaths so close together. Maybe, it was we had lost three giants so close in succession. Maybe, it was because I had just lost another dear friend.

We had spent more time together, in so many different venues across the world. I met Felder for the first time at the Collegeville gathering in the second year. He was not present the first year we convened. Of all the people that started out in this group, I have remained close, dear friends and crossed paths the most with Felder and Renita Weems. They became like blood brother and sister to me.

Our friendship began at Collegeville when Cain and Clarice Martin gave me the best critique on my work. It was the first time I had ever received critical, but affirming engagement from a Black scholar, where there was no concern about racial overtones in the critique. I remember to this day the first comment Felder made about my piece. He said, "now here is a real, thorough, scholarly piece of research." We began a friendship and supportive relationship that lasted until the day he died. He lectured dozens of times at the Black Religious Studies Institute I founded and taught classes in the Black Church Studies program I founded at Ashland Seminary. He preached and lectured at my church many times. In fact, Cain preferred to stay at my home on many occasions for a week or more when he was in town doing something. And on one occasion, he and his daughter stayed an extended period of time.

We always met at AAR/SBL for lunch or dinner, alone or with friends. We shared our research with each other, giving honest and helpful critique. Felder was impressed with the work I was doing through the Black Church Studies Institute I'd founded in 1984, where all Black Church studies at every level at Ashland Seminary were being taught. He said he wanted to start something like mine, modeled similarly to what I was doing, but focusing on social change through biblical interpretation. We spent numerous hours across many years talking about that venture. It came to fruition as his Biblical Institute for Social Change.

Felder was one of our vanguards in biblical interpretation, having taught at Princeton Seminary and Howard Divinity School. I believe he was the first African American biblical scholar to teach at Princeton. In his own words, the treatment he received by colleagues in his department took a toll on him. He never felt more liberated than when he took the position at Howard. Thereafter, for more than three decades he gave his life to his students to the day he retired. Even after retirement, he came to my institute and taught.

On many different occasions, I would get a call from Felder about some research projects he was launching and asking me to participate. I collaborated with him on the *Original African American Heritage Bible*. We went to Israel for seven days, filming all over Palestine in an attempt to produce a video study on Ancient Africa and the Bible. I still have film that I personally shot on location. The Howard University Communications Department, which accompanied us and filmed the work we developed, retains that raw footage. All of it should be released for publication in some form. Felder received a few VCR tapes of aspects of our work, which were very small, thirty minutes or less, excerpts. They were insightful connections of Ancient Africa and the Bible, which, I believe, could be quite useful in the study of Black religious trajectories.

Upon his arrival in the second year, when we decided that a book should come out of this project, Felder made his presence known. He was working on his own book, which was eventually published as *Troubling Biblical Waters*. We elected Felder to be the editor of what we produced. If memory serves me correctly, he was the one who suggested we take the title from the African American National Anthem. Throughout our journey Felder was always pushing. His frequent phrase about completing the book was, "we need to fish or cut bait."

The students that Felder taught and mentored, his impact on their lives, as well as their accomplishments are noteworthy of his place in the Hall of Fame of biblical scholarship. None is more stellar than Brian Blount and his accomplishments. Blount's eulogy of Felder, which appears in this book, is classic Blount, but lying underneath all that is Felder, the troubler of biblical waters himself. Rest well, my dear friend and troubler, you reside now where you "ain't gonna trouble [water] no mo." I shall join you again after I stop troubling myself. But, not yet, not yet.

I conclude this part with a few honorable mentions, as well as a few regrets. I mentioned Hoyt and Felder, both deceased, in this tribute because they were key participants of the *Stony* project, one a convener, the other an editor, with whom I had a three-decade long friendship. Certainly, Charles Copher deserves honorable mention. He too is deceased since this project was completed. I did not know Copher like I knew the other two. My association with him was limited to the time of the project and directly thereafter. Yet, he too was a vanguard in biblical studies before any of us and helped pave the way for us all. Some of his students have gathered some of his works together and published them. Perhaps others who knew him far better than I will say more, somewhere, sometime. Rest well, Charles. We thank you for just being there, all alone, by yourself.

TENSIONS

I am passionate about my love and concern for the continued existence of the Society for the Study of Black Religion. More important to me than what publications it produces is its existence. That we assemble as a group of sisters and brothers who support each other, who support those who will carry on when we are gone, and who just get together to be together and celebrate our unique interests and being-ness.

I often wonder, most especially now that the founders have all left us to join the "ancestors," about the dynamics of starting SSBR. We know some of the history and the rationale. However, what were the untold dynamics and tensions they had to work through as they started on this new necessary journey? What was the study of "Black" religion? Who or what did it include or exclude? What were the power dynamics and personalities at play that had to be navigated as it was being conceived? I don't know. I don't know if anyone knows, now that the founders are gone. Maybe it was discussed; maybe it remained between the founders.

I do not want to memorialize all of the tensions, issues, idiosyncrasies, and irritations that were manifested at the inception of what became one of the most important, foundational, ground-breaking projects in biblical interpretation ever to see the light of day. I do not share this information to out anyone. We were all a part of it. We all had/have our own issues, idiosyncrasies, and irritations.

This is not a memoir, nor a chronicle of all aspects of the history of the *Stony* project. It is singularly my memory of selected dynamics that occurred, to humanize the undertaking that became iconic. Although I intentionally omit names, some who participated will, no doubt, be able to identify specifics of which I speak, even if their memories differ slightly from mine. That is unavoidable. I do not attempt to harm, underhandedly, anyone or the project itself. My objective in the entirety of this piece is to shed light on the humanity that was at work in the project.

In the summer of 1986, twelve African American biblical scholars were invited to gather in Collegeville, Minnesota, on the St. John University campus for a conversation. The participants consisted of Thomas Hoyt, John Waters, Vincent Wimbush, Clarice Martin, Charles Copher, Randall Bailey, Stephen Reid, Tom Scott, Lloyd Lewis, John Greene, Mel Peters, and William H. Myers. We were also joined by our host from the Ecumenical Institute, Patrick Henry. In the second year, three others joined our group, namely Renita Weems, Cain Hope Felder, and David Shannon.

Questions arose at once. What is meant by Black, African American biblical interpretation? Who does it include or exclude? From my estimation, I don't know if any of us had thought about that. I know I certainly had not, until one brother who was present the first year and did not return raised the question. This Caribbean Black brother asked, who are you talking about when you say "African American biblical interpretation"? Are you talking about North America only, or are you including me? That had to be wrestled with. Perhaps, the brother never returned or participated in the project for other reasons. Or maybe, the problem was in the way the project was defined, or both. I do not know, because I never saw him again. The question was raised again at an SBL annual meeting when Itumeleng Mosala published his book entitled *Black Biblical Interpretation* and was soundly grilled by the panel that included Felder. His work focused on South African Blacks. This issue was also carried over in another way when a brother who clearly identified himself as a self-avowed atheist and taught Bible in a university was interrogated about how he could participate in this project. Like the Caribbean brother, and perhaps for similar reasons, he did not return after that first year.

Gender tensions emerged as well. In the first year, Clarice Martin was the only female in attendance. Renita Weems attended in the second year. There was speculation about Weems's reasons for not attending that first year, but not about the males that failed to attend, which I found unnecessary. Martin, on the other hand, endured the misogyny alone in that first year. As a very dear friend and colleague, Kelly Brown Douglas, once remarked in a class she taught at my institute in Cleveland, "all men are recovering chauvinists." At first I bristled at the thought, but the more I considered Douglas's statement, given the culture of our times, I realized she was probably correct. Given that Martin participated as the only woman, we could have and should have been better. She was forced to correct our behaviors, and I learned immensely from those moments. For example, Martin pushed us to use more gender-inclusive language.

Weems arrived in the second year, and one would have thought we would be better prepared for two women scholars, given the dynamics of the first year, but as Brown asserted, we were still recovering. I had not met Martin or Weems before their arrival to the project. In fact, I had not met any of the participants before our gathering, except Hoyt, who invited me. However, Martin and Weems became two of my closest friends; Weems remains perhaps the dearest to this day. We have intersected more than any of them in numerous places across this country. She has become like the dearest sister I never had. I learned more than I can ever repay from these two sisters. Weems, in particular, has always helped me to be more gender-and denominationally inclusive in all aspects of my work and ministry.

At a crucial moment in the first year, I left before the session was over. Two small children of a woman I grew up with in our church had drowned. The little girl was around seven years old and her brother was nine years old. They were visiting a park with the mother's sister. Neither could swim. The little girl fell into a pond, and the little boy jumped in to save her, knowing he could not swim. They both drowned. I had to leave. The weight of this tragedy was overwhelming, and more important to me than any project. Honestly, I was looking for a reason to leave. The weight of the tensions that arose among the participants was too much for me. I just wanted out, but I felt guilty about letting Tom Hoyt down. Somehow he found out and came knocking at my door, thinking the tensions were my reason for leaving. That big pastoral heart kicked in again. He pleaded with me not to leave and give up on the project. I told him about the deaths and that I needed to go. He said he understood and that by all means, I should go, but requested that I not abandon the project but return the next year. Apparently, he told the group that I left. Although I received encouragement from a number of the participants, Hoyt and Martin were the constant souls who would not let me go. Tom called me often thereafter, but it was a letter from Clarice, the most beautiful that I have ever received, that kept me connected. We went on to become dear friends. It was the care and concern for me the person, not the project participant, that tethered me to the project. And I returned to see it through.

The tensions were weathered and overcome by the humanity of the people and their love, friendship, and kindness that transcended and covered a multitude of sins. Those tensions made me a better, kinder, more observant, and caring person, I hope. But, if I have failed, it is not the fault of the project participants with whom I spent three summers in that wilderness experience. Sometime later, when the participants met in DC at Howard University, I was selected to present the sermon in the Chapel. I preached about that summer of crisis. Patrick Henry said it was one of the top sermons he had ever heard. Felder told me that my sermon must be published; he published it in the *Journal of Religious Thought*. Someone said, "it is rough seas that make the best sailors." Tensions have a way of shaping character for better or worse. However, it is love that wins over all else.

Yes, we experienced tensions and hurt feelings. Some threw in the towel, and others wanted to, but in the end the deep abiding grace imparted to us overflowed into super abounding grace for many others to come. In response to Felder's question—"Are we going to complete this publication or not?"—we did not "cut bait." We fished, and oh, the haul we caught.

TOUR DE FORCE

I started teaching in the field of biblical studies at Ashland Theological Seminary in 1984. I taught in the discipline of finance for seven years prior to arriving at Ashland and worked in the financial field for sixteen years concurrently. My life changed forever in 1986 when I joined a group of African American biblical scholars that I neither met nor knew existed. This would become a watershed moment in biblical interpretation, the likes of which I do not believe anyone envisioned at the beginning.

In 1986, a Lilly grant was awarded in conjunction with the Ecumenical Institute to assemble the entirety of African American biblical scholars in the nation, to convene in one place and to become acquainted with each other and share our journeys. Some left after the first year, never to return, as stated above. The rest of us spent two additional summers together in 1987 and 1988. The intense contact with each other continued, culminating with the publication of *Stony the Road* in 1991. While a total of fifteen people began this journey, only eleven contributed chapters to the book. A variety of reasons account for the reduced number of submissions, including other publication responsibilities, failure to meet the schedule as required, and so on.

There was no conversation about producing a book like *Stony the Road* either in the initial invitation or at the beginning of our conversations, at least not as I recall. Somewhere along the journey the idea of a book emerged. Initially, however, our time together centered around the stories we had shared, whether something could or should come out of those stories. We walked, ate, and worshipped together in a Catholic service on campus, and we fellowshipped at Patrick Henry's home. Together, we swatted away or ran from deer flies. I had never heard of or seen a deer fly. A deer fly is as large as a bee and delivers a bite. We sang, laughed, and cried together; we irritated the hell out of each other on more than a few occasions. Ultimately, we bonded together as a cohesive group to produce a feat of enormous proportions that cascaded across the discipline, disrupting everywhere it went.

The conversation had shifted to a publication of a critical engagement of how an African American hermeneutic differed from the dominant Eurocentric approach. What this group accomplished and engendered in those three summers and across that season of five years at that time in history is just phenomenal. I, for one, do not think what flowed from our meetings will ever be matched. The book itself may be surpassed, updated, and at some point seen only as a relic for another time. The production itself, what flowed from it and after it, cannot be surpassed. Such is the case with many vanguard achievements, many firsts. Let us consider the cascading ripples that flowed from that historic moment.

We published the first critical hermeneutical volume from a group of African American biblical scholars. It not only challenged the dominant approach, laying out the methodological, historical, and ideological issues, but demonstrated how it could be done differently, at a table of our making, centering our voices at the table.

One of the challenges we decided to face head-on was the lack of African American biblical scholars, male and, especially, female in biblical studies in the guild. Therefore, all the participants agreed unanimously to contribute all the proceeds to the FTE (then, the Fund for Theological Education, now the Forum) to be distributed equally to Black males and females going into the discipline of biblical studies. We held a celebration for the publication of the book in Washington, DC, called *Paving the Stony Road*. We invited students in seminaries across the country considering PhD studies. Our objective was to encourage more African American students to go into the discipline of biblical interpretation. The book became the fastest-selling book in Fortress Press history and remained a top seller for many years to come. I still remember the wonderful, glowing letters that I received from Oscar McCloud for years about how much the book contributed to the FTE. I recall many of the names of those the funds helped. Today, many of them remain a who's who in the study of the Bible with their own achievements.

We started the first African American Hermeneutics section in SBL that is still active today. We helped and supported many younger scholars get their footing in the guild through that section. Randall Bailey published an article entitled "Academic Biblical Interpretation among African Americans in the United States," many years after those summers, and listed by name all the scholars that had been produced to that date. The count was forty-five at that point, a 400 percent increase. Now, I think its well in excess of two hundred African American biblical scholars. The publications at the time were perhaps a couple dozen or so. Now they number in the thousands.

Many of the participants went on to achieve historic firsts in their own right. Vincent Wimbush became the first African American president of SBL. Cain Felder started his own Biblical Institute for Social Change. Wimbush started his own Institute for Signifying Scriptures. I became the first Black biblical scholar tenured at Ashland, and I founded the McCreary Center for African Religious Studies Institute where, across the years, many participants came to teach Black students and give public lectures. Renita Weems went on to become one of the most prolific writers and freelance public theologians of our times. Tom Hoyt became the Presiding Prelate of the entire CME denomination. The collective publications of this group alone are noteworthy. Other important works followed *Stony the Road*, of which many of the participants were contributors in those works as well, for example, *True to Our Native Land, The Africana Bible,* and this volume, *Bitter the Chastening Rod* (BTCR).

Yet, with all of these impressive accomplishments, it is the relationships that emerged from that moment, some lasting a lifetime, that matters above all else. These friendships, supporters, partners in the struggle are what matter most. Those summers in the wilderness bound us together in spite of tensions and allowed us to overcome even ourselves to do a greater work than these.

I find it rather fulfilling that many of us from the *Stony* project were involved in a variety of ways in the lives of many of the contributors to this work. The eulogist for Felder, Brian Blount, was a student of Felder and general editor of *True to Our Native Land*. The general editor of this work, Mitzi J. Smith, was a student and teacher's assistant of Felder. Life has a way of coming full circle sometimes. We are intersected and interwoven in ways we might never fully consider until someone leaves us. It is not lost on me, either, that the script has flipped in this work from ours in ways we not only fought for but contributed to. The males outnumbered the females in *Stony* by a large margin, but that gap has narrowed in this volume. Equity in gender is but one of the things we strove to achieve. This volume is one testament to that long, hard work.

Finally, in this Zoom bubble that we find ourselves in over this last year, perhaps this group was not destined to a face-to-face interchange together like the earlier group had. In one sense, the group that produced *Stony* was not able to Zoom in on the moment that produced *this* work. But we, then, had a different kind of "Zoom" interaction. Yet, I find in these BTCR contributions a similar desire for the same end result—"black [bodies] lives matter." May this group remember that their lives matter also, and not forget what they have achieved "together" in their own Zoom moment.

Cone, Cannon, and Felder have left us; so too have Long, Wilmore, Hoyt, and others. Nevertheless, we who are left behind must carry on. Yet, their memories remain with us. The beauty of this work is that it is self-evident that there are those ready to take up the mantle and carry on. Let us not, however, overlook the relationships that we create as we do this work. In fact, as Weems reminds us well, what transcends it all is to remember "[Our] Friends." I hope this group remembers, whatever this work accomplishes, those precious friends we gain are more important than any notoriety this work can create. Don't forget, they are only with us for a moment. From one generation to another, as long as there remains someone to take up the mantle, the struggle for liberation will go forth. Carry on, then! I will be watching, cheering you on. So too, will that great cloud of witnesses.

PART II

God's Black(ened) People in the World—Thugs, Slaves, and Criminals

Chapter 4

God's Only Begotten Thug

Allen Dwight Callahan

> It is naturally impossible for me to prove that the deterioration in the position of humble citizens—and indeed of poor free men in general—during the first two centuries of the Christian era was due to the deliberate desire of the upper classes to reduce their legal rights, with the aim of making them less able to defend themselves against increased exploitation: but it was . . . the direct effect.
>
> —G. E. M. de Ste. Croix (1981)

> In common law, a denizen was not a full citizen but had a status similar to that of a "resident alien" today; the law followed the ancient Roman idea of granting someone a right to live in a place but not to participate in its political life. Later, the word . . . was also used to refer to non-slave blacks in the United States before the abolition of slavery.
>
> —Guy Standing (2011, 93)

> A deep-seated ambivalence has always characterized the official response to the political prisoner. Charged and tried for the criminal act, his guilt is always political in nature. . . . It is not surprising that Nazi Germany's foremost constitutional lawyer, Carl Schmitt, advanced the theory which generalized this a priori culpability. A thief, for example, was not necessarily one who had committed an overt act of theft, but rather one whose character renders him a thief.
>
> —Joy James (2004, 66)

As a historian, I confess to a certain amusement when I hear the Judeo-Christian tradition praised as the source of our concern for human rights. In fact, the great religious ages were notable for their indifference to human rights in the contemporary sense.

—Arthur Schlesinger, Jr. (1989, 1)

Criminals, it turns out, are the one social group in America we have permission to hate. . . . When we say someone was "treated like a criminal," what we mean to say is that he or she was treated as less than human, like a shameful creature. Hundreds of years ago, our nation put those considered less than human in shackles; less than one hundred years ago, we relegated them to the other side of town; today we put them in a cage.

—Michelle Alexander (2012, 141)

The top decile always owns more than 60 percent of the wealth available for inheritance, while the bottom half of the population owns nothing.

—Thomas Piketty (2014, 616n.7)

Me and my niggas are on some Black Jesus shit. Not a new religion or anything, but the saint for thugs and gangstas—not killers and rapists, but thugs. When I say thugs, I mean niggas who don't have anything.

—Tupac Shakur (1996, T7)

HOW THE OTHER HALF LIVES

Half of all the people in the world inherit nothing from their parents, accumulate nothing for themselves, and leave nothing to their children. Half of all the people in the world—"the bottom half"—are born with nothing, live with nothing, and die with nothing.

And all four of the Gospels agree that it is in that bottom half that we find Jesus of Nazareth. In all the Gospels, Jesus is represented as penniless, landless, and homeless. He is without a patrimony, for he neither inherits anything from his forebears nor bequeaths anything to his survivors. He lives in the shadow of political violence. He is arrested, convicted of a capital offense, and crucified, a mode of capital punishment the Romans considered too degrading to be inflicted upon Roman citizens. All the Gospels are aware of these things, yet show little interest in any of them.

Jesus is a denizen: not a citizen of the Roman Empire, but one of its tributary subjects. He is what the rap artist Tupac Shakur defined as a thug, one of that great majority of criminalized denizens without a patrimony. Shakur coins what philosophers of language call a "stipulative definition" of a thug:

"not killers and rapists. . . . I mean niggas who don't have anything." It is a definition based on neither what one is nor what one does, but on what one has—or rather, what one does not have.

"Nigga" is the twenty-first-century variant pronunciation of the word "nigger." Until recently, a nigger was a denizen of the United States who was the descendant of American chattel slaves. This remains, of course, its primary meaning. But now, after the disestablishment of American apartheid, features of this status, even a variant of the term itself, "nigga," may be applied to others whose rights and status as citizens are effectively denied or nonexistent. Such people are, in effect, "niggarized."

Niggarization is a complex of policies: a priori criminalization, illegal search and seizure, suspension of habeas corpus, torture, rape, and summary execution. It is inflicted upon detainees in Guantanamo; upon the prisoners in the shocking photos from Abu Ghraib; upon immigrants held in detention by ICE, upon American Muslim communities infiltrated by FBI informants. And it has been inflicted on the working-class descendants of American chattel slaves for a century and a half before it was inflicted upon any of these others.

Niggarization serves as foreign as well as domestic policy. Invading American soldiers are known to have called Iraqi inhabitants "sand niggers": a perversely apt sobriquet, for the invasion of Iraq and the occupation of Afghanistan—the martial law, the militarized policing, the assassinations, the surveillance, the wanton destruction of civic life—may be seen as the niggarization of an entire region.

The denizen is, by definition, niggarized. The denizen's putative guilt, asserted by the so-called criminal justice system, is a travesty, because criminality is not a question of behavior but of ontology: that is to say, a matter of what one is, not what one does. The birthright of denizens is a prison sentence. They are born guilty.

Consequently, it is very, very easy for denizens to catch a case, and very, very hard for them not to. For them, there is no shorter distance between two points. Thus, denizens are either struggling to get out of jail or struggling to stay out of jail. And it is a struggle, a perverse game with marked cards and the deck stacked against them, for the lavish infrastructure for their incarceration is much more amply endowed than those for their health, safety, education, accommodations, or employment—more amply endowed than all of these combined.

The denizen is a criminal by fiat. In the Bottom Half, people are what they are and have what they have by fiat: they are what they are and have what they have because the People Who Matter say so. Titles, whether in the sense of a status designation or in the sense of a deed to land, matter. On the other hand, what people are and what people have bear little or no relation to what they make or what they do. What is decisive is who they are to the People

Who Matter. Thus the nepotism, the favoritism, the cronyism that honors elites and dishonors all Others—the inevitable, inescapable effects of inherited wealth, hereditary privilege, and private property.

Jesus is in that cohort that has no wealth to secure, having inherited nothing and having nothing to pass on to those surviving him: that cohort of denizens, of "niggas who don't have anything." Indeed, this is a recurring feature of the stories told about Jesus: he is a subject, subject to poverty, violence, and disrespect throughout his life—the life of a thug—from cradle to grave.

BORN UNLUCKY

The Gospel of John gives the following account of the popular response to Jesus as he holds forth in the courtyard of the Jerusalem Temple:

> When they heard these words, some in the crowd said, "This is really the prophet." Others said, "This is the Messiah." But some asked, "Surely the Messiah does not come from Galilee, does he? Has not the scripture said that the Messiah is descended from David and comes from Bethlehem, the village where David lived?" So there was a division in the crowd because of him. Some of them wanted to arrest him, but no one laid hands on him. (John 7:40–43)

The controversy is a conflict of opinions about Jesus's origin, and whether it disqualifies him from being a messiah. The messiah is expected to work "signs," that is, to be a miracle-worker, which Jesus is. But the messiah is also expected to be a descendant of David, and so from Bethlehem, David's hometown—which Jesus is not.

The Gospel of Luke opens with an elaborate story that, in its own way, addresses Jesus's controversial origins. The birth of Jesus is announced by juxtaposing it with and so dignifying it by references to the Emperor Augustus and Quirinius, governor of Syria—people in power, people who make history, People Who Matter. Though Jesus's parents live in Nazareth, and though Jesus is raised there (see Luke 1:26; 2:3–4, 39; 4:15–16), it is precisely because Joseph, the father of Jesus, is a descendant of King David that he is required by Roman imperial decree to be registered in the census in David's ancestral home town, Bethlehem. Joseph makes the trek to Bethlehem with his expectant fiancée, Mary, in tow. Soon after they arrive in Bethlehem, Mary gives birth to Jesus (Luke 2:4–7). It is Bethlehem, then, not Nazareth, that comes to be stamped on Jesus's birth certificate, as it were.

In this way, the Gospel of Luke has it both ways. It acknowledges that Jesus hails from the otherwise undistinguished hamlet of Nazareth. At the same time, the Gospel claims that Jesus as a scion of the House of David, born in the City of David, and so is qualified to be the Messiah.

The Gospel of Luke further validates the claim that Jesus is the messiah by showing the piety of Jesus's royal but impoverished family. Jesus bears his congenital poverty in accordance with Mosaic Law: "This is the law for her who bears a child, male or female. If she cannot afford a sheep, she shall take two turtledoves or two pigeons. one for a burnt offering and the other for a sin offering; and the priest shall make atonement on her behalf, and she shall be clean" (Lev 12:1–8). The Gospel of Luke knows of this rite, knows that there is a two-tiered pricing structure, and that the family of an artisan from Nazareth could only have fulfilled its requirements at the lower rate. The point here is not the poverty of Jesus's family: that is a given. The point is that the family's poverty is scrupulously law-observant. The poverty of Jesus is, according to the Gospel of Luke, kosher.

That Jesus hails from Nazareth is common knowledge in the Gospel of Matthew. Jesus is popularly known as "the prophet Jesus from Nazareth in Galilee" (Matt 21:11). But the Gospel of Matthew opens with the premier claim that it makes throughout: that Jesus is a born messiah: "An account of the genealogy of Jesus the Messiah, the son of David, the son of Abraham" (Matt 1:1). Like the Gospel of Luke, the Gospel of Matthew too wants to show that Jesus's birth certificate is issued in Bethlehem (Matt 2:1–12), for Jesus is that "one who is to rule in Israel," as foretold in the scriptures. And those scriptures speak of that ruler as coming from "Bethlehem, in the land of Judah."

Only later does the Gospel of Matthew note that Jesus makes his home in Nazareth. But this too is in fulfillment of the scriptures: "There he made his home in a town called Nazareth, so that what had been spoken through the prophets might be fulfilled, 'He will be called a Nazorean'" (Matt 2:23), though it is unclear just what a "Nazorean" is—if it is supposed to mean "Nazarene," the atrocious spelling is a *hapax legomenon*—or which "prophets" are being referred to.

The upshot: Jesus is from both the storied village of Bethlehem *and* the impoverished village of Nazareth. The Gospel of Matthew, too, has it both ways.

Then there is the other side of the question.

THUG LIFE

The Gospel of John knows that Jesus is not from "Bethlehem, in the land of Judah." The Gospel's messianic claims for him are challenged, however, because of where he *is* from—Nazareth, a jerkwater in the impoverished northern region of ancestral Israelite territory called Galilee. The messiah is expected to be a descendant of David from Bethlehem, David's hometown. David is mentioned in the entire Gospel only here, and Jesus is not addressed as "son of David" anywhere by anyone in the Gospel of John. The Gospel tacitly concedes that Jesus is not a "son of David."

The Gospel of John introduces Jesus as the "son of Joseph from Nazareth." The name "Jesus of Nazareth" appears in official proceedings against him: it is the name of record on his arrest warrant and on his death sentence (John 18:3–8, 19:19–21). The charge that Jesus is "the King of the Judeans" is disputed (see John 19:21). But none dispute that he is the Man from Nazareth. Nevertheless, the Gospel of John concedes that Nazareth is not only not the "right" place for a messiah. Indeed, it is not even a good place: "Can anything good come out of Nazareth?" (John 1:45).

The Gospel of Luke, its insistence on Jesus's Judean pedigree notwithstanding, acknowledges that the parents of Jesus live in Nazareth, and that Jesus is known to have grown up there (Luke 2:39; 4:16). According to the Gospel of Mark, Jesus begins his public career after having come from Nazareth to be baptized by John. Throughout the narrative, everyone knows that Jesus is from Nazareth. Even the demons know it (see Mark 1:21–24).

Later in the Gospel of Mark, the native son returns home, only to be rejected by his own people (6:1–6). The townsfolk "knew him when," and regard what he is now as effrontery. Their words drip with disdain. Jesus is "the carpenter, the son of Mary": that Jesus is identified as the son of his mother and not the son of his father, whom the Gospel of Mark never mentions, is an odd way to refer to a grown man in a traditional, patriarchal society. The word rendered here as "carpenter," *tektōn*, "artisan, craftsman," signifies a peasant who does not work his land for a living because he has no land to work. That is why he is an artisan: he has been reduced to working with his hands, his marketable skill—and the market for it—the only thing between him and destitution. The rebuff leaves Jesus not only "amazed" but incapacitated: "he could do no deed of power there" (Mark 6:5).

In the Gospel of Luke's lengthier version of the episode (Luke 4:16–30), the homecoming is a near-death experience. But Jesus is violently rejected at Nazareth because of what he says, not because of what he is—and is not. Jesus is "Joseph's son": there is no mention either of Jesus's mother or his siblings. Neither Joseph nor his son is identified as a *tektōn*. It is Jesus's tough talk, not his humble status, that offends his audience. And here, in contrast to the account in the Gospel of Mark, it is the audience, not Jesus, that is amazed—before things get ugly, that is. Jesus's hasty retreat affords him no time for miraculous cures, for none are reported. According to the Gospel of Luke, Jesus is shut down in Nazareth not by unbelief, but by attempted murder.

In the Gospel of Matthew's version of the homecoming, Jesus is not "the carpenter" but "the carpenter's son," an oblique reference to Jesus's father that distances Jesus from manual labor (Matt 13:54–58): it is Jesus's father, not Jesus himself, who is the *tektōn*. There is no word of his amazement at the people's unbelief. But even in this kinder, gentler version of the episode, Jesus is rejected and disrespected. He is a prophet without honor in his own country.

A Lean and Hungry Look

And on occasion, he is also a prophet without lunch. For Jesus, daily bread was precarious. The episode of an improvised meal on the go, in which Jesus's disciples snatch up and eat ripe grain on the Sabbath while passing through a farmer's field, is similarly recounted in three of the Gospels (Luke 6:1–5; Mark 2:23–28; Matt 12:1–8). The Pharisees condemn the hungry men for violating the blanket prohibition in Mosaic Law against all forms of labor on the sabbath (Exo 31:14–15).

Yet ancient Israelite law granted to indigent people the right to glean fields, that is, to collect the residue of crops already harvested (Lev 23:22). The landowner was even prohibited from doubling back to try to collect any remaining fruit. Whatever was left behind after the first pass of the harvesters belonged to the poor by right. And hungry passers-by were allowed, within limits, to help themselves to ripe grain: "If you go into your neighbor's standing grain, you may pluck the ears with your hand, but you shall not put a sickle to your neighbor's standing grain" (Deut 23:24–25).

None of the three versions of this episode mentions these Mosaic provisions. It is simply taken for granted that, due to their poverty, Jesus's companions are reduced to finding their meals in the grainfields of others by hand—and that they were entitled to do so by law. What is controversial in this controversy story, then, is not what the disciples are doing, or how they are doing it, but when. They are plucking grain, to which they otherwise have an ancestral right, on the wrong day of the week.

The accusation of violating the sabbath, of course, catches Jesus and company red-handed. Jesus's defense is to appeal to what he claims to be a venerable precedent: all three versions allude to the same legendary episode from the life of David, at a moment in his multifarious career when, as a gangsta on the run, he seeks asylum at a sanctuary in the Judean town of Nob (see 1 Sam 21:1–6).

Several narrative flourishes appear in all three retellings that are not found in the account in First Samuel as it has come to us. All three Gospels mention that David is accompanied by a goon squad, and that David and his gang were in urgent need of victuals and already famished. All three versions refer to the shrine in Nob as "the house of God," an epithet identified exclusively with Jerusalem. The shrine is attended not by a mere priest but by a "high priest." In the more ancient account, David demands bread, but does enter the shrine—suggesting that it was the fearful priest who comes out of the shrine to meet *him* ("the priest . . . was afraid at the meeting of David," 1 Sam 21:1). Nothing is said of David eating the bread. But the Gospels represent David as taking the sacred bread, dividing it among the members of his gang, and eating it on the spot. The Gospel of Luke specifically says that David took the bread and divvied it up personally (Luke 6:4).

The Gospel of Mark adds two further details. Neither the Gospel of Matthew nor the Gospel of Luke mention the name of the priest. The Gospel of Mark does: "Abiathar." This is contrary to notices elsewhere in the Bible that the priest at Nob is named Ahimelech, and that Abiathar is the name of Ahimelech's son, a priest who officiates not in Nob but in Jerusalem. The other detail that the Gospel of Mark adds is Jesus's declaration, "The sabbath was made for humankind, and not humankind for the sabbath." Neither the Gospel of Matthew nor the Gospel of Luke goes this far. In the Gospel of Mark, Jesus makes a pronouncement that authorizes not only Jesus but anyone who hungers may eat what is at hand—even on the sabbath.

The Gospel of Matthew calls attention to the priests' lawful violation of the sabbath, and adds to Jesus's rebuttal yet another proof text: "But if you had known what this means, 'I desire mercy and not sacrifice,' you would not have condemned the guiltless." Jesus quotes an oracle of mercy as divine imperative found in the book of the prophet Hosea, though Jesus, true to form, does not cite chapter and verse (see Hos 6:6). A recurring critique of the Gospel of Matthew is that the Pharisees, the supposed custodians of "the Law and the Prophets," do not read them rightly and do not apply them justly. Jesus turns the accusation against the gleaners into a teachable moment to school the Pharisees on the right interpretation of the Scriptures—Jesus's interpretation, that is.

In none of the three versions of the sabbath controversy is there any reference to the Mosaic provisions for those who are hungry and those who are poor, though all the versions suggest that Jesus is both, and that to travel with him made for precarious meals.

On The Road

All the Gospels also agree that Jesus travels a lot. And that, too, could be precarious.

The Jesus of the Gospel of John is never at home. His first recorded journey with his disciples is a trip from Judea to Cana in Galilee for a wedding. Later, after celebrating a festival in Jerusalem he and his disciples go into

Aenon in Judea to compete with John the Baptist: "After this Jesus and his disciples went into the Judean countryside, and he spent some time there with them and baptized. John also was baptizing at Aenon near Salim because water was abundant there" (John 3:22–24).

But Jesus's compulsive traveling is also a security measure. In Jerusalem, Jesus becomes the target of a murder conspiracy after healing a cripple on the sabbath (John 5:1–18). Even in his native Galilee, among members of his own family, Jesus is ill at ease. Nowhere does the Gospel of John suggest that Jesus stayed with his Galilean relatives. As pilgrims prepare to make the southward trek to Jerusalem, Jesus's family urges him to accompany them on the pilgrimage. The tension is occasion for stealth, and even, it would appear, dissimulation.

> After this Jesus went about in Galilee. He did not wish to go about in Judea because the Judeans were looking for an opportunity to kill him. Now the Jewish festival of Tabernacles was near. So his brothers said to him, "Leave here and go to Judea so that your disciples also may see the works you are doing; for no one who wants to be widely known acts in secret. If you do these things, show yourself to the world." (For not even his brothers believed in him.) Jesus said to them, "My time has not yet come, but your time is always here. The world cannot hate you, but it hates me because I testify against it that its works are evil. Go to the festival yourselves. I am not going to this festival, for my time has not yet fully come." After saying this, he remained in Galilee. But after his brothers had gone to the festival, then he also went, not publicly but in secret. (John 7:1–10)

Where Jesus says, "I am not going to the feast," an ancient manuscript tradition reads "I am not going to the feast yet." Other ancient manuscripts read that Jesus followed his family, going to the feast after them "as though in secret." These early variants attempt to rescue Jesus from appearing to be dissembling. On any reading, Jesus misleads his family, whom he distrusts, about his whereabouts.

On several other occasions Jesus is constrained to leave Jerusalem because of attempts on his life, arrest warrants, and death threats. Later he absconds to Bethany, a small suburb several miles outside of Jerusalem, where he finds some short-lived relief. But even there, he is not safe.

According to the Gospel of Mark, it is the ominous report of the arrest of John the Baptist that spurs Jesus's initial return to Galilee: "Now after John was arrested, Jesus came to Galilee, proclaiming the good news of God" (Mark 1:14). The Gospel of Matthew, too, notes that Jesus goes to Galilee after learning of John's arrest, though the journey is but the fulfillment of a prophetic oracle (Matt 4:12–17).

In the Gospel of Luke, however, Jesus comes and goes without subterfuge and without anxiety. Jesus heads to Galilee a hale fellow well-met under the power of the Holy Spirit. There is no mention of the arrest of John the Baptist, and Jesus's sole motive is his mission. Later Jesus is warned about Herod Antipas, who by this time has had John beheaded. Jesus spurns the warning with prophetical swag: "At that very hour some Pharisees came and said to him, 'Get away from here, for Herod wants to kill you.' He said to them, "Go and tell that fox for me, 'Listen, I am casting out demons and performing cures today and tomorrow, and on the third day I finish my work'" (13:31–32). Jesus has already set his course for Jerusalem (9:51) because, as he explains, "it cannot be that a prophet perish out of Jerusalem" (13:33), and so is stoically resolved to perish there.

The Gospels, then, ascribe various motives at various times to Jesus's frequent changes of venue. But they agree that Jesus is a man without a permanent address. At no time, even when he is at home in Nazareth, is he ever at home. He is a son of man with no place to lay his head.

You're Under Arrest

Jesus's enemies in Jerusalem have sought to capture and kill him, and eventually they do. The Gospels agree that Jesus is betrayed in Jerusalem by a paid informant in his own inner circle, and is arrested in the middle of the night by an armed detail. While in custody, he is tortured and interrogated. Following a brief hearing, the Roman governor of Judea, Pontius Pilate, passes sentence and condemns the prisoner to be summarily executed.

All four Gospels agree that Jesus was crucified along with two other men who were known criminals. They tell a story about three convicted criminals as a story about two convicted criminals and Jesus. The narrative sleight-of-hand sets Jesus apart, obscuring the brute fact that his conviction juridically certifies him as a thug.

As it does with the infamy of Jesus's Galilean origin, the Gospel of John makes the best of Jesus's execution as a thug among thugs by acknowledging what the audience must already know. The Gospel does so, nevertheless, without calling the criminals criminals.

So they took Jesus; and carrying the cross by himself, he went out to what is called The Place of the Skull, which in Hebrew is called Golgotha. There they crucified him, and with him two others, one on either side, with Jesus between them (John 19:16–18).

According to the Gospel of Luke, Jesus is not really a thug, and there is nothing at all thuggish about what he or his associates are up to (see 23:13–25, 39–42). Jesus is executed between two "malefactors" (23:32,33, 39): Jesus is not one himself, but merely a lotus floating unsullied atop a mud pond of seditious thuggery. The Gospel of Mark (15:27) and the Gospel of Matthew (27:38) report that Jesus was crucified between two "thieves," *lēstai*, a word used to describe the banditti of the Palestinian outback who, for want of work and bread, take up a life of highway robbery.

All the Gospels tell different, bowdlerized versions of the same story: that Jesus was accused as a thug, arrested as a thug, charged as a thug, tried as a thug, found guilty of a thug's crime, and condemned to a thug's death.

The King Is Dead

Jesus is homeless. He lives that way. And he dies that way.

The Gospel of John, which shows little interest in the material conditions of Jesus's life, nevertheless relates some of the material conditions of his death:

> When the soldiers had crucified Jesus, they took his clothes and divided them into four parts, one for each soldier. They also took his tunic; now the tunic was seamless, woven in one piece from the top. So they said to one another, 'Let us not tear it, but cast lots for it to see who will get it." This was to fulfill what the scripture says,"They divided my clothes among themselves, and for my clothing they cast lots."
> And that is what the soldiers did. (John 19:23–25)

Jesus's only personal effects at his time of death were his clothes: no wallet, money, jewelry, tools, or weapons. Jesus's tunic is gambled away as he dies, in fulfillment of a line of poetry found in Psalm 22, interpreted here as an oracle. In ancient Israelite tradition, this psalm is the cry of a king who suffers the scorn and derision of his enemies while weakened and defenseless. It appears in the narrative just after the announcement of the text of the placard that Pilate orders placed over the cross, "Jesus of Nazareth, the King of the Judeans." He is a king of shreds and patches; but that Jesus died owning only the clothes on his back afforded the narrator the opportunity to read Jesus's poverty as prophecy.

A soldier pokes Jesus's dead body—his only inalienable possession—with his spear, and "blood and water" issue from the postmortem wound. "For these things were done," explains the narrator, "that the scripture should be fulfilled, . . . 'They shall look on him whom they pierced'" (John 19:34). The impalement of Jesus's body on the cross, alleges the narrator, thus fulfills the prophetic oracle of a coming day of lamentation in Jerusalem:

> And I will pour out a spirit of compassion and supplication on the house of David and the inhabitants of Jerusalem, so that, when they look on the one whom they have pierced, they shall mourn for him, as one mourns for an only child, and weep bitterly over him, as one weeps over a firstborn. (Zechariah 12:10)

The grisly scene is revisited in Bach's *St. John's Passion*; in the figure of the angel catching in a chalice the blood and water that spurts from Jesus's wounded side in Raphael's altarpiece *Crucifixion*; in the plaintive lyrics of the Negro Spiritual "Were You There?" ("Were you there/ When they pierced him in the side?/ Oh, sometimes it causes me to tremble, tremble, tremble"). Later ages would make art of this desecration of a poor man's dead body.

> And so Jesus dies, having little personal property. And no real property.
> Meanwhile, standing near the cross of Jesus were his mother, and his mother's sister, Mary the wife of Clopas, and Mary Magdalene. When Jesus saw his mother and the disciple whom he loved standing beside her, he said to his mother, "Woman, here is your son." Then he said to the disciple, "Here is your mother." And from that hour the disciple took her into his own home. (John 19:25–27)

Jesus is not a citizen of the Roman Empire: he is a denizen. He is a criminalized denizen: crucifixion was the capital punishment of rebels and slaves. And he is a denizen without a patrimony, for he neither inherits a house from his father nor bequeaths one to his surviving mother who, homeless, is a denizen as well. The Gospel of John knows neither her name nor the names of any of her other children, who are absent in her destitution at the foot of the cross.

The scene is a grim contrast to the felicitous gathering at the home of Lazarus in Bethany only a week before, where Jesus is feted, celebrated, and even anointed with expensive aromatic oil by Mary, sister of the recently-resurrected Lazarus (John 12:1–8). "Jesus loved Martha and her sister and Lazarus," notes the narrator (John 11:5). And apparently they loved him, too. Mary, her sister Martha, and their brother Lazarus are non-priestly elites who welcome Jesus's criticism of the corrupt Jerusalem priesthood, and they afford him social and material support. They are not denizens: they are privileged, propertied, upper-class Judeans. At their dinner parties, they are the hosts, not the help.

The arch-traitor Judas, who complains about Mary's extravagance, holds the money for Jesus and his entourage. Later the narrator editorializes, "Some thought that, because Judas had the common purse, Jesus was telling him . . . that he should give something to the poor" (John 13:29). According to the Gospel of John, Jesus and his partisans give alms; they do not receive them. The poor people of the Gospel are nameless: "poor," the adjective, has become a substantive, a collective noun for anonymous mendicancy—the "the poor" of Catholic encyclicals, of Evangelical piety, of neoliberal welfare reform, the poor "you always have with you" (John 12:8). It is a view of poverty from the vantage of the well-off, well-connected Friends of Jesus, whom the Gospel features by name: Mary, Martha, and Lazarus, Nicodemus, and, later, Joseph of Arimathea. In the Gospel of John, "the poor" have no names.

With one important exception, of course. Jesus, indigent in death as in life, becomes a homeless cadaver. Someone must donate a tomb for a proper burial. All four Gospels report that that someone is Joseph of Arimathea. It is Joseph who saves the pauper's corpse from a pauper's grave.

According to the Gospel of John, Joseph is a secret disciple of Jesus. He is joined by Nicodemus, another crypto-disciple who, the audience is reminded, came to Jesus under cover of darkness (19:39; see 3:1–2). Together, Joseph and Nicodemus have the body of Jesus embalmed in costly spices and placed in a nearby empty garden tomb that has not been sullied by the ritual impurity of a dead body.

Further, according to the Gospel of John, Jesus is condemned before Pilate's judgment seat, after the Jerusalem authorities make it clear that Jesus's mass appeal poses a threat the security of Jerusalem, the regional seat of Roman imperial power in Palestine. But in the Gospel of Luke, Jesus is brought up for a hearing before a council of Jerusalem leaders, which after questioning him formally condemns him of blasphemy and remands him to Roman custody (22:66–71, 23:1). Joseph is a pious member of this "assembly of the elders of the people, both chief priests and scribes" who has dissented from the decision to condemn Jesus: whether he is a scribe or a priest is not specified. Joseph petitions Pilate for the body, which Joseph has taken down from the cross, wrapped in linen, and put in a pristine tomb.

The Gospel of Mark explains that Joseph is an esteemed member of the Jerusalem council that condemns Jesus before he is sent to Pilate. The condemnation of the council is unanimous: the Gospel of Mark makes no mention of Joseph's dissent. Joseph "boldly" approaches Pilate for the body, which he is permitted to bury after Pilate has made sure that Jesus is dead. Joseph handles the funeral arrangements with dispatch: Jesus has died on the very eve of the Passover, and so everything must be done before all work is suspended in observance of the sabbath. What Joseph does he does quickly, having the unembalmed body wrapped in a linen shroud and deposited it in a nondescript rock-hewn tomb, which is then sealed shut with a stone.

The Gospel of Matthew tells us that Joseph is a wealthy disciple of Jesus, with no apparent relation to the council of Jerusalem leaders. Joseph has the unembalmed body of Jesus wrapped up in a "clean linen" shroud and placed in his own "new" rock-hewn tomb that he then has closed up with a heavy stone to prevent theft of the body (Matt 27:62–66).

All four Gospels offer variations on and embellishments of a single account to the effect that the family of Jesus does not bury him; that the funeral arrangements are handled by strangers; and that Jesus's body is laid to rest in a donated tomb. The details common to the four accounts of Jesus's burial agree that Jesus's poverty did not end with his life.

The Jesus of the Gospels is a pauper, a vagabond, a convict—a denizen. The Gospels take for granted that Jesus is born, lives, and dies as a thug. He inherits nothing and bequeaths nothing. He is without means and without a patrimony, subject to the disrespect and violence that attend his precarious poverty.

Jesus is like half of all the people in the world—the Bottom Half. In his birth, his life, and his death, the Gospel writers catch a brutal glimpse of how the other half lives.

And they look away.

WORKS CITED

Alexander, Michelle. 2012. *The New Jim Crow: Mass Incarceration in the Age of Colorblindness*. New York: The New Press.

James, Joy. 2004. *Imprisoned Intellectuals: America's Political Prisoners Write on Life, Liberation, and Rebellion*. New York: Rowman & Littlefield.

Piketty, Thomas. 2014. *Capital in the Twenty-First Century*. Cambridge, MA: Harvard University Press.

Ste. Croix, G. E. M. de. 1981. *The Class Struggle in the Ancient Greek World*. Ithaca, NY: Cornell University Press.

Schlesinger, Arthur Jr. 1989. "The Opening of the American Mind." *New York Times*, July 23, Section 7.

Standing, Guy. 2011. *The Precariat: The New Dangerous Class*. London: Bloomsbury Academic.

Tupac Shakur, *Tupac*. 1996. Quoted in Rob Marriott. "Last Testament." *Vibe Magazine*, November.

Chapter 5

Abolitionist Messiah
A Man Named Jesus Born of a Doulē

Mitzi J. Smith

You can kill a revolutionary, but you can't kill a revolution. You can kill a freedom fighter, but not freedom.

— Fred Hampton (1948–1969), Black Panther, African-American Activist

To know Jesus is to know him as revealed in the struggle of the oppressed for freedom. Their struggle is Jesus' struggle.

— James H. Cone (1938–2018)

Let's begin our abolitionist journey not with the question "What do we have now, and how can we make it better?" Instead, let's ask, "What can we imagine for ourselves and the world?" If we do that, then boundless possibilities of a more just world await us.

— Mariame Kaba (2021, 3)

PROLOGUE

Africana peoples have testified that God is a God of liberation, freedom, justice, and love. God is a God who hears, sees, and responds to the cries of the enslaved and oppressed (Ex 2:23–25). The Hebrew Bible exodus event demonstrated and reminds Israel that Yahweh is a liberator, and not an enslaver.

As a God of liberation, freedom, justice, survival, and love, God stands firmly on the side of the enslaved, the criminalized, brutalized, and dehumanized in every era. Inspired by the civil rights and Black power movements, James Cone (1997) declared that God sides with the oppressed. Cone wrote that "Black theology cannot accept a view of God which does not represent God as being for oppressed blacks and thus against white oppressors. Living in a world of white oppressors, blacks have no time for a neutral God" (1970, 70). In the Black interpretive tradition, Black people deployed Scripture to describe God and Jesus in ways consistent with the Black struggle for liberation (Cone 1997). Not all Scriptures are unequivocally liberative or liberative at all, and some are only descriptive of foreign events and narratives with little or no contemporary significance. To be contextually relevant, all Scriptures require interpretation or translation to function as good news for a particular person or community. Martin Luther King, Jr. insisted on the hermeneutical, moral and ethical relationship between the civil rights movement and the gospel of Jesus (Cone 2006, 127). God demonstrates God's solidarity with the oppressed through God's interventions and God's anointed revolutionary and abolitionist prophets, messiahs, hermeneuts, and movements. Further, Cone declared that God is a Black man. God is also a Black woman.

Stated differently, God is a Black(ened) man or woman. Black(ened) people, to use Zakiyyah Jackson's (2020) concept in *Becoming Human*, signifies the creation of and imposition of blackness on people of African descent as having stigmatized plastic flesh that is neither human nor animal *and* both human and animal, never fully either. In analyzing the "violence of humanization" in Toni Morrison's "neo-slave narrative," Jackson argues that "*Beloved* suggests that animalization and humanization of the slave's personhood are not mutually exclusive but mutually constitutive . . . the slave's humanity (the heart, the mind, the soul, and the body) is not denied or excluded but manipulated and prefigured as animal and whereby Black(ened) *humanity* is understood, paradigmatically, as a state of abject *human* animality" (2020, 46–47). Jackson asserts that "blackness" has been essential to "liberal humanism" and not excluded from it (ibid, 46). The "slave's humanity was cast in the terms of a globally expansive debate over what *kind* of human black(ened) people represented. To put it plainly, the discourse of race is a discourse of speciation" (ibid., 49). Slavery produced a "kind of human" on the "scale of being" (ibid., 46–48; *see* Douglass 2000, 312).

Within the ideo-theological and pseudo-anthropological economy of blackness, Africana peoples must sift through the broken shards of whitened Scriptures and biblical interpretations pressed and impressed upon us as God's Word to re-imagine and repurpose the useful remains and resurrect a God who created all human beings equal and free. Hugh Page asserts that Africana peoples "through the radical act of 'picking up pieces' and building assemblages—for example, 'pieces' of ideas, memories, traditions, texts, peoples, and so on— . . . continually formed, occasionally modified, and at times refashioned" a liberationist Christology (2010, 62). Cone (1997) argued that Scripture limited white people's use of Jesus Christ to sanction Black oppression. But boundaries have been and can be crossed under the pretense of true and correct interpretations and with an appeal to whiteness under the guise of exegesis and rigorous approaches to Scripture. Mainstream dominant white biblical scholars ask, "how do you know when you have crossed the line, gone too far?" It is the Black interpreter, the interpreter of color, or the woman to whom this question is put. And with that question, we are rendered fungible and Black(ended) because we overtly contextualize our readings, which are replaceable with other darkened bodies and readings that do not transgress the boundaries of whiteness.

Black life from enslavement through the present remains fungible—easily displaceable from life to death and replaceable as in dispensable and like any other Black(ened) body—precarious, exposed, traumatized, and tortured. In this chapter, I argue that Luke's Gospel presents Jesus as the child of an enslaved woman. Jesus is born in Nazareth of Galilee; he and his mother are Galileans (1:26; 2:39; 4:14). Josephus describes the Galileans (pejoratively?) as "fighters virtually from birth" and whose men have never lacked courage (2017, 3.42). God chose a Galilean *doulē* (enslaved female) named Mary to conceive a male child called Jesus whom the Spirit anointed in her womb to be an abolitionist, as announced in his inaugural sermon: "The Spirit of Yahweh is upon me because he has anointed me to bring good news to the poor . . . sent me to proclaim release to the captives and recovery of sight to the blind [conscientization is the precursor to activism] and to let the oppressed go free" (4:18 NRSV). All of these social categories encompass the plight of the average enslaved person: captive/enslaved, poor, and oppressed. In response to his courageous sermon and hermeneutics, Jesus is driven from the synagogue by attendees who attempt to kill him. He was in modern parlance "blackballed," as opposed to "whiteballed" (i.e., ostracized, outcast, stigmatized) that day. Put differently, Jesus was Black(ened), but the blackening of Jesus began before birth.

Any child born of an enslaved woman, is a slave, living but always dying in stigmatized Black(end) flesh.[1] Luke expressly identifies Jesus as an enslaved human being using the markers of a slave society. I propose that Jesus's story as a Black(ened) or enslaved male has been lost in translation. Modern readers euphemistically translate and spiritualize the text's linguistic signifiers of Jesus's enslavement. Particularly instances of the word *doulē* or *doulos* are strategically translated as "servant" in Luke. Clarice Martin responds with an emphatic "no" when asked whether it is better to translate *doulos* euphemistically (2015, 23). Martin (2015) further argues biblical translators and other modern interpreters who render *doulos* as "servant" obscure the fact that "rendering service" was "not a matter of choice" for the enslaved and thus translators promote an unrealistic view of the slave's lived reality. Further, a euphemistic translation of *doulos* "minimizes the full psychological weight of the institution of slavery itself" (Martin 2015, 25; see Lettsome 2021).

This chapter argues that Jesus lived in somatic and existential solidarity with other enslaved persons. I build on Winsome Munro's work in *Jesus Born a Slave* (1998) where she contends that Jesus was a slave because his birth mother, Mary, was an enslaved woman.[2] In *Black on Both Sides: A Racial History of Trans Identity*, C. Riley Snorton writes that "Flesh is, above all else, a thing that produces relations—real and imagined, metaphysical and material" (2017, 40). Munro wrote, "[no] amount of evidence for the metaphorical and allegorical use of the slave image, whether for Jesus or any others, automatically refutes the possibility that Jesus was an actual, literal slave" (1998, 68). Like Munro, I begin with a discussion of the historical context of Roman and Jewish enslavement. Second, I examine the Christological hymn in Philippians 2:6–11 that predates Luke's Gospel (and perhaps Paul's letters) and compare it with Mary's song in Luke, noting linguistic and theological similarities. As Munro asserts, the hymn "is either very close to, or close enough in time to the historical Jesus for the composer to have known that Jesus' social status was that of a slave, if he was one" (1998, 164). Third, I explore Luke's birth narrative and the beginnings of Jesus's public career in the historical context of enslavement. Finally, I address the significance of the phrase "sinners and tax collectors" and how viewing Jesus as an enslaved man might impact our understanding of that phrase. Luke's Gospel narrates Jesus's embodied solidarity with the enslaved who subsisted at the base of the paterfamilias or household structure. Interpreters can imagine Jesus as being of humble social status, but he cannot be situated at the bottom.

CONTEXT OF ROMAN SLAVERY AND JEWISH ENSLAVEMENT

Slavery across time and cultures is always dehumanizing and violent for the purpose of nation-building, productivity, and profits. Rome became a slave society—rather than a society with slaves—between the late second century and first century BCE (Joshel 2010, 7, 53, 56); it conquered, captured, traded in, and bred human flesh. People and nations were enslaved primarily through war, especially during the earliest years of the empire. However, in the first century CE, the enslaved population was replenished through the wombs of enslaved women as well as by war (Joshel 2010, 65–67). Slaves are treated as commodities and tools by which slave masters built and expanded empires, sustained socioeconomic status, and maintained extravagant and leisurely lives. The enslaved are fungible property—tradable, interchangeable, and replaceable commodities (Joshel 2010, 80–81). Some were manumitted or freed; most were not. In every slave or post-slavery society, the formerly enslaved carry the stigma of their enslavement in their bodies and in relation to oppressive structures and systems of society dominated by the progeny and heirs of enslavers. For freedpersons, that stigma was manifest in the continued patron relationship between freedpersons and their former masters. Slave masters are loath to relinquish their grip on the formerly enslaved, especially the most loyal and productive ones.

Rome enslaved thousands of Jewish people when the Roman general Pompey conquered Jerusalem in 63 BCE (before Jesus's birth) and during the first (66–73 CE) and second (132–35 CE) Jewish wars (Josephus 2017, 1.293, 1.305).[3] Captured Jewish women and boys were sold on the slave market as prostitutes (Hezser 2005,180). Yet, in the late first BCE and in first century CE, children born to enslaved women were a significant source for replenishing and maintaining the slave population, as stated (Glancy 2006, 74; Joshel 2010, 71; Hezser 2015, 197; Mouritsen 2015, 16).

Some Jewish people, including priests, owned the enslaved. In the Gospels, including Luke, the ear of the high priest's slave (*doulos*) is cut off when the soldiers arrest Jesus (22:50). Slaves were everywhere, including in rural areas where *rustica* (rural slaves) labored on farms and in fields. The populace of Galilee, where Jesus was born and ministered, did not escape the wrath of Rome and the concomitant violence of enslavement. According to Josephus, a large part of the population was enslaved in the first century BCE to first century CE (2017, 2:68–69, 3.60–62). This is the empire and region that Jesus was born into and where his mother lived.

PHILIPPIANS 2: A SLAVE SONG OF COUNTERCULTURAL HUMANIZATION

Prior to Luke's Gospel, the Christ-hymn in Paul's letter to the Philippians offers some evidence for Jesus as an enslaved man. Munro (1998) argues that the hymn is confirmation that the historical Jesus was born into slavery. Differently, Jennifer Glancy argues the hymn contains a "reference to [Jesus's] participation in the moral human condition" and not "an oblique clue that he was born and raised a slave" (2006, 101). I agree with Munro that the hymn pinpoints the particular social condition into which Jesus was born. The Christ-hymn states that "existing in the form [*morphē*] of God, Jesus did not consider [*hēgeomai*] the state of being equal to God something to unyieldingly possess" (2:6). "But [*alla*; strong adversative] he emptied [*ekenōsen*] himself taking on the form [*morphē*] of an enslaved man [*doulos*], becoming in the likeness of human beings and in outward appearance [*schēmati*], he was found as a human being [*anthrōpos*]" (2:7). Jesus willingly became a species or kind of a human being, a slave and in a form ostensibly discernable by other human beings in his context. The unmitigated description of Jesus as a *doulos* (i.e., without possessives "of God" or "of the Lord") was likely conceived "to deal with the fact that Jesus was quite unequivocally and literally a slave" and recognized as one (Munros 1998, 173). However, Munro argues that Jesus was "a unique kind of slave, . . . a divine being" who deprived himself of equality with God (Munro 1998, 175; contra, Briggs 1989 views the hymn metaphorically). By calling Jesus both a *doulos* (enslaved) and a human (*anthrōpon*), the hymn subverts attempts to view *doulos* metaphorically *and* rejects the ideology that the slave is simply a tool and not human in God's eyes. The use of *doulos* and *anthrōpos* in reference to his form (*morphē*) is also subversive to Rome or any slave society that considered the enslaved as property to be owned, used, or useful, and counted among one's livestock (see Philemon v.11; Patterson 2018; Vasser 2018). Munro argues that "the name call *doulos*, not being capable of refutation, is sublimated into a badge of honor, like the battle scars that a [seriously injured] warrior displays" (1998, 175).

Paul's reference to himself and Timothy as "slaves [*douloi*] of Christ Jesus" in Philippians 1:1 is performative of their humility and solidarity with the historical Jesus's incarnate material reality (cf. Rom 1:1). Even though Paul adds the words "of Christ" to the identification of himself as a prisoner in the salutation, we do not treat his imprisonment metaphorically. Paul's solidarity is also demonstrated in the rhetoric of sharing (*koinōnia*) of the same mind and humility (*tapeinophrosynē*)—there is nothing shameful about being born a slave—which Paul expects the Philippians to imitate in Christ (2:1–5).

Philippians 2:8 deploys language typically associated with the enslaved: he humbled himself (*tapeinoō*) and became obedient (*hypēkoös*) up to [his] death, death by crucifixion. These behaviors—unmitigated humility and obedience—are the marks of faithful and loyal enslaved (Luke 12:42–48; 14:15–24; 16:1–13). Mary Sommar (2020) argues that the Romans did not believe in the inherent inferiority of enslaved persons but objected to the tasks the enslaved performed that involved serving other people. A person of honor would not be caught serving another person. Sommar states that "since no real man would submit himself to another in this way, then someone who did this, who [yielded himself to another person] must be less than a real man . . . The Romans really seem to have believed that slaves were inferior beings for the simple reason that if the slaves had not been inferior, they would never have submitted themselves to their masters," despite the circular reasoning, and despite the mobility sometimes allowed from enslaved to freedperson, and even Roman citizenship status (2020, 17).

The Christ-hymn states that after Jesus humbled himself by taking on the form of an enslaved human being up until death, God did two things simultaneously: (a) elevated or exalted him (2:9a); and (b) granted him the name that is above every name, as opposed to the fungible names normally imposed upon enslaved by their enslavers (2:9b), so that at the name of Jesus every knee (on earth, in the heavens, and in Hades) *should* bow (*kamptō*) (2:10) and every tongue should acknowledge openly (*exomologeō*) that Jesus Christ is *master* (*kyrios*) to the glory of God the Father. Jesus will be exalted and acknowledged as the ultimate master after having lived as a slave (2:11). Munro asserts that the hymn alone provides "a viable possibility, approaching probability" that the historical Jesus was a "literal slave" (1998, 183). The Lucan birth narrative places us in the proximity of probability.

LUKE'S BIRTH NARRATIVES: JESUS, BORN OF A *DOULĒ*

Again, a significant way that the enslaved population increased in the first century CE was through the wombs of enslaved women. Munro insists that "it is highly probable that Jesus served as a slave, and that his career outside his household of origin was not as a freeman, but as a slave, or *de facto* slave only conditionally freed, who had abandoned his slave or quasi-slave state" (1998, 2). I propose that Jesus was a freedman manumitted at thirty years of age and then began his public itinerancy. We can imagine a freedman (and even an enslaved man) healing and pronouncing oracles, similar to the enslaved Pythia girl in Acts 16 who is an itinerant prophetess.

In the Lukan birth narratives, Mary identifies herself as a "virgin" and as an enslaved female or *doulē* when the angel Gabriel informs her that God, in God's favor, has impregnated her without her knowledge, choice, or desire. Mary is the Spirit's surrogate womb. An enslaved woman has no surrogates—nobody carries or absorbs the violence of her enslavement. She can be, often is, everyone else's surrogate. When Mary is notified—not asked—that she has been impregnated, she is a virgin espoused/engaged (*mnēsteuō*) to a man named Joseph. Enslaved women can be virgins too, before they are penetrated against their will at an early age.[4] She must have been quite young. Mary's status as an engaged *doulē* (unmarried enslaved girl) does not change before she gives birth (1:27; 2:5). Luke records no marriage between Mary and Joseph. Her child inherits her low social status (Hezser 2005, 109).

The naming of Jesus by Gabriel circumscribes Joseph's power to name the enslaved child himself; he is perhaps Mary's master/enslaver (Hezser 2005, 117). Jesus is circumcised as an enslaved male child living in a Jewish household.[5] The Torah instructs that every male in a household, including slaves born in the house or purchased from a foreigner, be circumcised at eight days old (Gen 17:12–13; Hezser 2005, 30). Hector Avalos (2015) argues convincingly that circumcision can serve as the mark of an enslaved man; the circumcision of Mary's child could serve two purposes: the fulfillment of the Torah and the mark of a household slave. As also required for all male children, enslaved or free, in a *paterfamilias*, Mary and Joseph, as Jesus's parents, take him to the temple for the rite of purification (in contrast to antebellum US slavery, where white slave masters did not claim the children they fathered with enslaved women). It is important that Luke show that Jesus is circumcised and immersed, otherwise a male slave born into a Jewish master's household is considered a gentile; the enslaved child is cleansed from any previous involvement with idolatry (Hezser 2005, 36). Hezser states that circumcised and immersed slaves were considered to "have been brought 'under the wings of the *Shekhinah*,' that is, saved from leading a life of idol worship" (ibid, 38). Jesus will not worship the *diabolos* during his testing in the wilderness; he will only worship God (Luke 4:5–8). The Torah does not mention purification rites for enslaved female, and they were not required "to convert . . . or be manumitted before marriage" (Hezser 2005, 31).[6] The children of an enslaved woman (Jewish or Gentile) and an Israelite male are considered proper Israelites whether the mother is manumitted or not before birth or marriage (ibid.). But it remains that the child of an enslaved woman is born a slave. Manumission of an enslaved girl was not required for a Jewish slave master to become engaged to or enter a concubinage relationship with her (ibid., 192–93). However, Josephus expresses opposition to such unions (ibid., 195–96). Some Pharisees asked Hyrcanus to relinquish his high priesthood due to rumors his mother was enslaved during the reign of Antiochus Epiphanes, according to Josephus (Josephus 1995, *Ant.* 4.244).

I propose that Joseph could have been a freedman or free born master. Either way, Joseph would have owned *and* been engaged to the young virginal *doulē*, Mary. Both enslaved and freed persons sometimes owned slaves in antiquity. Neither Joseph nor Mary can afford more than a poor person's offering when they take Jesus to the Temple for the rites of purification (Luke 2:24). As the enslaved of a poor enslaver, Mary was among the poorest of the poor. In his slave narrative, Frederick Douglass discusses how slaves of wealthy slaveowners considered themselves better off than enslaved persons of poor masters: "It was considered as bad enough to be a slave; but to be a poor man's slave was deemed a disgrace indeed!" (2000, 294).

SONG OF A *DOULĒ*

The second time Mary identifies herself as a *doulē* is in her praise song, also known as the Magnificat (1:48). Jane Schaberg and Sharon Ringe state that the "Magnificat is the great New Testament song of liberation—personal and social, moral and economic—a revolutionary document of intense conflict and victory" (2012, 504). Further, Schaberg and Ringe argue that the song envisions for women and the oppressed "concrete freedom from systemic injustice"; the oppressors are political rulers, the arrogant, and the rich (ibid.). They do not read references to the wealthy metaphorically, and yet regard Mary's self-designation as a *doulē* as contributing to a portrait of female passivity deployed for "shock value"; Mary bears the honorary title "slave of God" upon whom God's spirit is poured in the last days (ibid., 503).[7] In the second century CE text *The Shepherd of Hermas,* the Shepherd is both an enslaved man whom his master sold (*pepraken*) to a certain mistress named Rhoda in Rome *and* he is called "the servant [*doulos*] of God" (1913, 1.1, 2.4). The addition of the words "of God" does not automatically preclude the material reality of his enslavement.

I argue that readers who treat Mary's self-identification as a *doulē* metaphorically should also consider references in her song to the "rich" similarly. Luke's Gospel is often praised for not spiritualizing or metaphorizing poverty or wealth, yet translators interpret references to enslavement differently even when juxtaposed with the rich, if only in the birth narratives. If we read "the rich" as signifying the materially wealthy, then we should translate *doulē* as a reference to Mary's material reality and social status, from which she experiences and expects a reversal along with others. Interestingly, the NRSV interprets the Greek word *doulos* as *slave* thirty-five times in Matthew. And in Luke, it is translated thirty-one times as *slave, except* in the birth narratives. The Greek noun, *doulē* (feminine)/*doulos* (masculine), is translated as *servant* in Luke's birth narrative in reference to Mary and Simeon (1:38, 48; 2:29).[8]

We find a number of linguistic connections between Mary's song and the hymn in Philippians. She is humble (*tapeinōsis*) or of lowly status as an enslaved woman (1:48) Similarly, Jesus humbled himself to become a slave in the Philippians 2 hymn. Perhaps, through the hymn, the early Jesus movement sought to redeem the humiliation of Jesus's crucifixion and social status with the claim that Jesus *chose* solidarity with the enslaved over equality with God; it was not forced upon him.

In both the Philippians hymn and Mary's song, we find status reversal; Jesus is exalted from enslaved human being to Christ for the glory of God (Phil 2:10–11). Mary's exaltation is based on the chosenness and future destiny of her son (Luke 1:30–35; 2:25–35). Similar to Hagar, God did not free Mary but promised that her son would be great and freed. God lifted up (*hypsōo*) the humble, Mary sings (1:52). But the rich are sent away empty (*kenos*); and in Philippians 2, Jesus empties (*kenoō*) himself of an exalted status of equality with God to become an enslaved human being. Born a slave, Jesus was "born empty" (Munro 1994, 181). Clarice Martin argues "the significance of portraying Christ as a slave derives both from a loss of status and also from the degradation of being a slave" (2015, 29). Perhaps these two hymns (Christ-hymn and Mary's song) derive from the same community, or Jesus's status as a child born of an enslaved woman was known or shared knowledge in several communities; others preferred to erase it from memory.

Another significant individual in the birth narratives who is called a *doulos* is Simeon (2:25–32). He lives in Jerusalem and is twice called a human (*anthrōpos*, not unlike the use of *anthrōpos* and *doulos* of Jesus in Phil 2:7) and a just and devout one, upon whom the Holy Spirit rested. The Spirit promised him that before his death he would see the Messiah. The Spirit guided Simeon into the temple at the same time that Mary and Joseph arrived with the infant Jesus. Simeon recognizes Jesus as the Messiah and, while holding the baby, announces, "Master [*despotēs*], you are now releasing [*apolyeis*] your slave [*doulos*] according to your word [*rēma*] in peace because my eyes have seen your salvation" (2:29–30, my translation). This story may be a manumission pronouncement and a prologue to Jesus's public abolitionist ministry under the anointing of the Spirit (4:18). The emphasis on Simeon's humanness while naming him as a slave is reminiscent of the Philippians 2 Christ-hymn and *The Shepherd of Hermas*.

THIRTY AND MANUMITTED: JESUS, A FREED ABOLITIONIST PREACHER

Luke is the only Gospel informing readers that Jesus began his public ministry at about the age of thirty years (3:23). The *lex Aelia Sentia* (4 CE) established the age requirement for manumission: a master must be at least twenty years old to manumit and the enslaved male he desires to manumit must be thirty years old, unless the enslaved is manumitted by *vindicta* or rod and for good cause shown (Mouritsen 2015, 34–35). Significantly, Jesus's age is revealed immediately before Joseph's genealogy. This genealogy signifies Joseph's proximate death, as we find with Abraham in Genesis 25:7–18. Thus, the mention of Jesus's age as thirty is an allusion to an eligible age for manumission. This allusion to manumission coincides with Joseph's genealogy (and perhaps death). It may very well indicate that Joseph freed Jesus by last will and testament, so as not to deprive Joseph's *familia* of Jesus's services during his father/master's lifetime (see Hezser 2005, 306). Hezser asserts that "[a] s quintessential 'others,' slaves and gentiles had to be excluded from membership in the genealogically [unchallengeable] Jewish family" (ibid., 199). Family boundaries must be preserved. The genealogy expresses uncertainty about Jesus's paternity because his mother was a *doulē* and his parents never married: "Jesus was the son (as was thought) of Joseph" (3:1 NRSV).[9]

Luke emphasizes Joseph's connection with the house of David at 1:27 and in the genealogy. But Joseph is one of three Josephs mentioned in the genealogy (3:23–37); until the mention of David, the men in Joseph's genealogy are unknown and not traceable. Luke's genealogy, different from Matthew's Gospel, does not list Mary as Jesus's mother. Again, this signifies that the child Jesus belongs to the slave master-father, the *paterfamilias*, Joseph. In Ishmael's genealogy, he is the son of Abraham "whom Hagar the Egyptian Sarah's slave-girl [*paidiskē*, Septuagint] bore to Abraham" (Gen 25:12, NRSV). Hagar is mentioned as the womb, the surrogate, and not as the mother. But again, Mary's name is absent from Jesus's genealogy in Luke.

It is difficult to know what task or services the Lucan Jesus performed as an enslaved boy and man during the first thirty years of his life. Luke is the only Synoptic Gospel that does not identify him as a carpenter (Mark 6:3; Matt 13:55). Some enslaved persons served as carpenters and shepherds (*pastoris*) (Columella 2010, 3.5–8; see MacDonald 2000, Jesus was a carpenter like Odysseus). Perhaps, Jesus was a healer as might be indicated by his own words at Luke 4:23 when the synagogue attendees identify him as Joseph's son: "Doubtless you will quote to me this proverb, 'Doctor, cure yourself!' And you will say, 'Do here also in your hometown the things that we have heard you did in Capernaum.'" Enslaved persons were permitted to work as independent craftsmen, and prominent persons hired them as bodyguards and policemen (ibid., 86). Epictetus was a slave and a philosopher, a rarity. More commonly, slaves could be pedagogues, bookkeepers, actors, athletes *and physicians* (ibid., 87). It is not impossible that Jesus was known as a "physician" or healer.

The enslaved population was "diverse and fragmented," which served to scatter and not unite them (Hezser 2005, 89), even in terms of assigned duties and skills. Among landowning wealthy rural slave masters, the enslaved could perform the duties of field hands, overseers, supervisors, vineyard workers, and a large majority were shepherds (and head shepherds) or farmhands (Hezser 2005, 299; Joshel 2010,167–8). In Luke's birth narrative Jesus's birth is announced to lowly perhaps enslaved shepherds living in the fields, as opposed to magi bearing expensive gifts in Matthew (Luke 2:8; Matt 1). Enslaved persons ranked and were counted among the animals, including sheep, as property. In his slave narrative, Frederick Douglass regards the cruel treatment of his grandmother as affirmation of the "infernal character of slavery," which filled him "with unutterable loathing of slaveholders" (2000,

313). When his old master died, not one of his enslaved persons were freed but left with "strangers." Under the ownership of strangers, Douglass's grandmother "saw her children, her grandchildren, and her great-grandchildren, divided, like so many sheep" with no say in their fate (ibid.).

AT HOME AMONG SINNERS AND TAX COLLECTORS

As a freedman, Jesus did not share the fate of every enslaved person; many were never manumitted but died in unmitigated enslavement. Jesus spent considerable time as a freedman in the company of his friends; he is known as a "friend [*philos*] of tax collectors and sinners" (7:34). The phrase "tax collectors and sinners" is a significant phrase in Luke. The job of tax collector was also often performed by enslaved persons whose master was the state. Jesus is criticized for continually eating with "tax collectors and sinners" (5:27–30; 6:32–36; 7:36; 11:37–38; 14:1). Jews and Gentiles could be tax collectors. Josephus mentions a leading Jew in Caesarea who was a tax collector (*Jewish War* 2.287, p. 120). Some tax collectors amassed wealth through extortion. It was those that John the Baptist and Jesus call to repentance (3:10–14; 5:31–32). The status reversal that Mary sang about, Luke preaches and promotes in the present life when he admonishes wealthy tax collectors and other rich people to cease extorting the poor and to help alleviate poverty (18:18–30). When Jesus visits Zacchaeus, a wealthy tax collector, he happily announces that he will gift half of his possessions to alleviate poverty and provide restitution to anyone he defrauded (19:1–10).

Included among the so-called "sinners" are other enslaved persons as well, who were forced into prostitution or who performed unpleasant duties and even violence, at the command of their masters or to prevent death and exposure (e.g., 16:1–13). Instructively, Josephus views captivity/enslavement as punishment for sin. When the Roman general Pompey sieged and captured Jerusalem, he asked whether it was their own internal strife and actions that made them unworthy of freedom and caused God to subject them to the Romans? Josephus further says, "When [Herod] was king God inflicted another capture of their city on an errant people. Herod the son of Antipater brought in Sosius [first century CE Roman politician] and Sosius brought in a Roman army, which encircled the besieged city for six months, until in punishment for their sins the people were captured and the city sacked by the enemy" (2017, 5.398). Thus, in Josephus' mind, the enslaved is understood to be a sinner because he succumbed to enslavement or he was permitted to be captured because of some sin he or she (or perhaps his mother) committed.

Jesus does not require the "tax collectors and sinners" he befriends to repent. The woman labeled a sinner in Luke 7 is not asked to repent; she could have been an enslaved woman raped and forced into prostitution like other Black(ened) women and boys. Jesus did not treat or call her a "sinner"; he did not condemn her or extract repentance from her or other so-called "sinners." I propose that Jesus is comfortable among "sinners" because he is one of them, namely, the son of a *doulē*. Being an enslaved man made him a sinner in the view of people. Greg Carey concludes that Jesus's compromised masculinity—he was not married, fathered no children, and was not a *paterfamilias*—invited disdain from some neighbors (2009, 69). Enslaved men could not marry unless the master consented, fathered no children of their own, and could not be a *paterfamilias*! When freed at thirty years of age, Jesus was preoccupied with ministry and close to death. As son of a *doulē*, Jesus would have been the object of ridicule by freeborn persons of every socioeconomic class, but especially the wealthy across ethnicity and religion, including among his own people.

EPILOGUE

In addition to the many parables and stories about the wealthy—most of who, if not all, likely owned slaves, Luke (like Matthew) has a plethora of slave parables, compared with Mark and John. Historical Jesus scholars agree that Jesus taught using parables. Concerning slave parables in particular, I have disagreed (Smith 2017). Regardless, *Luke's* Jesus teaches with slave parables, which is problematic and symptomatic—symptomatic of hybridity that neither enslaver nor enslaved escape; slavery shapes and diminishes both.

How do the slave parables function? What is their purpose or what do they do? According to Munro (1998), the NT slave parables demonstrate a slave's standpoint (contra Glancy 2006, 127–28, who argues they represent the master's perspective). I suspect that the Lucan slave parables offer a freedman's intimate insider perspective of master-slave relationships. Clarice Martin asserts that slave masters "were not actively conscious of . . . the hidden transcript of the dissident subculture of the slave life. Slaves were props," despite their pervasiveness and visibility (2005, 224). Eyes were always on them; but the enslaved also had ears "on the ground." Although always under the M/master's gaze (Divine and human, as they were taught), the enslaved did resist, sometimes in plain view or in "safe" spaces within spaces of captivity (Snorton 2017; Joshel and Peterson 2014, 140). The slave parables reflect the status quo but are also subversive and performative of slave resistance. Enslavers did not want their cruelty toward the enslaved publicized and forbade slaves from disclosing it under threat of death or re-enslavement; the enslaved were expected to speak well of masters at all times, especially in their absence (because the Master is omnipresent). Frederick Douglass reveals that the enslaved were expected to lie about their condition and the kindness of their masters; thus, "[t]hey suppress the truth rather than take the consequences" (2000, 293). Luke's Gospel tells the truth about master-slave relationships without naming particular masters and thereby exposing the cruelty of their enslavement.

Even as a freedman, Jesus must navigate his "freedom" in stigmatized, black(ended) flesh. Quoting Saidiya Hartman, Snorton writes that "spaces of freedom" can be simultaneously "spaces of captivity" for the formerly enslaved or of the fugitive (Snorton 2017, 68). Black(ened) peoples are always fugitives in unjust, violent spaces. Jesus died like many enslaved persons, the criminalized, and criminals by the shameful spectacle of crucifixion (Smith 2021). Similar to the lynched Black men and women in the US antebellum South, Jesus was stripped, flogged, sexually violated, and even castrated (ibid.).

It still matters who interprets and/or translates the biblical texts and characters (see Vasser 2018; Martin 2015; Avalos 2011; Harrill 2006; Meeks 1996, 249–50; Felder, 1990; Bradley, 1987, 19). The crucifixion did not initiate Jesus's suffering and humiliation; it is where it culminated. Jesus's dehumanization began in the womb of his enslaved birth mother, Mary. Snorton writes that "the [enslaved] mother is the maker and marker of boundaries . . . her function is to reproduce, through offspring, the life of the border" (2017, 104). Jesus, as Thomas Hoyt argued, "serves as an analogue to black suffering" in "birth, life, death" and beyond (1991, 29). Jesus lived in a black(ended) body that society stigmatized—a body subjected to violence from birth to the point of death—as he ate and visited with friends, as he wielded a whip in the Temple, as he disputed with Pharisees or as he slept, walked the neighborhood eating Skittles, stood on a street corner, barbecued in his own yard. After Jesus exhaled his last breath, pressed from his lungs as his body hung from the lynching tree, his spirit left him (Luke 23:46). And after he died, like George Floyd, the centurion, a representative of the state, declared Jesus innocent/just (*dikaios*) and a human being (*anthrōpos*) (23:47). A crowd formed to see the horrible spectacle (*theōria*) of Jesus's death as the breath escaped his Black(ened) body, like George Floyd (24:49).

George Floyd's life was meaningless to Derek Chauvin and the other officers who knelt, like patriots at a football game, on Mr. Floyd's shackled body. Chauvin stared into the Black and white people who pled for Floyd's life, but he saw only a "black(ened) mob" and refused to stop killing Floyd. In the final nanosecond, Floyd called out to his deceased mother through whose womb he entered this life, a Black(ended) child. Not all lynched Black bodies are hung from trees, but all enter this racialized world through the wombs of Black(ened) mothers. Jesus—God's Black(ened) son—and God, the Father of a Black(ened) child in the world affirm—at birth, from life to death, and in resurrection—that Black lives matter. African Methodist Episcopal Church Bishop Henry McNeal Turner (1834–1915) imagined the Divine in Black flesh when he declared that "God is a Negro" (see Johnson 2015). If God is a Negro in a racialized world, so is his son. Womanism affirms Jesus, God, and Spirit's solidarity with the least, particularly enslaved and/or poor Black women as unconditionally human and worthy of quality of life. This affirmation, Jacquelyn Grant argues, "is not an exercise in romanticized contentment with one's oppressed status in life. For as the resurrection signified that there is more to life than the cross for Jesus Christ, for Black women [and their Black(ended) children] it signifies that their [multi-dimensional] oppressive existence is not the end [or all there is], but it merely represents the context in which a particular people struggle to experience hope and liberation" (Grant 1989, 217). Today, we choose hope; we write, speak, sing, work, march, walk, and run in our liberty and toward unmitigated freedom unmitigated by "whiteness."

NOTES

1. I do not reject the possibility that the historical Jesus was an enslaved and later freed man.

2. Winsome Munro (1925–1994), a South African feminist biblical scholar, received notice from Mellen of the decision to publish her book a few days before her untimely death. Munro's colleague William Poehlmann prepared the manuscript for publication.

3. When Titus and his army attacked the Galileans, men were slaughtered but 2,130 infants and women were enslaved (2017, 1.305). Josephus writes "It must have been God giving the Romans the present of a Galilean tragedy. God who at this critical time had these townspeople shut out by their friends and delivered up abandoned to a murderous enemy, with not a man surviving the wholesale destruction" (ibid. 1.293).

4. Under the *lex Iulia de adulteriis*, female slaves who had intercourse with their masters (raped or coerced) were not charged with adultery (Hezser 2005, 191).

5. Hector Avalos (2015) offers this explanation for circumcision wherein Yahweh is the slave master.

6. Circumcision should not be regarded "as a conversion rite, since the circumcised slave did not" become a proselyte (Hezser 2005, 31).

7. The only woman in Acts who prophesies is the Pythian enslaved girl whom Paul silences (16:16–18). Philips' daughters are eclipsed and muted when Agabus arrives from Judea (21:8–11).

8. In Luke's prologue we find the Greek noun *hyperetai* translated servants and in Mary's song the Greek noun *pais* translated servant in the phrase "Israel his servant" (1:2, 54, 69 NRSV; cf. Isa 52:13–53:12 LXX).

9. A female slave, even if freed, was not theoretically permitted to marry a priest (Hezser 2005, 109). It is not impossible to imagine Joseph as a priest.

WORKS CITED

Avalos, Hector. 2011. *Slavery, Abolitionism, and the Ethics of Biblical Scholarship.* Sheffield: Sheffield.

———. 2015. "Circumcision as a Slave Mark." *Perspectives in Religious Studies* 42, no. 3: 259–74.

Briggs, Sheila. 1989. "Can an Enslaved God Liberate? Hermeneutical Reflections on Phil 2:6–11." *Semeia* 47: 136–53.

Bradley, Keith R. 1987. *Slaves and Masters in the Roman Empire: A Study in Social Control.* New York: Oxford University Press.

Carey, Greg. 2009. *Sinners: Jesus and His Earliest Followers.* Waco, TX: Baylor University Press.

Columella. 2010. *De Re Rustica*: Books X–XII. Translated by E. S. Forster and Edward Heffner. Loeb Classica Library. Cambridge, MA: Harvard University Press.

Cone, James H. 1970. *A Black Theology of Liberation.* Maryknoll, NY: Orbis.

———. 1997. *Black Theology and Black Power.* Maryknoll, NY: Orbis.

———. 2006. *Malcolm, Martin and America: A Dream or a Nightmare.* Maryknoll, NY: Orbis.

Douglass, Frederick. 2000. *Narrative of the Life of Frederick Douglass, an American Slave. Written by Himself.* In *Slave Narratives,* edited by William L. Andrews and Henry Louis Gates, Jr., 281–368. New York: Literary Classics.

Felder, Cain Hope. 1990. *Troubling Biblical Waters. Race, Class and Family.* Maryknoll, NY: Orbis.

Glancy, Jennifer A. 2006. *Slavery in Early Christianity.* Minneapolis: Fortress.

Grant, Jacquelyn. 1989. *White Women's Christ and Black Women's Jesus: Feminist Christology and Womanist Response.* Atlanta: Scholars.

Harrill, J. A. 2006. *Slaves in the New Testament: Literary, Social, and Moral Dimensions.* Minneapolis: Fortress.

———. 2020. "Revisiting the Problem of 1 Corinthians 7:21." *Biblical Research* 65: 77–94.

Hartman, Saidiya. 1997. *Scenes of Subjection: Terror, Slavery, and Self-Making in Nineteenth-Century America.* New York: Oxford University Press.

———. 2007. *Lose Your Mother: A Journey Along the Atlantic Slave Route.* New York: Farrar, Straus and Giroux.

Hezser, Catherine. 2005. *Jewish Slavery in Antiquity.* New York: Oxford University Press.

Hoyt, Thomas, Jr. 1991. "Interpreting Biblical Scholarship for the Black Church Tradition." In *Stony the Road We Trod,* 17–39.

Jackson, Zakiyyah Iman. 2020. *Becoming Human: Matter and Meaning in an AntiBlack World.* New York: New York University Press.

Johnson, Andre. 2015. "'God is a Negro': The (Rhetorical) Black Theology of Bishop Henry McNeal Turner." *Black Theology* 13, no. 1: 29–40.

Joshel, Sandra R. 2010. *Slavery in the Roman World.* New York: Cambridge University Press.

Josephus. 2017. *The Jewish War*. Translated by Martin Hammond. Oxford, UK: Oxford University Press.

Kaba, Mariame. 2021. *We Do This 'Til We Free Us. Abolitionist Organizing and Transforming Justice*. Chicago: Haymarket.

MacDonald, Dennis R. 2000. *The Homeric Epics and the Gospel of Mark*. New Haven, CT: Yale University Press.

Martin, Clarice J. 2005. "The Eyes Have It: Slaves in the Communities of Christ-Believers." *Christian Origins*, edited by Richard Horsley, 221–39. Minneapolis: Fortress.

———. 2015. "Womanist Interpretations of the New Testament: The Quest for Holistic and Inclusive Translation and Interpretation." In *I Found God in Me: A Womanist Biblical Hermeneutics Reader*, edited by Mitzi J. Smith, 19–41. Eugene, OR: Cascade.

Meeks, Wayne A. 1996. "The 'Haustafeln' and American Slavery: A Hermeneutical Challenge." In *Theology and Ethics in Paul and his Interpreters: Essays in Honor of Victor Paul Furnish*, 232–53. Nashville, TN: Abingdon.

Mouritsen, Henrik. 2015. *The Freedman in the Roman World*. Cambridge: Cambridge University Press.

Munro, Winsome. 1998. *Jesus, Born of a Slave: The Social and Economic Origins of Jesus' Message*. Lewiston, NY: Edwin Mellen.

Page, Hugh R. Jr. 2010. "Early Hebrew Poetry *and* Ancient Pre-Biblical Sources." *The Africana Bible. Reading Israel's Scriptures from Africa and the Africa Diaspora*, edited by Hugh R. Page, et al., 61–69. Minneapolis: Fortress.

Patterson, Orlando. 2018. *Slavery and Social Death. A Comparative Study*. Cambridge, MA: Harvard University Press.

Shepherd of Hermas. 1913. Translated by Kirshopp Lake. *Apostolic Fathers*. Vol. II. Translated by Kirshopp Lake. *Loeb Classical Library*, no. 25. Cambridge, MA: Harvard University Press.

Smith, Mitzi J. 2017. "Historical Jesus, Slavery and the Problem of the Kingdom of God." Presentation at Historical Jesus Section, Society of Biblical Literature Conference.

———. 2018. *Womanist Sass and Talk Back: Social (In)Justice, Intersectionality and Biblical Interpretation*. Eugene, OR: Cascade.

———. 2021. "He Never Said a Mumbalin' Word": A Womanist Perspective of Crucifixion, Sexual Violence and Sacralized Silence." In *When Did We See You Naked? Jesus as a Victim of Sexual Abuse,* edited by Jayme Reaves, David Tombs, and Rocio Figueroa, 46–66. London: SCM.

Snorton, C. Riley. 2017. *Black on Both Sides: A Racial History of Trans Identity*. Minneapolis: University of Minnesota.

Sommar, Mary E. 2020. *The Slaves of the Churches. A History*. London: Oxford University Press.

Vasser, Murray. 2018. "'Bodies and Souls: A Case for Reading Revelation 18.13 As a Critique of the Slave Trade." *New Testament Studies* 64: 397–409.

Weems, Renita J. 2015. "Re-Reading for Liberation. African-American Women and the Bible." In *I Found God in Me: A Womanist Biblical Hermeneutics Reader*, edited by Mitzi J. Smith, 42–53. Eugene, OR: Cascade.

Chapter 6

Reading with the Enslaved

Placing Human Bondage at the Center of the Early Christian Story

Emerson B. Powery

> Critical writers and readers have a responsibility not to be too polite or too fearful to notice a disrupting darkness before its eyes.
>
> — Toni Morrison (1993)

> I wake up every morning in a house built by slaves.
>
> — Michelle Obama

Nicole Hannah-Jones, an investigative journalist and creator of *The 1619 Project*, wrote a lead essay for the project titled "America Wasn't a Democracy, Until Black Americans Made it One," for which she won a Pulitzer Prize for Commentary in May 2020. *The 1619 Project* attempts to reframe the stories the USA tells about its origin "by placing the consequences of slavery and the contributions of black Americans at the very center of our national narrative" (Hannah-Jones 2019, n.p.). Any effort to rethink a national story for the sake of a more inclusive and complicated narrative is worth the creative struggle.

Just as *The 1619 Project* has argued for the fundamental impact slavery (and, Black life) had on the "founding" of this nation, so must readers of the Bible recognize how fundamental human bondage was to the early years of the Christian movement. The New Testament collection did not attempt to hide the impact of people enslaving other people. Later commentaries do. It is not uncommon for commentaries and introductory textbooks to obfuscate (or, ignore altogether) the role these enslaved characters had on the larger developing religious movement. What might the story of the early Christian movement—and the myths that surround it—reveal if we were to place the stories of enslavement (implicit and explicit) and those most affected by this colonial activity at the center of the movement?

Strabo (d. 24 CE), an ancient historian and philosopher, recalled a popular proverb when describing the ancient slave markets in Delos: "Merchant, sail in and unload your ship, your cargo (of slaves) is already sold" (*Geography* 14.5.2). He reported that Delos would import and export thousands of enslaved people daily. In this environment, it is no surprise that many early Christ-followers were enslaved. Paul wrote to the Christ-followers at Corinth, "For in the one Spirit we were all baptized into one body—Jews or Greeks, slaves or free—and we were all made to drink of one Spirit" (1 Cor 12:13). Other NT passages also highlight the presence of enslaved people within these new religious communities (cf. 1 Cor 1:26; Gal 3:28; Eph 6:5; Col 3:22). Perhaps, more distressingly for contemporary readers, *enslavers* were prominent members of early Christianity. Philemon, a prominent church leader in Colossae, was an enslaver and Paul's "dear friend, and co-worker" (Phm 1:1).[1] We should assume the presence of the enslaved throughout the larger households associated with the new religious network. Acts reports the households of Cornelius, Mary, Lydia, and Crispus as all connected to the Way (Acts 10, 12, 16, 18). Paul greets the households of Aristobulus and Narcissus in Rome (Rom 16:10, 11). We hear about the households of Chloe and Stephanas in Corinth (1 Cor 1:11, 16). Those persons who advocated for obedience from the enslaved must have been either household enslavers themselves or, at least, advocates for maintaining on a local level the colonizing hierarchies of the Empire (cf. Eph 6:5; Col 3:22; 1 Tim 6:1–2; 1 Pet 2:18–19).

Enslaved Christ-followers were commonly depicted in the documents that comprised the early Christian communities of the first century. More difficult to imagine is the omnipresence of the enslaved. They appear in Jesus's parables as examples of loyal and obedient (and, disloyal and disobedient) "disciples." In Jesus's imaginative constructions he could portray an alert enslaved individual as one—in an odd reversal of roles—who may be served by the enslaver himself (Luke 12:37). Then, just a few verses later, Jesus could also depict the significant violence that could befall a condemned enslaved person, if that one failed to carry out the expectations of the enslaver (Luke 12:42–47). The enslaver "will cut him in pieces" if the enslaved carried out his own desires and not that of his enslaver's (Luke 12:46). Furthermore, even those "bodies"—a common reference for the enslaved of this period (cf. Rev 18:13)—who lived out their activities unaware of the rules also would "receive a light beating" (Luke 12:48). In either case in this story, whatever action the enslaved performed, intentionally or unintentionally, physical violence greeted the enslaved!

Sadly, the enslavers in the (North) American landscape prominently repeated these same words of Jesus (from Luke 12). Numerous slave narratives—including those of Frederick Douglass, Solomon Northup, and William Wells Brown—detail stories in which enslavers summoned the words of the Lukan Jesus to carry out their violence (see Powery and Sadler 2016, 156–58).

Nineteenth-century slavery, during the period of the trans-Atlantic slave trade, was distinctive from its first-century counterpart in the Roman Empire in a number of ways, not the least of which surrounds the category of "race." Gay Byron (2002) has shown that racial and ethnic biases did exist among ancient people, even if those distinctions were not (necessarily) the (sole) cause for the enslavement of other people groups. Classical scholar Shelley Haley (2009) would agree. Many scholars, rightfully, admit that interpreting ancient slavery through the lens of its USA version "distorts" our understanding of the ancient world. Yet, as classicist Keith Bradley notes, "Distorted vision may be imperfect vision, but it is preferable to no vision at all" (1992, 134). The analogy opens up a possibility for developing a hermeneutical *sensitivity* that is necessary for dealing with ancient slavery, especially as it dovetails with biblical literature. Even if it is impossible to know for sure what the enslaved thought or felt, it is worth a hermeneutical risk (duBois 2003; Kartzow 2018; Charles 2020).[2] When attempting to read "with the enslaved," the passages on slavery should challenge us not only to identify with the enslaver but also with those held in bondage (duBois 2003). Attention to the "darkness" requires recognition of the trauma that accompanies the life of one bound to another human (Wimbush 2000). Slavery haunts the early records of the Christian movement. To deal only with the surface of the text fails to account for the hauntings of the human bondage system in ancient Rome. Staying on the surface of the text—that is, providing straightforward exegetical observations based only on what is stated (supposedly) plainly on the surface of the text—fails to do justice to the hauntings of slavery that the textual surface elides. Each enslaved character (real or imagined life) represents embodied memories that may only be alluded to in the way they functioned in the story. These hauntings are part of the memories they represent. As Morrison reminds us in another vein, critical writers and readers have a responsibility not to be "too polite or too fearful to notice a disrupting darkness before [their] eyes" (1993, 91).

Within this essay, we will explore the stories of two named, enslaved Christ-followers from their perspective (as much as possible). The early Christ-following movement, as expressed within the pages of the NT, was also a "house built by slaves" (Michelle Obama). My own reading strategy is to place less emphasis on what Paul or Luke says than on what others might hear, especially those among the more marginal groups within the early church communities. I am less interested in Paul's or Luke's view of slavery or their views of enslaved believers and believing enslavers than how the rhetoric might have affected the various persons who made up these communities. To put it another way: it is not only what is explicitly said that is important; what is left unsaid is equally important (Charles 2020). If Tertius was an enslaved scribe in reality (Dunn 1988, 912–13), what might he have wondered as he penned Paul's metaphors about "bondage" and "freedom"? If Rhoda was an enslaved doorkeeper in reality, what might she have wondered as the church in Mary's house disbelieved her report?

Reading with the enslaved entails the following:

- It requires a hermeneutical *commitment to read from the margins* (even from within the early circles of Christ-followers);
- It compels us to *take the physical body seriously*, as well as investigate the religious "ideas" (i.e., intellectual history) that impact those bodies; real ideas effect physical realities;
- It encourages us to *consider who benefits from a particular interpretation*; if it dehumanizes anyone, then we should question whether our scholarship has upheld a so-called neutral, so-called objective position to the detriment of human bodies, Black bodies, queer bodies, differently abled bodies.

RHODA AND TERTIUS: THEIR COMMON LOT

In addition to Onesimus, who has received much attention in Black biblical scholarship (Lewis 1991; Callahan 1997; Johnson, Noel, and Williams 2012; Smith 2012), other enslaved, *named* characters present in the early texts of the movement give us insight into the general lives of what it might have meant to be members of this new movement and still enslaved to earthly masters. We will look at two of those characters in this short essay: Rhoda and Tertius (Acts 12; Rom 16).

Their stories are distinctive in many ways (see below). One of their stories (Rhoda's) was told through the pen of another; the other (Tertius) wrote out his own greeting. Nonetheless, there are also common features these two enslaved characters share.

The tradition remembered their names. Slavery was ubiquitous in the Greco-Roman world and the system of human bondage oftentimes left most of those lives burdened by this violence unnamed. The NT collection usually attends to the domestic context; these accounts rarely relay stories about the masses of enslaved bodies working in agriculture, in the mines, or at sea. Yet, whenever domestic labor was performed, it would not be surprising if enslaved persons were performing these activities, even if unmentioned. Many households included enslaved persons. Among the numerous stories, few enslaved characters were named. Rhoda and Tertius were two of them.

Rhoda and Tertius played key roles within their respective stories, despite the "minor" nature of their characters. It would be easy to overlook their roles, since each one occurs in only one short biblical passage. Their stories, however, serve as decisive moments in the movement. The Acts 12 story sets the stage for the fundamental shift in Luke's narrative, a shift from the labor of Peter to the labor of Paul. Peter will make only one final appearance after this account (see Acts 15:1–7). Rhoda is the truth-teller that stands between these two key male apostolic leaders. The Romans letter, penned by Tertius, was the longest letter within the larger collection and an appeal to the assembly at Rome for a hoped-for mission westward to Spain.

Both "served" leading characters within the larger story: Peter and Paul. Unsurprising is scholarship's concentration on these central male characters. Applying her observations to ethnic and class distinctions, literary novelist Chimamanda Ngozi Adichie (2009) notices how the telling of a story from *only* one vantage point does not make the story untrue; but the story remains incomplete. Making assumptions about their (unintentional?) silences is not the point of this exercise. Rather, I wish to highlight the efforts to fill in the gaps of the story in ways that attempt to salvage Luke's (positive?) message. By doing so, many (white?) interpreters ignore—or, at best, explain away—the trauma of the conditions that lay behind the other characters of the story. Much scholarship on Acts 12 and Romans 16 pays particular attention to the individual male hero that dominates so much Western scholarship. Attractive to these scholars is Peter (and, Herod and John Mark) and Paul as the central (and, in many ways, only) true figures worth discussing in these interpretative constructions of a so-called history of the early Christ-following communities.

Both had "voice," albeit within a contrived setting. Although Rhoda "announced" and "insisted," we hear no specific words from her lips (Acts 12:15, 14). Luke did not allow his audience to hear the logic of this *paidiskē* ("enslaved girl"). On the other hand, the debate continues whether Tertius only penned Paul's dictated words or contributed more to the construction of Paul's religious and cultural ideas. It is difficult enough to determine the ancient functions of these characters. Yet, contemporary resources do not always aid in our efforts.

Finally, both are frequently hidden from plain view within English translations and modern commentaries. As one enslaved (*paidiskē*), Rhoda's status is often concealed with translations like "maiden" (NRSV), "damsel" (KJV), or "young woman" (The Message), even though the NRSV and The Message will use the terms "slave girl" when the same Greek word appears in Acts 16:16. As for Tertius, most English translations will combine the phrase "in the Lord" (*en kyriō*) to the greetings Tertius offered rather than, as in the Greek word order, to the writing process itself. More importantly, it is rare for an English translation to translate *kyrios* as "master," which would be a common designation in the first century and may have direct bearing on its usage in Tertius's personal greeting.[3]

RHODA, LUKE-ACTS, AND SLAVERY

Among the early Christ-following communities, there were free, freed (in liminal positions), and enslaved. Some of the enslaved participants had multiple identity-markers. A person could be immigrant, female, and enslaved (a dangerous confluence, if one fell into the hands of the wrong enslaver). The situation could be precarious for many enslaved Christ-followers who served earthly enslavers (some fellow believers, some not), who prepared for the activities of these house church gatherings. The story of Acts 12 reveals how complicated it could be.

Luke provides the names of several people connected to this prominent house-church community. Peter sought out this conspicuous community after his miraculous release from prison. Mary was named as the one most responsible for this community and she was the mother of another prominent figure, John Mark, whose brief introduction here will set up the end of the chapter, when John Mark joins Barnabas's and Saul's travelling party (12:12, 25). But it was Rhoda whose actions moved the plot within this short account.

Violence surrounds this story, as Acts 12 opens with Herod's desire to shut down the movement. With the murder and imprisonment of leaders from the Way—James and Peter, respectively—at the hands of the State, Herod sets the stage for the possibility of more suffering and violence. Even though it turns out well for Peter, his disappearance from Luke's narrative (with only one final appearance) suggests the power such despotism has to alter plans of those who speak out against it (Acts 15:7–11). And, Rhoda was caught in the middle of this movement.

What do we learn about ancient slavery from Rhoda's (*paidiskē*) "sisters"? In the two-part Lukan narrative, we find other enslaved female characters in Luke-Acts. All are enslaved domestic workers in one way or another. The Greek term *paidiskē* is a synonym for *doulē* ("female slave") and may refer to a younger enslaved female, which would account for the NRSV's translation of "servant-girl" for the courtyard "slave" at Luke 22:56.[4] Enslaved females were not exempt from vicious beatings (Luke 12:45). The *paidiskē* of the courtyard, enslaved to the high priest according to Mark, challenged Peter's alliances, but her testimony was not readily believed and required confirmations (14:69). Did her (enslaved) status make her untrustworthy? Could the truth come only from the enslaved via torture, as the ancients believed (duBois 1991)? Another *paidiskē* made money for her masters through (spiritual) ability to relay future events (Acts 16:16). Among Luke's *paidiskē* references, the only named character was "Rhoda" (the gatekeeper) an enslaved female who was part of the Christ-following community.[5]

Her status haunts the religious community, since it was a reminder of the different means for enslavement in the ancient world.[6] Some ancients could oppose the slave *trade*—as some early Christian pro-slavery advocates would—even while participating wholeheartedly in the slave institution itself, since enslavers could acquire the enslaved by infant exposure or births to enslaved women (1 Tim 1:10, Scheidel 2011). In light of some apparent opposition to the market trading in human bodies, we might assume that enslaved Christ-followers in these communities were born into their roles in an attempt to forego the agora about which Strabo spoke.

Children received their assigned status from their birth mothers, which frequently placed younger enslaved females in precarious situations with household patriarchs. If an enslaver could not secure slaves from the marketplace, then one way to guarantee sufficient slave labor to work the fields and manage the households was through "slave-breeding" practices (Bradley 1992; Joshel 2010; Hezser 2011). (To explain Rhoda's presence in Mary's household, Margaret Aymer raises the possibility that John Mark may have fathered Rhoda [2016, 275])! These hauntings tear open the silence.

What do we learn from Luke's depiction of Rhoda here? How does "Rhoda" serve Luke's narrative? Her name is remembered as an important member of the Christ-following community. Her actions are key: (1) she recognized Peter's voice, which seems to imply that she has heard him before. (2) She responded with "joy" after hearing his voice, revealing her to be (potentially) a Christ-follower herself (Smith 2011, 126; contrast Aymer 2016, 275). (3) Third, her "joy" sent her to share the news with others rather than perform her servile duty (i.e., open the gate). The excitement made her forget her duty. Although we know that she shared her news, Luke fails to report exactly what she said; readers must imagine what she said and how she said it. (4) Her announcement was challenged: "You're crazy!" Despite this reaction, she persisted, until they revised their assessment saying it must be an "angel." Similar to the scene in Luke 22, another enslaved person was disbelieved. Do these responses indicate the common lot of the enslaved? (5) Likely, she was part of the "they" who eventually opened the gate.

What else is there to know beyond the surface of the text? What has Luke omitted? Lots of scholarship attempts to fill in gaps within these ancient biblical stories by downplaying the trauma of ancient human bondage. It is not uncommon to read comments like the following even though absent from the accounts themselves: (1) The enslaved of the household were, usually, better off (financially) than "free peasants" and "had far better chances of improving their positions, including gaining freedom" (Keener 2014, 356); (2) many commentators feel certain that no sexual harassment entered the earliest communities of Christ-followers, especially in one headed by a female (Keener 2014). Aymer, rightfully, calls this assumption into question; (3) Ben Witherington finds a positive word for female empowerment: "Thus Luke presents Rhoda as an example to his audience that the testimony of a woman, even a female servant, can be trustworthy. He may be intentionally countering tendencies to devalue the word of a woman by showing that even a servant girl like Rhoda can be trusted" (1992, 719). Within the Acts 12 story itself, however, Rhoda's witness to the truth was *not* believed. The others had to witness the event for themselves; they did not trust the word of a *paidiskē*. Scott Spencer also acknowledges this rejection despite Luke's earlier advocacy for the prophecies of enslaved women (2004).

Black scholarship has turned its attention to Rhoda to provide a more nuanced description of this Lukan character (Martin 1994; Williams 2007; Smith 2011; Aymer 2016). Although acknowledging Peter's presence, Clarice Martin focuses her comments on the two women in the story. Mary's prominent home-ecclesia "functioned as a place of communal nurture, restoration, and renewal" (1994, 783). Martin interprets the Rhoda announcement in light of an earlier Lukan announcement by other women, "the women disciples' experience, following the resurrection of Jesus in Luke (Luke 24:9–11)" (1994, 783). For Martin, the primary difference, in Rhoda's account, was that she "was disbelieved by *women and men*" (1994, 783; Martin's italics). Furthermore, the lack of trust in Rhoda's word was, likely, due to her enslaved status (Martin 1994, 784).

In another (short) commentary, Demetrius Williams questions the common interpretive tradition of the comedic nature of the story, in light of this portrayal of the Rhoda character: "While certain elements of this episode are comedic . . . Rhoda is portrayed as a stereotypical 'slave' as perceived in Greco-Roman culture" (2007, 232; see Dunn 1988; Harrill 2006).

Mitzi Smith takes this discussion one step further, critically questioning the gendered nature of Luke's portrayal, since the author "acknowledges women's presence, but women's speech or lack thereof and women's activity or inactivity foregrounds men's presence, speech, and authority, particularly Peter's authority" (2011, 96). For Smith, contrary to Witherington, Rhoda's gender is the problem for Luke: "Only the male voices count. Rhoda's voice is othered as representing madness and as unreliable. Seeing is believing. In the end, it did not matter what Rhoda said" (ibid., 127). In the final analysis,

Smith acknowledges that "A female of slave status is the first to announce Peter's liberation to the *ekklēsia*" (ibid., 126–27).

The most extensive work engaging Rhoda's enslavement derives from Margaret Aymer's (2016) recent essay in which she attempts to attend to the trauma that lays behind the enslaved circumstances of Rhoda's life (real or imagined). Similar to how Onesimus functioned in relationship to Philemon (see Phm 1:13), Rhoda served as Mary's "body double" and, in the midst of persecution, could have suffered physical harm (Aymer 2016, 271, 279). Her description as a *paidiskē* highlights Rhoda's youth and allows Aymer to focus on the experience of trauma on children, certainly different from that experienced by adults especially for those displaced from their homes. As an enslaved female, she would have known of the potential for sexual abuse, even if not her own: "if a girl like Rhoda is not facing this, she probably knows other slave girls in Jerusalem who are" (ibid., 274). Attentive to her own contemporary experience, Aymer recognizes the potential of an ancient migrant story here: "Rhoda" may derive from the island city "Rhodes," which, in turn, leads to Aymer's summation that "Rhoda is not part of Mary's 'people.' We cannot assume that she or her people come from Palestine. She may well have been a gentile girl," whose status occurs before the decision of Gentile inclusion in Acts 15. "Thus, we cannot assume that she is a member of the Way" (ibid., 275). It is necessary to (re)imagine the story of Rhoda and not think of her only as a textual bridge within the story of Acts (ibid., 283). Her character also reveals much about the early Christ-following movement.

The scholarly debate continues on the nature of the "stock character" in ancient stories (Harrill 2007; Glancy 2007; Aymer 2016; Cobb 2019). A stock character in a narrative like Acts only works if its audience knew what it was like for "slaves" to exist, to operate under the will of a "master" since the institution was central to the Roman way of life. For some, they knew what it was like because they themselves were enslaved to earthly enslavers. For even a third group, as freed persons, formerly under the control of an enslaver and transitioning to a client-patron existence, they would know what it meant to pay obeisance to a (former) "master."

Why does Luke's "God" open the prison gates for Peter but not break the chains of Rhoda? Why did one form of abolition receive divine sanction and not the other? Why did Luke write his way into particular kinds of freedoms but not others? What did "release to the captives" mean (Luke 4:18)? Why was Luke's "Spirit" limited—willing to challenge the State on some forms of bondage and not on other forms of bondage . . . which may have ramifications for the contemporary—to a mixed story, a mixed Gospel, a partial freedom? To be fair to Luke (and, to ourselves), all writing toward freedom is partial.

In the end, Luke's accounts on the early religious movement enforce the distinction between the public and the private. In the public square, Luke's

"God" will "set the captives free" and participate in the freeing of those falsely imprisoned. On the other hand, within its private settings of the house churches of the ancient world, the church could continue to maintain its distinctions in social status between the free and the unfree. Breaking the chains of the prison cell did not lead to the broken chains of one enslaved, even to one enslaved to a Christ-following enslaving woman. Luke's depiction in Acts maps the discourse and practice of the empire with respect to human bondage. "Slaves obey your masters" continued to exemplify the rhetoric and custom of the common house codes within the newly developing religious communities. Whatever else may have been thought about the baptismal formula—neither slave nor free—most of these early Christ-followers did not anticipate an immediate restructuring of the human relationships of those bound by two masters. The prophet Joel, the Apostle Peter, and Luke might be able to imagine an enslaved woman as a prophet, but could they imagine her freedom (see Acts 2:18)?

TERTIUS, ROMANS, AND SLAVERY METAPHORS

The first-century communities of Christ-followers benefitted from slave labor. This ancient cultural fact lies behind Paul's words to Philemon with respect to the transaction of Onesimus: "I wanted to keep him with me, so that he might be of service to me" (Phm 1:13). Lloyd Lewis acknowledges a more passive Paul in this letter: "we wish he would demand or order: he chooses to appeal (v. 9)" (2007, 438). This "appeal" was to Philemon and not to Onesimus. What additional service Paul desired remains undefined. Likely, other house church communities profited from the presence of the enslaved as well. If the members met in house-churches, then the enslaved were present—whether specifically mentioned in the literature or not. Some, like Rhoda, were doorkeepers (Acts 12). There were many unnamed others who carried out duties. If the "Lord's supper" was served, the enslaved likely served the bread and the wine (1 Cor 11). If common meals were shared, the enslaved likely cooked the fish, baked the bread, and poured the lentil soup. If members traveled from afar for the religious gatherings, the enslaved likely washed their feet and cared for their garments.

Paul's regular visits to large households provided access to enslaved bodies. In the wider network of this developing religious movement, the Pauline traveling team often stayed in contact with these households (e.g., Chloe's, Gaius's, Narsicuss's, Philemon's). The language of *kyrios* was not a term reserved only for the *Lord* Jesus. It was a common term for the "master" of any household. Whether at Rom 14:4 (as part of an example of good discipleship) or at Rom 16:22 (in the mouth of the enslaved), the term suggests a religious culture in which the broader images of status and power intertwined with the complexities of an ancient economic and political system that gave linguistic and ideological shape to the developing religious community known as the Way.

Along these lines, what has often been obscured is the vital role many of the enslaved—some Christ-followers and some not—played in the religious community. For example, the production of a written document was often a communal affair. A letter written to an *ekklesia* required more than the individual thought-leader. The apostle also needed support, including one (or, more?) who could transcribe his words, perhaps in ways (now difficult to decipher) that later interpreters struggle to distinguish the *kyrios*-dictator from the *doulos*-transcriber. Both become important to the letter's completion. Of course, communication with a letter required even more assistance than these two. For example, the letter to the Romans commended Phoebe, who was likely the one responsible for transporting the letter to Rome and its public reader (16:1). Were there others involved in the construction of this letter? What about Gaius, Paul's "host"? Or, "our brother Quartus," arguably another enslaved body in the household? What instrumental roles did they play, so much so that Paul desired to utilize their names in this rhetorical game of you-may-not-know-me-but-you-know-my-friends?

On the presence of the enslaved in the Roman church, Wayne Meeks stipulates that an unidentifiable number of freedmen and freedwomen constituted significant positions within Pauline congregations (1983; Patterson 1991, 323). While some, we may presume, were formerly enslaved, other Christ-followers were still enslaved. Although Sheila Briggs focuses on Philippians 2 in her essay "Can an Enslaved God Liberate?," her attention to a first-century enslaved Christian audience as the hearers of Paul's words is relevant for other Pauline communities (such as Romans) (1989). James Dunn imagines just such a scenario for the *doulos*-language of Romans 6: "For the Christian slaves and freedmen and freedwomen in the Roman congregations the emotional force of the metaphor (of enslavement) must have been very strong" (1988, 354). The literary evidence for these suggestions may come from Paul's greetings, in chapter 16, to the "households" of Aristobulus and of Narcissus (cf. Rom 16:10–11). Certainly, these households included enslaved bodies. At the very least, we should imagine that the Roman church shared Rome's population distribution. According to classical scholars, one out of every five persons in Rome were enslaved (Scheidel 2011).

Always attentive to the contemporary marginalized reader, Mitzi Smith warns that whatever Paul's intention, African Americans, in particular, and all interpreters, more generally, "cannot uncritically appropriate metaphors for slavery just because they are theologically contextualized as part of exemplars for the Christian's relationship with Jesus and/or God" (2007, 19).

Nonetheless, Paul did his thinking with "slave" language, even if he did not always reason from the perspective of the enslaved. As Thomas Hoyt reminds us, "For Paul, all human beings are slaves" (2007, 259). Rhetorical ambivalence toward Empire is evident in his *doulos*-discourse. Even so, Monya Stubbs (2004) argues that Paul's subjugation language in Romans 13 should be read in light of his advice not to conform to the world order, an (un)intentional ambiguity at best (Rom 12:2). For the enslaved (Christ-follower), this ambiguity may suggest that Paul desired "to be patient with the weakness of those who don't have power" (Stubbs 2004, 181).[7] Angela Parker and Mitzi Smith make similar points—though in different ways—in their interpretations of the letters to the Corinthians and Galatians, respectively (2020).

Imagine if the "Letter to the Romans" was told from the perspective of the "weak" within this community (cf. Rom 14:1–15:6), or if Tertius had a more active role in the words on the scroll. As the debate continues, it is difficult to prove historically how much independence Tertius had as a scribe, but most scholars have attempted to protect the spoken word (dictation) of the "master," Paul (see Elmer 2008; Cadwallader; 2018). Suppose we did not focus so much on the "hero" of the story but engaged the words through some imaginative license thinking through how others may have been impacted by these words. One of Kartzow's forceful reminders is that "some slaves of the Lord were more slaves than others," which should force us all to read the texts more critically (2018, 102).

To be a full participate in the body of Christ, that is, to be "God's slave," required control over one's own body (cf. Rom 6:22). As he penned Paul's words, Tertius must have discovered the irony in light of his own condition. Most explicitly, Tertius offered his own greeting: "I Tertius, the writer of this letter, *greet you in the Lord*" (emphasis mine). The NRSV obscures the personal words of this laborer even as his body was not his own. The Greek word order places the phrase "in the Lord" more closely with the labor: "I greet you, I, Tertius, the one who *writes the letter in the Lord*" (Rom 16:22; emphasis mine).

First, the association of the phrase *en kyriō* (in the Lord) with the verbal adjective ("the one who writes") fits the pattern of its usage in the remainder of the chapter. Within the immediate context of Romans 16, the prepositional phrase usually follows a noun in the sentence (16:8, 11, 12, 13). The emphasis is *less* on the action ("to greet") and more on those who are "workers" (etc.) "in the Lord" (= Christ-followers?). This syntactical construction matches Tertius's use, since the phrase follows a participle (or, verbal adjective) in his construction. That is, the phrase modified his writing activity (*hō grapsas*).

Second, the exact meaning of the prepositional nature of the phrase "in the Lord" is not easy to discern. Apparently, it means something like to write a letter "in (the name of/for the sake of) the Lord." The construction of Romans

16:11 is instructive, since the phrase also immediately follows a participle. The NRSV's translation places the phrase in the appropriate position in this translation relative to the Greek word order: "Greet *those in the Lord* who belong to the family of Narcissus." The emphasis should fall more on greeting those *who come in the Lord* (= Christ-followers) than on greeting (by means of the Lord) them (whoever they may be).

Finally, and more significantly, the meaning of *kurios* (as mentioned above) should always be judged by its cultural and linguistic context. What might it have meant for Tertius to acknowledge publicly that he wrote this letter *en kyriō*? It could mean "Lord" (Jesus) but it could also mean "master." Oddly, some scholars suggest that he could not have been both enslaved and a Christ-follower (Elmer 2008). That suggestion, however, is a false dichotomy. It would be unsurprising if Tertius (the *doulos*) implied that he wrote on behalf of a "master" (*kyrios*)? Could the reference to the *kyrios*, in the mind of this enslaved scribe, be a double entendre, a reference to Paul (or, Gaius) and God? A double-consciousness provokes his imagination and his use of *kurios* allows the scribe to inscribe a word that captures a multiplicity of meanings, seizing the intersectional nature of his labor in the service of a *kyrios* (an earthly one and, possibly, a heavenly one).

Such a plausible reality might well underlie the double-consciousness of this enslaved scribe when he pens words surrounding the metaphor of slavery. When reflecting on the religious discourse of "sin" and "grace," Paul offered this analogy: "Do you not know that if you present yourselves to anyone as obedient slaves . . . ?" (6:16) This language—"Do you not know . . . ?"—implied that they knew all too well the experience that Paul discussed here about enslavement. When this phrase occurred elsewhere, it implied that the audience understood clearly the nature of this discussion—for example, that they "know that a little yeast leavens a whole batch of dough," or that they "know that in a race the runners all compete, but only one receives the prize" (cf. 1 Cor 5:6; 9:24).[8] Are all his listeners (in Corinth) bakers and athletes? Of course not! More than likely, however, some served their enslavers (or, former enslavers) as bakers and as athletes. Of course, the Roman audience may have understood these things cognitively and not experientially. As Jennifer Glancy starkly concluded, "to be a slave was to be the body of another" (2002, 85). Indeed, some within the Roman congregation—like Aristobulus and Narcissus—as enslavers understood what it meant to hold absolute authority over the body of another person! Others, like Tertius, comprehended the opposite all too well.

Presumably, the metaphor of slavery would fall differently on the ears of those whose status included bondage to another. Before penning Paul's words, whether Tertius cringed after he heard them, for example, would depend on his experience under Gaius and how harsh his master was to the other bodies Gaius controlled. Perhaps it is the physical presence of Tertius—to whom Paul dictates—that causes Paul's hesitancy when utilizing the slavery metaphor as Romans 6:19 seems to suggest: "I am speaking in human terms because of your natural limitations" (NRSV). The ambiguity surrounding Paul's views on slavery continues (Martin, 2010).

This language exposes how crucial bondage language was for religious discourse in the early Christian period. Slavery was fundamental for how Paul thought about relationships of all kinds. Other early Christian theologians developed their own *slave*-thinking from Paul's language in this area, as Chris de Wet argues convincingly with respect to John Chrysostom, the 4th–5th century archbishop (2015). When reflecting on the "weak" and "strong" members of the community, Paul offers the analogy of the "household slave" (*oiketēs*) who should receive judgment only from the one in charge of his bodily production: "Who are you to pass judgment on the servant of another? It is before his own master that he stands or falls" (Rom 14:4, ESV). Again, the analogy is ambivalent, at best, since it emphasizes that, in this case, the "master" (i.e., the "strong") was the only one who may determine the outcome of the "slave" body (i.e., the "weak"). The violence invoked by all types of authorities was well-known (Rom 13:4). As Tertius pens these words on Paul's behalf, it is possible that the amanuensis senses the reality of their truth in a distinct, bodily way. The lived reality of a colonized self is always more complicated than what appears on the literary surface in the midst of a new movement within an empire (Liew 2007, 97). Although space does not allow for further exploration here, one fundamental question belies the language of this religious discourse: despite the confession of the earliest believers within the formation of this new religious movement, why did Paul's "God" (still) need "slaves" (Gal 3:28)? Unlike in 1 Corinthians (7:21–22), Romans does not appear to address enslaved believers directly, although he may greet several at the end of the letter (e.g., Tertius and Quartus). The closest language in the letter to the baptismal formula of Gal 3:28 appears in Rom 10:12, which drops the enslaved from the litany: "For there is no distinction between Jew and Greek; the same Lord is Lord of all and is generous to all who call on him." Perhaps, Paul intentionally dropped the status distinction from the Galatian formula because he was staring directly at an enslaved scribe who was penning his words on behalf of his *kyrios*.

For some scholars of Paul, the Pauline communities may have been more successful in promoting an egalitarian community than others (Sanders 1983). Was Tertius one example of this possibility? Yet, it remains unclear whether Paul fully apprehended "the moral harm of slavery to the slave" (Glancy 2011, loc. 424). Paul may have never heard anyone pray as Epictetus confessed: "it is the slave's prayer to be made free immediately." What has become a grand ethical concern for contemporary believers was simply not part of the moral universe of one of Christianity's founding moral teachers. Whatever Paul's intention, I still agree with Mitzi Smith's warning that African Americans, in particular, and all interpreters, more generally, should not appropriate these *doulos* metaphors uncritically (if at all).

SUMMARY

Sylvester Johnson (2010) is right that the Bible is not innocent. In the summer of 2020, a former President summoned military forces to push back (with tear gas and physical force) a group of peaceful protesters opposing police brutality in the recent death of George Floyd. Trump's primary objective was to create access to St. John's Episcopal Church (across the street from the White House) so that he could initiate a photo opportunity with a Bible in his hand. Trump's Bible—held high over his head—was a symbol on the side of power, governmental authorities, and military force. As bell hooks suggested years ago, "From slavery on, white supremacists have recognized that control over images is central to the maintenance of any system of racial domination" (1992, 2).

Will it ever be time to call into question the ancient "sources" that we read—and, not just *how* we read them—even when those same sources support (and, even foster) cultural practices that separate and divide one group from another or limit the full human capacity of some for the elevation of others? We ourselves need to be freed from textual bondage, enslaved to the texts that benefit the powerful. Surely, the God we imagine is not as limited in desiring a world of justice and peace for all, as are some of these ancient (and, contemporary) Christian thinkers. One way into these sources is to bring to the forefront the texts about human bondage. Hannah-Jones acknowledges in an interview on *The 1619 Project*: "it's also an entire project about slavery, the thing that we don't ever really want to grapple with" (Louis 2019).

Early Christian slave practices is also one of those areas "that we don't ever really want to grapple with." Those attuned to the legacy of violence, abuse, dishonor, lack of volition, loss of a communal self that was associated with human bondage may still sense the indignity of being/becoming enslaved even to God. To conceive of a "god" who needed "slaves" also seems to flow into the contemporary desire to continue to place human bodies inside cages as a supposedly humane practice in a "just" society (Dubler and Lloyd 2019). I assume the metaphors of human bondage wrapped in religious rhetoric were complicated for ancient enslaved Christ-followers, although we never hear from them directly. It is likely that no literature of the canonical New Testament was written by any enslaved disciple (unless Tertius's contribution was more instrumental than traditionally imagined), although it is possible that Christ-following enslavers may have contributed to the collection (Huzienga 2016).

Contemporary readers should not be fooled. The power structures of every age will attempt to control the narrative. How should we utilize the influence we have to challenge those narratives—even the biblical ones—that perpetuate harm against Black bodies in order to hinder the well-being of all?

With respect to the Bible—which does not speak—African American interpreters must use our agency to give it "voice." We must speak on its behalf; we must make it stand on our side. When it does not, we must be willing to say so! As Nancy Ambrose (Howard Thurman's grandmother) modeled for us long ago: some biblical texts do not need to be read aloud ever again.

NOTES

1. Equally striking is Paul's familial language about the enslaved Onesimus: "my child" (v. 11); "a beloved brother" (v. 16).

2. In an odd historical analogy, the written production of nineteenth century "slave narratives" often required the enslaved "author"—such as Sojourner Truth or J. H. Banks (who dictated his account to James Pennington)—to dictate their stories to white or Black editors. In the first century Paul would dictate his words for the *ekklēsia* through the hand of Tertius, one enslaved to the household church.

3. Perhaps this is the implication of the *The Message*'s translation, in which the *kurios* apparently refers to Paul: "I, Tertius, who wrote this letter at Paul's dictation send you personal greetings" (Rom 16:22).

4. The NRSV varies its translation on *paidiskē*: Luke 12:45 ("slaves . . . women"); 22:56 ("servant-girl"); Acts 12:13 ("maid"); and 16:16 ("slave-girl").

5. John's courtyard *paidiskē* was specifically listed as a "gatekeeper" (John 18:17), similar to Rhoda.

6. Warfare was the main supplier, but other avenues existed too: slave trade, kidnapping, infant exposure, births to enslaved women, and punishment for criminals. None of these consider the possibility that a person might sell themselves (or, family members) into debt slavery.

7. Taking Monya Stubbs's lead, it is possible that Paul's discourse about enslavement to an earthly enslaver was more ambivalent than it appears, in light of the apostle's desire for fellow Christ-followers to be (like himself), primarily if not exclusively, enslaved only to God.

8. See also Rom 11:2; 1 Cor 6:9; and 9:13.

WORKS CITED

Adichie, Chimamanda Ngozi. 2009. "The Danger of a Single Story." October 16, 2009. https://www.ted.com/talks/chimamanda_ngozi_acichie_the_danger_of_a_single_story.
Aymer, Margaret. 2016. "Outrageous, Audacious, Courageous, Willful: Reading the Enslaved Girl of Acts 12." In *Womanist Interpretations of the Bible: Expanding the Discourse*, edited by Gay L. Byron and Vanessa Lovelace, 265–89. Atlanta: Society of Biblical Literature.
Bradley, Keith. 1992. "The Regular, Daily Traffic in Slaves": Roman History and Contemporary History." *The Classical Journal* 87, 2:125–18
Briggs, Sheila. 1989. "Can an Enslaved God Liberate?: Hermeneutical Reflections On Philippians 2:6–11." *Semeia* 47: 137–53.
Byron, Gay. 2002. *Symbolic Blackness and Ethnic Difference in Early Christian Literature*. New York: Routledge.
Cadwallader, Alan H. 2018. "Tertius in the Margins: A Critical Appraisal of the Secretary Hypothesis." *New Testament Studies* 64: 378–96.
Callahan, Allen. 1997. *Embassy of Onesimus: The Letter of Paul to Philemon*. Valley Forge: Trinity.
Charles, Ronald. 2020. *The Silencing of Slaves in Early Jewish and Christian Texts*. London/New York: Routledge.
Cobb, Christy. 2019. *Slavery, Gender, Truth, and Power in Luke-Acts and Other Ancient Narratives*. Palgrave MacMillan.
de Wet, Chris. 2015. *Preaching Bondage: John Chrysostom and the Discourse of Slavery in Early Christianity*. Oakland: University of California Press.
DuBois, Page. 1991. *Torture and Truth: The New Ancient World*. New York: Routledge.
———. 2003. *Slaves and Other Objects*. Chicago: University of Chicago Press.
Dubler, Joshua and Vincent Lloyd. 2019. *Break Every Yoke: Religion, Justice, and the Abolition of Prisons*. New York: Oxford University Press.
Dunn, James D. G. 1988. *Romans 9–16*, WBC 38B. Waco, TX: Word.
Elmer, Ian. 2008. "I, Tertius: Secretary or Co-author or Romans." *Australian Biblical Review* 56:45–60.
Glancy, Jennifer. 2002. *Slavery in Early Christianity*. New York: Oxford University Press.
———. 2007."Slavery, Historiography, and Theology." *Biblical Interpretation* 15: 200–11.
———. 2011. *Slavery as a Moral Problem: In the Early Church and Today*. Minneapolis: Fortress.
Haley, Shelley P. 2009. "Be Not Afraid of the Dark: Critical Race Theory and Classical Studies." In *Prejudice and Christian Beginnings: Investigating Race, Gender, and Ethnicity in Early Christian Studies*, edited by Laura Nasrallah and Elisabeth Schüssler-Fiorenza, 27–49. Minneapolis: Fortress.

Hannah-Jones, Nicole. 2019. "America Wasn't a Democracy, Until Black Americans Made it One." *New York Times Magazine*. August 14. https://www.nytimes.com/interactive/2019/08/14/magazine/black-history-american-democracy.html.

———. "The 1619 Project." https://www.project1619.org/.

Harrill, J. Albert. 2006. *Slaves in the New Testament: Literary, Social, and Moral Discussions*. Minneapolis: Fortress.

———. 2007. "The Slave Still Appears: A Historiographical Response to Jennifer Glancy." *Biblical Interpretation* 15: 212–21.

Hezser, Catherine. 2011. "Slavery and the Jews." *The Cambridge World History of Slavery*, edited by Keith Bradley and Paul Cartledge, 438–55. Cambridge: Cambridge University Press.

hooks, bell. 1992. *Black Looks: Race and Representation*. Boston: South End.

Hoyt, Thomas. 2007. "Romans." *True to Our Native Land: An African American New Testament Commentary*, edited by Brian Blount, Cain Hope Felder, Clarice Martin, and Emerson Powery, 249–75. Minneapolis: Fortress.

Huizenga, Annette Bourland. 2016. *1–2 Timothy, Titus*. Wisdom Commentary 53. Collegeville: Liturgical.

Johnson, Matthew V., et al., editors. 2012. *Onesimus Our Brother: Reading Religion, Race, and Culture in Philemon*. Minneapolis: Fortress.

Johnson, Sylvester. 2010. "The Bible, Slavery, and the Problem of Authority." *Beyond Slavery: Overcoming Its Religious and Sexual Legacies*, edited by Bernadette J. Brooten with the editorial assistance of Jacqueline L. Hazelton, 231–48. New York: Palgrave MacMillan.

Joshel, Sandra R. 2010. *Slavery in the Roman World*. Cambridge: Cambridge University Press.

Kartzow, Marianne Bjelland. 2018. *The Slave Metaphor and Gendered Enslavement in Early Christian Discourse: Double Trouble Embodied*. London/New York: Routledge.

Keener, Craig. 2014. *The IVP Bible Background Commentary: New Testament*. Second Edition. Downers Grove, IL: Inter Varsity.

Lewis, Lloyd A. 1991. "An African American Appraisal of the Philemon-Paul-Onesimus Triangle." *Stony the Road We Trod: African American Biblical Interpretation*, edited by Cain Hope Felder, 232–46. Minneapolis: Fortress.

———. 2007. "Philemon." *True to Our Native Land: An African American New Testament Commentary*, edited by Brian Blount, Cain Hope Felder, Clarice Martin, and Emerson Powery, 437–43. Minneapolis: Fortress.

Liew, Tat-Siong (Benny). 2007. *What Is Asian American Biblical Hermeneutics? Reading the New Testament*. Honolulu: University of Hawaii.

Louis, Pierre-Antoine. 2019. "No People Has a Greater Claim to That Flag Than Us" (An Interview with Nicole Hannah-Jones). September 6. https://www.nytimes.com/2019/09/06/us/nikole-hannah-jones-interview.html).

Martin, Clarice. 1994. "The Acts of the Apostles." *Searching the Scriptures; Volume 2: A Feminist Commentary*, edited by Elisabeth Schüssler-Fiorenza, 763–99. New York: Crossroad.

———. 2007. "1–2 Timothy, Titus." *True to Our Native Land: An African American New Testament Commentary*, edited by Brian Blount, Cain Hope Felder, Clarice Martin, and Emerson Powery, 409–36. Minneapolis: Fortress, 2007.

———. 2010. "The Eyes Have It: Slaves in the Communities of Christ Believers." In *The People's History: Christian Origins*, edited by Richard Horsley, 221–39. Minneapolis: Fortress.

Meeks, Wayne. 1983. *The First Urban Christians: The Social World of the Apostle Paul*. New Haven: Yale University Press.

Morrison, Toni. 1993. *Playing in the Dark: Whiteness and the Literary Imagination*. New York: Vintage.

Parker, Angela N. 2020. "Feminized-Minoritized Paul?: A Womanist Reading of Paul's Body in the Corinthian Context." *Minoritized Women Reading Race and Ethnicity*, edited by Mitzi Smith and Jin Young Choi, 71–88. Lanham: Lexington Books.

Patterson, Orlando. 1991. *Freedom: Volume I: Freedom in the Making of Western Culture*. Cambridge, MA: Harvard University Press.

Powery, Emerson B., and Rodney S. Sadler. 2016. *The Genesis of Liberation: Biblical Interpretation in the Antebellum Narratives of the Enslaved*. Louisville: Westminster John Knox.

Sanders, E. P. 1983. *Paul, the Law, and the Jewish People*. Minneapolis: Fortress.

Scheidel, Walter. 2011. "The Roman Slave Supply." *The Cambridge World History of Slavery*, edited by Keith Bradley and Paul Cartledge, 287–310. Cambridge: Cambridge University Press.

Smith, Mitzi. 2007. "Slavery in the Early Church." *True to Our Native Land: An African American New Testament Commentary*, edited by Brian Blount, Cain Hope Felder, Clarice Martin, and Emerson Powery, 11–22. Minneapolis: Fortress.

———. 2011. *The Literary Construction of the Other in the Acts of the Apostles: Charismatics, the Jews, and Women*. Princeton Theological Monograph Series. Eugene, OR: Pickwick.

———. 2012. "Utility, Fraternity, and Reconciliation: Ancient Slavery as a Context for the Return of Onesimus." *Onesimus Our Brother: Reading Religion, Race, and Culture in Philemon*, edited by Matthew V. Johnson, James A. Noel, and Demetrius K. Williams, 47–58. Minneapolis: Fortress.

———. 2020. "Hagar's Children Still *Ain't* Free: Paul's Counterterror Rhetoric, Constructed Identity, Enslavement, and Galatians 3:28." *Minoritized Women Reading Race and Ethnicity*, edited by Mitzi Smith and Jin Young Choi, 45–70. Lanham: Lexington Books.

Smith, Mitzi, and Jin Young Choi, eds. 2020. *Minoritized Women Reading Race and Ethnicity: Intersectional Approaches to Constructed Identity and Early Christian Texts*. Lanham: Lexington Books.

Spencer, F. Scott. 2004. *Journeying Through Acts: A Literary-Cultural Reading*. Peabody, MA: Hendrickson.

Strabo, *Geography*. https://penelope.uchicago.edu/Thayer/E/Roman/Texts/Strabo/14E*.html.

Stubbs, Monya. 2004. "Subjection, Reflection, Resistance: An African American Reading of the Three-Dimensional Process of Empowerment in Romans 13 and the Free-Market Economy." *Navigating Romans through Cultures: Challenging Readings by Charting a New Course*, edited by Yeo Khiok-khng (K. K.), 171–98. New York/London: T & T Clark.

———. 2013. *Indebted Love: Paul's Subjection Language in Romans*. Eugene, OR: Pickwick.

Williams, Demetrius. 2007. "Acts." *True to Our Native Land: An African American New Testament Commentary*, edited by Brian Blount, Cain Hope Felder, Clarice Martin, and Emerson Powery, 213–48. Minneapolis: Fortress.

Wimbush, Vincent L. 2000. "Reading Darkness, Reading Scriptures." *African Americans and the Bible*, edited by Vincent L. Wimbush with the assistance of Rosamond C. Rodman, 1–43. New York/London: Continuum.

Witherington, Ben. 1992. "Rhoda." *The Anchor Bible Dictionary*, Volume V, edited by David Noel Freedman, 719. New York: Doubleday.

Chapter 7

"I am a Human"

Racializing Assemblages and Criminalized Egyptianness in Acts 21:31–39

Jeremy L. Williams

In Acts 21:31–39, the Roman police commander Claudius Lysias arrests Paul after he has been criminalized. Directly before this passage, Paul is falsely charged with violating the law and desecrating the Jerusalem Temple for inviting a non-Jewish Ephesian into the area preserved for Jewish people. Claudius Lysias swoops in with his Roman police force, apprehends Paul, mistaking him for a criminal Egyptian? He does not learn that Paul is not an Egyptian criminal until after he arrests him and Paul asks a question in Greek, to which the police commander responds, "So you know Greek? You aren't the troublemaking Egyptian who recently caused unrest and led four thousand knife-carrying assassins into the desert, huh?" Paul declares, "I am a human, [*Egō anthrōpos men eimi*] a Jew, from Tarsus in Cilicia, a not insignificant city, of which I am a citizen. I request of you, that you permit me to speak to the people." This leads to a central question for this essay: what made Lysias, the police commander, assume that Paul was a criminal Egyptian?

To analyze this scene, I employ critical race theory (CRT) and Alexander Weheliye's concept of racializing assemblages that engages Black feminist thought. I hone in on what Richard Delgado and Jean Stefancic identify as a hallmark of CRT: a critique of liberalism (2012, 26). Particularly, I focus on how Weheliye's racializing assemblages capture Sylvia Wynter's and other Black feminists' critique against the liberal category of the "human." This essay demonstrates how these frameworks not only help to contextualize this scene in Acts 21, but also provide tools for reading Josephus, Philo, and other Roman texts that elide particular understandings of Egyptianness with criminality. Furthermore, I present how interrogating sociopolitical processes like policing, ethno-political rhetoric, and respectability politics exposes how texts, including biblical passages like Acts 21, understand humanity to be hierarchized and imagine that justice should be measured out accordingly. My interrogation seeks to read the power arrangements of the world that produced Acts in order to present Acts as a tool to critique our world. I conclude with questions for how considering new understandings of what it means to be human can lead to a more capacious category that does not render some people as subhuman or nonhuman.

I begin this essay with my translation of Acts 21:31–39, which contributes to the argument.

While they were seeking to kill him, a report rose to the police commander of the (Jerusalem) police force that all of Jerusalem was stirred up Immediately, he took militarized police and the sergeants and ran down to them. When they saw the police commander and the militarized police, they stopped beating Paul. Then, coming near, the police commander arrested him and ordered him to be bound with two chains, and he inquired about who he was and what he had done. Some in the crowd shouted this and others shouted that, and since he could not understand the facts through the uproar, he ordered Paul to be taken into the precinct. When he came to the stairs, it happened that on account of the violence of the crowd, he had to be carried by the militarized police, for the throng of people that followed were crying, "Away with him!" As Paul was about to be taken into the precinct, he said to the police commander, "Is it lawful for me to speak to you?" The police commander responded, "So you know Greek? You aren't the Egyptian who recently caused unrest and led four thousand knife-carrying assassins into the desert, huh?" Paul replied, "I am a human, a Jew, from Tarsus in Cilicia, a not insignificant city, of which I am a citizen. I request of you, that you permit me to speak to the people."

A CRITIQUE OF LIBERALISM AND THE CATEGORY OF THE "HUMAN" AND ACTS

My translation and interpretation of this passage are informed by CRT's critique of liberalism and Wynter's critique of the category of the "human." Both frameworks shed light on ancient Roman sociopolitical and contemporary processes.

Alexander Weheliye uses the term "racialized assemblages" to expose how sociopolitical relations create hierarchies within the category of the human to expose that race is not only or primarily about phenotypic difference, but it is a combination of factors (an "assemblage") ultimately meant to hierarchize humans (2014, 8). For Weheliye,

> if racialization is understood not as a biological or cultural descriptor but as a conglomerate of sociopolitical relations that discipline humanity into full humans, not-quite-humans, and nonhumans, then blackness designates a changing system of unequal power structures that apportion and delimit which humans can lay claim to the full status and which humans cannot. Conversely, "white supremacy may be understood as a logic of social organization that produces regimented institutionalized, and militarized conceptions of hierarchized 'human' difference" (2014, 3).

Weheliye relies on Sylvia Wynter's critique of the category of the human in Western philosophy to inform his discussion about how white Man has saturated the category of the human, rendering others as not-quite-human or subhuman (2003, 257–337). Wynter claims that "the struggle of our new millennium will be one between the ongoing imperative of securing the well-being of our present ethnoclass (i.e., Western bourgeois) conception of the human, Man, which overrepresents itself as if it were the human itself, and that of securing the well-being, and therefore the full cognitive and behavioral autonomy of the human species itself/ourselves" (Weheliye 2003, 260). Wynter persuasively argues how the category of the human evolves from Enlightenment transformations of the Christian lay people into secular humans. She exposes that a secular understanding of humanity demanded new borders to define who was within, at the limits, and beyond the category of humanity. Wynter presents that race in some ways replaces religion as a tool to forge the boundaries of this humanity. She argues that many Enlightenment thinkers and those who follow them wield race in a way that does not necessarily exclude Black humans, but instead places their humanness at the very margins of the concept of humanity. Zakkiyah Jackson reads Wynter in these terms:

> Within the structure of much thought on race there is an implicit assumption that the recognition of one as a human being will protect one from (or acts as an insurance policy against) ontologizing violence. Departing from a melancholic attachment to such an ideal, I argue that the violence and terror scholars describe is endemic to the recognition of humanity itself—when that humanity is cast as black. A recognition of black humanity, demonstrated across these pages, is not denied or excluded but weaponized by a conception of "the human" foundationally organized by the idea of a racial telos. For Wynter, the Negro is not so much excluded from the category Man and its overrepresentation of humanity but foundational to it as its antipodal figure, as the nadir of Man. (2020, 19–20)

For Wynter and Jackson, liberalism understands humanity as hierarchized to the point that some have oversaturated the category and put others, Black humans at the very margins, literally serving as the defining limit of humanity. Hence, "blackness has been central to, rather than excluded from, liberal humanism" (Jackson 2020, 48).

In *Race: A Theological Account*, J. Kameron Carter (2008) reads Immanuel Kant's "Of the Different Human Races" as the first scientific theory or philosophical account on race. In Kant's text, the destiny of the human species is global perfection and the spread of whiteness (Carter 2008, 39–78). CRT and Black feminists like Wynter critique this notion and suggest that if this is how humanity is considered then the entire category should be reconsidered. Black studies scholar Ashon Crawley notes that in discourses that follow Kant, "'the body' is a conceptual abstraction produced through normative theological and philosophical discourses" (2016, 92). To counter those discourses, especially those about Black bodies, he proposes what he calls an *atheologial-aphilosophical* approach that does not privilege Kant's framework but instead begins otherwise and critically analyzes what a human is in Western thought, who is considered human, who gets to determine another's humanity, and what responses to dehumanization arise. Weheliye, Crawley, Wynter, and others transform "the human into a heuristic model and not an ontological fait accompli" (Weheliye 2014, 8). Therefore, Weheliye, Black studies, and Black feminists offer "the human" and blackness as sites to evaluate racializing assemblages.

Racializing assemblages, as a theoretical framework, offers resources for examining ancient sociopolitical processes around militarized policing, respectability politics, and ethno-political invective against Egyptianness. This framework exposes operative understandings that consider some humans as fully human, others as not-quite-human, and some as nonhuman in Acts and other texts entangled in the Roman hegemonic imagination.

In the verses directly preceding Lysias' entrance into the scene, Paul's antagonists claim that he is

> the person [*anthrōpos*] teaching all against the people, the Law and this place. And now he brought a Greek into the Temple and has defiled this holy place. [29] For they had seen Trophimus the Ephesian in the city with him, whom they supposed that Paul had brought into the Temple. [30] The whole city was shaken and the people tumultuously came together. They detained Paul and dragged him out of the Temple and immediately the doors were shut.

They accuse him of being a lawbreaking human that desecrates sacred spaces. He rejects those allegations and after Lysias misidentifies him as an Egyptian criminal, Paul declares the type of human that he is. He is one who deserves to be treated better than a criminal (lawbreaker) or Egyptian insurrectionist. Acts wants it to be clear that Paul is not just any kind of human, he is the highest kind of human with rights to be protected. Thus, Acts is not interested in an egalitarian humanity but understands humanity as hierarchized. For Acts, it is not wrong for the Roman police or mobs to attack or beat an *anthrōpos*, but it is not acceptable to mistreat *certain anthrōpoi*. Now I return to key features in my translation that provide clues into the sociopolitical processes at work in criminalizing Egyptianness and Paul.

MILITARIZED POLICING AS SOCIOPOLITICAL PROCESS

Above, I translated Acts 21:31–39 to capture aspects of policing and institutions that police as sociopolitical processes. Philosopher and activist Frank Wilderson sheds light on how policing functions as a component of a racializing assemblage. He argues that a major component of the Black experience both in the United States and abroad is persistent policing (Wilderson 2003, 18–27; also see Hattery and Smith 2021, Muhammad 2010, and Hinton 2017). Black bodies are constantly under surveillance, like Foucault's *délinquant* in the panopticon prison (Foucault 1977, 73–103). Black humans are policed both via state agents and by white people more broadly who are deputized by the presence of Black people. Steve Martinot and Jared Sexton make this point: "Police impunity serves to distinguish between the racial itself and the elsewhere that mandates it . . . the distinction between those whose human being is put permanently in question and those for whom it goes without saying" (2003, 174). Wilderson analyzes that quotation this way: "In such a paradigm, white people are, ipso facto, deputized in the face of Black people, whether they know it (consciously) or not. Whiteness, then, and by extension civil society, cannot be solely 'represented' as some monumentalized coherence of phallic signifiers, but must first be understood as a social formation of contemporaries who do not magnetize bullets" (2003, 20). Black humans are subject to perennial policing and the policing can come from state-sponsored entities or from people who presume the authority to arrest and execute because they consider their humanity to be more valuable than or exclusive from Black bodies. This directly contributes to the disproportionate rates of imprisonment of Black humans in the US Nikia Robert (2016, 181) notes that

> while people of color make up about 30 percent of the United States' population, they account for 60 percent of those imprisoned. The prison population grew by 700 percent from 1970 to 2005 where 1 in every fifteen African American men and 1 in every 36 Latino men are incarcerated in comparison to 1 in every 106

White men. Comparably African American women are among the fastest growing prison population, where the number of women incarcerated has increased by 800 percent over the last three decades. African American women are three times more likely to be incarcerated, while Latina women are 69 percent more likely than White women to be incarcerated. Similarly to brazed cattle it is as if laws were virtually written on the backs of the oppressed as a mark of punishment to effectively slaughter the poor and vulnerable in a penal system of sacrifice.

Policing participates in legal systems that mark some people for punishment and functions as a sociopolitical process that separates and hierarchizes humans.

The above insights on policing inform my translation of Acts 21:31–39. I translate five terms to capture aspects of their policing function and to explore how Acts wields policing and institutions that police as sociopolitical processes. The term *stratiōtai* is traditionally translated as soldiers; I translate it "militarized police." Frequently, Roman governors commissioned members of this group to resolve intercity conflicts, punish offenders, and capture delinquents or insurrectionists (Fuhrmann 2012, 102). The Romans and their deputized subjects worked to maintain order for Roman interests. Roman people also understood that a *stratiōtēs* could resolve a non-military dispute. A papyrus from the Egyptian port city Euhemeria captures a moment when a son tells his father to repay a debt less he send the *stratiōtēs* to place him in prison (P.Fay.135). Although that text is dated later than Acts, it demonstrates how *stratiōtai* did more than wage war; they policed communities as the sheriffs (*stratēgoi*) do in Acts 16:19–40.

The police in Acts 21:31–39 are led by a *chiliarchos*, which I render as police commander. This translation of *chiliarchos* as "police commander" aligns with Holladay's suggestion that "commander" is a viable translation of the term *chiliarchos* (Holladay 2016, 419). The Latin equivalent of *chiliarchos* is *tribunus militum* in the Roman military. In the first and second centuries, the position of *chiliarchos* or *tribunus militum* was normally occupied by a nineteen-or twenty-year old elite who served for one or one-and-a-half years before beginning their path of social mobility (*cursus honorum*) (de Libero 2006). An audience hearing the term *chiliarchos* would have imagined a young, inexperienced, high-born person who received the position without necessarily earning it. Tacitus in *Agricola* also notes that those who acquired this position did not always take their roles very seriously. In Acts 22:22–29, the young commander almost mishandles Paul and suggests having him flogged, because he has classified him as a not-quite-human, as a criminal Egyptian.

The police commander brings *hekatontarchai* and a *speira* with him to investigate the commotion at the Jerusalem Temple. I translate *hekatontarchai* as sergeants to align with my translation of Lysias as police commander and to capture the role that would have been subordinated to a *chiliarchos*. The oft-used translation of "centurion" is not extremely accurate, because this position did not lead 100 men, but more likely 80. I translate *speira* as police force. This group would have called to mind for the earliest readers of Acts an armed cohort of approximately 80–500 subordinates. A legion of approximately 5,000 was divided into these units.

Lysias' force was headquartered at the Antonia Fortress to keep order as occupying police. In line with my previous translations, I interpret the term describing Antonia Fortress, *parembolē*, as "precinct" or "headquarters." The occupying presence of Lysias' Roman militarized police force headquartered in the Antonia Fortress supposedly functioned to keep order in Jerusalem, especially during festivals (Josephus 2014, 5.238–245 and 1943, 15.403–409). Although scholars are suspicious of Josephus' large-scale depiction and agree that Antonia was much smaller than previously imagined, the headquarters still represented surveillance (Magness 2012, 157–8). Along with protecting and serving from foes, the presence of the Roman military, in Judea—a hotbed of dissent—was to keep the people in line. Archaeologist Jodi Magness writes, "The Antonia was a deterrent (message to the Jews: you are being watched!), and housed troops to quell any uprisings or trouble" (2012, 157). The work of this precinct was to regulate the people who lived in, visited, or did not belong in Jerusalem. In that way these militarized police had to hierarchize humans and to handle humans and groups of humans that they classified as criminal.

The precinct's location on the Jerusalem Temple Mount also shows Rome's investment with protecting the financial and political interests of the Roman Empire in the particularly tumultuous Judean province (Smallwood 1981, 206–10). It was particularly important to keep this community under surveillance, since it had a history of revolt and discontent with the imperial government. The precinct and the presence of the police literally represent military violence.

The militarized police and their young police commander operate as imperial agents imbued with power to criminalize and punish; they arrest (*epilambanō*) Paul who they prejudge as a criminal Egyptian. This type of policing would have been familiar to Acts' audience, whether in Jerusalem or elsewhere. The militarized police criminalized people that the Empire deemed as delinquents, but we have not yet clarified why the police commander presumed that Paul was a delinquent or an Egyptian.

ETHNO-POLITICAL RHETORIC AS SOCIOPOLITICAL PROCESS

Gay Byron's analysis in *Symbolic Blackness and Ethnic Difference in Early Christian Literature* presents the widespread disdain and criminal profiling of Egyptians in literature. She explores how Greek and Roman elite literature discussed Egyptians' differences, especially with regard to color differences. Byron refers to this discussion as "ethno-political rhetoric" which she defines as "discursive elements within texts that refer to 'ethnic' identities or geographical locations and function as political invective" (Byron 2002, 2). Ethno-political rhetoric marks certain humans as other and inferior and frequently moves beyond language into laws and thus onto bodies. Robert using Michel de Certeau notes that "brown bodies become a juridical corpus—a body of laws—an enfleshment of lingual politics. Similarly to Logos, as in God violently entered into history to occupy human flesh, jurisprudences coercively disrupt embodied 'otherness' to mark Black bodies for punishment. The result is a bodily discursive violence that replaces paper for pigmented peripheral people" (2016, 182).

Ethno-political invective appears on bodies. Hence, such rhetoric participates in a sociopolitical process that transforms human beings into delinquents prime for punishment, castigation, and mistreatment. Byron helpfully explains that this process is not new; its roots extend to antiquity.

Contemporary classicists consider how the Roman elite produced the "Egyptianness" of people and objects. (Swetnam-Burland 2015; Nasrallah 2019, 179–223). In *Beyond the Nile*, Miguel Versluys notes that ancient writers used Egypt for their own agenda as a tool to depict Rome in a certain light (2018, 230–37). Therefore, one must always evaluate the function of "Egyptianness" in light of the image that the author or craftsperson wants to portray about Rome. For example, if the author wanted to portray Rome as strong, then it was important to show Egypt as weak, but not too weak; it had to also be portrayed as a place that was a worthy adversary, even if only temporarily. Roman authors used Egypt and Egyptians for Roman self-understanding and self-legitimization (Leemreize 2016).

Josephus sets the table for Acts' racializing assemblage of Paul and the ethno-political invective that combines "Egyptianness" with criminality. Josephus rhetorically uses "the Egyptian" in *Jewish War* 2.261, which influences Acts (Pervo 2006, 161–66; Haenchen 1971, 621–22; Holladay 2016, 418). Josephus uses "the Egyptian" trope similarly to how he wields the term *lēstēs* (robber, bandit, or delinquent) in *Jewish War* 2.21.

For Josephus, *lēstai* are both popular troublemakers and his political rivals. Classicist Thomas Grünewald argues that Josephus always uses *lēstai* in a politicized way that resembles how Greek novelists crafted dramatized depictions of *lēstai* (2004, 11). Writers filled the term with its meaning, and for Josephus the term depicted a bandit, an insurrectionist, or to use Foucault's term a *délinquant* or delinquent. Foucault is relevant here because he argues that a delinquent is created by society's institutions through what Weheliye would call sociopolitical processes (Foucault 1977, 73–103). In this way, what constitutes a delinquent is not objective, but societies and individuals like Josephus create the criteria for assessing someone as such. For example, in his discussion of events after Herod I's death in *Jewish War* 2.4.1, he writes: "At Sepphoris in Galilee and of Judas in Galilee. Judas, son of Ezechias, the chief delinquent (*archilēstou*) who in former days infested the country and was subdued by King Herod, raised a considerable body of followers, broke open the royal arsenals, and, having armed his companions, attacked the other aspirants to power."

Josephus applies the term *lēstēs* to individuals who gathered groups of people and aspired to power or kingship, and in *Jewish War* 2.21 he also resorts to using a prominent topos that views *lēstai* as plunderers and violent opportunists to portray his opponents as criminals. Josephus also weds the term *lēstai* with Egyptian identity. This usage occurs in *Jewish War* 2.254–65 to which Acts 21:38 alludes:

> Then while the country was thus cleared of these, another kind of delinquent [*lēstōn*] was springing up in Jerusalem, those called knife-carrying assassins who killed people in the middle of the day in the middle of the city. . . . More than this blow, *the Egyptian* false prophet, who was a deceiver, did the Jewish people evil. He gathered thirty thousand in the countryside by putting the trust of a prophet on himself. He gathered those deceived and led them round from the wilderness to the mountain, which was called the Mount of Olives. From there, he intended to go to Jerusalem to press into it, and after overpowering the Roman garrison and the people, he would tyrannize them by attacking with those guards that were rushing along with him. But Felix prevented his assault and met him with his Roman armed troops. All the people assisted the defense with the result that the Egyptian fled with only a few, while the greatest part of those that were with him were utterly destroyed or taken alive. The rest of the multitude scattered to their own homes to escape notice. Now, when these affairs were put in order, another part of the body became inflamed as happens in a sick body. The deceivers and delinquents [*lēstrikoi*] got together, and led many to resist, and exhorted them to assert their liberty and exact death on those continuing in obedience to the Roman leadership. They said that those who willingly prefer slavery ought to be snatched with force.

Josephus uses the following strategies to criminalize the Egyptian: characterizations of deception, plundering, and the term *lēstai* (*Jewish Wars* 2.264).

Josephus portrays the Egyptian leading 30,000 people out into the wilderness. He compares the Egyptian to the delinquents who similarly reject Roman leadership and the knife-carrying assassins who kill people in broad daylight, both of which Josephus denounces. The parallels to Acts' narrative appear in the Egyptian leading knife-carrying assassins into the wilderness, although Acts claims that the Egyptian led out 4,000 instead of 30,000.

Beyond *Jewish War*, Josephus shows his disdain for Egyptians in his *Against Apion*, where he challenges Apion for labelling Jewish adversaries as Egyptians. He writes:

> That he should lie about our ancestors and assert that they were Egyptians by race [*to genos Aigyptious*] is by no means surprising. He told a lie, which was the reverse of this one about himself. Born in the Egyptian oasis, more Egyptian than them all, as one might say, he disowned his true country and falsely claimed as an Alexandrian, thereby admitting the ignominy of his race. It is therefore natural that he should call persons whom he detests and wishes to abuse Egyptians. Had he not had the meanest opinion of natives of Egypt [*Aigyptious*], he would never have turned his back on his own nation [*to genos*]. (Byron 2002, 36; author's emphases)

Josephus suggests that identifying an individual as Egyptian was to present the person as detestable. Josephus elides Apion with all Egyptians in order to portray him as duplicitous (Isaac 2004, 352). Josephus views Egyptians as a group loaded with criminal potential, and labelling someone as such could serve to portray a person as worthy of incarceration, punishment, execution, or penance. Josephus' understanding of Egyptians impacts the "history" that he conveys. The way that Josephus engages Egyptians and negative stereotypes about Egyptians should be taken into account when considering his influence on the milieu that shaped Luke-Acts. By referring to Josephus and appealing to "the Egyptian," Luke-Acts not only discusses a delinquent but alludes to a portfolio of criminality, a racializing assemblage, associated with Egyptians. Other Romans, beyond Josephus like Philo, Cicero, Tacitus, Pliny the Younger, Plutarch, Cassius Dio, Juvenal, also castigate Egyptianness to portray Roman identity as a *telos* of humanity. Philo provides a useful complementary example to our previous conversation on Josephus.

Philo, another Jew under Roman rule was from the Hellenized capital of Egypt, Alexandria, which Romans described as "by" Egypt (Cohen 2006, 355–81). Philo's *Legatio ad Gaium* and *In Flaccum* negatively stereotype Egyptians for his own political purposes. These treatises are direct and often vitriolic appeals to castigate those who oppose his Jewish community in Alexandria. Alexandria was understood to be culturally superior to the rest of Egypt (Cohen 2006, 356). As an Alexandrian, Philo is careful to further separate himself and his Jewish community from their Egyptian neighbors. Philo uses Egyptian identity as a marker for inappropriate worship, mischievousness, and low status.

Philo uses "Egyptians" as an ethnic instrument against which he and his community could define themselves. Philo argues in *In Flaccum* 79–80 that Roman governor Flaccus mistreats his community. Philo explains that there are tiers of punishment that Flaccus and his henchmen violently ignore. One of Philo's primary concerns is that his people were being treated like they are Egyptians; indeed, the elders (*gerousia*) were being treated worse than the lowest Egyptians: "Surely then it was the height of harshness that when commoners among the Alexandrian Jews, if they appeared to have done things worthy of stripes, were beaten with whips more suggestive of freemen and citizens. The magistrates, the elders (*gerousia*), whose very name implies age and honor, in this respect fared worse than their inferiors and were treated like Egyptians of the meanest rank and guilty of the greatest iniquities." Here Philo employs "Egyptians" as a place holder of value—the lowest value. Philo uses "Egyptian" to hyperbolically express how mistreated his people were by Flaccus. His rhetorical elision of Egyptians with criminality participates in a sociopolitical process that renders Egyptian as nothing (not-quite-human), and his own people as something (human). Philo's negative use of "Egyptians" was a component of his own project of self-definition for his diasporic Jewish community in Roman Egypt. He attacked the "Egyptian" in order to create a space and notion of self-worth in opposition to Alexandrians and Roman officials continually attempting to humiliate him and his community. His fight was to define his people, but the Egyptians were collateral.

With such negative ethno-political rhetoric against Egyptians, one cannot overlook Paul's mistaken identity. By incorporating Egyptian identity into this narrative, Acts generates several interpretive possibilities. Acts could have introduced "the Egyptian" in Acts 21 for the general effect that "Egyptians" generated in readers and as a rhetorical term that often portrayed dubious, mischievous, impious, low status persons. Lysias' confusion could be a nod to Paul's phenotypic similarity to Egyptians, a group whom elite writers negatively stereotyped. Regardless, Acts has Paul misidentified as an Egyptian to indicate how a Roman policing official understood him as a delinquent, a criminal. Acts' Paul was viewed as one that was not fully human, especially not on Roman terms. For one reason or another, he was mistaken as one who did not look like he deserved justice afforded to full humans. To that end, Lysias, functioning as the commander of the Antonia precinct, polices Paul's not-quite human body.

RESPECTABILITY POLITICS AS SOCIOPOLITICAL PROCESS

One solution that minoritized people explore in order to avoid the pitfalls of racializing assemblages is to participate in respectability politics. Mitzi Smith introduces the concept of respectability politics into New* Testament studies[1] and Luke-Acts scholarship (Smith 2018). She defines it as

> the notion that if a member of a subordinated, marginalized, or oppressed group exhibits acceptable and submissive behaviors, is socially compliant in her appearance and ways of being (e.g., attire, hair style, language, voice, sexuality, marital status, and so on), achieves some measure of success regardless of any systemic obstacles, and according to the standards of the dominant culture, she will be accepted by the dominant group; she will be treated justly and equally and will earn access to the same privileges and protected rights enjoyed by the dominant group. (Smith 2018, 10)

Unfortunately, respectability politics ultimately reinforce the racial stratification imposed by the hegemonic group through using the dominant group's standard for humanity and "civilization" to gauge whether people should be treated as human or not. This type of politics suggests that people minoritized through racialization, immigration status, language, sexuality, gender non-conformity, ability, class, or other status markers can behave in a way that can prove their human value (Harris 2003, 212–20). However, one cannot behave like the dominant group enough to gain automatic entry into its ranks, even if said minoritized person performs more like the dominant group than members in the dominant group. When the goal is to have one's humanity treated equally to that of the dominant group, the dominant group retains the power to determine who it extends humanity to and the extent of humanity that minoritized people can receive. Furthermore, many versions of respectability politics uncritically presume that the dominant groups' understanding of humanity is superior or worth emulating, and that must be interrogated.

In Acts, Paul operates in a framework that closely resembles respectability politics, but respectability is still not enough to save him from being policed and treated as subhuman or nonhuman by Roman police. After Paul is arrested by the police commander, he makes a request of Lysias in Greek, which Lysias interprets as an indication that Paul is not the criminal Egyptian. Pervo, following Conzelmann, suggests that what Acts may signal here is "Paul's Greek accent, since a Jewish rebel from Egypt was likely to have spoken some Greek. Paul exhibited the fluency of an educated native speaker" (2009, 553).

Paul's knowledge of Greek presents one marker that he was not just some common yokel and that he had a certain amount of education in classical arts and literature and elite status (Neyrey 1984, 210–24). This is not to suggest that many in antiquity would not have been multilingual (Mullen and James 2012). However, here Paul's multilingualism functions as a display of ancient respectability politics. Throughout the text, Acts presents Paul as a well-trained elite. Most notably, Acts 17:16–34 places Paul in Athens, an intellectual center of the Roman world and the infamous home of Socrates. Acts 17:28 depicts Paul quoting a Greek poet as he exegetes an inscription to the Unknown God. Paul states in Acts 18:28, "In God we live, are set in motion, and exist" (*en auto zōmen kai kinoumetha kai esmen*). Pervo draws parallels in Paul's quotation to *Aristeas to Philocrates* (2009, 101–103). Others have drawn connections to Cleanthes, *Hymn to Zeus*, 4–5 (see Conzelmann 1987, 247–8). In Athens, Paul debates with philosophers and stands trial on the Areopagus as Socrates also had done, criminalized as Socrates had been (Pervo 2009, 427). By Lysias acknowledging Paul's Greek speech, Acts activates how Paul's Greek speech has been a major catalyst that demonstrates the validity of his claims and the value of his life, especially in trials in which his interlocutors challenge his status.

After Lysias hears Paul's Greek speech, he asks Paul a rhetorical question about being an Egyptian criminal, to which Paul states "I am a human [*Egō anthrōpos men eimi*], a Jew, from Tarsus in Cilicia, a not insignificant city, of which I am a citizen." Hence, as Paul's life has been capriciously assaulted by state-sanctioned discrimination, he asserts "I am a human"; "My life matters." However, the Roman elite like Lysias and Philo could wield Egyptianness to portray someone like Paul as a low-status human.

Acts demonstrates its own respectability politics as it presents Paul as the type of *anthrōpos* who deserves to be treated properly, and the text links *anthrōpos* to citizenship status to depict that. Acts only uses the term *anthrōpos* with a nation or ethnic marker as substantive three times (16:37, 21:39, 22:25). Acts places all these usages in Paul's mouth, and two of those times, Paul identifies as an *anthrōpos Rōmaios* to protest how Roman police forces mishandle him in relation to his status as a Roman citizen (16:37 and 22:25). In Acts 21:39, Paul claims that he is an *anthrōpos Ioudaios* at the Jewish Temple in front of a murderous mob, and he also claims that he is an *anthrōpos Tarseus*, which is an important city. The audience already knows that Paul is also an *anthrōpos Rōmaios* from his unjust treatment in Philippi (16:37); yet, in the present scene in Jerusalem, he does not immediately reveal this identity (22:25). Paul states that he is an important *anthrōpos* by linking the term to national citizenship as he faces mistreatment by Roman policing forces. By connecting *anthrōpos* to citizenship status as an appeal to how they should treat him, Acts also suggests that there are *anthrōpoi* who are not to be treated properly by Roman authorities. Although humans, they do not have access to all the privileges of the elite and their humanity is depreciated. Ultimately, even Acts illustrates that respectability politics are not enough, because although Paul has education and citizenship and, even after he declares that he is a human, he remains in Roman custody for the remainder of Acts' narrative.

CONCLUDING QUESTIONS

Policing, ethno-political rhetoric, and respectability politics hierarchize people within the category of the human. The contemporary framework of racializing assemblages provides strategies for analyzing ancient sociopolitical processes. Acts simultaneously portrays Paul as criminalized while using a notion of hierarchized humanity to present Paul as misidentified. Acts points to injustice but does not seek to remedy the structures and anthropological scaffolding that make that injustice possible. Acts gets some parts right and others not so much. My assessment primarily sought to examine how texts like Acts hierarchize humans and how they can teach us to be suspicious of sociopolitical processes that render human beings as not fully human, as subhuman, nonhuman, or delinquent. The theoretical framework applied in this essay helps us to read the power arrangements of the world that produced the texts in the Bible, and then in turn presents the Bible as a resource to closely read and exegete our world.

The mistaken police, the harmful ethno-political rhetoric, and ineffective respectability politics in Acts should lead us to questions like the one posed by Weheliye: "what different modalities of the human come to light if we do not take the liberal humanist figure of Man as the master-subject but focus on how humanity has been imagined and lived by those subjects excluded from this domain?" (2014, 3). How might the story of early Christianity be told differently if our understanding of humanity did not privilege some with full human status and others as subhuman, some as saved and others as damned, some as holy insiders and others as heathen outsiders, some as Christian believers and others as Jewish antagonists, some as citizens and others as delinquents? How might ancient history be told from the perspective of the criminal Egyptian and those in Josephus' *Jewish War* 2.264 who "led many to resist and exhorted them to assert their liberty and exact death on those continuing in obedience to the Roman leadership"? How do we work to create a humanity that is capacious enough that no one has to argue that they are human and that their lives matters? Here, I sought to expose assumptions at work in our understandings of humanity to hopefully lead us to imagine a humanity that is not policed, vilified in rhetoric, or forced to perform to preserve its life.

NOTE

1. Elisabeth Schüssler Fiorenza (2017) inserts asterisk to create the phrase "New* Testament," troubling the supersessionist and anti-Jewish implications of the designations "New" and "Old" Testaments and signifying the complicated history behind describing a collection of writings in Christian bibles as "new."

WORKS CITED

Byron, Gay. 2002. *Symbolic Blackness and Ethnic Difference in Early Christian Literature*. New York: Routledge.

Cohen, Getzel M. 2006. *The Hellenistic Settlements in Syria, the Red Sea Basin, and North Africa*. Los Angeles: University of California Press.

Conzelmann, Hans. 1987. *Acts of the Apostles: A Commentary on the Acts of the Apostles*. Hermeneia. Philadelphia: Fortress.

Crawley, Ashon. 2016. *Blackpentecostal Breath: The Aesthetics of Possibility*. New York: Fordham University Press.

de Libero, Loretana, Thomas Franke, and Kirsten Groß-Albenhausen 2006. "Tribunus." *Brill's New Pauly, Antiquity*, edited by Hubert Cancik and Helmut Schneider. https://referenceworks.brillonline.com/entries/brill-s-new-pauly/tribunus-e1220120?s.num=167&s.start=150.

Delgado, Richard, and Jean Stefancic. 2012. *Critical Race Theory: An Introduction*. New York: New York University.

Fiorenza, Elisabeth Schüssler. 2017. *1 Peter: Reading Against the Grain*. New York: T&T Clark.

Foucault, Michel. 1977. *Discipline and Punish: The Birth of the Prison*. Translated by Alan Sheridan. New York: Pantheon.

Furhmann, Christopher J. 2012. *Policing the Roman Empire: Soldiers, Administration, and Public Order*. New York: Oxford University Press.

Haenchen, Ernst. 1971. *The Acts of the Apostles: A Commentary*. Louisville: Westminster.

Harris, Paisley J. 2003. "Gatekeeping and Remaking: The Politics of Respectability in African American Women's History and Black Feminism." *Journal of Women's History* 15: 212–20.

Hattery, Angela J., and Earl Smith. 2021. *Policing Black Bodies: How Black Lives are Surveilled and How to Work for Change*. Lanham: Rowman & Littlefield.

Hinton, Elizabeth. 2017. *From the War on Poverty to the War on Crime: The Making of Mass Incarceration in America*. Cambridge, MA: Harvard University Press.

Holladay, Carl. 2016. *Acts: A Commentary*. Louisville: Westminster John Knox.

Isaac, Benjamin. 2004. *The Invention of Racism in Classical Antiquity*. Princeton: Princeton University Press.
Jackson, Zakiyyah. 2021. *Becoming Human: Matter and Meaning in an Antiblack World*. New York: New York University Press.
Josephus. *Jewish Antiquities. Volume VI: Books 14–15*. 1943. Translated by Ralph Marcus, Allen Wikgren. Loeb Classical Library 489. Cambridge, MA: Harvard University Press.
———. *Against Apion*. 2007. Translated by John M. G. Barclay. Boston: Leiden.
———. *The Jewish War*. 2014. Translated by H. St. J. Thackeray. Loeb Classical Library 203. Cambridge, MA: Harvard University Press.
Leemreize, M.E.C. 2016. *Framing Egypt: Roman Literary Perceptions of Egypt from Cicero to Juvenal*. PhD. Dissertation. Leiden: Leiden University.
Magness, Jodi. 2012. *The Archaeology of the Holy Land from the Destruction of Solomon's Temple to the Muslim Conquest*. Cambridge: Cambridge University Press.
Martinot, Steve, and Jared Sexton. 2003. *Social Identities* 2, vol. 9: 169–81.
Muhammad, Khalil G. 2010. *The Condemnation of Blackness: Race, Crime, and the Making of Urban America*. Cambridge, MA: Harvard University Press.
Mullen, Alex, and Patrick James. 2012. *Multilingualism in the Graeco–Roman Worlds*. Cambridge: Cambridge University Press.
Nasrallah, Laura. 2019. *Archaeology and the Letters of Paul*. New York: Oxford University Press.
Neyrey, Jerome. 1984. "The Forensic Defense Speech and Paul's Trial Speeches in Acts 22–26: Form and Function." *Luke-Acts: New Perspectives from the Society of Biblical Literature Seminar*, edited by Charles H. Talbert, 210–24. New York: Crossroad.
Pervo, Richard I. 2006. *Dating Acts: Between the Evangelists and the Apologists*. Santa Rose, CA: Poleridge.
———. 2009. *Acts: A Commentary*. Hermeneia. Minneapolis: Fortress.
Philo. 1941. *Every Good Man is Free. On the Contemplative Life. On the Eternity of the World. Against Flaccus. Apology for the Jews. On Providence*. Translated by F. H. Colson. Loeb Classical Library 363. Cambridge, MA: Harvard University Press.
Robert, Nikia Smith. 2016. "A Lingual Politic: Power and Resistance in Sacred Secular, and Subaltern Narratives in an Age of Mass Incarceration." *Horizontes Decoloniales* 2: 163–201.
Smallwood, E. Mary. 1981. *The Jews Under Roman Rule: From Pompey to Diocletian*. SJLA 20. Leiden: Brill.
Smith, Mitzi J. 2018. *Womanist Sass and Talk Back: Social (In)Justice, Intersectionality, and Biblical Interpretation*. Eugene, OR: Cascade Books.
———. 2019. "Paul, Timothy, and the Respectability Politics of Race: A Womanist Inter(con)textual Reading of Acts 16:1–5." *Religions* 10, vol. 3: 1–13.
Swetnam-Burland, Molly. 2015. *Egypt in Italy: Visions of Egypt in Roman Imperial Culture*. New York: Cambridge University Press.
Tacitus. 1914. *Agricola. Germania. Dialogue on Oratory*. Translated by M. Hutton, W. Peterson. Revised by R. M. Ogilvie, E. H. Warmington, Michael

Winterbottom. Loeb Classical Library 35. Cambridge, MA: Harvard University Press.

Versluys, Miguel. 2018. *Beyond the Nile: Egypt and the Classical World.* Los Angeles: The J. Paul Getty Museum.

Weheliye, Alexander. 2014. *Habeas Viscus: Racializing Assemblages, Biopolitics, and Black Feminist Theories of the Human.* Durham: Duke University Press.

Wilderson, Frank III. 2003. "The Prison Slave as Hegemony's (Silent) Scandal." War, Dissent, and Justice: A Dialogue *Social Justice* 30, vol. 2: 18–27.

Wynter, Sylvia. 2003. "Unsettling the Coloniality of Being/Power/Truth/Freedom: Towards the Human, after Man, Its Overrepresentation—An Argument." *The New Centennial Review* 3, vol. 3: 257–337.

Yoder, Joshua. 2014. *Representatives of Roman Rule: Roman Provincial Governors in Luke–Acts.* Boston: De Gruyter. (Beihefte zur Zeitschrift für die neutestamentliche Wissenschaft und die Kunde der älteren Kirche; Beiheft 209.

Chapter 8

The Terror of White Hermeneutics

Black and Enslaved Bodies Interpreted in the Context of Whiteness

Marcus W. Shields

INTRODUCTION: WHITE INTERPRETATION OF BLACK BODIES

In March 2008, Democratic Illinois Senator Barack Obama delivered a speech on race and the role it played in the presidential campaign. During his soliloquy, Obama offered personal testimony about his white grandmother as a woman who raised him, sacrificed for him again and again, and loved him, but included she was "a woman who once confessed her fear of black men who passed her by on the street, and who on more than one occasion has uttered racial or ethnic stereotypes that made me cringe" (Obama 2008). During the trial of Michael Brown, Ferguson police officer Darren Wilson issued a grand jury testimony about his interaction with him. Wilson described his racialized prejudice interpretation of eighteen-year-old Brown as a demon with superhuman strength. The trial of Trayvon Martin heard George Zimmerman describe the young man as a real suspicious guy as Martin dwelled in a space that Zimmerman felt did not belong. Nineteen-year-old Renisha McBride was seeking help after a car crash and knocked on the door of Theodore Wafer, and he shot her in the face. Wafer told investigators that he shot her in the face because he feared that she was trying to break into his house. In each instance the white body reacted to an interpretation of the black body through the hermeneutic of whiteness that resulted in violence and often death to Black bodies.

The hermeneutic of whiteness uses ingrained stereotypes about black bodies to render a misinterpretation about them. George Yancy indicates that the interpretation of black bodies is linked "to the history of whiteness, primarily as whiteness is expressed in the form of fear, sadism, hatred, brutality, terror, avoidance, desire, denial, solipsism, madness, policing, politics, and the production and projection of white fantasies" (2017, xxx). M. Shawn Copeland argues that the hermeneutic of whiteness produces a negrophobic society in which "blackness mutates as negation, nonbeing, nothingness; blackness insinuates an 'other' so radically different that her and his very humanity is discredited" (2010, 19). Just as black bodies are subject to violence due to the hermeneutic of whiteness so are enslaved bodies in the biblical text subject to violence because of whiteness in historical criticism. Whiteness in historical criticism is the failure to acknowledge existential dynamics of enslaved bodies in the biblical text. That is, interpretive concentration is geared toward analyzing grammar and syntax, which renders enslaved bodies invisible.

The hermeneutic of whiteness and historical criticism intersect as lenses of interpretation that impact black and enslaved bodies. The former maintains stereotypes about black bodies through the lens of whiteness. The lens of whiteness interprets these bodies with a hermeneutic of suspicion. Within the context of whiteness black bodies are interpreted as criminal, violent, unworthy, savage, inferior, worthless, and dangerous. The latter, historical criticism, operates in the confines of the literary environment concentrating on white questions and concerns discounting enslaved bodies. The lens of historical criticism interprets biblical texts as literature. Within the operation of historical criticism, the critic is to engage in literary features of the biblical text rather than in existential realities. The hermeneutic of whiteness and the white interpretive practice of historical criticism establish an exclusiveness that does not include the bodies of the "other." Both establish a standard signaling a white gaze that communicates that "other" bodies do not belong in the white space which contributes to the death of black and enslaved bodies. The hermeneutic of white gaze specifies that black and enslaved bodies live under the scrutiny of possible misinterpretation "by a hostile or simply uncomprehending onlooker (Yancy 2017, x). In this chapter, I argue that black bodies face literal death while enslaved bodies within the biblical text face a literary death when interpreted through white gaze.

WHITENESS AND IMMIGRANT BODIES

Whiteness has a long and complex history. David R. Roediger (2007) in his work *The Wages of Whiteness* examines the arduous history of whiteness through economic theory, histories of integration, psychology, industrialization, slavery, and class formation. Whiteness was a problem among white bodies and black bodies were grafted into their problem. Whiteness is the tentacle of white supremacy and racism is the manifestation of attitudes and oppressive acts upon black bodies embedded in a system of social and structural injustice. The construction of whiteness is constantly at work in society and examples of this social and structural injustice are ubiquitous. When a white person receives a job and a well-qualified Black person is rejected, whiteness is at play. When a white person has access to resources that a Black person does not, whiteness is at play. When a white person can live after murdering people at a church and a Black person is murdered on a traffic stop, whiteness is at play. When white bodies clothed in blue, walking under the rhetoric "protect and serve," are not charged with a crime when violence is inflicted upon black bodies, whiteness is at play. Whiteness benefits whites whether they acknowledge it or not. Why is whiteness problematic for the black body? The problem is that those who are white are protected in the space of whiteness but black bodies become endangered bodies in that same space.

Whiteness arose when European immigrants were trying to figure out how to take advantage of their white skin. Millions of immigrants, namely Irish and Germans, who arrived on the shores of the United States, looked white but were not actually white. America was not purely a white nation but an immigrant nation that attracted people from eastern and southern Europe due to the existential crisis of extreme poverty they encountered. Matthew Frye Jacobson, in his monograph *Whiteness of a Different Color*, observes that in the mid-nineteenth century the landscape of the American republic began to change. This was evidenced in the census taken after the famine in Ireland because it ushered a new era in the meaning of whiteness in the United States (1998, 43). Roediger (2018) argues that whiteness is a historical phenomenon in the United States that ethnicities now considered white were not considered white initially. Immigrants identifying, as white negotiated their "inbetweenness" (Roediger 2018, 10–13) through "real life context and social experience" distanced themselves from black bodies while acquiring security, power, and American identity (Conzen and Gerber et al.1992, 5). The common denominator shared between Anglo-Saxons and immigrants was their white skin. Possessing white skin served as an advantage for immigrant bodies. Immigrant bodies functioned in whiteness to distinguish themselves from black bodies while seeking acceptance from Anglo-Saxons. Immigrant bodies reasoned that "the worst thing that one could be in this Promised land was colored" (ibid., 14).

Immigrant bodies understood their "white skin" as a wage. Because they possessed white skin, they had the ability to function in duality, establish a distinction of difference from black bodies, construct white identities, and trade in their heritage to become white. The intellectual prowess of immigrant bodies allowed them to understand their white skin as racialized privilege and treasured property (Harris 1993, 1741). The racialized privilege that accompanied white skin carried material benefits especially for the white worker. White workers did not see themselves on the same level as black workers but more in line with the capitalist class who owned most of society's wealth. The social critic W.E.B. Dubois noted in his classic work *Black Reconstruction* that "the group of white laborers while they received a low wage, were compensated in part by a sort of public and psychological wage. They were given public deference and titles of courtesy because they were white. They were admitted freely with all classes of white people to public functions, public parks, and the best schools" (Dubois 1998, 700). In this manner, Dubois draws attention to how the identification of whiteness by white bodies materialized its value in society while also communicating that black bodies did not have the privilege, nor any advantages based on the color of their skin. In fact, the opposite was true for black bodies because of the attitude of inferiority displayed by white bodies toward black bodies.

Whiteness as treasured property also poses a threat to black bodies. According to Cheryl Harris, whiteness "is treasured property in a society structured on racial caste" (Harris 1993, 1741). Whiteness as treasured property protects white bodies from being chattel and is the marker that communicates that white bodies are superior people. Harris notes that the status of being "white became an asset that whites have sought to protect. Whites have come to expect and rely on these benefits and over time these expectations have been affirmed, legitimated, and protected by law" (ibid., 1713). Whiteness excludes and creates distance between itself and people of color—especially black bodies. In other words, while the value of whiteness soared, the value of black bodies plummeted. Whiteness as treasured property granted license for black bodies to be subjected to violence.

BLACK BODIES IN THE CONTEXT OF WHITENESS

Dubois was one of the first to articulate whiteness and how it shaped social reality and the climate for black bodies. In his essay, *The Souls of White Folk*, Dubois (1999) wrote about whiteness through his experience with "white" souls in society. Dubois notes that the racial identity we call white was "the discovery of personal whiteness among the world's peoples" (1999, 17). Whiteness created a state of opposition for black bodies. Dubois argues that whiteness is a system that works well for white people if black bodies are compliant with the system, as long as they are "humble black folk, voluble with thanks, and receiving old barrels of old clothes from lordly and generous whites" (ibid., 18). When black bodies cease to comply with whiteness, insist on their human rights, and advocate for the restoration of their black dignity, "the spell is suddenly broken and the philanthropist is ready to believe that Negroes are impudent" (ibid., 19). If the disrespect of whiteness is conjured up in the minds of white bodies, then the climate of death looms over black bodies. Dubois calls whiteness a descent into hell for black bodies because whiteness and white bodies are the writers of black human hatred that equal murder for the bodies of Negro descent (ibid., 18).

The ideology of whiteness perceives black bodies as a threat to society. Black bodies are deemed dangerous by the ideology of whiteness. As a result they have endured more than their share of violence, which includes castration, rape, mutilation, harassment, policing, and death. Some scholars note that one does not need to trace the annals of history to search for the blood that has been spilled because of the terror of whiteness. Violence committed against black bodies results from transgressing white space, which is a guaranteed death sentence. George Yancy notes, "black existence constitutes the threat, leading to the conclusion that the nullification of Black being is the only sure prerequisite to white safety" (2017, xxxvi).

The value of whiteness heightens because it prevents and protects white bodies from being owned or commodified. Black bodies as chattel serve as the fundamental difference between the white body and the black body. This suggests that black bodies are not treasured properties as white bodies are but commodified bodies that do not have rights to control their own bodies. Freedom is not an option for those who belong to another but rather they are controlled for someone's use. Harris notes, "the racial line between white and black was extremely critical; it became a line of protection and demarcation from the potential threat of commodification" (1993, 1720–21). Unfortunately, commodification is not just being owned by another, but it reinforces the fact that black bodies do not have any rights. George Yancy acknowledges the part the white gaze plays in the curtailment and/or loss of rights for black bodies. White gaze is the hermeneutical lens in which white bodies perceive that all others except white people do not belong. In other words, black bodies do not possess freedom. To be free, according to James Cone, "means that human beings are not an object, and they will not let others treat them as an 'it'" (2012, 95). However, as Dubois (1999) observes, when black bodies are not compliant with the rules of the white establishment, a death blow is dealt to the black community which can result in the loss of black life.

WHITENESS AND HISTORICAL CRITICISM

Exegetical tyranny is committed when enslaved bodies are ignored in the interpretive practice of whiteness in historical criticism. This type of interpretation began in the seventeenth century and gained traction in the nineteenth and twentieth centuries. This branch of criticism investigates the origins of ancient texts to understand the world-behind-the-text. To access this "world," it is necessary for the interpreter to establish primary and secondary goals. The primary goal of this interpretive grid is to discover the text's original meaning in its original context and its *sensus literalis historicus* (literal sense). The secondary goal is to reconstruct the historical situation of the author and recipients of the text. These goals serve to determine the text's historical origin inquiring about items such as location, date, and occasion. This method is dominant in biblical scholarship because it concerns itself with ancient literary and grammatical questions and not the materiality of enslaved bodies in the ancient texts or contexts. Dismissal of this kind of critique is the "white" standard in biblical interpretation. The aim of "white" biblical interpretation is to compile sources that formed the biblical text while concentrating on literary function because it does not involve itself with existential affairs. The dismissal of existential affairs by this interpretive method places whiteness on display because it cares for textual and not bodily matters. Majority white biblical interpretation in its preoccupation with constructed literary patterns callously reinscribes and treats enslaved bodies as tools or hermeneutical textual fodder and not as oppressed human beings whose precarious existence or materiality has implications for contemporary and ancient texts and contexts.

TEXTUAL MATTERS, WHITENESS, AND 1 CORINTHIANS 7:17–24

Various New Testament (NT) scholars place emphasis on textual matters using historical criticism while interpreting 1 Corinthians 7:17–24. They begin with the assumption that the Bible is literature and proceed to use tools of literary criticism to determine how this pericope operates in the chapter. Some NT scholars note that this text behaves as a *digressio* and supports the main idea of marriage. A *digressio* is a literary device that is used by authors to support the main argument in a text. That is, a *digressio* does not wander from the main theme but rather intensifies it. In this text, this literary device contains circumcised, uncircumcised, and enslaved bodies that are used as illustrations to undergird Paul's instructions on marriage and celibacy.

For some NT scholars, the enslaved bodies do not present any real problem in Corinth. The mention of "slave" as noted in verse 21b is representative of the existential crisis surrounding these bodies. The appearance of "enslaved" in the text should alert the reader that this body is the legal property of another, and it poses a problem to the Corinthian community. It is a problem because Paul acknowledges that freedom is something that can be obtained. In this section, it is necessary to examine the application of historical criticism with an awareness of the white hermeneutical act putting to death enslaved bodies by relegating them to mere illustrations.

S. Scott Bartchy's monograph, *First-Century Slavery and 1 Corinthians 7:21*, introduces the reader to the thought pattern of 1 Corinthians 7:17–24. Bartchy (1973) argues that this passage has an A-B-A chiastic pattern. A chiastic pattern features two ideas together with a variant. Chiastic patterns commonly appear in ancient literature. The motion of the chiastic structure is circular or cyclical. It is an idea that is introduced at the beginning of a composition and repeated at the conclusion, so that the whole passage is framed by identical content being illustrated by the variant in the passage. Relying on J. J. Collins's research on the usage of this literary structure, Bartchy observes that Paul frequently interrupts his main thought to give an illustration or clarification of a general principle. While Bartchy details how the structure is performed in this text, he disregards enslaved bodies. He states, "there is no evidence that Paul's choice of examples in 7:17–24 was influenced by actual problems in the Corinthian congregation. No particular activity of Jews or the slaves in the congregation had moved Paul to write 7:17–24" (Bartchy 1973, 140). He also opts to dwell in the space of historical criticism by searching for the literary function of the pericope instead of asking questions about the concrete situation of those enslaved.

Hans Conzelmann exegetes this pericope by examining particles, verbs, nouns, forms of expression, and articulation of calling while adding his own hermeneutical flavor as he writes about grace creating freedom (1975, 126). While unpacking verse 21, he suggests versus 21–24 are a self-contained section (ibid., 127). He writes, "verse 21 explains the principle of v. 20 by reference to the example of the slave" (ibid.). Conzelmann participates in the whiteness of historical criticism as he analyzes the usage of words and phrases in their literary environment to prove that this section supports Paul's advice on marriage.

However, the astute reader must pay attention to what Conzelmann writes in his quote referenced previously (ibid., 5). He suggests that v. 21 explains the principle of v. 20 through the means of an example or illustration through enslaved bodies. Why does he describe the functionality of vv. 20 and 21?

Conzelmann makes a hermeneutical move that places importance upon textual matters referring to this pericope as a diatribe. A diatribe is a literary device that takes many forms and does not have a typical structure (Stowers 1988, 71–83) but its functionality exemplifies distinctiveness through literary performance in ancient works of Greek or Roman philosophy. The literary performance of this device in these ancient works contain a teaching element. Stanley Stowers highlights a diatribe is useful "when understood as a term for teaching whether in schools or writings employing pedagogical and rhetorical styles" (ibid., 73). For Conzelmann, Paul takes the opportunity to teach the Corinthians to remain in the situation in which they have been called noting that the diatribe offers supporting argumentation for the paraenesis Paul gave those married and unmarried in 1 Corinthians 7 by using enslaved bodies as an illustration to solidify his point.

Will Deming also concentrates on the literary writing of the apostle suggesting that he "casts his thoughts in a diatribal style and specifically made use of it by employing the hallmarks of the diatribal pattern by conforming to a distinctive syntactical formula" (1995, 130–37) citing examples from Hellenistic authors (Teles, *Fragments* 2.10.65–80; Philo 1929, *Jos*. 24.144; Seneca 1932, 4.3–4; Epictetus 1928, *Enchiridion* 15). According to Deming, the syntactical formula is "a statement of fact given in the form of a rhetorical question, often in the direct address of the second person singular, followed by an imperative that denies that the statement of fact has any significance for a person's life. An explanation is sometimes added to demonstrate why the statement of fact should be treated with indifference" (Deming, 130–31). Deming's study is primarily concerned with how Paul employs a rhetorical pattern through his letter-writing by comparing his style with other Hellenistic patterns in the Greco-Roman world. Deming does not recognize that there is a fine line between rhetoric and reality. He does not demonstrate any concern for enslaved bodies as evident by concluding "Christian slaves regard their disenfranchised state as a matter of indifference" (ibid., 137).

Gordon Fee considers 1 Corinthians 7:17–24 a guiding principle like most NT scholars. Fee admits that Paul's paragraph "appears to move afield a bit" (1987, 307). He suggests chapter 7 is about status and its significance to the Corinthians. Even though his point is one of many interpretations concerning this text, he argues that Paul proves his point by drawing from two other social settings namely circumcision and slavery. He does not name this section as a literary device instead he reduces the existential settings to mere illustrations in support of a larger argumentation presented in the chapter. For Fee, there was a lack of urgency in circumcision and slavery because there was no problematization concerning these social spaces.

Raymond F. Collins, like Bartchy, calls this passage a chiastic pattern recognizing the A-B-A structure. He argues that vv. 17–24 is the B element that "serves as a supporting argument for the paraenesis Paul has offered to the married in vv. 1–16 and for the exhortation he will address to the unmarried in vv. 25–40" (Collins 1999, 274). For Collins, God's call is Paul's theological thrust throughout his letter. Collins uses his exegetical adroitness to indicate that God's call is important to the chiastic structure of the argument in this pericope (vv. 17, 18 [2x], 20, 21, 22 [2x], 24). Collins is blinded by his white hermeneutic because he spiritualizes the reality of social dimensions by hiding behind the rhetoric of God's call. He notes that "the real life of any human being is characterized by gender, ethnicity, and social class, but suggests that God's call in Christ relativizes all social conditions" (1999, 275). Collins does not address the concrete problems that slavery inherently promotes, as a result, he creates the dismissal of enslaved bodies in his textual analysis.

In her monograph, *The Corinthian Women Prophets*, Antoinette Clark Wire's study reconstructs "as accurate a picture as possible of the women prophets in the church of first-century Corinth" (1990, 1). Although the primary aim of her study is women prophets in the church, she still contributes to the present study by offering insight into the Pauline paragraph. Wire also agrees with NT scholars that suggest that Paul establishes a general principle to remain as they were called. She notes that Paul pulls from two areas of church life, as Fee mentioned in his analysis, circumcision and slavery. According to Wire, circumcised and enslaved bodies are examples used to support the rule of remaining in one's state (ibid., 86). She also falls into the white space of historical criticism while interpreting this passage because she labels enslaved bodies as examples indicating the purpose of the areas of church life is to support the marital argument Paul presents to the Corinthians. Furthermore, Wire develops a phraseology called "rhetoric of equality" (ibid., 86). Wire develops this phrase built on the Greek adjective "each one" that appears in vv. 17 and 20. She remarks that "the rhetoric of equality is clear throughout—it is 'each one' who is to remain as called" (ibid., 86). It is difficult to reconcile equality and enslaved bodies while these bodies are owned and subject to violence. Wire neither considers the significance nor the situation of enslaved bodies and what these bodies have had to endure in Corinth. She follows the exegetical road and stays true to the theme of 1 Corinthians 7 which is status and sexual conduct (ibid., 86).

Gregory W. Dawes (1990), in his article "But If You Can Gain Your Freedom," contributes to the discussion reiterating what previous scholars have specified about 1 Corinthians 7:17–24. Dawes recognizes that most commentators find the role of vv. 17–24 puzzling. Dawes embarks on a mission to find the function of this pericope by understanding its role within the chapter and how it helps us understand marriage and celibacy (1990, 681–97). According to Dawes, literary importance has been placed on reading Paul "in light of the science of rhetoric because it dominated the education and thinking in the ancient world" (ibid., 683). He focuses on the ancient technique known as *digressio*. As written earlier in this article, a *digressio* uses illustrations to support the main idea of this text. He argues that the use of this literary device is frequent in the Pauline corpus (Rom 7:2–3; 9:21–23; 11:16–24; 1 Cor 3:5–17; 9:25–27; 12:14–27; 14:7–8; 15:36–44; Gal 4:1–2). Paul's usage of illustrations in his letters are deliberate and have a role to play in his argumentation. However, as Dawes analyzes the illustrations used in this pericope by the apostle, he surmises that the second illustration highlighting enslaved bodies is indifferent and simply relegated to playing a role in supporting the idea of marriage and celibacy. Dawes attempts to figure out the function of the Corinthian pericope but does not assess the difficulty enslaved bodies suffer nor the possibility of being granted freedom. As argued above, few NT scholars consider the abuse of enslaved bodies in this passage.

Other NT scholars who have exegeted 1 Corinthians 7:17–24 understand slavery as a violent institution and place it at the center of their existential hermeneutical agenda. These NT scholars do not depend on the white hermeneutic to render an interpretation of this pericope but incorporate the violence inflicted on enslaved bodies into the reading of the biblical text to give insight to the lived realities of enslaved bodies. Slavery was far from a positive experience because these bodies were in danger of being exploited, tortured, and killed. The following section surveys the hermeneutical practices of NT interpreters who interrupt the spin when enslaved bodies become the starting point for the academic study of the Bible (Wimbush 1998, 61–76).

Clarice J. Martin (2005), in her essay *The Eyes Have It: Slaves in the Communities of Christ-Believers*, discusses enslaved bodies as background in ancient literature and society. She provides some reasons why the "white" standard of biblical interpretation became the dominant hermeneutical key for interpreting enslaved bodies in ancient literature. Knowledge and perpetuation contributed to the "white" standard of interpretation for slavery. Martin observes that the basis for the hermeneutical key for interpreting slavery and enslaved bodies was knowledge acquired from classicists. Classical historians promoted slavery as an institution flowing with promise and opportunity for enslaved bodies. Martin writes, "knowledge about slaves and slavery in Greek antiquity and Roman imperial slavery was long obscured and mystified by classicists. In search of sources of classical humanism, historians and literary interpreters idealized antiquity as a golden age, a mythical utopia" (2005, 222). Classical scholars were not concerned with exploring "the extent, the brutality, or the dehumanization involved in slavery in Western antiquity" (ibid.).

Dependence on classical scholarship perpetuated a benign ideology about slavery that infiltrated New Testament studies. New Testament scholars did nothing but "replicate this uncritically benign view of ancient slavery" (ibid.,

222). A critical approach to slavery was introduced by classicist M.I. Finley and sociologist Orlando Patterson to feature the "more critical investigations of the complexities and contradictions of one of the most repressive, dehumanizing, violent and exploitative social arrangements in history" (ibid.). This critical examination brought by these two scholars heightened the reality enslaved bodies were not "mere props" (ibid.) but real people that participated in the landscape of life. Martin recognized the existential reality of enslaved bodies and emphasized that "brutality could be a matter of daily routine for the enslaved" (ibid., 239) and other NT interpreters identified the importance of this type of existential exegesis and contributed to the reading of slavery with the experience of enslaved bodies at the center of their hermeneutical task.

J. Albert Harrill (1995), in his monograph *The Manumission of Slaves in Early Christianity*, does not approach 1 Corinthians 7.17–24 as a benign institution but as a violent institution that recognized enslaved bodies who were subject to violence at any time. Harrill is not concerned with how the pericope functioned literarily in 1 Corinthians 7, rather he is concerned with placing emphasis on the "actual situations in which early Christians lived and the reality of their experiences especially with chattel slavery" (1995, 5; 2020). Brad R. Braxton argues that vv. 17–24 highlights real concerns in the Corinthian community. He notes the mistake made by NT interpreters of this text, is that this pericope is "singled out as a theoretical digression: having little to do with social issues in the community" (Braxton 2000, 56). In fact, he contends that these "illustrations" in v. 18 and vv. 21–23 might be concrete concerns in the Corinthian congregation (ibid., 36). Braxton suggests that enslaved bodies are not simply illustrations as proposed by some interpreters; they were real bodies that experienced tangible social realities.

Jennifer A. Glancy in her work *Slavery in Early Christianity* examines 1 Corinthians 7:17–24, observing that some commentators do not address the sexual vulnerability of enslaved bodies (2002, 68). Glancy does not spend time tracing the white traditional reading of this passage because she realizes that there is an existential threat attached to the noun "slave." The noun "slave," as mentioned earlier in this article, denotes that enslaved bodies do not belong to themselves but rather are owned by a master making them the object of their desires and abuse. If the enslaved failed to comply then torture and death was an imminent threat to their bodies.

David Garland understands the literary function of this passage as a *digressio* in his commentary, *1 Corinthians*, but he knows that enslaved bodies are not solely illustrations. He highlights the existential situation of enslaved bodies in his commentary by incorporating the humiliation enslaved bodies suffered in his interpretation of the passage noting that "one third of Corinth's populations were slaves" (Garland 2003, 307). He also issues eye-opening comments reacting to Paul's worry rhetoric writing "there were plenty of things to worry about. Slaves were not legally persons, and consequently they had no legal or human rights and were classified as things and tallied as living pieces of property. Slaves were constantly subject to the whip. Since they lacked human worth in the world's eyes, they could easily anguish that they also lacked worth before God" (ibid.).

CONCLUSION

The hermeneutic of whiteness creates a situation where the loss of life is an existential threat because black and enslaved bodies are not accepted in the white context according to the interpretation of the white gaze. In addition to being a social construct and operating in invisibility, the hermeneutic of whiteness contributes to the death of black bodies. Likewise, historical criticism contributes to the death of enslaved bodies preferring the importance of grammar and syntax over the violence that these bodies are subjected to. Whiteness is an ideology structured to grab power while fostering racist attitudes toward black bodies. It is a branch of oppression that is conveyed as a nonexistent categorized norm against which all other persons of difference are critiqued and evaluated. Black bodies who have experienced violent and tragic encounters include Trayvon Martin, Eric Garner, Eric Harris, Renisha McBride, Michael Brown, Tamir Rice, Sandra Bland, Jordan Davis, and George Floyd. Too many black bodies to mention—some will remain unknown—have lost their lives through the gaze of whiteness.

WORKS CITED

Bartchy, S. Scott. 1973. *First-Century Slavery and The Interpretation of 1 Corinthians 7:21*. Eugene, OR: Wipf and Stock.

Braxton, Brad Ronell. 2000. *The Tyranny of Resolution 1 Corinthians 7:17–24*. Atlanta: Society of Biblical Literature.

Collins, Raymond F. 1999. *First Corinthians*. Edited by Daniel Harrington Jr. Minnesota: Liturgical.

Cone, James H. 1986. *A Black Theology of Liberation*, 2nd ed. New York: Orbis.

Copeland, M. Shawn. 2010. *Enfleshing Freedom: Body, Race, and Human Being*. Minneapolis: Fortress.

Conzelmann, Hans. 1975. *1 Corinthians: A Commentary on the First Epistle to the Corinthians*. Philadelphia: Fortress.

Conzen Kathleen Neils, David A. Gerber, Ewa Morawska, George E. Pozzetta, and Rudolph J. Vecoli. 1992. "The Invention of Ethnicity: A Perspective from the U.S.A." *Journal of American Ethnic History* 12, 1: 3–41.

Dawes, Gregory W. 1990. "But If You Can Gain Your Freedom (1 Corinthians 7:17–24)," *The Catholic Biblical Quarterly* 52, 4: 681–97.
Deming, Will. 1995. "A Diatribe Pattern in 1 Cor. 7:21–22: A New Perspective on Paul's Directives to Slaves." *Novum Testamentum XXXVII*, 2: 130–7.
Dubois, W. E. B. 1998. *Black Reconstruction in America 1860–1880.* New York: The Free Press.
———. 1999. *Darkwater: Voices from Within the Veil.* New York: Dover.
Epictetus. 1928. *Discourses, Books 3–4. Fragments. The Encheiridion.* Edited and translated by W. A. Oldfather. LCL. Cambridge: Harvard University Press.
Fee, Gordon D. 1987. *The First Epistle to the Corinthians.* Grand Rapids: Eerdmans.
Garland, David E. 2003. *1 Corinthians.* Grand Rapids: Baker.
Glancy, Jennifer A. 2002. *Slavery in Early Christianity.* New York: Oxford University Press.
Harrill, J. Albert. 1995. *The Manumission of Slaves in Early Christianity.* Tübingen: Mohr.
———. 2020. "Revisiting the Problem of 1 Corinthians 7:21." *Biblical Research* 65: 77–94.
Harris, Cheryl L. 1993. "Whiteness as Property," *Harvard Law Review* 106, 8: 1707–91.
Jacobson, Matthew Frye. 1998. *Whiteness of a Different Color. European Immigrants and the Alchemy of Race.* Cambridge, MA: Harvard University Press.
Lipsitz, George. 2018. *The Possessive Investment in Whiteness: How White People Profit from Identity Politics.* Pennsylvania: Temple University Press.
Martin, Clarice J. 2005. "The Eyes Have It: Slaves in the Communities of Christ-Believers," in *Christian Origins.* Vol. 1. A People's History of Christianity. Richard A. Horsley and Denis R. Janz, eds., 221–39. Minneapolis: Fortress.
Obama, Barack. 2008. "Barack Obama's Speech on Race," transcript, NPR, online, https://www.npr.org/templates/story/story.php?storyId=88478467.
O'Neil, Edward. 1977. *Teles: The Cynic Teacher.* SBLTT 11/SBLGRS3. Missoula: Scholars.
Philo. 1929. Translated and edited by F. H. Colson. Vol 6. LCL. Cambridge: Harvard University Press.
Roediger, David R. 2007. *The Wages of Whiteness: Race and the Making of the American Working Class,* 3rd ed. New York: Verso.
———. 2018. *Working Toward Whiteness: How America's Immigrants Became White: The Strange Journey from Ellis Island to the Suburbs.* New York: Basic Books.
Seneca. 1932. *Moral Essays.* Edited and translated by John W. Basore. Vols 2–3. LCL. Cambridge, MA: Harvard University Press.
Stowers, Stanley K. 1988. "The Diatribe." In *Greco-Roman Literature and the New Testament: Selected Forms and Genres*m, ed. David E. Aune, 71–83. Atlanta: Scholars Press.
Wimbush, Vincent L. 1998. "Interrupting the Spin: What Would Happen Were African Americans to Become the Starting Point for Biblical Studies." *Union Seminary Quarterly Review* 52, 1–2: 61–76.

Wire, Antoinette Clark. 1990. *The Corinthian Women Prophets*. Eugene, OR: Wipf and Stock.

Yancy, George. 2017. *Black Bodies, White Gazes: The Continuing Significance of Race in America*. 2nd ed. New York: Rowman & Littlefield.

PART III

Africana Hermeneutical Strategies, Pedagogy, Translation, and #BLM

Chapter 9

Hoodoo Blues and the Formulation of Hermeneutical Strategies for Contemporary Africana Biblical Engagement

Hugh R. Page, Jr.

PROLOGUE

What follows is an experimental and avowedly "messy" theoretical intervention in the domain of biblical studies, with a weird backstory.[1] It began some seventeen years ago as a paper prepared for a session of the African American Biblical Hermeneutics Section in the Society of Biblical Literature (SBL) and read at the 2004 Annual Meetings of the American Academy of Religion (AAR) and SBL in San Antonio, Texas. Several years later (in 2012, if memory serves) it was subsequently submitted to a journal for possible publication. The peer review suggested revision and resubmission. A number of helpful changes were recommended, for which I remain grateful. Some have been incorporated below. Other dimensions of the feedback received were unsettling, insofar as they intimated that the genre and tone of the piece were not sufficiently academic. Wanting to contribute to the larger conversation about theoretical interventions in biblical studies, I set about making the necessary changes, but the notion that the type of intellectual experimentation being advanced in the essay, which selectively incorporated first person narration and nontraditional interlocutors, was somehow inappropriate for a disciplinary journal, was disconcerting. That uneasiness—and other administrative responsibilities—slowed the process of revision and it remained on my *curriculum vitae* as one of several pieces in preparation. Torn between the pressures associated with embracing the journal's sense of what the article should contain on the one hand, and the feeling that those standards ought to be resisted on the other, part of me wondered whether the piece would ever see the light of day. It seemed increasingly that it would become one of many essays anthologized in some collection at my career's twilight. The invitation to submit an entry for this volume breathed new life and *àshe* into this project.[2] It empowered me to close the door on one venue and to accept the invitation to enter another. I am grateful to the editors for their timely invitation and acceptance of this essay.

METHODOLOGY AND THE FUTURE OF AFRICANA BIBLICAL HERMENEUTICS

Over the past two decades or more, we have witnessed remarkable growth and expansion in Africana biblical engagement. For example, to cite just a few representative exemplars, there are now three major one-volume commentaries—that is, those edited by Adeyamo (2010), Blount et al. (2007), and Page et al. (2010); several major works focusing on African (West and Dube 2000, Dube 2001, West 2016) and Caribbean (Thomas 2014) interpretation; groundbreaking monographs in the area of Womanist hermeneutics (Smith 2015, 2018; Byron and Lovelace 2016; Gafney 2017; Junior 2015); a literary and theological introduction to the Christian Bible (Fentress-Williams 2021); a study of the intersection of Africana Studies and Africana Biblical Studies (Smith 2020); works challenging the methodological orthodoxies of biblical research (Wimbush 2011, 2012); and a retrospective introduction to African American biblical interpretation in the twentieth and twenty-first centuries (Smith 2017). These and related works, too numerous to mention here, have set the stage for additional scholarly interventions focused on several distinct yet related tasks, for example: (1) defining further the specific object(s) of study—that is, what Africana hermeneutics of the Bible entails as an enterprise; (2) cataloging the various endeavors that can be so categorized; (3) mainstreaming Africana hermeneutical strategies within the guild so as to increase the extent to which they are tested, refined, and adapted; and (4) providing support and encouragement for experimentation aimed at the creation of new interpretive methods woven from various Africana cultural strands.

The current study takes up the fourth and final task by advocating derivation, from the crucible of Black life, of a new paradigm for the interpretive engagement of the Bible based on a subgenre of American Blues music known as Hoodoo Blues. The compositions falling within this subset of the larger Blues genre are well known for their mention of physical artifacts used in the amalgam of African American healing and ritual practices given names such as *hoodoo*, *rootwork*, and *conjure* in popular lore and scholarship. It is hoped that this intervention and others akin to it will, in time, lead to the development of a body of Africana interpretive theory focused on the Bible with a breadth comparable to that which already obtains for the study of African American literature (cf., Napier 2000). Such would help enrich conversations between fields such as Biblical Studies, Africana Studies, and Ethnic Studies. Clarice Martin's (1998) pioneering article, "'Somebody Done Hoodoo'd the Hoodoo Man': Language, Power, Resistance, and the Effective History of Pauline Texts in American Slavery," demonstrated long ago the liberating interpretive possibilities that emerge from applying the paradigm of conjure in the engagement of biblical texts. This study continues in that vein.

For some time there has been increasing interest in the relationship between theoretical constructs and the sociocultural settings in which they are created. Such concern has a direct bearing on the way in which one delimits the principal aims of Biblical Studies as a discipline. It also has an impact on the selection of existing methods and the development of new ones used in the reading and interpretation of the biblical canon in its various forms. Within the specific realm of Africana (i.e., African American and African-Diasporan) biblical hermeneutics, an area of continuing interest is the identification of interpretive models generated within Africana contexts in the Americas, the Caribbean, and elsewhere that can be used in scholarly and other forms of Bible reading. The extent to which such paradigms have been either the primary tools of Bible scholars or the focus of academic inquiry within the profession to date has been increasing. One hopes that such approaches will continue moving from the methodological periphery to the academic mainstream. They have much to tell us about the constantly evolving topography of the Black intellectual landscape and the place that the Bible occupies within it.

An analysis of the dynamics that give rise to such paradigms promises to be a most fruitful academic enterprise in the coming years. Moreover, efforts on the part of Bible readers within African and African Diasporan communities to formulate interpretive strategies based on the intellectual, artistic, philosophical, mythic, and literary traditions of Africa and the African Diaspora ought to be part of the agenda of scholars for whom the Black experience worldwide is of central rather than marginal import. The implications of such work for the vitality and relevance of Biblical Studies generally, and that branch focusing on culturally conditioned interpretive strategies in particular, are enormous. The same can be said for the well-being and continued development of the heterogeneous community of Black Bible readers in the Americas, Europe, and elsewhere.

The work of scholars such as Smith (1994) and Yvonne Chireau (2003) has shed new light on African American religious *praxis* and its impact on ethnogenetic impulses in the Black Diaspora. Moreover, both raise awareness of the complex relationship that exists between African American "conjure" and the Blues musical tradition. Chireau's research, in particular, has noted the ways in which one Blues subgenre, so called Hoodoo Blues, served as a mechanism for the reclamation of indigenous conceptions of the supernatural and the construction of what amounted to a modern Blues faith (2003, 144, 145, 148–49). The current study builds on the work of Chireau by examining the implications of the use of this subgenre for: (1) the formulation of principles for the hermeneutical engagement of the Bible and other ancient Near Eastern texts; (2) scholarship on the nature and scope of esoteric traditions in the Black Diaspora; and (3) the construction of twenty-first century Africana spiritualities of resistance.[3]

The essay begins with a brief description of the genre of Hoodoo Blues. It then enumerates a list of topics derived from analysis of a random sample of twelve songs in the *Hoodoo Blues Lyrics* archive maintained by author Catherine Yronwode (1995–2019a, b). This is followed by a set of personal observations and a list of hermeneutical *maxims* generated from an analysis of the sample. Some reflections on the ways in which Hoodoo Blues may shed light on the place that Christian and other forms of *esotericism* occupy in the Black Diaspora in North America follows. The study concludes with a few words about the contribution that interpretive protocols derived from *Hoodoo Blues* may offer for the development of spiritualities that resist oppressive social, religious, and other hegemonies.

The major proposal flowing from this study is that such protocols can be used in the formulation of what I would term "Textual Healing Algorithms" (THAs) that facilitate the use of a broad array of Africana literary sources as *materia medica* in the treatment of social ills. The concept of the healing algorithm is borrowed from the burgeoning field of energy psychology (cf. Hover-Kramer 2002: 122–123) where it is used in reference to strategic points along acupuncture meridians that are "tapped" to alleviate physical and emotional problems. In this study it refers to principles governing the selection and appropriation of texts for the purposes of eliciting thoughtful reflection on issues of currency in Africana life.[4]

Hoodoo Blues as Sub-Category

Technically, *Hoodoo Blues* can be said to consist of those songs within the larger Blues universe that allude to or make direct mention of elements in the African Diasporan tradition of "hoodoo" or "conjure."[5] The latter is defined by Chireau as a complex of traditions and manipulative ritual practices, "in which supernatural power is invoked for various purposes, such as healing, protection, and self defense" (2003, 12). It is a dynamic *mélange* or amalgam whose boundaries cannot be delimited with precision. Early on, its magico-religious and botanical repertory consisted of indigenous African, Native American, and Christian elements. It is organic and its inventory of ritual practices and paraphernalia continue to grow as contemporary adherents adapt and expand it. Some of the more easily recognizable allusions to "conjure" in this genre include mention of *mojos*, *mojo hands*, John the Conqueror root, *goofer dust*, black cat bones, sacred numbers, and references to practitioners themselves, i.e., Hoodoo Men and Hoodoo Women (see the list provided in Yronwode 1995–2019b). The corpus itself is large and continues to evolve as new artists embrace and work in the genre. Audiences today are perhaps most familiar with exemplars such as Willie Dixon's "Hoochie Coochie Man," Muddy Waters' (McKinley Morganfield) "Got My Mojo Workin," and Junior Wells' "Hoodoo Man Blues." However, artists such as Bessie Smith, Sonny Boy Williamson, Ma Rainey, Robert Johnson, and a host of others have songs that could be included under this classification as well (for song lists see Yronwode 1995–2019b).

Hoodoo Blues—Its Taxonomy of Pivotal Issues

Chireau illustrates the major social and religious themes addressed in Hoodoo Blues lyrics (2003, 144–49). The goal of the current study is not to reproduce hers, but selectively to reengage the corpus in an effort to discern themes, tropes, and ideas suggestive of interpretive *maxims* that can be used to inform a twenty-first century Africana biblical hermeneutic consistent with the particularities of the African American experience. In so doing, a random sample of twelve of the songs found in Yronwode's online database of Hoodoo Blues lyrics was used. Moreover, the sorting and analysis of the sample was done from two personal vantage points. The first was from that of classical biblical scholarship. The second was from that of the Blues spiritual *matrix* itself. In the former capacity, a traditional social-scientific modality was employed. In the latter, a paradigm more akin to that of auto-ethnography and anthropological poetics was deployed (for descriptions and examples, see Ellis and Bochner 1996; Goodall 2000; Jones 1998; Denzin 1997). Both were reflective of my *locus* as researcher.

Hoodoo Blues—Tropes and Hermeneutical *Maxims*

The random sample of lyrics surveyed consisted of the following: "Bad Luck Woman Blues," by Papa Charlie Jackson; "The Duck Yas Yas Yas," by Tampa Red and Georgia Tom Dorsey, "Fogyism" by Ida Cox; "Hoo

Doo Blues," by Harry Chatmon; "Hoodoo Man Blues," by Victoria Spivey; "Hoodoo Hoodoo," by John Lee "Sonny Boy" Williamson; "Hoodoo Man," by Albert Williams; "I'm a Mojo Man," by Lonesome Sundown; "The Ins and Outs of My Girl," by Bo Carter; "Jinx Blues," by Casey Bill; "Little Queen of Spades," by Robert Johnson; and "Louisiana Hoo Doo Blues," by Ma Rainey.[6]

The survey confirmed much of what Chireau says about the issues addressed in *Hoodoo Blues* lyrics. It also supported her contention that they are reflective of a coherent spirituality that reclaims an indigenous African and Black Diasporan heritage and fosters self-empowerment and liberation (2003, 148–49). With regard to the engagement of the Bible, the authors of these songs present ideas suggestive of a thoroughly transgressive hermeneutical agenda. Several things can be immediately said of the *corpus* itself.

First, it almost completely *ignores* the Bible. None of the songs in the sample allude to biblical books or characters. Neither do they engage in extended "God talk," with the single exception of an exclamatory "good Lord" in "Bad Luck Woman Blues." This is not to say that themes and issues of perennial human concern addressed in the First and Second Testaments are not referenced, because they are. However, the biblical text itself is not the primary point of reference for the discussion of cosmological, anthropological, theological, ontological, or soteriological concerns.

Second, the lyrics reinforce the notion that the highs and lows, joys, pains, triumphs, and disappointments of human experience are the primary text to be read and interpreted by the human family. They place relational issues having to do with the construction, maintenance, protection, and dissolution of social aggregates such as families in the foreground. They also call attention to individual and communal concerns such as indigence, jurisprudence, and the agonistic nature of social interactions. Throughout, one can detect, as Chireau has noted, a concern with wholeness and human well-being as well as an implicit belief in the cathartic power of word and melody (2003, 148). Such emotive release is clearly vital given some of the theological dilemmas addressed in the lyrics such as unjust suffering, the vagaries of luck, and the ongoing quest for economic self-sufficiency.

Third, the sample also evidenced a strong didactic function not unlike that of biblical wisdom books and ancient Near Eastern inventories or lists. The taxonomy of "conjure" *praxis*, the names of personnel, and the traits and capacities of individual practitioners—e.g., the manipulation of time, precognition, and the ability to manifest desires—are crucial. Moreover, they suggest that there is no established *hierarchy* of "conjure" practitioners. Women and men undertaking the work are presented as *liminal* figures whose social *cachet* is derived from their professional "track record." Nonetheless, access to power, supernatural and earthly, is understood to be available to all. The clear message is that both the *materia medica* and rubrics needed to create, harm, and heal are available to everyone.

Fourth, the sample reveals that certain geographical locations are understood as places from which "conjure" practitioners originate, where supernatural assistance can be obtained, or where *numinous* encounters occurred. Spain, Louisiana (both the state and Algiers in particular), Alabama, and Memphis, Tennessee are mentioned. These references have the effect, one could argue, of sacralizing space and establishing a mythopoeic landscape within the Africana Diaspora. Finally, one song, "Fogyism" by Ida Cox, indicates a self-critical impulse in the tradition of "conjure" as constructed by Blues practitioners, one that applies a hermeneutic of suspicion to the belief in signs, omens, and portents central to Africana cosmologies.

These data suggest several Africana hermeneutical *maxims* for twenty-first century Bible research, all of which can be said to emerge from a Blues-oriented ideology: (1) make as the starting point for research the lived experiences, social challenges, ontological ruminations, and socioreligious concerns of the peoples of Africa and the African Diaspora worldwide; (2) set the Bible within a larger set of African, Black Diasporan, and global ecologies of sacred texts, traditions, and social *realia*; (3) use a "soft gaze" when reading that permits one to appreciate the interpretive implications of cultural boundaries within and outside of the Africana *milieu* that are permeable; (4) conceive of the interpretive task as a creative one intended to elicit catharsis and wholeness—i.e., as a healing art rather than as a science; (5) democratize access to the interpretive process by writing in accessible idioms; (6) juxtapose incongruous texts and reading strategies to promote randomness and give rise to intuitive insights; and (7) experiment, test, and "prove" (in the *homeopathic* sense) all reading strategies.

Some of these proposals have been presaged by the work of Copher (1989, 1974), Felder (1990, 1991), Bailey (1991), Kirk-Duggan (2001, 2004), hooks and West (1991), and a host of others who have advocated placing issues of import in the Black community at the center of Africana research in Biblical Studies and cognate disciplines. The tradition of activist scholarship is, in sum, already established. However, one issue deserves highlighting at this point: that Africana artists have played a pivotal role in preserving, adapting, reclaiming, and reshaping religious ideas in the Black Diaspora and have important things to say about the history and future place of the Bible within it. To suggest that the tradition of African American "conjure," as mediated through the lyrics, music, and performances of Blues practitioners can serve as a basis for the development of modern Africana interpretive models, is to ask that twenty-first century scholars return to an ancient paradigm of investigation, teaching, and social transformation. It is to urge biblical scholarship to reembrace the creative impulses, tools, and evocative media of storytellers, *bards*, *griots*, and poets. As for the second and third maxims, Wimbush (2000, 2008) has noted the importance of problematizing the relationship between marginalized peoples and the scriptures they create and with which they interact. The tradition of "conjure," as reflected in the textual sample used in this study, reflects a worldview that acknowledges, with some reservations, the reality of *numinous* phenomena. The miraculous is not rejected. The "soft gaze" advocated above is actually derived from the martial arts, where it refers to a relaxed state of heightened awareness in which one can perceive energies both overt and subtle.[7] Biblical reading and interpretation that employ this skill involve opening oneself to the rhythms of life that obtain in the larger Africana world and entering into dialogue with the textual, artistic, musical, and other resources that have been used for community building, identity construction, and nurture. One goal of such encounters should be to broaden perception so as not to carry Enlightenment ideals of dispassionate objectivity to an extreme, but to approach the several interlocking tasks of exegesis, exposition, etc. with a passionate commitment to social transformation. This sets the stage for what is suggested in the fourth and fifth maxims. By conceiving of biblical interpretation as an artistic endeavor that affirms the emotions and inner life of the scholar—rather than as one that obliterates the self—the way is opened for a paradigm oriented toward the promotion of wholeness and the democratization of access to knowledge. For a Bible scholar to conceive of herself or himself as chiefly engaged in the promotion of human wholeness through translation and other interpretive artistic performances could be seen as a significant departure from extant models for responsible academic *praxis*. However, when one looks at the long list of luminaries who are usually credited with having shaped the parameters of modern biblical scholarship—e.g., Origen, Spinoza, Astruc, Wellhausen, deWette, Albright, and others—there are in fact passionately held beliefs and agendas woven intricately as subtexts into the fabric of their various endeavors.[8] By stating our presuppositions explicitly, we demystify the scholarly and creative processes, thereby paving the way for a more egalitarian spirit with regard to biblical reading and exposition to emerge.[9]

The sixth and seventh *maxims* concern the generation of new ideas pertaining to longstanding interpretive dilemmas in biblical research and the testing of new ideas for effectiveness. The former is derived from the tradition of divination at home in "conjure." Some cross-cultural researchers have supported the proposition that divination is a means of deploying the principle of randomness as a human survival technique (Moore 1957: 73–74). This concept, when applied to the choice of secondary and tertiary media employed as dialogue partners in the interpretive enterprise, can be used as a way of accessing the literary, artistic, musical, and other cultural riches of Africa and the African Diaspora, the entirety of which no single scholar can control. By allowing oneself to read texts not necessarily considered standard fare in Hebrew Bible or New Testament research, and by selectively, impressionistically, or randomly exploring more deeply the warp and weft of the Black experience worldwide, one is able to engage a broad spectrum of Africana sources and epistemological domains that can be utilized in the interpretive process. The final maxim, related to testing, puts forward the idea that Africana scholarship should have an activist dimension oriented toward communal healing and that hermeneutical encounters with texts—as well as the development and selection of methodologies to facilitate the same—should be subject to the equivalent of homeopathic "proving" to assess the extent to which they are able to promote communal wellness.[10] This notion of the Bible scholar as healer is crucial, especially given the number of texts and interpretive methods that have had a demonstrably negative impact on Black life over multiple generations.

CONCLUSION—TOWARD A *TEXTUAL HEALING ALGORITHM*

Textual Healing Algorithms for Africana biblical interpretation derived from Hoodoo Blues—i.e., flexible sets of procedures for bringing issues and cultural artifacts from either the African or African Diasporan *ethos* into more direct conversation with Biblical texts, themes, and cruxes—are sorely needed as Africana Biblical Criticism continues to mature as a subfield. Such promise to expand the range of cultural artifacts and lore from African, Afro-European, Afro-Asian, Caribbean, African American, and other Africana settings brought into conversation with the Bible. They also have the capacity to raise awareness of the role that *esoteric* cosmologies and modes of thinking—Africana, Christian, Jewish, Muslim, and other—have played in the shaping of personhood, the development of reading strategies and life ways, and the promotion of freedom and self-determination in the larger Africana community.[11]

The implications of such algorithms for the African American community are considerable. To date, its religious ecology has been one in which client-based faith systems have co-existed with congregationally centered church structures. By and large, the former are viewed as less normative and less orthodox than the latter. Conventional modes of biblical engagement, particularly those of a decidedly Christian theological orientation are by and large geared to promote the interests of established ecclesial organizations. It could be argued that the model proposed in this study will help to level the proverbial playing field and allow a broader sweep of concerns and a larger collection of voices within the Africana community to be heard when biblical research is undertaken.

If this occurs, then the immediate future will witness an increase in the generation of interpretive modalities emerging from the mining of Africana philosophies, ideologies, and literatures. There will also be an expansion of the database for exemplars of Africana biblical interpretation so as to include: the library of primary sources used by "conjure" practitioners (e.g., Gamache 1983); the oral lore of nineteenth, twentieth, and twenty-first century *root workers* (see, for example, the anecdotes in Mitchem 2007, 51–74, 141–62); the *hoodoo* inventory of candle shops;[12] and the lyrics, personal ruminations, and performances of Hoodoo Blues artists. It will also further destabilize existing notions of biblical scholarship and reframe it as liberative praxis in service to humanity. One hopes it will also succeed in leading those with an interest in Africana encounters with the Bible to take on the challenge issued by Wimbush in his 2010 Presidential Address to the Society of Biblical Literature (2011, 24), that is:

> to run—away from the feigned solid canonical self, onto "the ghost-story train," into a "disrupting blackness," down into what Howard Thurman called a "luminous darkness" where the process of the hard work of self-criticism can take place.

One can only hope that such will lead, perhaps even encourage, a few attendees at future Annual Meetings of the Society in Chicago, Illinois, or elsewhere to venture out of pricey hotels and overcrowded meeting rooms to social venues and night clubs where ordinary folk struggling to survive gather for healing and restoration; and where transformational epistemologies that offer freedom and hope continue to foment.

EPILOGUE

Essays like this one are, on the one hand, time-bound and context-specific accounts of intellectual conversations. On the other, they are often snapshots or fragments of discussions that actually unfold over the course of a career or lifetime. Much of my thinking about Hoodoo Blues and biblical interpretation has remained consistent since 2004. Some of it has evolved. My appreciation of Blues, resistance, and hermeneutics has deepened and responses to earlier versions of this article—enthusiastic and muted—have influenced my approach to reading Early Hebrew Poems (Page 2013) and continue to shape the ways I think about texts, authority, and the precariousness of Black Lives. Returning to this piece: as the COVID-19 pandemic continues its ravages; in the era of both the SayHerName and MeToo movements; almost a year after the #BlackScholarsMatter virtual panel discussions sponsored by the Society of Biblical Literature (August 2020); not long after the sentencing of Derek Chauvin for the murder of George Floyd; and on the very day (July 6) that Nikole Hannah-Jones made public her rejection of the fraught and delayed offer of tenure at the University of North Carolina, Chapel Hill, in favor of an endowed chair at Howard University, one of our nation's premier HBCUs, the urgency I feel about interpretive efforts that honor Africana intellectual resources and Black genius—wherever they are to be found—is palpable. The same can be said of the need to raise serious questions about knowledge production and various forms of "gatekeeping" not only in biblical studies but in the academy at large. Much work remains to be done and it is my hope that the "messy" foray above will elicit others akin to it that redefine the nature and scope of scholarship.

NOTES

1. Here and in other endeavors, I have found Norman Denzin's concept of the "messy text" as a genre encouraging risk taking and empowering authors both to be "part of the writing project" and to "move back and forth between description, interpretation, and voice" to be particularly useful (Denzin 1997, 224–25). I use the word "weird" intentionally to honor the uncanny nature of this reengagement of an older essay.

2. On the concept of *àshe*, see Thompson (1983, 5–9).

3. The relationship between conjure, hermeneutics, and resistance is also a theme that Martin engages (1998, 228).

4. Some may take issue with the inclusion of concepts from the realms of music, energy psychology, homeopathic medicine, and the martial arts as interlocutors in a discussion of methodology in Biblical Studies. I would argue that the bringing together of disparate ideas and practices in the creation of life ways and interpretive strategies that mitigate the challenges of exclusionary discourse such as Biblical Studies is characteristic of Africana life in diaspora.

5. See, for example, Chireau (2003, 144–49) and Spencer (1994, 14–18).

6. Unfortunately, copyright restrictions prohibit my reproducing the lyrics of the songs in this paper. Readers are invited to access them *via* the online archive noted above.

7. See, in particular, Hatsumi's description of the need to appreciate "the aesthetics of space" and "read between the lines" in order to understand the martial arts and the essence of his own work on *Ninpo Taijutsu* (2004, 30–32).

8. See for example Long (1997) on the impact of context on the work of Albright.

9. Such was a major feature of *The Africana Bible* (Page et al. 2010).

10 For a simple explanation of homeopathic proving, see Marks (1997, 8).

11 For a recent example of how such work can enrich our understanding, see Page and Finley (2021).

12. See, for example, Grandma's Candle Shop in Baltimore, Maryland.

WORKS CITED

Adeyemo, Tokunboh, ed. 2010. *The Africa Bible Commentary*. Grand Rapids, MI: Zondervan.

Bailey, Randall C. 1991. "Beyond Identification: The Use of Africans in Old Testament Poetry and Narratives." In *Stony the Road We Trod: African American Biblical Interpretation*, edited by Cain Hope Felder, 165–84. Minneapolis: Fortress.

Blount, Brian K., Cain Hope Felder, Clarice J. Martin, and Emerson B. Powery, eds. 2007. *True to Our Native Land: An African American New Testament Commentary*. Minneapolis, MN: Fortress.

Byron, Gay L., and Vanessa Lovelace, eds. 2016. *Womanist Interpretations of the Bible: Expanding the Discourse*. Semeia Studies 85. Atlanta, GA: Society of Biblical Literature.

Chireau, Yvonne P. 2003. *Black Magic: Religion and the African American Conjuring Tradition*. Berkeley, CA: University of California Press.

Copher, Charles. 1989. "Three Thousand Years of Biblical Interpretation with Reference to Black Peoples." In *African American Religious Studies: An Interdisciplinary Anthology*, 105–128. Durham, NC: Duke University Press.

Copher, Charles B. 1974. "The Black Man in the Biblical World." *Journal of the Interdenominational Theological Center* 1, vol. 2: 7–16.

Denzin, Norman. 1997. *Interpretive Ethnography: Ethnographic Practices for the 21st Century*. Thousand Oaks, CA; London; New Delhi: Sage Publications.

Dube, Musa, ed. 2001. *Other Ways of Reading: African Women and the Bible*. Atlanta: Society of Biblical Literature.

Ellis, Carolyn, and Arthur P. Bochner, eds. 1996. *Composing Ethnography: Alternative Forms of Qualitative Writing*. Edited by Carolyn Ellis and Arthur P. Bochner, *Ethnographic Alternatives Book Series*. Walnut Creek/London/New Delhi: Alta Mira.

Felder, Cain. 1990. *Troubling Biblical Waters*. Maryknoll, NY: Orbis Books.

———, editor. 1991. *Stony the Road We Trod: African American Biblical Interpretation*. Minneapolis: Fortress.

Fentress-Williams, Judy. 2021. *Holy Imagination: A Literary and Theological Introduction to the Whole Bible*. Nashville, TN: Abingdon.

Gafney, Wilda C. 2017. *Womanist Midrash: A Reintroduction to the Women of the Torah and the Throne*. Louisville, KY: Westminster John Knox Press.

Gamache, Henri. 1983. *The Master Key to Occult Secrets*. Reprint of 1942 ed. Bronx, NY: Original Publications.

Goodall, H. L., Jr. 2000. *Writing the New Ethnography*. Walnut Creek: AltaMira.

Hatsumi, Masaaki. 2004. *The Way of the Ninja: Secret Techniques*. Translated by Ben Jones. New York: Kodansha International.

hooks, bell, and Cornel West. 1991. *Breaking Bread: Insurgent Black Intellectual Life*. Toronto, Ontario: Between the Lines.

Hover-Kramer, Dorothea. 2002. *Creative Energies: Integrative Energy Psychotherapy for Self-Expression and Healing*. New York: W. W. Norton.

Jones, Stacy Holman. 1998. *Kaleidoscope Notes: Writing Women's Music and Organizational Culture*. Walnut Creek: AltaMira.

Junior, Nyasha. 2015. *An Introduction to Womanist Biblical Interpretation*. Louisville, KY: Westminster John Knox.

Kirk-Duggan, Cheryl. 2001. *Refiner's Fire: A Religious Engagement with Violence*. Minneapolis: Fortress.

———, ed. 2004. *Pregnant Passion: Gender, Sex, and Violence in the Bible*. Semeia Studies 44. Leiden: E. J. Brill.

Long, Burke O. 1997. *Planting and Reaping Albright: Politics, Ideology, and Interpreting the Bible*. University Park, PA: Pennsylvania State University Press.

Marks, Cassandra. 1997. *Homeopathy: A Step-By-Step Guide*. Boston, MA: Elements Books.

Martin, Clarice J. 1998. "'Somebody Done Hoodoo'd the Hoodoo Man': Language, Power, Resistance, and the Effective History of Pauline Texts in American Slavery." *Semeia* 83–84: 203–34.

Mitchem, Stephanie. 2007. *African American Folk Healing*. New York: New York University Press.

Moore, Omar Khayyam. 1957. "Divination—A New Perspective." *American Anthropologist* 59, vol. 1: 69–74.

Napier, Winston, ed. 2000. *African American Literary Theory: A Reader*. New York: New York University Press.

Page, Hugh R., Jr. 2013. *Israel's Poetry of Resistance: Africana Perspectives on Early Hebrew Verse*. Minneapolis, MN: Fortress.

———. (Gen. ed.), Randall C. Bailey, Valerie Bridgeman, Stacy Davis, Cheryl Kirk-Duggan, Madipoane Masenya, Nathaniel Samuel Murrell, and Jr. Rodney S. Sadler, eds. 2010. *The Africana Bible: Reading Israel's Scriptures from Africa and the African Diaspora*. Minneapolis, MN: Fortress.

———, and Stephen C. Finley. 2021. "'What Can the Whole World Be Hiding?': Exploring Africana Esotericisms in the American Soul-Blues Continuum." In *New Approaches to the Study of Esotericism*, edited by Egil Asprem and Julian Strube, 168–81. Leiden/Boston: Brill.

Smith, Abraham. 2020. *Black/Africana Studies and Black/Africana Biblical Studies*. Leiden: E. J. Brill.

Smith, Mitzi, J., ed. 2015. *I Found God in Me: A Womanist Biblical Hermeneutics Reader*. Eugene, OR: Cascade.

———. 2017. *Insights from African American Interpretation*. Minneapolis, MN: Fortress.

———. 2018. *Womanist Sass and Talk Back: Social (In)Justice, Intersectionality, and Biblical Interpretation*. Eugene, OR: Cascade.

Smith, Theophus. 1994. *Conjuring Culture: Biblical Formations of Black America*. New York: Oxford University Press.

Spencer, Jon Michael. 1994. *Blues and Evil*. Knoxville, TN: University of Tennessee Press.

Thomas, Oral A. W. 2014. *Biblical Resistance Hermeneutics within a Caribbean Context*. Abingdon, UK: Routledge.

Thompson, Robert Farris. 1983. *Flash of the Spirit: African and Afro-American Art and Philosophy*. 1st ed. New York: Random House.

West, G. O., and Musa W. Dube, eds. 2000. *The Bible in Africa: Transactions, Trajectories, and Trends*. Leiden: E. J. Brill.

West, Gerald O. 2016. *The Stolen Bible: from Tool of Imperialism to African Icon, Biblical Interpretation Series*. Leiden, Netherlands: E. J. Brill.

Wimbush, Vincent. 2000. "Introduction: Reading Darkness, Reading Scriptures." In *African Americans and the Bible: Sacred Texts and Social Textures*, edited by Vincent L. Wimbush, 1–43. New York: Continuum.

———. 2008. "Introduction: TEXTures, Gestures, Power: Orientation to Radical Excavation." In *Theorizing Scriptures: New Critical Orientations to a Cultural Phenomenon*, edited by Vincent Wimbush, 1–20. New Brunswick, NJ: Rutgers University Press.

———. 2011. "Interpreters—Enslaving/Enslaved/Runagate." *Journal of Biblical Literature* 130, vol. 1: 5–24.

———. 2012. *White Men's Magic: Scripturalization as Slavery*. New York: Oxford.

Yronwode, Catherine. 1995–2019a. "All The Pages in Blues Lyrics and Hoodoo by Catherine Yronwode." [Website], accessed 06 July 2021. http://www.luckymojo.com/allblues.html.

———. 1995–2019b. "Blues Lyrics and Hoodoo." http://www.luckymojo.com/blues.html.

Chapter 10

Reflections on Teaching Biblical Interpretation through a Black Lives Matter Hermeneutic

Wil Gafney

INTRODUCTION: WHEN I BEGAN . . . DAUNTE WRIGHT WAS STILL ALIVE

"When I began this [assignment] Daunte Wright was still alive."[1] This deeply disturbing first line of a final project in the course rocked me to my core. The day I graded that project I learned that police in Mesquite, Texas, killed a Black man named Ashton Pinke earlier that very same day. In other words, when I began grading the assignment marking the death of Daunte Wright, Ashton Pinke was still alive. This vignette illustrates the trauma attendant upon engaging a subject matter composed of (violently killed) dead and dying persons while the teaching and learning community attempts to engage the substance and implications of those lives and deaths as fully embodied human beings with our own emotional responses and religious and political commitments. In this essay I will reflect upon the origination of this upper-level elective in biblical interpretation, "The Bible and Black Lives Matter," its course design and pedagogy, observations from the first offering, and assessment of some of the work produced for the second offering as viable examples of a BLM hermeneutic.

The impetus for this course and its 2017 predecessor was the murder of Mike Brown[2] in the summer of 2014, the summer that I moved to Fort Worth, Texas, to take up my appointment to the faculty of Brite Divinity School.

While I was aware of and enraged by earlier police killings—Amadou Diallo in 1999, Sean Bell in 2006, Oscar Grant III in 2009, seven-year-old Aiyanna Stanley-Jones sleeping on her couch in 2010, the "citizen's" execution of Trayvon Martin in 2012, the killings of Rekia Boyd in 2012, and Renisha McBride, Miriam Carey, and Kimani Gray in 2013—the summer of 2014 brought with it a spate of killings at the hand of the police in very short succession.

Less than thirty days after I moved to Fort Worth, Eric Garner was strangled to death on a public street by NYPD on July 7, 2014. Nineteen days later, police in Beavercreek, Ohio, killed John Crawford on August 5, 2014, and four days later, the execution of Michael Brown and public display of his body for four hours, like a recumbent lynching, in Ferguson, Missouri, brought me back to my feet and back into the street with a passion and intensity that has not faded. Those experiences left me with a question that resulted in the initial design for these courses, "what does my training and scholarship have to say to the present moment?" In addition, Sandra Bland's in-custody death in Waller County, Texas, in July 2015, while not officially deemed a police-killing, weighed heavily as a harbinger of my individual relative lack of safety in Texas.

I had difficulty as professor and pedagogue articulating how my training and research agenda prepared me for the moment, but had significantly less difficulty as pastor, priest, and preacher. I decided to teach a course that would prepare students to engage the BLM movement, more specifically, the ethical, moral, and spiritual issues raised by the continuing extra-judicial slaughter of Black women, men, and children by police and citizens acting as police. It was my intention to teach BLM hermeneutics, an approach I had been developing for my own preaching in the aftermath of Mike Brown's killing. In this hermeneutical approach, as with other interpretive paradigms I taught and used myself, the scriptures would be read and communicated authoritatively and contemporarily contextually, mindful of their originating contexts, to respond to the present moment. The vehicles of those hermeneutics would be varied: academic papers and projects, sermons and congregational curricula, and scholarly writing and presentations. In the spring of 2017, I first taught "The Bible in the Public Square: Interpreting the Bible in the Age of #BlackLivesMatter" at Brite Divinity School as an upper-level first master's course.

The bulk of the reflection and analysis in this essay will be on the second edition of the course in the spring of 2021. This was a multilevel course with students undertaking their first master's degree and students in the DMin and the PhD programs. The student demographics included Black, Latinx, white, and Asian students, women, men, and nonbinary students, and LGBTQIA students. Between registration fluctuation and the presence of an auditor, the class maintained consistent numbers of ten to twelve students for the majority of the semester. The students were clergy, clergy in formation, and laypersons. All student work was done with a specific context in mind, chosen by the student and reflective of their current vocational setting and ambitions. For those students engaged in congregational work, there were white pastors of white congregations and Black pastors of Black congregations in addition to Black pastors of white and multiethnic congregations. Some students were in secular and theological educational contexts or preparing for them; those contexts were in primarily white settings. The presence of PhD students in biblical interpretation meant that some written work was shaped for academic engagement of a BLM hermeneutic. These students engaged the assigned biblical texts at a deeper level, including original translation and textual studies to support their writing. Rather than producing for a congregation, these students were writing for academic readers.

There were significant differences between the two semesters due to a redesign of the course. One was the participation of members of the Black Lives Matter community, who were on the ground in Ferguson, in the later course via Zoom. Our guests included the Rev. Traci Blackmon (then a community pastor in the area),[3] the Reverend Dr. Starsky Wilson (then a local pastor in St. Louis),[4] the Rev. Dr. Pamela Lightsey (who went to Ferguson repeatedly in response to multiple requests),[5] the Rev. Dr. Valerie Bridgeman (who was also called to Ferguson),[6] and the Rev. Mike Kinman (who served as Dean of the Episcopal Cathedral in St. Louis, in which he sheltered protestors). Another noteworthy new development was the intentionality that some of the preaching and educational material developed was suitable for children and youth. And this semester, there was much more attention to the role of journalism in not only covering protests and the shootings to which the protests respond—in that order, as the shootings are often unknown until the protests—but also the role of journalism in perpetuating the trauma of seeing these murders, shootings, and killings over and over and over again. The volume *They Can't Kill Us All* was particularly helpful here (Lowery 2016).

Finally, given the prominence of art in the movement, memorial art and protest art at the site of these executions and their curation by the Museum of African American History, this iteration of the course also attended to art. First, in the presentation by the Rev. Dr. Valerie Bridgeman, a painter and poet, and secondly by providing space for students to create art in an in-class project and as an option for their final assignment. A number of us contributed poetry to individual class sessions as well. Some of the students found producing their own art quite moving. Reflecting on each individual class in the end of semester exercise, one student wrote of his own earlier artistic endeavor, "[T]he artistic exploration of lament at the end of class was more helpful for me than I imagined. I have very few practices of grief and I felt a weight lifting from my head as I drew. I will incorporate a bit of artistic exploration into my daily life now."

Connecting the two iterations of the course was one distinctive phenomenon that occurred during the first offering (and continued to and through the second) for which I had not been and was not prepared. Black women, men, and children continued to be killed by police at an alarming rate, those deaths gaining national attention primarily through the repeated looped broadcasts of their deaths. I was frequently called on to address these deaths in writing, and preaching adding to the weight of this work, making the weekly pedagogy infinitely more difficult.

LITANY OF THE DEAD

Between the deaths of Mike Brown and Eric Garner in 2014 was the killing of Tyree Woodson (Baltimore, Maryland). Between those killings and the first day of class were the executions of Yvette Smith (Anderson, Texas), Aura Rosser (Ann Arbor, Michigan), Akai Gurley (New York, New York), twelve-year-old Tamir Rice (Cleveland Ohio), Victor White III (Iberia Parrish, Louisiana), and Ariel Levy (Hayward, California), just in 2014.

In 2015, police killed Anthony Hill (Chamblee, Georgia), Jamar Clark (Minneapolis, Minnesota), Christian Taylor (Arlington, Texas), India Kager (Virginia Beach, Virginia), Sam Dubose (Cincinnati, Ohio), Alexia Christian (Atlanta, Georgia), Raynette Turner (Mount Vernon, New York), Redel Jones (Baldwin Hill, California), Tony Robinson (Madison, Wisconsin), Bettie Jones (Chicago, Illinois), Barbara Dawson (Blountstown, Florida), Nuwnah Laroche (Secaucus, New Jersey), Kindra Chapman (Homewood, Alabama), Joyce Curnell (Charleston, South Carolina), and Icarus Randolph (Wichita, Kansas).

In 2016, police killed Kisha Michael (Inglewood, California), Alfred Olango (El Cajon, California), Terrence Crutcher (Tulsa, Oklahoma), India M. Beaty (Norfolk, Virginia), Gynnya McMillen (Shelbyville, Kentucky), Deborah Danner (Bronx, New York), Korryn Gaines (Baltimore, Maryland), Deresha Armstrong (Orlando, Florida), Laronda Sweatt (Gallatin, Tennessee), and Jessica Williams (San Francisco, California).

Police killed Patrick Harmon in Salt Lake City, Utah, in 2017, before the first iteration of the course began. During the course of the semester, Jordan Edwards was murdered by an officer in Balch Springs, Texas, in April 2017. The amount of trauma, processed and unprocessed, carried by myself and the Black and Latinx students enrolled in the course was incalculable. Between the 2017 and 2021 editions of the course, police (and policing civilians) killed Alteria Woods (Gifford, Florida), Jonie Block (Phoenix, Arizona), Charleena

Lyles (Seattle, Washington), Morgan London Rankins (Austin, Texas), Sandy Guardiola (Canandaigua, New York), and India N. Nelson (Norfolk, Virginia) in 2017.

In 2018, police killed Stephon Clark (Sacramento California), Shaheed Vassell (New York, New York), Antwon Rose (East Pittsburgh, Pennsylvania), Botham Jean in his apartment (Dallas, Texas), Geraldine Townsend (Tulsa, Oklahoma), Dereshia Blackwell (Missouri City, Texas), Cynthia Fields (Savannah, Georgia), Crystalline Barnes (Jackson, Mississippi), April Webster (Darlington County, South Carolina), Shukri Ali Said (Johns Creek, Georgia), Tameka Simpson (Calhoun, Georgia), LaJuana Philips (Victorville, California), and Angel Decarlo (Hopewell, Virginia).

In 2019, police killed Atatiana Jefferson in her home, in front of her nine-year-old nephew (Fort Worth, Texas), Brittany McLean (Dorchester County, South Carolina), Nina Adams (Greensburg, Pennsylvania), Elijah McClain (Aurora, Colorado), Pamela Turner (Baytown, Texas), Latasha Walton (Miami, Florida), and Ronald Greene (Monroe, Louisiana).[7] The killings of Botham Jean in Dallas in 2018 and Atatiana Jefferson in Fort Worth in 2019 were particularly impactful on the seminary community by virtue of being local and because each of them were killed by police in the supposed safety of their respective homes

In 2020, police killed Breonna Taylor (Louisville, Kentucky, George Floyd (Minnesota, Minnesota), Jonathan Price (Wolfe City, Texas), Walter Wallace Jr. (Philadelphia, Pennsylvania), and Jacob Blake (Kenosha, Wisconsin). Also in 2020, marauding citizens acting as police executed Ahmaud Arbery in Glynn County, Georgia. Death, grief, anger, rage, and trauma were among our primary texts for this class. With this cloud of witnesses, I revised the design of the second offering based on lessons learned from the first.

As noted previously, police killed Daunte Wright (Brooklyn Center, Minnesota) mid-semester during the 2021 course and Ashton Pinke (Mesquite, Texas) near the end of the course. Between them, police killed Andrew Brown Jr. (Elizabeth City, North Carolina) and sixteen-year-old Ma'Khia Bryant (Columbus, Ohio). Also mid-semester, police killed thirteen-year-old Adam Toledo in Chicago. And during the course, anti-Asian violence reached a particular crescendo and began receiving prominent nationwide coverage followed by the murder of eight people at two Atlanta spas: Delaina Yaun, Xiaojie Tan, Daoyou Feng, Paul Michels, Elcias Hernandez-Ortiz, Hyun Jung Grant, Soon Chung Park, Suncha Kim, and Yong Ae Yue.[8]

Exodus famously begins *v'elleh shemoth*, "these are the names" (of the Israelites who went to Egypt). However, that list is woefully incomplete, as only the names of narratively significant characters are included. Similarly, the foregoing list of the most publicized victims of police and civilians lethal violence cannot by any means be considered complete. These are not all of the names.

PEDAGOGY

Both editions of the course were multilevel including master's and doctoral students with auditors. The readings included the RCL texts for the coming Sunday so that those students in congregational ministries might use the fruit of their exegeses in their own settings. There was also an option for students who did not use a lectionary to bring an additional passage. The assigned texts differed significantly between iterations.[9] There was overwhelming negative reaction to *America's Original Sin* (Wallis 2016) in the first instance, so it was removed from consideration for any future version of the course. The second edition of the course benefitted tremendously from new scholarship, including two volumes of sermons employing BLM hermeneutics and the reflections of a journalist. The teaching objectives and learning goals (slightly modified from the previous course) were as follows:

- We will explore the emergence of the Black Lives Matter (BLM) movement in order to be able to speak about it responsibly. *Students will be able to define the BLM movement and its aims succinctly and in depth.*
- We will analyze the American cultural context from which the BLM movement and its call was first issued in order to identify the precipitating issues of BLM. *Students will be able to articulate the justice issues emerging from the BLM movement.*
- We will assess the American cultural context(s) in which the call continues and the contemporary provocations to which the call responds in order to identify spaces for social engagement and justice work. *Students will learn to identify the justice issues consistent with the BLM movement present in unfolding current events.*
- We will interpret the canons of Jewish and Christian scriptures in light of the call and its precipitations in order to be able to speak to the justice issues raised by BLM using the words and witness of the scriptures as illuminating, inspiring, and where appropriate, authoritative. *Students will explore assigned scripture selections and those of their own choosing to identify texts that can be read or interpreted as speaking to BLM issues.*
- We will address the justice issues raised by the call, in light of the scriptures. *Students will craft sermons, blog posts, editorials, and other communiqués to respond to BLM concerns raised by assigned reading and current events.*

In this second semester the course was offered, I sought to expand the framework of the course beyond Black and white by assigning as our very first reading Potawatomi author Kaitlyn Curtice's (2020) theological memoir *Native,* to keep present the scope and legacy of white supremacist Christianity in this country. We were also helped in expanding our conversation by the presence of students who had neither African nor European heritage. One very fruitful ongoing conversation was how to translate the BLM movement and its concerns into an Asian context, specifically, a student's home context. From these conversations, the Korean notion of *han,* intergenerational grief, sorrow, resentment, and fear, gave voice to the multigenerational emotional legacy of police killings in the United States. In addition, during the course of the semester, national attention turned to the ongoing problem of violence against Asians, Asian Americans, and Pacific Islanders in the United States. I diverted the syllabus and assigned a research project documenting the stories of persons who had been targeted, brutalized, and killed because of their Asian appearance and identity. We took time to situate anti-Asian violence in the context of white supremacist violence in conversation with the BLM movement.

The artifacts of the course through which student learning was facilitated and assessed included: (1) weekly journals engaging the readings due twenty-four hours before class, (2) in-class discussion curated around student observations and questions, (3) an oral presentation defining BLM and its aims to their constituency, (4) brief exegetical papers, (5) a cumulative journal in which students could supplement their previous submissions with a final end of course reflection, (6) a choice between final papers and a substantial exegetical paper for Maryland MDiv and DMin students, and (7) a final substantial exegetical paper for PhD students (who were not assigned shorter exegeses). My primary learning from the first class that shaped the second class was that students needed more processing time, which led to the process of early submission of first thoughts followed by a more nuanced collective discussion, with intentional space between the due date and class engagement.

BLM HERMENEUTICS

I had begun to think through the textual grounds for a BLM hermeneutic in 2016 when I was invited to the Austin Presbyterian Seminary in Austin, Texas, to give their annual Hesed Lecture, that year entitled, "Which Lives Matter?" In the earliest form of the hermeneutic I simply maintained that the lives that are imperiled and disdained in the text are the ones that matter. That was my first articulation of the hermeneutic which I continued to develop and presented as a starting place on the first day of class in each iteration.[10] The following year I reflected on the BLM movement and its impact on scholarship, offering a *"meturgemanic"* reading of Isaiah 53.[11] My subsequent BLM hermeneutical work centered heavily on Habakkuk's "How long, O Lord?" (and its parallels in Psalms 90:13; 94:3). I have preached on these verses, and written on them in the aftermath of Breonna Taylor's killing (Gafney 2020).

A Black Lives Matter hermeneutic begins with the world in which the biblical texts are translated, read, heard, and interpreted. In that world, Black lives are imperiled by white supremacy and institutionalized structural racism including lethal over-policing and disparate outcomes for Black, Brown, and poor folk in the justice system. Those imperiled lives are in the United States of America (and to some degree in the United Kingdom and other parts of Europe, notably France and Germany), those lives are Black lives in all their plurality, Black women's lives, Black queer lives, Black trans lives, Black Muslim lives, the lives of Black disabled folk, and the lives of Black folk living with mental illness among others. The hermeneut brings multivalent Black identity to the text or, reads the text in solidarity with those who do.

Blackness transcends the world of the hearers, readers, and interpreters of scripture and the worlds of the scriptures themselves. The settings of the scriptures of Israel and of the Jesus movement are the ancient Afro-Asiatic world. The great tectonic plates of Africa (West) and Asia (East) meet in the Jordan River, which is part of the Great Rift Valley system extending down through East Africa to Lake Victoria. Israel is on the west, African side, with its neighbors; Jordan and Syria are on the east, Asian side. These facts are immutable in spite of enduring claims of white supremacist biblical scholarship.[12] The world of the scriptures is an African world, a Black world. Yet, the category of race does not exist in the world of the scriptures. While racism does not exist in the Hebrew Scriptures, there is vicious ethnic conflict that can function as an analog for contemporary race-based conflict.

Moreover, the occupation setting of most biblical literature extends itself readily to the American context in both straightforward and inverted readings. From the perspective of Native Americans, the conquest of Canaan can be read as the conquest of the Americas, rejecting the traditional reading that valorizes the Israelites; reading with native peoples inverts the intended (Israelite) reading of the text. Black folk in the African diaspora tend to read the exodus straightforwardly with and as Israel, while postcolonial African readers may well read with the peoples of Canaan along with other indigenous readers. A Black Lives Matter reading therefore may read with or against the text or its intended protagonist, the ancient Israelites and the emerging nation of Israel with its own imperial and colonizing agenda.

As in the world that reads the text, there are inequities between peoples in the text, inequities between people who subjugate, colonize, and occupy other people. A Black Lives Matter hermeneutic privileges the colonized and occupied whether they are the heroes of their own story, Israel and Judah, or those whose subordination they have justified in religious terms, the many peoples of Canaan. The lives that are at risk, the lives that do not matter to those with power in the text, the lives that those on the downsides of power curve in the texts, those are the lives that matter in a BLM reading of the scriptures. From the perspective of the canon shapers, authors, and editors of the scriptures, Israelite lives matter in the scriptures of Israel. Occasionally, other lives matter too. But it cannot be said that all lives matter in the Bible, nor can it be said that of those lives that do matter that they matter equally. It cannot even be said that all Israelites lives matter equally.

In my teaching, a BLM hermeneutic is also a womanist praxis which requires looking at the full complexity of interwoven effects stemming from different components of identity. We looked for those lives that were at risk, subject to oppression (occupation/colonization), economic exploitation, death, physical and sexual violence, enslavement and/or being relegated to the margins of the text and/or discounted as disposable, particularly as a result of an intersecting element of identity. The intersecting identities we considered were largely gender and ethnic identity, Israelite/non-Israelite primarily, supplemented by class and economic indicators where available. In addition, we attended to cultural status indicators such as fertility and infertility. In doing so, we regularly read against the text in which the Israelites and their vulnerability to external imperial powers are the central perspectival subject, to disrupt the normative Christian interpretive practice of reading with the Israelites and co-opting that identity to wield against indigenous peoples in colonization, enslavement, and genocide. We progressed from somewhat reductionist "who is oppressed in the text" readings to asking how any text could be read through a BLM hermeneutic in the students' identified contexts, utilizing the definitions crafted earlier.

Before the first attempt at constructing a BLM hermeneutic the students had to define the Black Lives Matter movement and its goals briefly and succinctly to a constituency they identified as the one for whom they were producing their work, in which they might teach or preach, provide Christian education or, offer scholarly papers and writing.

DEFINING BLM

Students were assigned definitions of the Black Lives Matter movement by its founders and tasked with translating them to their identified contexts. The primary definition of the Black Lives Matter movement that we considered was: "Black Lives Matter is an ideological and political intervention in a world where Black lives are systematically and intentionally targeted for demise. It is an affirmation of Black folks' contributions to this society, our humanity, and our resilience in the face of deadly oppression" (Garza 2014). Non-Black students supplemented their definitions of the BLM movement with an articulation of their relationship to it. Some wrote "BLM allied" readings and hermeneutics; others wrote "in conversation with" BLM; my suggested language was "in collaboration/conversation with" and "co-conspiratorial." A few moved beyond simply rearticulating the assigned definition, crafting new ones such as: "BLM is intersectional; Black Lives Matter firmly centers intertwining oppressions, centers those marginalized among and by the marginalized, and has as its core priority all Black lives." Another emphasized the role of the living as speakers for and on behalf of the dead: "Black Lives Matter is an organic liberation movement [arising] from the living matter of Black lives." (This was fleshed out in discussion.) One student questioned whether BLM is addressed to non-Black folk (not whether or not they have a place in the movement), "To whom is the cry 'Black Lives Matter' directed? Is it a call to Black folks to take our own survival in our own hands or is it a rebuke to the wider world, the whiter world?"

These definitions provided an additional scriptural text for the students to resource while doing their exegetical work. In the following section I present a series of student exegeses with commentary and analysis. The selections were made to demonstrate the diversity of student responses and represent the majority of the students across the course of the second course offering.

STUDENT EXEGESES

Students' initial efforts to read biblical passages through a BLM hermeneutic were individual assignments due prior to class.[13] Subsequently, they engaged in peer reflection with some facilitation by me and together we refined or rearticulated many of those early readings. It was important to continually contextualize the biblical texts in terms of their political settings, focusing on the state of the nation or monarchy and the nature and degree of their subjugation by foreign powers. Likewise, students began to articulate the necessity to situate their intended audiences with regard to the oppression the Israelites or Judeans were experiencing in a particular passage. That contextualization would necessarily vary depending on the social location of the congregation or classroom. These exegeses demonstrated a range of maturity dependent in part upon how many biblical studies courses the students had had previously; the only prerequisite was a single introductory course on either testament. Student preparation varied significantly, with some students only having had the single course while others had three or more, not counting the doctoral students. The following engagements of the biblical text with a BLM hermeneutic are illustrative of the scope of work submitted for this course.

As Holy Week and Easter fell during this semester, the liturgical season generated a number of readings. A shared reading offered by a number of students saw the women at the cross and at the tomb as women in the movement, whether the founders or the many, many women who march alongside them, or the mothers of the movement, the mothers of those women and men whose deaths loom large on the national stage, pushing their mothers into the national spotlight. Some of these women include Sybrina Fulton, the mother of Trayvon Martin, Lezley McSpadden, the mother of Mike Brown, and Lucy McBath, mother of Jordan Davis, among the most prominent. Students drew an analogy between the emotionally difficult labor of attending to the body of the murdered Jesus at the hands of the state and responding to the tidal wave of Black death, embodied particularly in the execution of Trayvon Martin. In these readings, both sets of women are catalysts for the movements that followed, the Jesus movement and BLM. The following examples of exegetical work offer more detailed insights into student work produced for the course.

EXEGESIS 1: 1 CORINTHIANS 1:18–25

A student uses the discourse in 1 Corinthians 1:18–25 about foolishness and wisdom to engage the discourse around "All Lives Matter" as a response to Black Lives Matter. The student argues that what sounds like foolishness, Black Lives Matter, is instead the wisdom of the wise as in vv.18–19. The student continues,

> The preaching of Christ crucified is proselytization that changes from generation to generation because Black America's understanding of the social actions of Christ dictates to always be on the side of the oppressed. This one idea will forever cripple White America because they can never live the Black experience. This final statement [to always be on the side of the oppressed] alone would be the interpretation I would use [for v 25, "*God's foolishness is wiser than human wisdom, and God's weakness is stronger than human strength*"].

This is an example of a hermeneutic targeted towards a white or multiethnic congregation in which the preacher is also white. The student, significantly influenced by James Cone, starts with a non-negotiable premise that God is on the side of the oppressed, a point as non-negotiable as the gospel for Paul. The notion that God is aligned with "the Black experience" positions white folk, in this case in the congregation hearing the sermon, as distant relations to the God they claim who will always be on the side of the oppressed, not theirs and likely engender conflict with the preacher and rejection of the sermon. Yet there is something in the proposition that is reminiscent of Hebrew Bible prophetic paradigms in which the chosen one (person or nation) or, elder sibling, is rejected for one not thought significant, competent or worthy.

EXEGESIS 2: JONAH 3:1–5

There were a cluster of exegeses on Jonah 3. In the first, a student engages the forty-day period allotted for Nineveh's repentance:

> Can we impose a time limit on Nineveh's reckoning? Can we impose a time limit on this "American reckoning with race" as the months following the murder of George Floyd and the protests into in response to that televised snuff film combined with response to Breonna Taylor's execution, among others, have been identified in the media? As with Jonah, self-appointed (forty-day) deadlines for transformation and premature talk of reconciliation have come and gone. There has been no divine intervention overthrowing this empire. What shall be our response? Shall we sit under the tree with the self-pitying prophet or, shall we overturn his empire ourselves.

Here, the student addresses frequent premature calls for "reconciliation" between Black and white folk emerging primarily from white churches (but also corporate deployment of BLM marketing), often without any confessional or reparative work and the phrase that entered public discourse in the aftermath of the murder of George Floyd, "reckoning with race." In the Jonah story, a divine threat provided the impetus for the conversion and confession of the people of Nineveh. In the world that reads the Jonah story, the world in which George Floyd was murdered, there is no sufficient threat to inspire or force a similar conversion. Missing from the argument was the specific mechanism punctuating such a time limit. However, in the broader scope of the course, we discussed disruptive protest, including those with accompanying property damage and loss, as strategy in the first case and inevitable consequences in the latter.

The potential overthrow of the Assyrian empire in Jonah 3:4 was the entry point into the passage for a number of students. One of the advanced students engages the key verb more deeply offering a response to the previous student's question:

> [Does *nehpaket*] have the connotation of being "overthrown" or "destroyed," as many translations have it, or the connotation of "transformed" (as in Exodus 7:15)?" The reading "transformed" makes the Jonah passage more readily available for a BLM proclamation to America. Rather than proclaim an eminent

cataclysm like so many failed and false prophets, the proclamation that America will be transformed in forty days (with the understanding that forty days is not a specific period of time in the biblical text) leaves room for the kind of national repentance that one my hope our recent national reckoning might generate. Yet, one might ask, "Forty days from whence?" Forty days from what prophetic outcry? What outcry, what protest, would be sufficient to transform this nation as Nineveh was transformed in Jonah's prophecy?14

This reading preserves the power of the passage without engaging in magical thinking. It enables the reader/hearer to hold on to a scriptural promise without trying to confine God to a specific set of actions in a specific period of time. It also anticipates a likely critique. At what point in the long history of white supremacist violence against Black folk did God issue such a proclamation? How far along are we on the countdown to transformation?

Yet another student focused on what it means for Black folk to read Nineveh as America, noting that Black folk in America, who are also Ninevites in this reading, will experience the repercussions of the prophet's message and any subsequent upheaval. This reading emphasized the cost of liberation, which is not fully paid by oppressors and colonizers, but often by those seeking liberation.

EXEGESIS 3: PSALM 31

A number of students found the Psalms to be a fruitful resource for BLM hermeneutics. In some cases, students rewrote the Psalm, in others they read it as is. For example, Psalm 31:9–16 functioned as a BLM lament for several students without intervention. Reading the same Psalm, one student offered a compelling exegesis of Psalm vv.11–16, reading the passage as a Black person reflecting on how they are perceived and engaged in white culture, particularly in v.11:

> I am the scorn of all my adversaries,
> a horror to my neighbors,
> an object of dread to my acquaintances;
> those who see me in the street flee from me.

"Horror" in the NRSV translation, though troubled, makes the point with which the student connected, the demonization and monstrification of Black folk.[14] The student writes, "Psalm 31:11 . . . just reached out and grabbed me when thinking of a BLM hermeneutical application. I immediately pictured white neighborhood crime watch patrols that target and target Black neighbors and children, even though they are doing nothing wrong, besides just being."

Another student offered a particularly poignant reading of Psalm 31:11 through the horrorscape of Mike Brown's body being left in the street. Having been abandoned in the street, the Psalmist has been slandered as was Michael Brown. And if a case against an officer for killing a Black person goes to trial, the victim and their family are likely to be slandered as well:

> The sense of abandoning a man in the street is strongly resonant with the body of Mike Brown, Jr., abandoned for hours in the streets of Ferguson, Missouri. Meanwhile, the slander was already beginning in the media, who portrayed him in the strongest possible terms as a violent, animalistic, out-of-control thug who "deserved" the death dealt to him by the cops who were, themselves, the ones out of control and violent.

These examples were representative of student work throughout the course at each enrolled level. Between the shorter and longer exegetical papers, presentations, and final projects and papers, all of the students demonstrated minimal to sufficient competency in interpreting the scriptures through the lens of the Black Lives Matter movement, and some quite simply excelled.

CONCLUSION

Brite Divinity School emphasizes contextual interpretation of the scriptures at all levels of biblical study. This course, "The Bible and Black Lives Matter," successfully introduced students to the founding narrative, self-definition, and articulate it goals of the BLM movement; students learned to translate those elements into their own contextual settings. Students successfully supplemented their previous studies in biblical scholarship and exegesis by developing a series of hermeneutic approaches to the scriptures, reading through the BLM movement and their own experiences of and responses to the ongoing killings of Black folk in the US by police and policing citizens. The final projects, papers, and artistic productions were exemplary. Most significantly, students were comfortably able succinctly and effectively to define and describe BLM and to read and teach scripture, writing on it in scholarly and theological voices, with mature and maturing BLM hermeneutics.

POSTSCRIPTS

One of the most significant events to occur during the course of the semester was the insurrectionist assault on the Capitol building in Washington DC. The obviously racialized dynamics and ostensibly Christian framework of white nationalist and supremacist belief and practice on display interrupted the syllabus. We spent quite a bit of time on the prayer offered in the well of the Senate by the trespasser known as the QAnon Shaman. We spent a portion of that class articulating responses to that prayer and its theology for use in congregational contexts. One suggestion was to read Luke 4, where Jesus demonstrates the importance of knowing scripture well and contextually as the foundation for commending deeper engagement with scripture and tradition so that people are less easily swayed by heretical movements; that is, the temptations Jesus faced were rooted in bad theology and worse exegesis.

At the end of the semester, the rapper Earl Simmons, known as DMX, died. His death had an impact on this class. In the aftermath of his death, we returned to the definitions of the BLM movement and its goals that we read and wrote at the beginning of the semester, focusing the conversation on the ability or inability of Black folk to flourish in this country. We discussed the full range of things that contribute to our flourishing, like art and culture and music, and those things that inhibit our flourishing, like addiction and the structural inequities that compound it, such as punitive responses and inequity in treatment for Black and white folk addicted to opioids. One student offered an inter-textual reading between the recently released volume of DMX's prayers and Psalm 4.

NOTES

1. This was the first line of a student final project in the 2021 edition of my Bible and Black Lives Matter course offered at Brite Divinity school in Fort Worth, Texas. This essay uses student anonymized materials with permission. The president of the Brooklyn Center (MN) police union killed Daunte Wright on April 11, 2021, in Brooklyn Center Minnesota. Police officers killed Ashton Pinke in Mesquite, Texas, on May 4, 2021.

2. I understand all of these killings to have been murders without regard to legal findings. And I intentionally do not name any killers, civilian or law-enforcement; this work is not about them.

3. Rev. Blackmon identified herself to the class as a "community pastor" in the narrative she related explaining how it was that she was called by a community member to respond to the death of Michael Brown. She contextualized her relationship with the community and with the observation that Michael Brown's killing was the 169th in that year.

4. Dr. Wilson served Saint John's Church (The Beloved Community), a congregation he described as "an inter-racial, inner-city congregation connected to the United Church of Christ."

5. Dr. Lightsey was then an administrator at Boston University.

6. Dr. Bridgeman then served and continues as the Dean of the Methodist Theological School in Ohio.

7. The story of Ronald Greene's killing is just emerging as I prepare this manuscript. It has taken two years for the body camera video of his final moments to be released.

8. At this point, I amended the syllabus to add an assignment researching the history of anti-Asian violence and violence in the United States and articulating its motivation in terms of the same white supremacist ideologies that manifest in structural institutional racist policies, including policing, and in interpersonal violence including that by police officers and civilians acting in their stead.

9. In the initial version of the course the primary assigned texts were: Bailey et al., 2009; Barber and Wilson-Hartgrove 2016; Douglas 2015; Gunning 2015;. Lightsey 2015; Wallis 2016.

10. A significant portion of the following paragraphs in this section are shared in common with the essay I wrote reflecting on the pedagogy of the inaugural offering of this course (Gafney forthcoming).

11. "*Meturgemanic*" signifies the work of a translator-prophet/interpreter and is rooted in the semantic range of *targum* and the form *metaturgemin* in Deuteronomy 27:8 in Targum Neofiti and Matthew 1:23 and Acts 13:8 in the Peshitta along with Ezra 4:7 in the MT (see Gafney 2017).

12. E.g., in his The Old Testament World published by Fortress, the press that would one day publish my first monograph, in the year of my birth Noth characterized the "races of the ancient world" as being "[e]xclusive of Negroes" (Noth 1966, 234). See also the "religious and moral authority" white supremacist biblical scholars granted the Nazi regime through their participation and the deployment of their scholarship (Heschel 2008, 11).

13. All of the quoted material in the following section comes from student writing in the course, used with permission. By agreement, they will remain anonymous.

14. *Me'od*, is an amplifier, meaning "very" in most contexts. Here, it modifies neighbors, yielding something like "my neighbors very much." The lack of verb is remedied in the NRSV by the addition of "horror" extended from the following verb, "to be in dread." JPS extends the previous verb into the phrase yielding, "I am the particular butt of my neighbors."

WORKS CITED

Agabond, Julian. 2014. "A List of Unarmed Blacks Killed by Police." https://abagond.wordpress.com/2014/08/26/a-list-of-unarmed-Blacks-killed-by-police/.

Bailey, Randall C., Tat-siong Benny Liew, and Fernando F. Segovia. 2009. *They Were All Together in One Place: Toward Minority Biblical Criticism*. Atlanta: Society of Biblical Literature.

Barber, William J., and Jonathan Wilson-Hartgrove. 2016. *The Third Reconstruction: Moral Mondays, Fusion Politics, and the Rise of a New Justice Movement*. Boston: Beacon.

Curtice, Kaitlyn. 2020. *Native: Identity, Belonging and Rediscovering God*. Grand Rapids: Brazos.

Douglas, Kelly Brown. 2015. *Stand Your Ground: Black Bodies and the Justice of God*. Maryknoll, NY: Orbis.

Edgar, Amanda Nell, and Andre E. Johnson. 2018. *The Struggle over Black Lives Matter and All Lives Matter*. Lanham, MD: Lexington.

Gafney, Wil. Forthcoming. "Reflections on Teaching the Bible and Black Lives Matter in a Divinity School." *Racism and Pedagogy*, edited by Shelly Matthews and Benny Tat-siong Liew. Atlanta: The Society of Biblical Literature.

———. 2020. "A Legal Perversion of Justice: Breonna Taylor's Death and the Lawlessness of Law and Order." https://divinity.uchicago.edu/sightings/articles/legal-perversion-justice.

———. 2020. "Jonathan Price's Shooting Was Not 'Reasonable.' Most Police Killings of Black People Aren't." https://www.nbcnews.com/think/opinion/jonathan-price-s-shooting-was-not-reasonable-most-police-killings-ncna1242463).

———. 2019. "The Atatiana Jefferson Shooting in Fort Worth Shows Black People, Again, that We Aren't Safe Here." NBC Think. https://www.nbcnews.com/think/opinion/atatiana-jefferson-shooting-fort-worth-shows-black-people-again-we-ncna1067831.

———. 2017. "A Reflection on the Black Lives Matter Movement and Its Impact on My Scholarship." *Journal of Biblical Literature* 136, 1: 204–7.

———. 2017. *Womanist Midrash: A Reintroduction to the Women of the Torah and of the Throne*. Louisville: Westminster/John Knox.

Garza, Alicia, Patrisse Cullors and Opal Tometti. 2014. "A Herstory of the #BlackLivesMatter Movement." http://www.thefeministwire.com/2014/10/Blacklivesmatter-2/.

Fisher-Stewart, Gayle. 2020. *Preaching Black Lives Matter*. New York: Church.

Francis, Leah Gunning. 2015. *Ferguson & Faith: Sparking Leadership & Awakening Community*. St. Louis: Chalice.

Heschel, Susanna. 2008. *The Aryan Jesus: Christian Theologians and the Bible in Nazi Germany*. Princeton, NJ: Princeton University Press.

Jennings, Willie James. 2020. *After Whiteness: An Education in Belonging, Theological Education Between the Times*. Grand Rapids: Eerdmans.

Lightsey, Pamela R. 2015. *Our Lives Matter: A Womanist Queer Theology*. Eugene, OR: Pickwick.

Lowery, Wesley. 2016. *They Can't Kill Us All: Ferguson, Baltimore, and a New Era in America's Racial Justice Movement*. New York: Little, Brown, and Company.

Noth, Martin. 1966. *The Old Testament World*. Philadelphia: Fortress.

#SayHerName Campaign In Memoriam page. https://aapf.org/shn-inmemoriam.

Snider, Phil. 2018. *Preaching as Resistance: Voices of Hope, Justice, and Solidarity.* St. Louis: Chalice.

Springfield (IL) Public Schools. Black Lives Matter chart. https://www.sps186.org/downloads/basic/636414/Black%20Lives%20Matter%20Timeline%20.pdf.

Wallis, Jim. 2016. *America's Original Sin: Racism, White Privilege, and the Bridge to a New America.* Grand Rapids: Brazos.

Chapter 11

Revisiting the Caananites and Contemporary *Ites*

Pedagogical Insights into Cheering for the Wrong Team

Theodore W. Burgh

Reading the biblical account of the Canaanite invasion is a challenge. Many who were reared in church, the Black church in particular, read the Joshua stories in Sunday School, in Bible study, or heard rousing sermons inspired by the miraculous fall of the Jericho walls and other underdog Israelite triumphs. The text shares how Joshua and the Israelites marched boldly into Canaan proclaiming that their god told them that the land was theirs, and they were to forcibly remove all who lived there: "And Joshua commanded the officers of the people, 'Pass through the midst of the camp and command the people, Prepare your provisions, for within three days you are to pass over this Jordan to go in to take possession of the land that the LORD your God is giving you to possess'" (Jos 1:10–11). The Israelites are set up from the beginning to "rightfully" colonize the land of Canaan and subdue its inhabitants.

Emboldened by a *cherem* (a divine decree said to come from a god to take or possess things or persons; and at times to destroy them) that they attributed to YHWH, the Israelites claimed this as a license to murder and to take possession of the land promised to their ancestors. To help establish justification for this undertaking, the writers carefully demonize and denigrate those living in Canaan at the time (e.g., Canaanites, Perizzites, Amorites, *et al.*) and paint them as dreadful, intimidating enemies. They make them appear less than human.

The invasion generates a number of questions: Are the killings of those living in Canaan justified? Are the colonizing actions of the Israelites a form of genocide or terrorism? Where is the perspective of the *Ites*—a term we employ to refer to the inhabitants of Canaan? Why are they not allowed to speak for themselves and tell their side of the story?

Exploring these questions, this article will briefly discuss how preconceived, unfounded biases must be curtailed when studying the Bible. We must also realize that we are often entering the biblical text with misinformation and corrupted data often from previous teachings, various skewed interpretations, and personal inferences and assumptions. This kind of information has generated misconceptions of peoples, as well as stoked unfounded stereotypes and biases, the result is the creation of perceived adversaries. More specifically, ill-informed teachings, blatant lies, and skillfully constructed propaganda manufactured from falsities have and continue to inspire and justify the mistreatment and murder of Black people. This discussion will present and examine some of these horrific instances in an attempt to challenge how stories from the biblical text may be interpreted effectively and better applied in navigating daily life.

"Any Canaanites in your family?" This is a question I often present to students in my Introduction to the Hebrew Bible/Old Testament class when we start to explore how the Israelites arrived in Canaan. I teach at a state university located in a geographical area where the Bible is extremely important in many of the students' lives. While some students in the course have no knowledge and experience with the Bible, most are white and come from evangelical, Bible-centered backgrounds. Active church lives at home and participation in local congregations during their time in school are the norm. Interestingly, a faction often feel they have so much of a grasp of the Bible that they develop a sense of arrogance and, at times, display a touch of condescension toward others in the class.

Nevertheless, I present my pedagogical question: "Any Canaanites in your family?" Like a competent attorney, I very seldom ask a question to which I do not already know the answer. With this query, my goal is to create a teachable moment about life and perspectives of living in the ancient and modern worlds. The response I receive initially to my Canaanite question from most students is silence. Many then present a perplexed look with their heads slightly tilted to the right and facial expressions displaying the countenance that says, "Huh?"

I follow up that inquiry with another: "What do you know about the Canaanites?" The students are usually more vocal and the responses are varied, ranging from "I don't know" to identifying them, without reservation, as heathens, pagans, giants, or "wrong god-worshiping" people. They never mention anything good about the Canaanites. It is an intro class, so I do not expect too many in-depth responses. In all the students' descriptions, they very seldom focus on ethnicity. I do, however, briefly introduce the "Curse of Ham/Canaan."[1] The explanation is often a shock and a bit overwhelming to most students, so it is difficult to go much beyond this point when it comes to race and ethnicity in antiquity.

In an attempt to challenge them to think critically about the labels they have attached to the Canaanites and others, I ask them if they think the biblical writers truly allow the Canaanites or the others to speak for themselves in this situation.[2] Some students start to realize that this group and the other *Ites* in the text do not have voices. Others, however, astutely point to Rahab the prostitute (*zona*) and argue that she is a Canaanite voice.[3] With a little prodding, they ruminate on the idea and determine that the Rahab figure does not speak for all Canaanites, and she may even be multidimensional. On one hand, she is quick-witted, smart, and shrewd, as she strikes a deal with the Israelite soldiers to save their lives in exchange for those of her and her family (Jos 2:12–33).[4] At times, students in the class view her actions as a demonstration of faith in YHWH. This is a popular perspective. They view Rahab assisting the Israelite soldiers as a sincere act of faith and doing what is right. Scholar William Lyons shares the following information and interpretations regarding Rahab that align with this perspective: "In the Book of Hebrews (11:31) we find Rahab listed in what might be called the 'Hall of Faith,' where she is remembered as an example of faith for later generations." Another observation highlights her treatment of the spies: "1 Clement (c. 96) claims that because of her faith and hospitality, Rahab was saved (12:1, 3, 8)." Lyons (2008) also explains how Origen thought Rahab's actions deserved a place of honor: "Origen (185–253/4) believed that by receiving the spies into her house she was placed in a position of high honor (something he refers to as one of the mysteries of faith [139]; *Homilies on Joshua* 3.3)." Mary J. Evans sees this in Rahab as well. She holds that Rahab's unique insight into the political/spiritual situation of her day apparently grew into a genuine commitment to the God of Israel and thus she was incorporated into the Israelite community of faith (Evans 2005, 990).

Hebrew Bible scholar Alice Bellis also considers Rahab a heroine and her actions as faithful. She explains that "the books of Joshua and Judges are filled with unusual women. Rahab, the first bona fide biblical harlot, is also something of a hero." This is an important point, as "hero" is not the first word that comes to mind when Rahab's name is spoken. Bellis elaborates on Rahab taking a big risk in protecting the Israelites. For her, the story shows her doing this because of her faith. "Rahab is a hero because she protects the Israelite spies. She is also heroic because she is a woman of faith who takes risks based on that faith. In addition, she is clever, like the midwives of Exodus" (Bellis 2007, 98–100).

Rahab's actions are understandable and admirable. But could we also ask if she is one who sells out her people to save herself and her family? She has heard the stories about the YHWH-assisted Israelite victories and does not think the Canaanites have a chance to survive the impending invasion. Before the men do what they came to do, Rahab confesses to them that she has heard about the Israelite victories. She knows that her people are afraid and thinks they do not stand a chance against them: "For we have heard how the LORD dried up the water of the Red Sea before you when you came out of Egypt, and what you did to the two kings of the Amorites who were beyond the Jordan, to Sihon and Og, whom you devoted to destruction" (Jos 2:8–10). However, could Rahab have alerted the Canaanite kings or other authorities of the spies' presence? By exposing them to the king, is it possible the Canaanites and other *Ites* could have united and prepared more for the coming Israelites? Could some have escaped?

Instead, Rahab takes the side of the colonizers. She is defeated before the invasion, but more importantly, through fear and the desire to survive among these coming inhabitants, her mind has been colonized. She has been convinced that the Israelites are correct in their annexation, so it is best to join them and save her and her families' lives. Rahab has bought into the Israelite propaganda and is seeking to find her "place" within the coming regime. Postcolonial feminist scholar Musa Dube explains that in this kind of indoctrination, "The colonizers narrativize themselves as exceptional chosen beings, while they also construct tales of derogation against their targeted victims as beings who deserve to be invaded, dispossessed, subjugated, and annihilated if need be" (2000, 70).

I conclude my inquiries with a designed scenario. I tell the students that they are all Canaanites, and I am an international news reporter in the country of Canaan to interview them about the impending Israelite invasion. I ask them if they think the coming invasion is justified or not, and why. Most of the responses say the invasion is not warranted, but some explain that because they, the Canaanites, do not worship YHWH like the Israelites, they deserve to be invaded. They also add that YHWH promised this land to the Israelites—His people. These individuals side with Rahab and also embrace the invading colonizers.

It is baffling to hear the students' calloused replies about the annihilation of peoples they do not know, and praise a group going into a land, taking it, and murdering the inhabitants because "their god" told them the land was theirs alone. This maneuver and attitude is similar to how some countries around the world originated or have been taken over. Thus, it is a consolation when I see students begin to reconsider what they have been taught, assumed, or have heard about colonizing, invasions, and people occupying the land.

There are placards, paperweights, and other religious regalia with Joshua 24:5 printed in bold letters: "As for me and my house, we will serve the LORD." The message that Joshua, the "new Moses," states is meant to be inspiring and to set a cultural standard for the Israelites. Preachers, pastors, and teachers have delivered countless sermons, references, and lessons incited by this passage and Joshua's undying obedience to YHWH. His willingness to institute the decreed *cherem*, which led the Israelites to victory, destruction, and defeat of those living in Canaan. The biblical writers painted these marginalized groups in the manner they wished, and their marginal voices are not readily present in the biblical stories. Yet, messages championing their demise are ubiquitous.

Scholar Uriah Kim presents excellent observations regarding this concern with the Israelite invasion in conjunction with actions in South Africa. He discusses how South African citizen Dora Mbuwayesango takes issue with the presentation of the celebrated biblical conquest and denigration of the marginalized inhabitants. Kim states that Mbuwayesango is a native of Zimbabwe and currently teaches in the United States. In light of the fact that the indigenous people of southern Africa suffered greatly at the hand of white settlers who used the Bible to justify the killing of the indigenous people and dispossession of their lands, Mbuwayesango asks, "What can the book of Joshua say to the Canaanites, the dispossessed, and the exterminated?" The question is apropos given what the biblical interpreters have done to them. Mbuwayesango goes on to ask, "Can the God of the dispossessor be the God of the Dispossessed?" The book of Joshua depicts God as God of Israel and not of others, and the identity of Israel is based on its exclusive relationship to God and the land. This is problematic for southern Africa, where people of different ethnicities and religions live together. This connects with the different ethnicities said to live in Canaan at the time of invasions. They appeared to coexist without major issues. Mbuwayesango further explains that "Such a religious exclusivism promotes intolerant attitudes toward others, making the 'other inhabitants' of the land, as Homi Bhabha would put it, 'unhomely' in their own land." Mbuwayesango rejects religious exclusivism and suggests that the book of Joshua "should serve only as a warning against such intolerant attitudes against those who are different" (Kim 2004).

Mbuwayesango's assessment describes perfectly the anxiety and uneasiness with the book of Joshua and produces an extremely important question: "What can the book of Joshua say to the Canaanites, the dispossessed, and the exterminated?" This query is crucial, particularly in light of colonizers' use of the Bible to explain and justify the killing of indigenous peoples, who are essentially perceived as the abhorred Canaanites and other degenerate *Ites*, and taking their lands in the name of their god. Where do readers such as aboriginal South Africans view themselves in this story? Why should they be considered others in a land they have occupied for centuries? Is the god of the dispossessing colonizer the god of the dispossessed indigenous South Africans?

WHAT DID THE CANAANITES AND OTHERS DO TO DESERVE MURDER, BE UTTERLY DESTROYED, AND HAVE THEIR LAND TAKEN?

Denigrating and demonizing one's opponent are useful tactics. It makes them appear less than human, if human at all, and thus it is easier to do away with them. They appear to get what is coming to them. Inflicting torturous pain and doing irreparable damage is not problematic when an opponent is presented as an inhuman menacing threat, and one that can potentially cause harm to you and your loved ones. Note the explanation Mbuwayesango shares regarding how an invader describes the native South Africans as others and "unhomely" in their own land. They are Canaanites and *Ites* in their own land, and they are not allowed to speak for themselves.

This strategy is often used in sports in the "pep talk" and inspirational statements. The "pep talk" or inspiration that YHWH gives Joshua (3:1–13) and Joshua gives to the Israelites (3:5) is no different than one of the rousing speeches an athletic coach and players give to their squad before, during, or after a crucial game. At times, pep talks and statements dehumanize the opponent and justify any kind of behavior to win:

> Kellen Winslow (NFL Player): It's war. They don't give a freaking you-know-what about you. They will kill you. They're out there to kill you. If I didn't hurt him, he'd hurt me. They're gunning for my legs. I'm gonna come right back at 'em. I'm a [bleep] soldier. (Media Education Foundation 2010)

> Alvin Mack: Let's open up a can of kick ass and kill 'em all, let the paramedics sort 'em out. (Stein 2011)

The ultimate desire is to raise the confidence of the team and stress the importance of the task ahead of them: "Then Joshua said to the people, consecrate yourselves, for tomorrow the LORD will do wonders among you" (Jos 3:5).

WHO WERE THE CANAANITES AND OTHER *ITES*?

Again, the Canaanites and others do not get to speak for themselves or share their thoughts about what is happening. The silence implies that they deserve all that happens to them. Instead, the biblical writers speak for them, and it is of course biased.

It appears that the Canaanites were made up of various ethnic groups and were not a single, political unit. Archaeologist Ann Killibrew (2005) explains that clear characteristics and cultural traits of other groups living in the land during this time (Late Bronze Age 1550–1200 BCE) are elusive. However, it is apparent that there are "general universals in architecture and ceramics" (Killibrew 2005, 12). Canaan was not made up of a single "ethnic" group "but consisted of a population whose diversity may be hinted at by the great variety of burial customs and cultic structures" (ibid.). Killibrew also states that "According to Rahab, the Canaanites are weak and fear the Israelites. Moreover, the Canaanites and others are viewed as pejoratively different from them although they are related" (ibid.). Killibrew supports this observation with Deuteronomy 23:3–8, which explains how "No Ammonite or Moabite may enter the assembly of the LORD." She also shared Ezekiel 9:1–4 as another example of the observed differences: "After these things had been done, the officials approached me and said, 'The people of Israel and the priests and the Levites have not separated themselves from the peoples of the lands with their abominations, from the Canaanites, the Hittites, the Perizzites, the Jebusites, the Ammonites, the Moabites, the Egyptians, and the Amorites'" (ibid.).

JUSTIFIED ORDERED GENOCIDE TO POSSESS AN OCCUPIED PROMISED LAND?

The controversies and blatant lies regarding Cristoforo Colombo's "discovery" of America still abound. Moreover, America continues to celebrate a national holiday for him based on a lie. How does one "discover" a land where people have been living for centuries or possibly longer? The description of his "discovering" America and the Canaanite invasion are the equivalent of someone kicking in your front door, saying that where you are living belongs to them because their god said so. And by the way, they are going to kill you and everyone living there because their god said they could. You are deemed unworthy of living in this space. I acknowledge whole-heartedly the continued plight of First Nation/Native American people due to colonization and a plethora of catastrophic atrocities at the hands of the people like Cristoforo Colombo. However, in this discussion I wish the focus to remain on the colonization, deprecation, and abuse inflicted on Black people.

The denigration of the people living in Canaan dehumanizes and casts unfounded aspersions. This calculated process makes the inhabitants disposable and easily eliminated. As mentioned, for some, the invasion and the genocide are justified and simple to explain. For example, scholar Robert Rothwell (2019) shares that the act was not genocide, and matters may have gone differently if they had just complied with the Israelites' requests: "The invasion of Canaan commanded by God and carried out by the Israelites under the leadership of Joshua has raised issues for Christians and non-Christians alike." He also observes that "Non-Christians have been quick to label the destruction of the Canaanites as an act of genocide. Yet, as we have seen in the first four parts of this series, this allegation cannot be sustained. One cannot honestly speak of the destruction of the Canaanites as a genocide." Rothwell (2019) goes further in explaining his justification: "Deuteronomy 12:10–15 instructs the Israelites that when they draw near to an enemy city outside of Canaan, they are first to offer terms of peace to it. The cities that agree to the terms and to serve Israel are not to be utterly destroyed. Instead, the people are to become servants of Israel." If they had simply followed instructions, they could have survived. Instead, "Those cities that will not agree to the terms of peace are to be conquered with the sword and the Israelites are to enjoy the spoil they get from defeating their enemies" (Rothwell 2019).

Theologian Don Stewart echoes this sentiment: "While the loss of innocent life is something that is to be deplored, the situation must be understood with the following background in mind. The nation of Israel was chosen to be a witness to the world of the true and living God." In other words, the Israelites are good and everyone else is not. According to Stewart, "The Israelites were to live in the Promised Land surrounded by the heathen nations, yet they were not to be influenced by the other nations' religions. God instructed His people that they were not to take to themselves any of the elements of the false pagan religions." Stewart (date unknown) further sullies the Canaanites stating why they could not live: "The Promised Land in which the Israelites were to settle was populated by the Canaanites who had corrupted and perverted God's truth. They had corrupted themselves to the place where they were beyond saving. Had any been permitted to live, they would have infected Israel with their moral depravity."

In both explanations, the murderous actions of the Israelites are justified (e.g., if they disagree with the Israelites' demands, they are to die by the sword; YHWH promised the land to the Israelites). Canaanites and others are denigrated (e.g., they are morally depraved; they had corrupted and perverted God's truth, practice false pagan religions, and corrupted themselves to the extent of being beyond redemption). It is interesting to note that the Canaanites and Israelites are very similar in their material culture and pantheon (e.g., Dever et al., 1995a, b; Lemche 1999; Buck 2019). While it is assumed by many that the Israelites contained a monotheistic majority, there were those within the culture that practiced henotheism or polytheism. For example, observe the following texts: Exodus 20:1: "I am the LORD your God, who brought you out of the land of Egypt, out of the house of slavery; you shall have no other gods *before* me (*emphasis mine*)." Psalm 82:1: "God has taken his place in the divine council; *in the midst of the gods* he holds judgment" (*emphasis mine*; see Smith 2001, Binger 1997, Avalos 2007).

BLACK PEOPLE VIEWED AS CANAANITES OR OTHER *ITES*

Even today, it is the practice of denigrating and dehumanizing that justifies and eases the killing of one's enemies, or anyone that a group or individual dislikes, hates, or fears. I offer that these sentiments are the foundation of a collective, often ignored, view of Black people by many across America. Carefully crafted, unfounded, threatening stereotypes, along with blatant lies of innate thuggery, hypersexuality, wanton violence, rapid drug use, and "black-on-black crime," transform Black men, women, and children into subhuman animals who can be easily disrespected, incarcerated, and killed with little remorse. In many instances, the Black person who is murdered is blamed. It is their fault because they did not comply, or they fit the description of at least one of the previously mentioned characteristics.

Black people have been deemed Canaanites and other *Ites* in their own land, a land we have occupied for centuries. We are a part of a country we have helped to build—for free. Yet, there are factions that want to see us wiped from the face of the earth or at least removed from the country. For them, we are the undesired inhabitants of their Canaan. Although we are the same people who have established creative practices in music, fashion, language, politics, religion, and countless other areas, we are tagged as lazy, shiftless, and lacking high intelligence. Therefore, we are dispensable and usually deserve any injustice that happens to us.

Consider the following deaths of Black people. The dominant society often treats these deaths as merely unfortunate, controversial, or even deserved (i.e., the person murdered bears some responsibility):

Breonna Taylor, a twenty-six-year-old Black female (killed March 13, 2020). White plainclothes officers Jonathan Mattingly, Brett Hankison, and Myles Cosgrove of the Louisville Metro Police Department shot Ms. Taylor as she slept in her apartment. They suspected her participation in illegal drug activity. Ms. Taylor was tried, convicted, and executed in her home as she lay in bed. She was stereotyped, profiled, and made worthy of death. She did not get a chance to comply or to share her part of the story. Armed with the authority of "I'm right and I say so," the officers invaded her space and executed her. Ms. Taylor was one of the *Ites*.

Philando Castile, a thirty-two-year-old Black male (killed July 6, 2016). Mr. Castile complied and recognized the authority of the police during a traffic stop. He had followed the rules and obtained a license to carry a weapon. Even after he stated this and complied with St. Anthony Police Officer Yanez's instructions, the officer still killed him. Stereotypes, fear, and ignorance pulled the trigger. Even in his willingness to comply, Mr. Castile was still one of the *Ites*.

Tamir Rice, a twelve-year-old Black male child (killed November 22, 2014). In Cleveland, Ohio, Tamir was sitting alone in a park playing with a toy gun. He had allegedly pointed the fake gun at people. Interestingly, the individual who called in the report to police stated that the gun/pistol was "probably fake" and the person was probably "a juvenile." Nevertheless, the officers had no verbal exchange with Tamir. Timothy Loehmann and Frank Garmback responded to the call. Loehmann killed Tamir. He was not given a chance to comply or share his story. This child was viewed as a dangerous, violent, Black man that posed a threat and had to be put down. He too was one of the *Ites*.

"The Emmanuel Nine," a group of Black men and women (murdered June 15, 2017). Rev. Clementa C. Pinckney, 41; Cynthia Graham Hurd, 54; Susie Jackson, 87; Ethel Lee Lance, 70; Depayne Middleton-Doctor, 49; Tywanza Sanders, 26; Daniel L. Simmons, 74; Sharonda Coleman-Singleton, 45; and Myra Thompson, 59. The Emmanuel Nine accepted Dylan Roof, an outsider, as a welcomed participant into their weekly Bible Study. They granted him permission to enter their sacred space to sit and commune with them. During the study, Roof stood up and pulled a gun from his fanny pack and said he was going to kill them. As members of the group asked him why he was doing this and tried to discourage his intentions, he stated, "I have to do it. You rape our women and you're taking over our country. And you have to go . . . Y'all want something to pray about? I'll give you something to pray about" (Borden, *et al.* 2015).

Dylann Roof demonized this group. From his rants read in court, Roof claimed:

> "Negroes have lower Iqs [sic], lower impulse control, and higher testosterone levels in general. These three things alone are a recipe for violent behavior" (O'Shea, et al. 2016). He alone sat in their space and determined these nine Black people were not worthy of life and had to be exterminated. Because they were *Ites*.

CONCLUSION

My hope is that those who establish interpretations and share thoughts that guide and assist readers navigating their way through the Bible will continue to develop innovative, probing hermeneutics that enter the text from unique, arduous perspectives. The Bible is not a pristine document that answers all of life's questions or addresses all of its problems. It is a curated, complex, prejudiced, inspiring, and contradictory collection of stories, wise sayings, and approaches to life from ancient cultures. Even with all of this, it remains a vital part of many lives. Scholars, preachers, and teachers should acknowledge the Bible's shortcomings and work to exhaust its strengths. Dora Mbuwayesango recognized the concerns with the book of Joshua, but did not say the Bible should be abandoned. Instead, Mbuwayesango presented challenging questions that must be considered: What can the book of Joshua say to the Canaanites, the dispossessed, and the exterminated? Can the God of the dispossessor be the God of the dispossessed?

Watching students wrestle with the enigmas of the biblical text and how it may skew perspectives of the world is inspiring. To see them begin to alter their views of the text and the world in which they live make teaching worthwhile. Yet, there is still much more to work to do.

History has documented the brutality and murder of innocent Black people in America for centuries. Lynchings, the flooding of Black-only towns, or our slaughter just for sport, still remain a part of American society. The dropping of bombs from planes on Black American citizens who created an affluent community in Tulsa, Oklahoma, is an event that remains unknown to many. Ironically, the Emmanuel Nine were practicing tenets of their faith and studying the Bible when they were slaughtered by an outsider whom they permitted in their space. Nevertheless, in most of these instances, the victims were villainized, dehumanized, and attempts have been made to justify their deaths—much like the Canaanites and others. Thus, although we know the outcome of the Israelite invasion, have you decided which team you're on?

NOTES

1. Many sources discuss the curse. However, Charles Copher presents a comprehensive explanation in his chapter, "The Black Presence in the Old Testament" in *Stony the Road We Trod: African American Biblical Interpretation* (1991, 146–53; also see Goldberg 2003).

2. Canaanites, Hittites, Hivites, Perizzites, Girgashites, Amorites, Jebusites, and Amalekites. See Jos 3:10, Num 13:29.

3. The books of Joshua and Judges are filled with unusual women. Rahab, the first bona fide biblical harlot, is also something of a hero (Bellis 207, 98).

4. In the Rahab story, the spies underscore the terms of the oath by qualifying that if any one of Rahab's kin were to go out into the street, that "his blood would be on his (own) head," Jos 2:19 (Scott 2016, 9). All Bible quotations are from the *NRSV*, unless otherwise stated.

WORKS CITED

Avalos, Hector. 2007. *The End of Biblical Studies*. Buffalo: Prometheus.

Bailey, Randall. 2004. "What Ever Happened to the Good Old White Boys?" Review of *Global Bible Commentary*, ed. Daniel Patte. Nashville: Abingdon.

Bellis, Alice O. 2007. *Helpmates, Harlots, and Heroes: Women's Stories in the Hebrew Bible*. Louisville: Westminster.

Binger, T. 2001. *Asherah: Goddesses in Ugarit, Israel and the Old Testament*. New York: Bloomsbury.

Borden, Jeremy, Sari Horwitz, and Jerry Markon. 2015. "Officials: Suspect in Church Slayings Unrepentant Amid Outcry over Racial Hatred." *The Washington Post*. June 19, 2015.

Buck, Mary Ellen. 2019. *The Canaanites: Their History and Culture from Texts and Artifacts*. Eugene, OR: Cascade.

Copher, Charles B. 1991. "The Black Presence in the Old Testament." *Stony the Road We Trod: African American Biblical Interpretation*, edited by Cain H. Felder, 146–64. Minneapolis: Fortress.

Dever, William G., T. L. Thompson, G. W. Ahlstrom, and Phillip Davies. 1995a. "Will the Real Israel Please Stand Up? Archaeology and Israelite Historiography: Part I." *Bulletin of American Schools of Oriental Research* 297 (Feb.): 61–80.

———. 1995b. "Will the Real Israel Please Stand Up? Archaeology and Israelite Historiography: Part II." *Bulletin of the American Schools of Oriental Research* 298 (May): 37–58.

Dube, Musa W. 2000. *Postcolonial Feminist Interpretation of the Bible*. St. Louis: Chalice.

Evans, Mary J. 2005. "Women." *Dictionary of the Old Testament: Historical Books*, ed. Bill T. Arnold and H. G. M. Williamson, 989–99. Downers Grove: InterVarsity.

Goldenberg, David M. 2003. *The Curse of Ham: Race and Slavery in Early Judaism, Christianity, and Islam*. Princeton, NJ: Princeton University Press.

Killibrew, Ann. 2015. *Biblical Peoples and Ethnicity*. Atlanta Society of Biblical Literature.

Kim, Uriah. 2004. *Pros and Cons of Contextual Biblical Interpretation: Critical Reviews of Global Bible Commentary: Methodological and Pedagogical Issues*. Nashville: Abingdon. https://www.vanderbilt.edu/AnS/religious_studies/GBC/proscons.htm.

Lemche, Niels Peter. 1999. *The Canaanites and their Land*. JSOTSup 110. Sheffield: Sheffield Academic Press.

Lyons, William. 2008. "Rahab through the Ages: A Study of Christian Interpretation of Rahab." *SBL Forum*, n.p. https://www.sbl-site.org/publications/article.aspx?ArticleId=786.

Media Education Foundation. 2010. https://www.mediaed.org/transcripts/Not-Just-a-Game-Transcript.pdf.

O'Shea, Keith, Darran Simon and Holly Yan. 2016. "Dylan Roof's Racist Rants Read in Court." CNN, December 14. https://www.cnn.com/2016/12/13/us/dylann-roof-murder-trial/index.html.

Patte, Robert, editor. 2004. Pros and Cons of Contextual Biblical Interpretation: Critical Reviews of Global *Review of Global Bible Commentary. Methodological and Pedagogical Issues*. Nashville: Abingdon. https://www.vanderbilt.edu/AnS/religious_studies/GBC/proscons.htm.

Rothwell, Robert. 2019. "The Gospel and Invasion of Canaan." https://tabletalkmagazine.com/posts/the-gospel-and-the-invasion-of-canaan/

Scott, B. Nogel. 2016. "Scarlet and Harlots: Seeing Red in the Hebrew Bible." *Hebrew Union College Annual*, vol. 87: 1–47.

Smith, Mark. 2001. *The Origins of Biblical Monotheism: Israel's Polytheistic Background and Ugaritic Texts*. Oxford and New York: Oxford University Press.

Stein, Matt. 2011. https://bleacherreport.com/articles/780120-the-38-best-quotes-in-football-movie-history.

Stewart, Don. "Why Did God Order the Destruction of the Canaanites?" https://www.blueletterbible.org/faq/don_stewart/don_stewart_1382.cfm.

Chapter 12

Reading Romans in Greek

Translating and Commenting on it in Haitian Creole

Ronald Charles

Traduttore, traditore. Translators are traitors. Translators are writers and interpreters. They are enmeshed in complex relationships by way of various ideologies, cultures, and interests (patrons, publishers, and social and political contexts). In their rewritings, translators show that texts are malleable; not only can they occupy new spaces, they can also convey new meanings. Translation, argues the postcolonial thinker Robert J. C. Young, is "a kind of metaphorical displacement of a text from one language to another" (2003, 139). Translation is linguistic negotiation as well as political and cultural mediation. Postcolonial translation theory recognizes that theoretical approaches to the problem of translation emerge from charged historical, theological, ideological, and political conditions. Translation, as Spivak understands it rightly, is an act of understanding the other as well as the self. For her, translation has a profound political dimension and translators should use strategies to build connection between the original or the source text and the translation (its shadow) (Spivak 2000, 397–416).

Reading is also interpreting or translating. It is a process by which one makes sense of what one reads and engages with one's own interpretative context(s). In this chapter, I reflect on what it means for me to read Romans in Greek and to translate and interpret it in Haitian Creole. Reading the Bible in Greek is to me, a Haitian-born scholar, a strange and beautiful experience. Writing about that experience in English is also an interesting enterprise. All of the aforementioned languages are foreign territories to me. English is my third language. Ancient Greek is my trade language, which I learned in seminary in my late twenties, in English. My second language (French), which I started to speak when I was about twelve, is a vestige of French colonization of Haiti. Haitian Creole is my first language. It is the language of my birth, the idiom of my heart. It is the language of my parents, my siblings, and everyone I knew while growing up in my impoverished land. French is the language of education in Haiti. I discovered reading, literature, and all I knew of books in French, before I went to study applied linguistics at the State University in Haiti. There I discovered many works in Haitian Creole and many scientific studies on Haitian Creole. Only then did I learn how to write in my native language and understand its linguistic complexities and beauty.

In this chapter, I show that the act of translating and reading is highly charged (politically and theologically) and that the exercise of commenting on the Bible in Haitian Creole is a subversive act. That is to say, the act of placing Haitian Creole in the position to engage in serious linguistic and theological reflections signifies an engagement for decolonization. The process of decolonization also entails that the linguistic training required of students in the field of New Testament studies, my principal area of scholarly enquiry, is woefully inadequate. The European logic of valuing certain languages for scholarship while other languages (non-European, but extremely useful, essential even, in specific contexts) are neglected or frowned upon is part of a colonial legacy that must be challenged.

This piece is written from my perspective as an immigrant/diasporic scholar, for whom questions of language(s) and of translation remain at the core of my work and identity. The impact of English as the dominant linguistic instrument by which so many of us do our scholarly work may hide the difficulty many scholars, who have to compete and excel in English—often their third or fourth language, face regularly. Having to navigate various social, cultural, and linguistic topoi is an aspect rarely reflected on in our scholarly productions.

Black lives matter, therefore languages spoken by Black people matter. Interpreting the Bible in and for Black communities of interpretation matters. It also matters to understand how the Bible is interpreted beyond the sphere of African American interpretation and in languages other than English. The global reach of the #BLM movement certainly points to areas of convergence in the struggles Black communities face, but it also directs attention to specific, local, and complex issues Black communities encounter.

This contribution focuses on the linguistic/social particularities of Haiti. Placing the analysis within this hostile and extremely violent climate (socially and politically) is an attempt to displace the conversation about #BLM away from a Euro-American context and reflect on it in a scape with the potential to help us question our own (linguistic) prejudices. I am grateful to the editors of this volume for inviting me to participate in a project that honors the legacy of *Stony the Road We Trod: African American Biblical Interpretation*, edited by Cain Hope Felder (1991). Clarice Martin, an original contributor to *Stony the Road*, has a significant and truly inspiring essay on the importance of holistic and inclusive translation entitled "Womanist Interpretations of the New Testament: The Quest for Holistic and Inclusive Translation and Interpretation" (1990). For Martin, "The quest for holistic and inclusive translations and interpretations must also include strategies for 'amplifying the whisper' of all persons who by virtue of race, class or other anthropological referents, are assumed to be 'morally bankrupt' or of negligible theological consequence within the narrative structure of biblical traditions" (1990, 56). I am very grateful for her body of work and for all the other contributors of this pioneer volume that we celebrate. We stand indeed on the shoulders of giants.

LANGUAGE AS CENTRAL TO POSTCOLONIAL DEBATES

Language is at the core of who we are (Pinker 1994). Thinking of language from a sociolinguistic point of view reveals how languages are part of, or made manifest within, social hierarchies and social divisions (Trudgill 1995). In the context of Haiti, French remains the perceived language of power and of privilege (Dejean 1993, 73–83). In many Haitian churches, especially in the capital city, Port-au-Prince, French continues to exercise its colonial grip over many. Certain ecclesial ceremonies, particularly weddings, are deemed very prestigious social gatherings where French is seen as the valued and *de rigueur* language in such moments. The songs, the Bible readings, the preaching, the exchange of vows are performed in French, regardless of the level of French comprehension of those in attendance. French plays a performative role as social capital that elevates those getting married to a higher social level than they may actually occupy (Clark 2006, 29–41). French is thus perceived and used for social advantage, to propel the people in the congregation into a higher plane of social meaning. French is also preferred, and often compulsory, for other ecclesial functions such as funerals and Sunday morning preaching in some churches, although that particular usage of the colonized language is not as pronounced as it is at weddings (Govain 2017, 155–77).

It is not that Creole is devalued in the Haitian context. In fact, all Haitians speak Haitian Creole. Haitians bathe naturally within the linguistic sea of their native language. It is the language of every imaginable activity. Haitians, as most native speakers, do not think much about their national language. Most Haitians, as most language speakers, do not have the formal linguistic tools to analyze their language, and they are unaware of the scientific work and intellectual value of their language for the purpose of education and development (DeGraff 2020).

Most Haitians do not speak or read French, yet many cherish the linguistic colonial vestige as important for social advancement. Many preachers or pastors value the use of French in certain "prestigious" ceremonies because they want to convey to a wider audience a sense of upper-class mobility and a sense of not being members of a church composed mostly or solely of poor and unsophisticated folks. The rationale behind this kind of linguistic inferiority complex is that these Haitian Christians want to impress upon others that although they may be Christians (fundamentalist Protestant Christians, who are the majority of Protestant churches in Haiti)—perceived in the Haitian context as composed of generally poor and uneducated people—they can also function in French. Many such Christians see this linguistic posture as a tool for drawing members from a larger and higher-status social pool into the fold. It is, of course, colonized thinking that justifies placing one language on a pedestal in order to imagine that it brings social group prestige and raises one's social status (Fanon 1968, 17–18; Ascroft et al. 1994). Decolonizing the minds and hearts of Haitians, particularly the thought processes and understandings of Haitian Christians, means displacing French and putting it where it belongs. The French language must be relegated to a colonial bin, for it is useless for the growth and independence of Haitians.

LINGUISTIC APARTHEID

Throughout Haiti's history, monolingual Creolophones have remained in marginalized positions economically and politically, whereas French-speaking Haitians, especially those of a tiny segment of the population who have spoken the language since birth and who are mostly of light skin pigmentation, have benefited socially, politically, and economically. This linguistic apartheid, which excludes monolingual Creole speakers in Haiti from social, economic, and political mobility and power, goes against the spirit of Article 5 of the Haitian Constitution that states, "all Haitians are united by a common language: [Haitian] Creole" (Hurbon 1987; Bellegarde-Smith 1990; Fick 1990; Danticat 2001; Farmer 2003; Wargny 2004; Debray 2004; Shamsie and Thompson 2006; Beaulière 2007).

It may appear understandable that members of the disenfranchised groups, which constitute the majority of the Haitian population, feel that they have to invest in the education of their children to acquire linguistic competencies in French. However, French-based (mis)education has perpetuated social inequalities and has held the majority of the Haitian people at a disadvantage both culturally and economically (Dejean 2003; Dejean 2006; Joint 2006). Francophilia, alongside the love of the cultures and languages of Euro(American) peoples, remain a strong draw to many Haitians (Price-Mars 1983). The corollary of such appreciation for what is foreign is the exclusion, misunderstanding, and even hatred of what is truly a product of the Haitian soul, namely, the people's language (Haitian Creole), culture and mores (Vodou, Haitian art, etc.). Here I am referring particularly to the general attitudes of those who have been (mis)educated in the system and not the outlook of poor Haitians, especially the peasants living in the countryside, who couldn't care less about anything beyond their immediate survival. Haitian Creole and Haitian Vodou remain important linguistic and fundamental cultural aspects of Haitian identity (Fils-Aimé 2007; Michel and Bellegarde-Smith 2006; Célucien and Cleophat 2016). This denial of one's culture and language in order to love and embrace what is other and foreign is part and sequel of colonization (Fanon 1968). It serves as a tool for maintaining class divisions and self-interests. It is problematic when a group of people is convinced, via (mis)education and propaganda, to internalize colonized language(s) and social/cultural and ideological values and interests irrelevant or even detrimental to their social, economic, and political advancements. It is also problematic when factions of a population that purport to represent the poor cannot fathom to represent them in ways that are respectful to their languages and mores. Whoever speaks French in Haiti (or English, Spanish and, in rarer cases, German) demonstrates his or her connection to other places and cultures that are perceived to offer more in terms of prestige and economic advancement. In Pierre Bourdieu's (1991) sense of language as social capital and symbolic power, the maintenance of various stereotypes and the cultivation of linguistic difference by the Haitian elites signifies that their economic, social, and symbolic "capital" can flourish at the expense or to the detriment of those who are monolingual Haitian Creole speakers.

To be clear, Haitians who are able to learn other languages should not cease attempting to do so. The problem is with structures (ideological, economic, and political) that are established to maintain the majority of Haitians in miserable conditions and to benefit the members of the tiny elite of Haitian society that have everything, usually those of lighter skin pigmentation, who are able to speak other languages than Haitian Creole. To move from abject poverty and to embark on dismantling the apparatus that works to their demise, Haitians, that is, the majority, must work from and with who and what they are, with their language and culture. The interests of the wealthy elites lie in the maintenance of the status quo. Six oligarch families (Brandt, Acra, Madsen, Bigio, Apaid, and Mevs), who migrated to Haiti mostly at the end of the nineteenth century and the beginning of the twentieth century, control Haiti's economic sector and, inter alia, Haiti's political life. Suzy Castor identified how Haiti's distinct political and financial elite share antidemocratic sentiments and how they work to maintain their position of power and privileges. For her, these elites are comprised of "factions of monopolistic bourgeoisie, businessmen who deal in smuggled goods, the landed and business oligarchy, drug dealers, mid-level executives, the military hierarchy, and officials of the Catholic and Protestant churches" (Castor 1992, 126–37). The truly revolutionary move is to expose them for who they truly are, namely, the purveyors and enablers of the misery of most Haitians, alongside the US government and commercial efforts that benefit those repugnant elite (Wilentz 2013).

THE POLITICS OF TRANSLATION

Before discussing some of the relevant issues concerning the politics of translation as related to Haitian Creole, I want to offer a brief history of the Bible in the Creole language, highlighting some key dates:

1. 1927: Publication of the first complete translation of a single book from the Bible in Haitian Creole: the Gospel of John (*Evangile à notre Seigneur Jesus Christ selon Saint Jean,* by Elie Marc).
2. 1944: Translation of the Gospel of Luke into Creole.
3. 1951: A complete translation in Creole of the New Testament and the Psalms.
4. 1966: Publication of *4 Ti liv evanjil yo* by Yves Dejean and Paul Dejean.
5. 1985: First publication or translation of the Complete Bible in Haitian Creole: *Bib la, paròl Bondié an Ayisyen.*
6. 2000: Publication of *Bib la*, a revised version of the 1985 translation.

In a previous work, I explored the politics of translation and linguistic prejudices that have influenced and marred the works of translators in translating the Bible in Haitian Creole (Charles 2015). I articulated a threefold objective in the book: (1) to identify the factors that have influenced Haitian translators; (2) to identify the theories and philosophy of translation that have influenced different versions of the Bible in Haitian Creole; and (3) to initiate a study which could serve as a critical reflection for future translations of the Bible in Haitian Creole.

Without my intimate familiarity with both the language of my homeland and the biblical languages, I would not have been able to conduct such research. The translation of the Bible will always be a work in progress. There is always room for improvement to achieve the ideal of intimate familiarity of any serious translator who wants to communicate the message of the original language to their audience in a way that is clear and faithful to the text in its contexts. It should be noted, however, that the translator/commentator might also have to leave an ambiguous passage in its ambiguity in the targeted language and not try to make everything crystal clear (Margot 1979, 57–163). By analyzing several Bible translations in Haitian Creole, I realized that some linguistic myths, habits, and prejudices have influenced the Haitian translators in their choice of words, sentences, and syntactic structures. I analyzed the myth of the so-called enrichment of the language and the myth of purported theological words.

The myth of the enrichment of language comes from the vestiges of colonization that Haitian Creole is an inferior and poor language that we must enrich. The myth of theological words, which allegedly need to be kept and conveyed in Haitian Creole, derives from the argument that for the sake of fidelity to certain Christian doctrines and providing readers a primer for Bible study, translations needed to be as close as possible to the original text. Terms such as justification, sanctification, and atonement are perceived as being part of universal theological discourse and that every translation should keep these words, whether or not they make sense in the targeted language. But what is a word if not a shortcut or a sign? Ferdinand de Saussure (1916) argued long ago about the arbitrariness of the linguistic sign. Each area of knowledge has its specialized jargon, but words are not magic. Why should one keep a word or phrase in French, or a word that sounds French, when one can express the same theological concept in terms that are equivalent and perfectly acceptable and understandable in Haitian Creole? The translators of the Bible into Haitian Creole should seriously consider the issue of accessibility of the text to the vast majority of Haitian Creole language speakers. For the common good, it is necessary to strive to liberate the people's language from the supremacy of the dominant language of the colonizer.

My hope in writing this book was to foster a theological vision that would contribute to an "authentically Christian church," which should eliminate the barbarian/civilized binary and, correspondingly, address the Haitian Christians in the language of all (Haitian Creole) in a clear medium accessible to all (Casséus 1987; Hurbon 1987). In this pivotal matter of Bible translation, I brought into conversation theology, indigenous ecclesiology, and a contextualized Christian identity. The Haitian church has suffered from colonialism, imperialism, classism, and demagogy. There have been a few voices of reason rising from various ecclesial denominations, but the general picture is disastrous. It seems to me that the situation today has never been so dire, with so many charlatans exploiting others. We need serious thinkers with a deep love for our people—not those looking to elevate themselves, but humble servants willing to be in struggle with everyone, learn from everyone, and share with everyone. This seems a dream that is very far from the current social and political reality in Haiti. We need an indigenous church, equipped with its own theological language embedded in the local context. What I mean by an authentically Haitian church is one that takes the time to reflect on what it means for communities of scriptural interpretation in Haiti to serve God within the context of poverty, cholera, Covid-19, exploitation, prostitution, political instability, unemployment, violence, traumas, ecological disaster, and other challenges. My study of the ancient world has confirmed a hunch I had early on in my studies that the variegated elements of life are linked and that one cannot pretend to preach the blessings of heaven by ignoring the "wretched of the earth" (to use the English title of Fanon's famous book) in their mess. Life is messy, and our scholarly work, as well as the work of those engaged in scriptural thinking and interpretation, must embrace or wrestle with this messiness.

TRANSLATING AND COMMENTING ON THE BIBLE IN HAITIAN CREOLE AS A SUBVERSIVE ACT

Commenting on the Bible in Haitian Creole, or in any language, means using the best tools of scholarship to grapple with the complexities of the text in its ancient contexts and its significance for our own contexts. Commenting on the Bible in a subversive way means probing its meanings for deconstruction. Deconstruction here implies unraveling the Bible's many tangled threads. The biblical text cannot be said to be simply a tool for liberation or for subjugation. It contains messages relevant to both projects. Thus, when commenting on a biblical text like Paul's letter to the Romans in Haitian Creole, which has been used in Haiti to subjugate various groups—or example, LGBTQ+ persons (1:26–27)—and to support the political status quo (ch. 13), the task of the subversive translator and commentator becomes even more arduous. I must add at this point that there is no tradition of biblical commentary in Haitian Creole. There are no existing commentaries on any book of the Bible in the Haitian vernacular. Hence, what I am attempting is a first. While engaging in this project, I remain clearly aware of some of the pitfalls related to the commentary as an intellectual project. The commentary as a genre limits the reader, especially the reader from/in the margins, from addressing some of the serious and broader matters that are problematic in and outside the text. The complexity of history, of broader contextual situations, both in and around the text(s) and related to communities of readers of texts, make the project of translation and the ensuing commentary a project that is still very limited, despite one's genuine efforts to include Others—in this case, my homeland, my language, and my culture.

Translation is important, but it is not easy. One may know both the source and target languages extremely well and still have serious difficulties in translating some terms, expressions, or nuances of a given language. That does not mean it is impossible to translate; it simply means that it can be extremely difficult to do so at times. No translation is "pure" or literal. In the process of translation/interpretation, two languages, two cultures (at least) come into contact through an interpreter and the result is necessarily hybridized, despite the new linguistic symbols. I started working on my Romans commentary by first translating the text anew for myself. I translated it into English (by default, since this is how I learned how to translate Greek), then into Haitian Creole, before embarking on the process of commenting on each verse in Haitian Creole. I continue that process until I reach chapter 8 of Romans, when I will send my commentary to some Haitian pastors I know and ask them to comment on my commentary. In this seminal project, I am both engaged in the production of a commentary on a book of the Bible in Haitian Creole, and simultaneously correcting available translations done in Haitian Creole.

Most Bible commentators or exegetes agree that Paul's letter to the Romans is a masterpiece, and a text that is difficult to fully understand. The letter is written to a community of Christ's believers that Paul did not found and to a city he has never visited (1:10–15). The introduction to Romans tells us a great deal about the missionary character of the letter and its whole purpose. Paul pictures himself as an eschatological person, who has been appointed to a proper place and for a particular task in the series of events to be accomplished in the final days of this world. Paul wanted to explain his gospel to this community and to receive financial assistance from them for the mission to Spain he was about to undertake (15:23–24).

In writing my commentary in Haitian Creole, I gave small hints to the context of the text. My audience consists mostly of Haitian pastors ministering in Haiti. I conducted small sessions on Bible translation for a group of Haitian pastors via Zoom. These pastors are well educated in French, and some in English. A few have master's degrees in various disciplines. I introduced the seminar by pointing out some of the difficulties of doing Bible translation. I gave them a few verses to translate from French or English to Haitian Creole. It was all fun, and they agreed on the difficulty of the task. I wanted them to see the porousness of the texts and the decisions Bible translators or commentators/exegetes must make in their work. Everything was going extremely well until I raised the question of contexts. I stated that any text taken out of its specific context might serve as a pretext to almost everything. The biblical text, as any other text, is a text to be interpreted in its own contexts (literary, political, sociological, religious, and/or theological), in conjunction with our own modern contexts. Many of the pastors in my seminar felt uneasy about placing the Bible within its various ancient contexts and studying it as a text one may deconstruct. Others questioned the various liberatory approaches of reading the Bible as well. To them, the Bible is a spiritual and atemporal text that gives life to anyone or everyone, regardless of one's social location, gender, racial background, ethnicities, or politics. To these ecclesial leaders, the task of translators and biblical interpreters is to draw the spiritual meaning of the scriptures and to explain it to the people for their spiritual growth. For pastors and Christians who regard the text as a sacred document whose content should not be questioned because it gives life in the midst of despair, translating and commenting is a serious challenge.

I do this work for them, and it is not intended to be in anyway disrespectful or sacrilegious. Yet, it is important to direct readers to the text in its contexts and to draw attention to the multivocality of the biblical record and the multiplicity of ways the text can be approached. Furthermore, although it is important to remain humble in how one approaches the task of translating and commenting on the biblical text, it is also imperative that one does so with the necessary critical distance and scholarly care that the task mandates. Few pastors in Haiti have developed any critical distance to the biblical text that they cherish. This may be because of the largely evangelical and fundamentalist theological training centers present in the country, which are in the majority sponsored by such groups located usually in the United States. Contextualizing the biblical text and questioning some evangelical and fundamentalist theological conclusions would mean losing much needed financial support for the existing seminaries. In general, there is a lack of sociological knowledge and analysis on the part of many Haitian pastors about the country's own history, language, and religion such as Vodou. The world in the imaginary of many Haitian pastors is a Manichean place, where the battle between good and evil, God and Satan, is raging. The sons of light (the Christians, especially the evangelical/Protestant ones) are engaging in spiritual and apocalyptic combat against the sons of darkness (the Catholics, the lost adepts of the Vodou religion, and all others) in order to go to heaven and escape the dread of hell (Charles 2011, 177–98).

In my commentary, I must address many specific and difficult questions. I will illustrate with three examples. For instance, here is how I comment on Romans 1:25–26:

> For Paul, the result of the sexual confusion he sees is related to all sorts of problems in the way people behave. It starts with sexual desires. For him and for many Jews of his day there are behaviors that are natural or normal, whereas there are other behaviors that are not natural and thus considered abnormal. One of the behaviors he sees as unnatural or abnormal is the same sex desire women have for women, or men have for other men. To him, these relationships are improper relationships and those in these relationships receive the punishment they deserve in their bodies for their mistakes. It is not clear what punishment

they receive in their bodies. Many people in Paul's day (Greeks and Romans) were in such a situation without seeing any problems in their relationship or without having anything happening to them.

My comments are brief and respectful of the context of the text. The reader will have to decide how to understand and wrestle with this text in the contemporary and specific sociological context of Haiti.

Another example of the challenges faced by an exegete is in determining how one should understand Paul's interlocutor in Romans 2:17–29. The question is one that remains a difficult interpretative issue for many interpreters. I have sided with the overall proposal made by Runar M. Thorsteinsson (2015) in his published doctoral dissertation (see Rodríguez and Thiessen 2016). The bulk of Thorsteinsson's argument in that monograph is that Paul's interlocutor in Romans 2 is a gentile who has been Judaized or is in the process of being Judaized. This line of reasoning cuts through any attempt at supersessionist or anti-Jewish conclusions based on these verses in Romans. This particular interpretation also allows an interpreter to (re)consider Paul's engagement with Judaism, the law of Moses, circumcision, and other aspects of Paul's ancestral tradition, which an anti-Jewish reading certainly precludes. My comments on Romans 2:17 read thus: "In verse 17 Paul is not addressing a Jewish person or a stereotypical Jew who exists everywhere at all times. Rather, he is engaging in conversation with a person who claims to be a Jew (who calls himself a Jew). Paul is talking to this person. This person is showing off how good he is because he has kept God's law." I try to sidestep two mistakes here. One, I avoid positioning a caricatured picture of a Jew as a rigidly stereotypical figure, a usual representation in the imagery of many Haitians (McAlister 2004, 61–81). Two, I indicate that Paul is engaging in a conversation, not with us today, but with a figure in his time, to make a specific argument. Thus, what I attempt in my work as a translator and commentator to my fellow Haitians is to make the best work of scholarship available to them, without necessarily mentioning the scholarly materials or sources informing my thoughts (Dunn 1988; Fitzmyer 1993; Schreiner 1998; Jewett 2006). I am also careful not to impose some of the scholarly concerns, agenda, and knowledge that have been produced in the West into the people in Haiti. I do my work as a cultural translator who is engaged in making connections between traditions, scholarship, and history. I try my best to always honor the lofty aspirations for peace, justice, love, and dignity of my Haitian sisters and brothers. My honest and moral wish is to bring the skills I have to empower my own community.

The last example is an illustration of how to render the theologically loaded term, "justification by faith"/"*justification par la foi*" in Haitian Creole. Already in the usual translations in modern European languages, the Greek term δικαιοσύνη (justification or righteousness) is problematic. Here is not the place to enter into this linguistic and theological debate. Most Haitian preachers will simply translate, "*justifikasyon pa la fwa*," basically a Creole phonological reading of the French phrase—which perpetuates the myth of the "untranslatability" of certain theological jargon prevalent within certain elite (evangelical) circles. My interest, however, is to do decolonizing work by speaking the language of the common folks, people who haven't learned French in school. The point is, how should a translator render this and related expressions in a way that makes sense in Haitian Creole and remains theologically sound?

The Greek text of Romans 3:24 reads, δικαιούμενοι δωρεὰν τῇ αὐτοῦ χάριτι διὰ τῆς ἀπολυτρώσεως τῆς ἐν Χριστῷ Ἰησοῦ. The participle δικαιούμενοι is passive, but Haitians don't use the passive voice much in Creole, and translating with the passive doesn't make much sense here. I propose to translate the verse by supplying the subject (God, "Bondye"), and translating in the active voice: "*Nan gras li, [Bondye] fè yo favè poutèt delivrans ki nan Jezikri.*" In English, "In his grace/by means of his grace, [God] favored them freely through the deliverance which is in Christ Jesus." Using *fe . . . favè* instead of *jistifiye* speaks more directly to Creole speakers who do not know French, and connects with the importance of honor and shame in Haitian culture. I also avoid the term *gratis,* used in the most common Creole translation, which bears a colonial undertone. In these ways, I seek to offer a clearer and more accessible translation to fellow Haitians who have never studied French; this is, then, a practical exercise in decolonizing the biblical language.

It is important we take the time to study the ancient languages alongside the modern and indigenous ones and, in humility and rigor, try our best in our works of translation and scholarship to be at the service of our own communities. It is also necessary to understand the important place of Haitian Creole (a specific language or languages) in Haitian self-definition and culture (in a particular cultural setting and identity).

LINGUISTIC DECOLONIZATION

Language competency is part of graduate studies in New Testament. One is usually required to study two or three ancient languages (Greek, biblical Hebrew and Latin, or Greek and Latin, or Greek and Coptic), and two modern languages (German and French). Developing linguistic expertise in these languages is important for serious and innovative scholarship in the field, although, admittedly, a lot of serious and innovative scholarship is or can also be done without engaging these languages. To master any of the aforementioned languages necessitates years of ongoing study and use or practice. It is important that minoritized faculty members engage in teaching these languages as well.

There are, however, other languages that should be studied but are usually not even mentioned in the training of graduate students The New Testament is taught primarily through the worldview of Greco-Roman people, places, and literature—with the Roman Empire being the primary or central frame of reference. In this regard, it is difficult to grasp other contexts and pockets of earliest Christianities in antiquity due to the lack of access to source material, and due to the lack of critical theoretical frameworks for raising questions about the polycentric nature of the earliest Christ groups. At around the same time when Christianity was becoming the official religion of the Roman Empire (Theodosius I declared Christianity the official religion of the Roman Empire in 380 CE), Christ groups were thriving in the ancient Aksumite kingdom (based in modern-day Ethiopia), especially with the conversion of Ezana, the son of Emperor Ella Amida, in Aksum. Ezana lived and converted to the Christian faith in the mid-fourth century CE. The earliest formal attestation of Classical Ethiopic, or Gəʻəz, appears in inscriptions related to him. Without Ethiopic sources, there is no sustainable way to engage the Axumite Empire and the questions that emerge when we consider other trajectories of Christianity south of the Roman Empire and into Nile Valley region of Africa. Granted, Coptic sources give us a glimpse of a different worldview of Christianity in Egypt, but these are not the same as Ethiopic or Gəʻəz sources, though they are often mistaken for the latter. By bringing these extracanonical sources in conversation with canonical sources, students and scholars may have access to different ways of conceiving of the spread of Christianity, not just around the Mediterranean Sea, but also along the Red Sea (Byron 2009, 161–90; Byron, 2010, 135–41).

Furthermore, especially for the graduate student from non-Euro/American centers of power, I would argue that beyond the linguistic requirements of the trade, alongside the inclusion of other important ancient languages for the study of earliest Christ groups, it is equally vital to know one's indigenous vernacular language(s), where possible, in profound and technical ways in order to question and decolonize one's own Euro/American training. That means understanding how one's language has been devalued and bastardized, and actively engaging in (re)appropriating the language of one's heart to do the necessary work of debunking theologies and ideologies that have no value for one's immediate context(s) of work. The suggestion here is to use other languages, indigenous languages, alongside the Western languages to do scholarship. It is a call to be involved in translation works, to provincialize the taken-for-granted European scholarship and show its limited scope (Dube 2018, 168–82; Dube 1999, 33–58; Dube and Wafula 2017; Yorke and Renju 2004).

Dube (2018) considers the importance of Bible translation in exploring ideologies and identities. Dube tells the story of the translated Setswana Bible, first translated between 1840 and 1857 by Robert Moffat, and how the first readers responded to that translation. She shows that the mindset behind this translation was entirely colonialist and ignorant of local culture. The people of Botswana (Batswana) read the Setswana Bible strategically and subversively and were able to decolonize the English Setswana version. Dube bemoans the lack of training in translation for biblical or religious studies scholars: "I still cannot explain why academic departments of the Bible and religion do not have full-fledged programmes on translation" (2018, 181). She argues that many students from the Two-Thirds World would benefit from such training and would advance scholarship and decolonial resistance within their own communities. There is a crucial need to reevaluate graduate training, especially in the context of decolonizing the academy. It is important to decolonize biblical studies and show its racist pitfalls. The texts that have been influential to my questioning of biblical studies as a discipline, which is still participating in a kind of colonizing enterprise, are Segovia 2004; Fiorenza 2009; Kelley 2002; and certainly Felder, *Stony the Road We Trod*, 1991.

CONCLUSION

Translation matters. Language matters. The languages of peoples and groups that inhabit impoverished corners of the world also matter. In a project that is interested in biblical interpretation in the context of Black Lives Matter, a focus on non-Western languages, such as Haitian Creole, is also urgent. Haitian Creole matters because Haitians matter. We matter for our ancestors, for ourselves, and for our children. As a Black Haitian-Canadian, my Blackness interrupts the Euro/American scenes and spaces, while simultaneously setting the stage for different representations of being a scholar and of scholarship. As someone interested in border crossing, in diasporic lives, histories, identities, and in the plurivocality of "Blackness" (social differences, class, ethnic origins and stories, linguistic varieties, gender, sexuality, intersectionality), my dreams are channelled through my scholarly work and my social activism.

It is a long and arduous journey to read Romans in Greek and to translate it in English, the language of Empire and the main linguistic instrument of today's (neo)colonization, while struggling to dust off the debris of another colonizing linguistic element (French), before finally translating it and commenting on it in my Haitian Creole language. My hope as a Haitian-Canadian biblical scholar, writing in my third language, is that I will continue to imagine a different world with new possibilities. As we endeavor to engage in robust scholarship, we may envision a world without any linguistic supremacy, without the violence of white supremacy, and a world where we can continue to struggle for expanding care within and outside of our narrow visions of communities.

In conclusion, I would like to offer the following points, which summarize my arguments in this contribution:

- Linguistic competencies in the languages of the trade are important;
- Linguistic analysis of other languages and of neglected languages (both ancient and modern) is also important;
- Grand Euro/American narratives and linguistic prejudices must be decentered and dismantled;
- Learning and becoming a scholar of the ancient world for minoritized scholars means learning in struggle, learning to struggle, and learning for struggle in our contemporary world.

WORKS CITED

Aimé, Jean-Fils. 2007. Vodou, je me souviens. Montréal: Éditions Dabar.

Ascroft, Bill et al. 1994. *The Empire Writes Back: Theory and Practice in Post-Colonial Literatures*. London and New York: Routledge.

Beaulière, Arnousse. 2007. "Haïti dans l'impasse économique et sociale: Une analyse en terme de gouvernabilité," edited by Louis Pierre, L. Naud. *Haiti: Les recherches en sciences sociales et les mutations sociopolitiques et économiques* Paris: L' Harmattan.

Bellegarde-Smith, Patrick. 1990. *Haiti: The Breached Citadel*. Boulder: Westview.

Bourdieu, Pierre. 1991. *Language and Symbolic Power*. Cambridge, MA: Harvard University Press.

Byron, Gay L. 2009. "Ancient Ethiopia and the New Testament: Ethnic (Con) texts and Racialized (Sub)texts." *They Were all Together in one Place? Toward Minority Biblical Criticism*, edited by Randall C. Bailey, Tat-siong Benny Liew, and Fernando F. Segovia 161–90. Atlanta: Society of Biblical Literature. Semeia Studies.

———. 2010. "Redrawing the Boundaries of Early Christianity: The Case of the Axumite Empire and Its Sources." *A New Day: Essays on World Christianity in Honor of Lamin Sanneh*, edited by Akintunde E. Akinade, 135–41. New York: Peter Lang.

Casséus, Jules. 1987. Pour une Église Authentiquement Haïtienne: *essai d'introduction à une théologie chrétienne haïtienne*. Limbé, Cap Haitien: Séminaire théologique baptiste d'Haïti.

Castor, Suzy. 1992. "Democracy and Society in Haiti: Structures of Domination and Resistance to Change." *Social Justice* 19: 126–37.
Célucien, L. Joseph, and Nixon S. Cleophat, editors. 2016. *Vodou in Haitian Memory: The Idea and Representation of Vodou in Haitian Imagination*. Lanham, MD: Lexington Books.
———. 2016. *Vodou in the Haitian Experience: A Black Atlantic Perspective*. Lanham, MD: Lexington Books.
Charles, Ronald. 2011. "Interpreting the Book of Revelation in the Haitian Context." *Black Theology: An International Journal* 9, vol. 2: 177–98.
———. 2015. *Traductions Bibliques Créoles et Préjugés Linguistiques*. Paris: L'Harmattan.
Clark, Tom. 2006. "Language as Social Capital." *Applied Semiotics* 8, vol. 18: 29–41.
Claudine Michel, and Patrick Bellegarde-Smith, eds. 2006. *Vodou in Haitian Life and Culture: Invisible Powers*. New York: Palgrave MacMillan.
Danticat, Edwidge, ed. 2001. *The Butterfly's Way: Voices from the Haitian Diaspora in the United States*. New York: Soho.
de Saussure, Ferdinand. 1916. *Cours de linguistique générale*, edited by Charles Bally & Alert Sechehaye, with the assistance of Albert Riedlinger. Lausanne—Paris: Payot.
Debray, Régis. 2004. *Haïti et la France: rapport à Dominique de Villepin*. Paris: Table ronde.
DeGraff, Michel. 2020. "Black Lives Will Not Matter until Our Languages Also Matter: The Politics of Linguistics and Education in Post-Colonies." ABRALIN—Associação Brasileira de Linguística, June 14, 2020; "The Politics of Education in Post-Colonies: Kreyòl in Haiti as a Case Study of Language as Technology for Power and Liberation." *Journal of Postcolonial Linguistics*, 3.
Dejean, Yves. 1993. "An Overview of the Language Situation in Haiti." *International Journal of the Sociology of Language* 102: 73–83.
———. 2003. "Créole, école, rationalité." *Chemins Critiques* 18. http://www.tanbou.com/2002/fall/CreoleEcoleRationalite.htm).
———. 2006. *Yon lekòl tèt anba nan yon peyi tèt anba*. Port-au-Prince, Deschamps.
Dube, Musa W. 1999. "Consuming a Colonial Cultural Bomb: Translating Badimo Into 'Demons' in the Setswana Bible (Matthew 8.28–34; 15.22; 10.8)." *JSNT* 21, vol. 73: 33–58.
Dube, Musa W., and R. S. Wafula, eds. 2017. *Postcoloniality, Translation and the Bible in Africa*. Eugene, OR: Pickwick.
———. 2018. "The Bible in the Bush: The First 'Literate' Batswana Bible Readers," in *Ethnicity, Race, Religion: Identities and Ideologies in Early Jewish and Christian Texts, and in Modern Biblical Interpretation*, edited by Katherine M. Hockey and David G. Horrell, 168–82. London/New York: T&T Clark.
Dunn, James D. G. 1988. *Romans 1-8*. Waco, TX: Word Books.
Fanon, Frantz. 1968. *Black Skin, White Masks*. New York: Grove.
Farmer, Paul. 2003. *The Uses of Haiti*. Monroe, ME: Common Courage.
Felder, Cain Hope, ed. 1991. *Stony the Road We Trod: African American Biblical Interpretation*. Minneapolis: Fortress.

Fick, Carolyn E. 1990. *The Making of Haiti: The Saint Domingue Revolution from Below*. Knoxville: University of Tennessee Press.
Fiorenza, Elisabeth S. 2009. *Democratizing Biblical Studies: Toward an Emancipatory Educational Space*. Louisville: Westminster John Knox.
Fitzmyer, Joseph A., SJ. 1993. *Romans. Anchor Bible Commentary*: New Haven, CT: Yale University Press.
Govain, Renauld. 2017. "Le symbolisme de la langue dans le protestantisme haïtien. Des pratiques linguistiques naturelles à la glossolalie" in Vijonet Demero/Samuel Regulus (dir.), *Deux siècles de protestantisme en Haïti (1816–2016). Implantation, conversion et sécularisation*. Québec, Éditions science et bien commun: 155–77.
Hurbon, Laënnec. 1987. *Le Barbare imaginaire*. Port-au-Prince, Haïti: Henri Deschamps.
———. 1987. *Comprendre Haïti: Essaie sur l'Etat, la nation, la culture*. Paris: Karthala.
Joint, Louis Auguste. 2006. *Système éducatif et inégalités sociales en Haïti: le cas des écoles catholiques*. L'Harmattan, Paris.
Jewett, Robert. 2006. *Romans. Hermeneia*: Minneapolis: Fortress.
Kelley, Shawn. 2002. *Racializing Jesus: Race, Ideology and the Formation of Modern Biblical Scholarship*. London: Routledge.
Margot, Jean-Claude. 1979. *Traduire sans trahir: La théorie de la traduction et son application aux textes bibliques*. Lausanne/Suisse: L'Age D'Homme.
Martin, Clarice. 1990. "Womanist Interpretations of the New Testament: The Quest for Holistic and Inclusive Translation and Interpretation." *Journal of Feminist Studies in Religion* 6, vol. 2: 41–61.
McAlister, Elizabeth A. 2004. "The Jew in the Haitian Imagination: A Popular History of Anti-Judaism and Proto-Racism." Race, Nation, and Religion in the Americas, edited by Henry Goldschmidt and Elizabeth McAlister. Oxford: Oxford University Press: 61–81.
Pinker, Steven. 1994. *The Language Instinct: How the Mind Creates Language*. New York: William Morrow.
Price-Mars, Jean. 1983. *So Spoke the Uncle (Ainsi Parla L'oncle)*. Translation and introduction by Magdaline W. Shannon. Washington, DC: Three Continents.
Rodríguez, Rafael, and Matthew Thiessen, eds. 2016. *The So-Called Jew in Paul's Letter to the Romans*. Minneapolis: Fortress.
Segovia, Fernando F. 2004. *Decolonizing Biblical Studies: A View from the Margins*. Maryknoll, New York: Orbis.
Schreiner, Thomas R. 1998. *Romans*. Grand Rapids, MI: Baker.
Shamsie, Yasmine, and Andrew S. Thompson, eds. 2006. *Haiti: Hope for a Fragile State*. Waterloo: Wilfrid Laurier University Press.
Spivak, Gayatri Chakravorty. 2000. "The Politics of Translation." *The Translation Studies Reader*, edited by Lawrence Venuti: 397–416. London and New York: Routledge.
Thorsteinsson, Runar M. 2015. *Paul's Interlocutor in Romans 2*. Stockholm: Almqvist & Wiksell, 2003; repr., Eugene, OR: Wipf & Stock.

Trudgill, Peter. 1995. *Sociolinguistics: An Introduction to Language and Society*. London: Penguin.
Wargny, Christophe. 2004. *Haïti n'existe pas!—1804–2004: deux cents ans de solitude*. Paris: Autrement.
Wilentz, Amy. 2013. "Letter from Haiti: Life in the Ruins." https://www.thenation.com/article/archive/letter-haiti-life-ruins/.
Yorke, Gosnell, and Peter Renju, eds. 2004. *Bible Translation & African Languages*. Nairobi: Acton & UBS.
Young, Robert J. C. 2003. *Postcolonialism: A Very Short Introduction*. Oxford: Oxford University Press.

PART IV

Black Rage and Protest in Times of #BlackLivesMatter and #MeToo

Chapter 13

Rage, Riots, and Rhetoric

Psalm 137 and African American Responses to Violence

Stacy Davis

On May 25, 2020, George Floyd died. He spent his last conscious moments pinned under the knee of a police officer. His death sparked national and international protests demanding police reform and substantive action to combat systemic racism. In Minneapolis, where Floyd died, there were calls to defund the police. In South Africa, people took to the streets to protest Floyd's death, seeing his death as a reminder of their own struggles against police brutality. As Ryan Lenora Brown wrote, "There has been both an outpouring of solidarity, and sharp calls to turn inward, to consider why violent policing of poor black South Africans remains common a generation after the end of apartheid" (R. Brown 2020). At one protest, those present sang an older anti-apartheid song: "What have we done? Our sin is that we are black? Our sin is the truth. They are killing us" (ibid.). How does a people respond to targeted extermination?

One response, exemplified by Psalm 137, is rage, defined by the *Random House Webster's Unabridged Dictionary* as an intense form of anger that is characterized by violence. Christian traditions often overlook the psalm because of the call for violent retribution in verses 8–9. Rage seems to be the antithesis of the Christian call to love the enemy. As a response to injustice, however, rage has regularly functioned in African American political activity, with the corresponding classification and condemnation of such rage as a riot in White American public discourse. This essay will examine Christian interpretations of Psalm 137, African American philosophical and theological works about anger, and media responses to African American and White rage.

Black rage has become synonymous with the word *riot* and is often defined as an "inappropriate" response of African Americans to systemic racism and racialized violence, but in light of political organizations like the Movement for Black Lives and the continued killing of unarmed Black people, rage not only is an appropriate response but a necessary one.

Psalm 137 expresses grief, longing, and rage in a short nine verses. Classified as a lament, the exiled speaker weeps with homesickness and promises to remember their home in the following lament:

> By the rivers of Babylon—there we sat down and there we wept when we remembered Zion. On the willows there we hung up our harps. For there our captors asked us for songs, and our tormentors asked for mirth, saying, "Sing us one of the songs of Zion!" How could we sing the Lord's song in a foreign land? If I forget you, O Jerusalem, let my right hand wither! Let my tongue cling to the roof of my mouth, if I do not remember you, if I do not set Jerusalem above my highest joy. (verses 1–6; NRSV)

The focus on memory has played a part in music, from the Jewish reggae artist Matisyahu to the early American composer William Billings, to Joel Barlow, to African American singer Roland Hayes, to the sermons of Moses Mather and Frederick Douglass (Stowe 2016, 61–62, 68, 71–73, 76, 85). The last three verses, however, hardly appear in any musical or theological analysis. The psalmist declares, "Remember, O Lord, against the Edomites the day of Jerusalem's fall, how they said, 'Tear it down! Tear it down! Down to its foundations!' O Daughter Babylon, you devastator! Happy shall they be who pay you back what you have done to us! Happy shall they be who take your little ones and dash them against the rock!" As David W. Stowe states, "Virtually no one sings the strange, final three verses of Psalm 137. They are silenced. Or forgotten. Or perhaps forgotten because we have silenced them" (2016, 120–21). In Jewish tradition, only the Orthodox recite the entire psalm; in other branches, "the vengeful final verses are simply expunged from prayers and services" (ibid., 121).[1] Psalm 137:7–9 has been recreated, if not sung, for example in a 1676 poem by John Oldman (ibid., 139). Today, however, "organized religion in the United States, with its hymns and liturgies, mainly steers clear of the language of imprecation sounded in cursing psalms like Psalm 137" (ibid., 148).

Yet, vengeance can and should have a place in religious discourse. According to Jennifer Geddes, "Redemptive religious language can be used to cover over in vaguely evocative language that which requires accurate reporting, the full force of justice, and the persistence of anger" (quoted in Stowe 2016, 164). And Cynthia Oziek argues, "What we call 'vengeance' is the act of bringing public justice to evil—not by repeating the evil, not by imitating the evil, not by initiating a new evil, but by making certain never to condone the old one; never even appearing to condone it" (quoted in Stowe 2016, 164–165). Robert Beckford describes two types of vengeance, punitive vengeance, which "focuses on retribution and retaliation," and corrective vengeance, which includes the wronged party being compensated for their injury (quoted in Stowe 2016, 167). Because it "ultimately [fails] to bring about social transformation on the part of the oppressor," Beckford prefers redemptive vengeance, with its emphasis on repentance (ibid., 167).[2] This raises two questions: what if the oppressor's redemption is not the oppressed person's problem, task, or responsibility? And how is such repentance supposed to happen? Related to these questions is the minimization of vengeance—the psalm's clear call for tit for tat retribution must be reconfigured in order to make it more palatable and less violent.

The reconfiguration of vengeance has been a part of African American theological discourse for decades, and there are two clear twenty-first century examples that utilize Psalm 137. Writing from a womanist hermeneutical perspective, Valerie Bridgeman notes that African Americans can fully relate to the disorientation that Psalm 137 describes (2017, 214). Focusing on verses 1–4, Bridgeman analyzes the concept of resistance both among exiled Jews in the sixth century BCE and protestors in Ferguson and across the US following the death of Michael Brown in 2014. She writes, "In 2016, a national football league player protested police brutality and violence against African Americans by sitting down on the national anthem and later by taking a knee. Similarly, hanging one's harps reflect the same defiant refusal to perform in a way that makes those who terrorize, oppress, or enslave others feel entertained. Remembering Zion is an act of cultural reintegration" (ibid., 217). The last verses of Psalm 137, however, "are hyberbolic prayer and taunting," so "readers must understand that the prayer or song for such violence is not the same as acting on that violence" (ibid., 221, 222). While the psalmist does not ask God to behave violently, there is a call for remembrance and retributive justice against those who have harmed Israel. Readers should be able to hear the rage without condoning it. And acting on rage would be bad, as Bridgeman argues in her conclusion: "Though rage may be normal and the desire for revenge may be human, in the end it is not productive. Venting the rage allows space for creative ways of confronting injustice to come forward, as even a precursory glance at the websites and vision statements of movement organizations will show" (ibid., 223). One can talk about rage, but *any* action motivated by it cannot be judged as positive, because there are acceptable and unacceptable responses to ill treatment. Esau McCaulley (2020) makes a similar argument. A priest in the Anglican Church in North America, McCaulley uses the psalms to talk about "the rage of the oppressed." Quoting Ps 137:8–9 and describing it as "an atrocity," he calls the song "a psalm of the traumatized" and argues that "for Christians, rage (Ps 137) must eventually give way to hope (Isa 49). And we find the spiritual resources to make this transition at the cross." For McCaulley, rage against those who have harmed you and hope that God will remember this harm and perhaps avenge it, which is the psalmist's cry, cannot occupy the same space. McCaulley, however, equates rage with hatred and argues that "it damages our own souls." Again, rage embodies a lower-level emotion that one must transcend.

Not all African American Christians, however, call for transcending rage. Utilizing Karl Rahner, Carmichael Peters argues that "rage 'expresses finitude from the inside' for those who belong to social locations which fundamentally and systematically deny or frustrate the indeterminateness of their finite transcendence. Unlike anger and hatred, rage is not related to specific things and cannot be conquered or remedied; it is ontological" (2003, 191–2). Because African Americans live in a world shaped by White supremacy, rage is a response to a world that often actively limits and denies their humanity (Peters 2003, 203, 205–6, 209). Peters notes that "in the process of being colonized in this country . . . black people have always been taught to deny or repress the mood of rage—that is, to opt for the mood of resignation"; this resignation has led to "all sorts of criminal and pathological possibilities whose primary impact is on black life itself—for example, physical and mental illness as well as black on black violence" (ibid., 210).

Rage, however, can be active resistance against the forces that limit Black life and can be used to bring change (ibid., 211, 213). In his response to Peters, Bryan Massingale observes that Whites and Blacks view Black rage differently: "The representation of 'black rage' on the part of the dominant culture, then, is that of an urban underclass that blindly lashes out in senseless acts of random violence. Such outbreaks occasion both demands for repression (e.g., more prisons and larger police forces) and cries of compassion (though from afar and at a safe remove)" (2003, 219). In contrast, for African Americans, "Black rage . . . is not the irrational outburst of urban menaces, but an intelligible response to the reality of racial terror and aggression experienced in myriad ways in daily life" (ibid., 219). Massingale argues that this rage can be weaponized to fight against the lie of white supremacy (ibid., 221).[3] Rage need not be an inherently destructive force that must be suppressed.

Instead, acknowledging rage can bring clarity. Mari Joerstad compares Ps 137:8–9 to Steve McQueen's film *12 Years a Slave* and native Canadian Joe David's totem pole *Cedar Man* to suggest that "violent texts can sensitize us to our own violence, and make visible patterns of oppression that we are accustomed to overlook" (2018, 2). Her conclusion is worth quoting directly:

> I believe Psalm 137 can help us think about contemporary ways in which land claims, cultural appropriation, and violence intersect. Consider, for example, the

Black Lives Matter movement and the Standing Rock protest ... Accusations of violence have been leveled against people representing both these movements. The Black Lives Matter protestors have been called looters, rioters, thugs, reverse racists, and so on. The Standing Rock protestors were accused of attacking workers and police, and neighbors said they disturbed the peace. These accusations redirect concerns about violence from those able to wield violence, in these cases, militarized police, and onto the victimized group. (Joerstad 2018, 12–13)

Characterization and language matter. When *any* political activity from a marginalized group can be dismissed as a riot, the language of protest becomes negative language. This makes any expression of rage dangerous for the marginal group and subject to criticism from the dominant group or anyone within the marginal group who sees rage and violent action as equally bad synonyms. The twentieth-century examples of Tulsa in 1921, various US cities in 1968, and Los Angeles in 1992, all covered by *The New York Times*, should demonstrate this point.

What is now called the Tulsa race massacre took place on May 31 and June 1, 1921. The June 1 headline in the *New York Times* declared, "Tulsa Riots: 30 blocks burned, military rule in city, angered whites surround negro quarter and set it on fire." The next day's headline, however, had a significantly different tone—"Tulsa in Remorse to Rebuild Homes. Dead Now Put at 30—Citizens . . . Voice Shame Over Riots that Razed Negro Quarter. Blame Police and Sheriff" (*New York Times* June 2, 1921). The article noted, "Some still believe that many other negroes perished in the burning of their section . . . and that those will never be known. There are vague reports also that negroes bodies were thrown into the river and that others were burned outside the city. There has been a tremendous revulsion of feeling as a result of the *outbreak* which [a US military commander in Tulsa] bluntly declares was caused by an impudent negro, a hysterical girl, and a yellow journal reporter" (ibid., 1; emphasis mine). While *outbreak* makes it sound like the violence was a virus, the article later said there would be an investigation to punish "those guilty of instigating the *riots*" (ibid., 1; emphasis mine). According to Judge Loyal J. Martin, the instigators were not "the real citizenship of Tulsa . . . but criminals who should have been shot on the spot" (ibid., 1). Blacks were forcibly detained and segregated at the fairgrounds in order to avoid a "crudescence of rioting" (ibid., 2), which began when a small group of Blacks went to the Tulsa courthouse to stave off a lynching and a much larger group of Whites "took a leading part in the rioting . . . content with what they regarded as just retaliation for the armed invasion of the city by the negroes" (ibid., 2). The article concludes with two observations: "Many of the ringleaders among the white rioters and men who did most of the shooting carried arms as special officers [and] 13 bodies of negroes were buried in the City Cemetery here today. The act was without ceremony, it being said that feeling possibly might flare up if the burial were attended by any show" (ibid., 2). Most mourners would not have been able to leave the fairgrounds at that time anyway. But the need to silence Black grief as a way to avoid rage became clear in the days after June 1, when "survivors reported seeing bodies tossed into the muddy Arkansas River or loaded onto trucks or trains, making it difficult to account for the dead" (D. Brown 2020). The civic support of White violence and the suppression of Black grief may explain how quickly the discourse about Tulsa changed and then went silent.

By June 4, the headlines blamed Blacks for their troubles. The main headline stated, "Military control is ended at Tulsa / civil law restored, one Negro agitator under arrest, Three Others sought / Plot by Negro Society?" A G.W. Gurley, "a wealthy negro," claimed Blacks were trying to organize "for the ostensible defense of the colored bootblack held at the courthouse" (*New York Times,* 1921, 1). Another man claimed that the armed African Blood Brotherhood organized the courthouse gathering and that their weapons exploded that night. The deflection of blame served its purpose—ignoring the white envy of Black prosperity and the reality that homes and not weapons exploded. As Gretchen Frazee wrote in 2020, "Some accounts indicate white residents used their private airplanes to drop firebombs onto black properties" (Frazee 2020). The white rioters disappeared, held harmless for decades, particularly among White Tulsans, for whom 1921 was simply unknown or ignored.

Only in the last several years has Tulsa, my hometown, begun to reckon with 1921, after earlier attempts in the 1970s. *The Oklahoma Eagle*, Tulsa's Black newspaper, published part of the 2001 Report by the Oklahoma Commission to Study the Tulsa Race Riot of 1921. Even the report itself challenges the use of the term *race riot* to refer to what was a sustained act of White violence against the Black community. Part of that report states, "Indeed, for a number of observers through the years, the term 'riot' itself seems somehow inadequate to describe the violence and conflagration that took place. For some, what occurred in Tulsa on May 31 and June 1, 1921 was a massacre, a pogrom, or, to use a more modern term, an ethnic cleansing. For others, it was nothing short of a race war. But whatever term is used, one thing is certain: when it was all over, Tulsa's African American district had been turned into a scorched wasteland of vacant lots, crumbling storefronts, burned churches, and blackened, leafless trees" (Franklin and Ellsworth 2001). And so many died that in 2020, scientists started digging for mass graves in Oaklawn Cemetery in a city where "a brutal race massacre took place" (D. Brown 2020). Mayor G. T. Bynum's decision met with opposition; one angry woman interrupted his family breakfast to complain that "'[he was] doing this to make white people feel bad'" (D. Brown 2020d). Scientists discovered a mass grave in October 2020 (D. Brown 2020b). It is irrelevant at this point whether White people feel bad or not. Those calling for the digging simply want to know what happened and to end what Mayor Bynum called "the conspiracy of silence" (D. Brown 2020a). The riot is now called a massacre (Marshall 2020), primarily because of the historical memory of Black Tulsans, including Dr. Olivia Hooker, who worked on the 2001 Commission Report and died in 2018 at the age of 103, one of the last survivors of what she called "'The Catastrophe'" (D. Brown 2020c).

When James Earl Ray assassinated Dr. Martin Luther King, Jr., on April 4, 1968, in Memphis, Black communities across the United States responded with rage and protest that was immediately characterized as rioting. In an April 5, 1968, article in the *New York Times*, Earl Caldwell quoted the Memphis police director as saying, "Rioting has broken out in parts of the city" (Caldwell 1968, 1). Caldwell's headline read, "4,000 Guardsmen Are Ordered Out / Curfew is Imposed . . . Windows Are Broken and Policemen Stoned." Those who "responded with bitterness and anger" were "Negro militants," according to Laurence Van Gelder's front page story (1). In New York City, "police reinforcements, including elements of the riot-trained Tactical Police Force, were rushed into both communities [Harlem and Brooklyn]" (Johnson 1968, 1). The following comments appeared under the headline "Widespread Disorders": "There were riotous outbursts and brief clashes with the police in Winston-Salem, New Bern, Durham, and Charlotte, North Carolina, and in Jackson, Mississippi, Boston, Hartford, New York City, and Memphis, when Dr. King was killed . . . the police [in Washington, DC] said riot squad officers used tear gas once tonight to open a path through a hostile crowd for fire equipment responding to an alarm" (1, 26). The top headline for April 6 was "Army Troops in Capital as Negroes Riot; Guard Sent Into Chicago, Detroit, Boston." In Donald Janson's April 6 *New York Times* article, "7 Die as Fires and Looting Spread in Chicago Rioting," he noted that "6,000 National Guard troops were called up yesterday as rioters pillage stores . . . in the Negro West Side . . . half of the armed guardsmen, in fatigues and riot helmets, began patrolling glass-littered West Side streets about 10 P.M . . . Dozens of automobiles that entered . . . emerged with smashed windows and dented hoods" (Janson 1968a, 1). By Palm Sunday, April 7, the top headline was "More Soldiers Sent to Control Washington and Chicago Riots; Capital Put Under 4 P.M. Curfew." Donald Janson, still in Chicago, filed the headline "5,000 Troops Are Flown to Chicago for Riot Duty" in order "to help quell rioting that spread yesterday from devastated West Side Negro slums to the South Side and near North Side of town" (Janson 1968b, 1). Notably, Janson described what was happening in Chicago as an insurrection (1). Yet, the *Times*' coverage focused almost exclusively on looting.[4]

The focus on the *what* at times made it difficult to focus consistently on the *why*.[5] The journalists who covered these events ranged from one of the paper's first Black journalists, Thomas A. Johnson, to Donald Janson, who marched with Dr. King, to Tom Wicker, an antiwar activist and requested observer to the 1971 Attica uprising, to Ben A. Franklin, who later wrote for the "independent, progressive" *Washington Spectator* (Martin 2008; McFadden 2011). In his April 5 article, Johnson quoted New York's Deputy Fire Chief George Fridell's response to fighting five separate blazes: "If they want to burn up their neighborhood, it's their business" (Johnson 1968, 26). It is unclear whether the comment is accepting or dismissive. Janson, writing about Chicago on April 6, stated that "several stores burned simultaneously on the dingy street . . . the murder of Dr. King in Memphis Thursday night touched off yesterday's rioting" (Janson 1968a, 23). This acknowledgment of the cause is brief but noteworthy.

The intersectionality of class and race affected not only how the events were reported but responses to those events. As the mayor of Detroit argued on April 6, "It is better to overreact than underreact" (Carroll 1968, 22). Tom Wicker described the scene in Washington as follows: "Rather, it seemed that the angry or vengeful actions of a few might have stimulated excitement in others and set them free of normal restraints. Most of the looters, far from appearing angry or mournful at the news from Memphis, appeared to be having a good time" (Wicker 1968, 23). The assumption appears to be that any response, whether from rage and/or the desire to acquire stolen property, must be incorrect. No one should take to the streets for any reason. And at least in DC, being out for any reason was dangerous, as "they were enforcing the curfew more vigorously against Negroes than whites" (Franklin 1968, 62). But for those who went out, "Negro looters, often in a laughing, holiday mood, made frequent comments indicating that some of their resentment against the stores they selected was focused on what they regarded as unfair credit and pricing policies" (ibid.). The description of affect minimizes both the violence being applied to those in the streets and folks' reasons for being in those streets. This was not a day off for random behavior but targeted, if illegal, action against economic discrimination. Personal affect, however, can be described more easily than systemic racism. In Chicago on the same day (April 7, 1968), Donald Janson wrote, "The mood in the West Side slum that has borne the brunt of the pillaging was ugly in some places, carnival in others" (Janson 1968b, 63). The words *carnival* and *holiday* contrast with *riot* and highlight the ways in which different groups responded to the same events. On April 8, Janson concluded, "All the riot damage was in Negro neighborhoods. The rioters had torn up and burned down the stores and apartments they needed for shelter and sustenance. No white neighborhood was touched by the destruction, and most Chicagoans have not seen any of it. They would not know a riot had occurred without radio, television and newspaper reports" (Janson 1968c, 30).[6] The reality of segregation meant that Whites could remain untouched by Black rage in any form, even though the actions of a White man, James Earl Ray, precipitated all of these events, and it is worth nothing that if the buildings destroyed were on those same already described dingy streets in a slum, a larger conversation about substandard living conditions very well could have been in order. Some Black political organizations "blamed the 'white power structure' for causing conditions that spark riots," including police brutality (Janson 1968c, 30). The conversation about economic and social justice, however, did not happen, and the conditions remained.

On April 29, 1992, four police officers were found not guilty of assaulting Rodney King; Los Angeles, where the assault but not the trial took place, literally and figuratively burned. Years of rage regarding police brutality culminated in people going out into the streets. In his May 1 article "Riots in Los Angeles: The Blue Line; Surprised, Police React Slowly as Violence Spreads," Robert Reinhold described the situation as "anarchy," or an absence of order, because the National Guard did not arrive until the afternoon of April 30. Unlike in 1968, when troops were in full force to keep Black rage in check, and unlike 1921, where the White police either stood by or actively raged against Black people, there was no significant law enforcement presence. Reinhold gave two reasons for the delay (1992):

> The police apparently gambled that restraint would result in less violence than an aggressive show of force. But by the time they mounted a more intense response, rioting, looting and burning had spread beyond containment. Mr. Gates [the Los Angeles police chief] today conceded that the police should have moved faster . . . At City Hall and Parker Center alike, the general assumption had been that the jury would return at least one or two guilty verdicts and that that would be enough to prevent unrest.

The *Times* kept its "Riots in Los Angeles" headline over the next several days, simply changing the subheadlines. Jane Fritsch noted that under Chief Gates, the Los Angeles Police Department became heavily weaponized (1992b). Fritsch concludes, however, that "[Gates'] departure from policing comes at a time when many of his views on the matter have been called into question by criminal justice experts and police officials who argue that hardware and efficiency are less valuable than building relationships within communities" (1992b).[7]

One shift between 1968 and 1992 media coverage is an increasing focus on the impact of the events on communities, and not simply a description of the events. As Los Angeles continued burning, psychiatrists and psychologists warned that children's response to the events would be race-based:

> Around age 8 or 9, children start defining themselves in terms of their peer group. Black and other minority children at this age are likely to feel that they have to be careful, lest what happened to Mr. King happened to them. And some white children from this age on will have a fear of retribution from *angry* blacks, psychologists say . . . "Teenagers in families on the right will be more likely to see the verdict as justified and interpret the rioting as confirming that there is a criminal element that needs to be restrained," said Dr. David Sears, a psychologist at the University of California at Los Angeles. But other teen-agers, especially members of minority groups, will come to a different conclusion. Dr. Roderick Watts, a psychologist at DePaul University in Chicago, said Thursday, "A black student in one of my classes today concluded the lesson was that you should avoid any contact with the police, because if they get you, your life isn't worth a damn." (Goleman 1992; emphasis mine)

The lesson was not lost on Tom Bradley, Los Angeles' first African American mayor.

Bradley's response to the Rodney King verdict showed his identity as an African American, if not necessarily political or judicial impartiality. It also showed his individual rage against the situation, even though he did not take to the streets as so many Black people would do later that day and night. As Jane Fritsch wrote,

> For a few moments on Wednesday, Los Angeles residents saw a side of the Mayor that was jarringly at odds with the patrician, almost bland, public image he has cultivated in his 19 years in office. Visibly angry, Mr. Bradley lashed out Wednesday afternoon at the jury that hours earlier had acquitted the officers. "I was outraged," Mr. Bradley said at a press conference at City Hall. "Today that jury asked us to accept the senseless and brutal beating of a helpless man." (Fritsch 1992)

Bradley's verbal rage led to criticism from John Ferraro, the City Council president, who stated:

> Mr. Bradley might bear some of the blame for the violence on Wednesday night. The Mayor's public expression of rage over the verdict was ill-considered and may have helped spark the rioting . . . "He probably was outraged," Mr. Ferraro said, "but he's the Mayor of the city and he's got to keep his cool and calm." The Mayor quickly got his anger under control, Mr. Ferraro said, adding, "I think he's shown some leadership since then." (Fritsch 1992)

Ferraro expected Bradley to be neutral, to not see himself or anyone who looked like him in Rodney King. Leadership becomes ignoring what you see, and any expression of Black rage means responsibility for riots, as opposed to the verdict itself. Mayor Bradley, however, held his position as mayor and as a Black man: "Asked whether he would now be afraid to be a black man in Los Angeles if he were not the Mayor, Mr. Bradley paused, then said: 'No, I would not be scared. I would be angry'" (ibid.). Characterizations notwithstanding, Bradley acknowledged the Black rage he saw and felt.

The year 1992 was also an election year, so both President George H. W. Bush and Governor Bill Clinton responded. Visiting the First AME Church in Los Angeles, Clinton "said repeatedly that the riots showed the need for a new President who could bind up and reunify a nation drifting apart along lines of race and income" (Pear 1992). Clinton accepted President Bush's response to the events, which included sending in "1,000 federal riot trained law enforcement officials" (Bush 1992). Calling repeatedly for restoring order, Bush rejected any association of events in Los Angeles with protests: "It's not a message of protest. It's been the brutality of a mob, pure and simple . . . The wanton destruction of life and property is not a legitimate expression of outrage with injustice. It is itself injustice" (Bush 1992). The president equated property damage with loss of life and suggested no physical action could be designated as a protest; however, he never called the events a riot. Similarly, Clinton "said many of the rioters in Los Angeles had used the acquittal of the four police officers as an *excuse* for looting and burning. The reaction, 'while understandable, is still unforgiveable,' he said" (Pear 1992; emphasis mine). The characterization is sobering—those who steal or burn are irredeemable. Clinton marginalizes the group further in a speech at First Baptist Church in Washington, DC: "'Just below the mainstream, there is another stream of Americans living apart from *our values*, apart from *our institutions*, apart from the warm embrace of a church like this, *with no connection to a society or a higher power*" (ibid.; emphasis mine). The assumptions shock. Those in the streets appear as antisocial, un-American atheists, which discredits them, what they did, and why they did it. Similar arguments will be made later by Catholics and evangelicals against the Black Lives Matter movement (Bruenig 2020; Molina 2020).

To see another view, one has to step outside White discourse. In a June 7, 2020, *New York Times* Podcast, Jon Caramanica interviewed James Bernard and Reginald Dennis, former editors of the hip-hop magazine *The Source*. Bernard flew to Los Angeles in May 1992 and interviewed people on the streets directly, embedding himself with the Crips. In the article the magazine published, he argued, "This was no riot. It was a rebellion" (Caramanica 2020). When asked to defend the thesis, Bernard responded, "Some of the activity was conscious . . . people were thoughtful about what they were doing

... 'The riots' were really a ... spontaneous cry for economic empowerment" (ibid.). Stores and hotels were targeted or ignored, for example, based on hiring practices.[8] Bernard noted that at the time, "Nobody's taking these folks seriously" (ibid.). Instead, the press focused on illegality and randomness and not the class struggle. Speaking in the summer of 2020, Bernard said, "The anger that's going on now is valid," confirming the wisdom of earlier warnings from rappers like NWA and Ice-T: "This always happens as a result of police brutality ... we always make the best of a bad situation" (ibid.). And Black people should stop doing that—"It's not really Black people's problem to solve" (ibid.). The shift in perspective enables one to rethink the language of riot and rage, which too often gets dismissed as random and unjustifiable violence and calls on the oppressed to be almost superhuman in their response to oppression. It may not be a coincidence that of the eleven journalists from *The New York Times* and the *Los Angeles Times* that reported on 1968 and 1992, ten of them are men. Out of those men, only two are Black. And those men were some of the earliest Black journalists at *The New York Times* in 1968. When there are so few people in a field who look like you, there are limits to how iconoclastic you can be, even when reporting on an incident that has caused your home community so much suffering.

Psalm 137:8–9 cries for retribution in the name of a suffering people, and too often that cry is dismissed or downplayed in the name of unity and justice that may suit the needs of those who are not suffering more than those who are. The exiled Israelites may not have had the power to kill Babylonian children as their little ones were killed, but they are not wrong or immoral to want that destruction. They respond as oppressed human beings. The cry cannot and should not immediately be explained away or criticized—it should be heard as it is. And for African Americans, the cry comes from centuries of living in and loving a country that, to quote Doc Rivers, "doesn't love us back" (Grant 2020). Ta-Nehisi Coates says that the [American]

> Dream is tree houses and the Cub Scouts. The Dream smells like peppermint but tastes like strawberry shortcake. And for so long I have wanted to escape into the Dream, to fold my country over my head like a blanket. But this has never been an option because the Dream rests on our backs, the bedding made from our bodies ... And all the time the Dreamers are pillaging Ferguson for municipal governance. And they are torturing Muslims, and their drones are bombing wedding parties (by accident!), and the Dreamers are quoting Martin Luther King and exulting non-violence for the weak and the biggest guns for the strong. (2015, 11, 131)

And herein lies the problem, or challenge, depending upon one's perspective. Peace and nonviolence have been glorified and idolized to the point that any expression of rage is perceived as violence, and heaven forbid if something gets broken. A shattered window somehow takes precedence over all else, including a Black person's life. In the long summer of 2020, Roxane Gay wrote about the impossible position that racism and extrajudicial violence places Black people in:

> They demand perfection as the price for black existence while harboring no such standards for anyone else. Some white people act as if there are two sides to racism, as if racists are people we need to deal with. They fret over the destruction of property and want everyone to just get along. They struggle to understand why black people are rioting but offer no alternatives about what a people should do about a lifetime of rage, disempowerment and injustice.

In the short term, one thing that Black people can do is to begin to undo the work of self-censorship and be unapologetically enraged. Psalm 137 is a lament, a response to tragedy. Grief can rarely be explained but it can be felt. And it need not be silenced to make others more comfortable. In an article for *The Christian Century*, Waltrina N. Middleton wrote about her relationship with her cousin Rev. DePayne V. Middleton, whom Dylann Roof killed in Charleston's Emanuel AME Church in June 2015. She stated,

> The inconceivable grief her children, parents, and siblings would bear—and still do five years later—would soon be lost in the forced narratives of forgiveness perpetuated by the media, by politicians, and even by the church, which was perhaps mesmerized by the spotlight or pressured to follow the script created for well-behaved black folks who say they love Jesus. . . . *To insist on a narrative of forgiveness is dehumanizing and violent, and it goes against the very nature of lament* . . . My family did not offer forgiveness in the courtroom. (Middleton 2020, 27; author's emphasis)

Middleton argued, "But we must be free to tell our own stories, speak our truths, and cry out with our rage and sorrow" (ibid., 29). Lament demands honesty, and honest confrontation with systemic racism has historically been in short supply.

George Floyd's death, along with the deaths of Ahmaud Arbery and Breonna Taylor and the shooting of Jacob Blake, brought one confrontation to the streets of the United States in the summer of 2020. The same narratives about protest versus riot appeared as well. This time, however, Black people pushed back not only against that dichotomy but against the narrative of respectability politics that makes some people "good" and others "bad."[9] Black people often are expected to distinguish between the good and peaceful protesters and the bad throwers of rocks. When one's life is on the line, however, "you must convince a stranger that you are in some amorphous way *good*. And at the same time you learn that it probably will not make a difference" (Thomas 2020). As R. Eric Thomas (2020) notes,

> It is a fool's errand to try to work out the arithmetic of how an incident with underlying racial bias begins or ends. To attempt to do so is to grant credence to the flawed logic that says a man like Jimenez or Floyd or Cooper, a woman like Sandra Bland or Breonna Taylor, a child like Trayvon Martin or Tamir Rice, is inherently dangerous to a system that has been designed to kill them since before they were born . . . And you think: "If it is futile anyway, if I am powerless over the reception that I get, what does it matter how I approach the world?" And there's a freedom in that, for it allows you to prioritize your own voice over the scolding one that speaks nothing but fear.

The freedom affirms Black rage without judgment. In a now viral video, "How Can We Win," Kimberly Jones (2020) challenges the dichotomy of rioting and looting versus peaceful economic protest by arguing that both are necessary. She says, "There are three types of people in the streets, the protestors, the rioters, and the looters." Her argument is to focus on *why* and not *what*—regarding looters: "Why are people that poor? Why are people that broke?" Because the US economic system is not designed for African Americans to succeed, they cannot win. The country where they live does not belong to them. Jones (2020) ends as follows: "Far as I'm concerned, they can burn this bitch to the ground. And it still wouldn't be enough. And they are lucky that what Black people are looking for is equality and not revenge."

While Black people are not calling for the killing of White children in retaliation for those lost to institutionalized violence, some physical buildings and institutional structures may fall. One building destroyed in the George Floyd protests was the Indian restaurant Gandhi Mahal in Minneapolis, owned by a Bangladeshi immigrant. The morning after the first, Hafsa Islam (2020) overhead her father saying, "'Let my building burn. Justice needs to be served. Put those officers in jail." Islam (2020) concludes as follows:

> I support peaceful protest above all—look at our restaurant's namesake—and I don't mean for my family to promote violence. But after the flash of pain, it is important to name what is happening to cause this in the first place, and to empathize with the fury and frustration of the people it's happening to. The protests and the violence and the fires will stop once we're rid of the system that oppresses, and maims, and kills people like George Floyd. So let it burn.

The Islam family's expression of empathy for Black rage, even at the cost of their restaurant, shows an emphasis on the *why* and not the *what* so often missing in studies about protests. Rage is not the problem but an expression of the problem; *racism* is the problem.

Any question that the combination of rage and racism equals toxicity that was not answered in Tulsa a century ago should have been answered with the storming of the US Capitol on January 6, 2021. Confederate flags flew, and some people the President called "great patriots" wore anti-Jewish sweatshirts (thetrumparchive.com; Bendix 2021; Perez 2021; Washington Post Staff 2021; Buchanan et al., 2021). While some news media called the incident a riot, and those involved rioters, the invaders were treated like guests, with an officer taking a selfie with one rioter and other officers helping rioters enter and leave the premises. The district that tear-gassed unarmed Black Lives Matter protestors in June 2020 effectively welcomed a large group of unauthorized White insurrectionists into a federal building (Leonig et al., 2021). The lesson is that not all rage is treated equally; White people enraged over a lie receive better treatment overall than Black people enraged over the truth.

Psalm 137 is an example of an enraged community shouting into the void and hoping for an answer. As a communal psalm of lament in a place of exile, the people declare their love for the home that they may not see again and declare their hope for vengeance. Historically, the exile ends but without the retribution wished for not only in Psalm 137 but in other exilic texts like Isaiah 47. The difference between then and now, at least theoretically, is that Black people lament and rage in a land that is supposedly their home, but it is often unsafe space where their very bodies can be seen and treated as a threat, whether their empty hands are up or holding a rock. White bodies are not envisioned in the same way, which may explain why Ashli Babbitt, killed during the January 6 Capitol riot, was praised in some circles as a "freedom fighter" (Bergengruen 2021). Psalm 137:3 asks, "How could we sing the Lord's song in a foreign land?" Black people ask, how they can sing *any* song in their *own* land. Yet as the Black Lives Matter movement and the centennial of the Tulsa Race Massacre make clear, the people remember, and they endure.

NOTES

1. Stowe repeats "vengeful" as a description of the verses (2020, 141).
2. Michael P. Jaycox, a Catholic ethicist, makes a similar argument (2016, 124).
3. Philosopher Mark Tschaepe argues that if directed and appropriated intentionally, anger bring awareness to microaggressions and what he calls epistemic injustice (2016, 87–101).
4. I counted thirteen references to looters or looting only *after* I realized the language was repetitive.

5. See Kimberly Jones's (2020) language in the same context describing the George Floyd protests.

6. Similarly, Franklin wrote about Washington, DC: "In the far reaches of the predominantly white Northwest residential section . . . the looting and burning seemed as if they were going on in a different city" (1968, 30).

7. The debate returned to the national stage with the 2014 Ferguson events. The shooting of unarmed Michael Brown by Officer Darren Wilson in itself would have been just another number in a growing pile of statistics. The militarized police response to the protests, however, made the event different. By the third night of protests, "summer rage pitted the people of Ferguson against those sworn to protect them. On Saturday, officers shot and killed 18-year-old Michael Brown. On Sunday, resident protests turned to riots, marked by looting and the burning of several local stores. And, taking to the streets again Monday night, locals were met with tear gas and rubber bullets" (Lowery 2014). By August 13, police were "in armored trucks"; by the 17th, tanks flooded on the streets (Cetinkaya et al. 2014).

8. The same argument appeared in 1968.

9. Ibram X. Kendi calls this "'uplift suasion.' The judges strap the entire Black race on the Black body's back, shove the burdened Black body into White spaces, order the burdened Black body to always act in an upstanding manner to persuade away White racism, and punish poor Black conduct with sentences of shame for reinforcing racism, for bringing the race down" (2019, 203).

WORKS CITED

Bendix, Aria. 2021. "A Harrowing Photo Shows a Trump Supporter Carrying a Confederate Flag Inside the US Capitol, Flanked by Portraits of Civil War-era Figures." *Business Insider*, January 6. www.businessinsider.com/photo-trump-supporter-riot-confederate-flat-us-capitol-2021-1.

Bergengruen, Vera. 2021. "'Our First Martyr': How Ashli Babbitt Is Being Used As a Far-Right Recruiting Tool." *Time*, January 10, https://time.com/5928249/ashli-babbitt-capitol-extremism/.

Bridgeman, Valerie. 2017. "'A Long Ways from Home': Displacement, Lament, and Singing Protest in Psalm 137." *Perspectives in Religious Studies* 44, vol. 2 (Summer): 213–23.

Brown, DeNeen L. 2020a. "A Century after a Race Massacre, Tulsa Finally Digs for Suspected Mass Graves." *Washington Post*, July 13, www.washingtonpost.com/history/2020/07/13/tulsa-digs-mass-graves-race-massacre-oaklawn-cemetery/.

———. 2020b. "Coffins Unearthed as the Search for Victims of the Tulsa Race Massacre Continues." *National Geographic*, October 26, www.nationalgeographic.com/history/2020/10/search-for-victims-tulsa-race-massacre-continues-mass-grave-unearthed/#close.

———. 2020c. "Olivia Hooker, One of the Last Survivors of the 1921 Tulsa Race Massacre, Dies at 103." *Washington Post*, November 22, www.washingtonpost.com/local/obituaries/

olivia- hooker-one-of-the-last-survivors-of-the-1921-tulsa-race-massacre-dies-at-103/2018/11/22/f5c03934-3371-11e8-8679-93412b53be52_story.html.

———. 2020d. "A White Republican Mayor Seeks the Truth about Tulsa's Race Massacre a Century Ago." *Washington Post*, March 13, www.washingtonpost.com/history/2020/03/13/tulsa-mayor-bynum-mass-graves/.

Brown, Ryan Lenora. 2020. "An Ocean Apart, Similar Stories: US Protests Hit Home in South Africa." *The Christian Science Monitor*, June 8, www.csmonitor.com/World/Africa/2020/0608/An-ocean-apart-similar-stories-US-protests-hit-home-in-South-Africa.

Brudholm, Thomas. 2009. "On the Advocacy of Forgiveness After Mass Atrocities." In *The Religious in Responses to Mass Atrocity: Interdisciplinary Perspectives*, edited by Thomas Brudholm and Thomas Cushman, 1–18. Cambridge: Cambridge UP.

Bruenig, Elizabeth. 2020. "'Racism Makes a Liar of God." *New York Times*, August 6, https://www.nytimes.com/2020/08/06/opinion/sunday/gloria-purvis-george-floyd-blm.html.

Buchanan, Larry, Lazaro Gamic, Christina Kelso, et al. 2021. "How a Pro-Trump Mob Stormed the U.S. Capitol." *New York Times*, January 7. www.nytimes.com/interactive/2021/01/06/us/trump-mob-capitol- building.html?referringSource=articleShare.

Bush national address. 1992. https://www.youtube.com/watch?v=ynoZY1npoYA. May 1, 1992

Caldwell, Earl. 1968. "4,000 Guardsmen Are Ordered Out / Curfew Is Imposed on City but Windows Are Broken and Policemen Stoned." *New York Times*, April 5, 1.

Caramanica, Jon. 2020. "How Did The Source Cover the 1992 Los Angeles Uprisings?" *New York Times*, June 7, https://www.nytimes.com/2020/06/07/arts/music/popcast-the-source-rodney-king-html?referringSource=articleShare.

Carroll, Maurice. 1968. "Philadelphia Bars Closed." *New York Times*, April 6, 22.

Cetinkaya, Karin, Celina Fang and Josh Williams. 2014. "Outcry and Confrontation in Ferguson." *New York Times*, August 17, www.nytimes.com/interactive/2014/08/17/us/ferguson-photos.html?referringSource=articleShare.

Coates, Ta-Nehisi. 2015. *Between the World and Me*. Spiegel and Grau.

Franklin, Ben A. 1968. "Calm is Restored; 9000 Troops Patrol Streets, with 3000 Held in Reserve." *New York Times* April 7, 1, 62.

———. 1968. "Capital Curfew Strict." *New York Times*, April 8, 1, 30.

Franklin, John Hope and Scott Ellsworth. "History Knows No Fences: An Overview." www.theoklahomaeagle.net/tulsa-race-riot.

Frazee, Gretchen. 2020. "What Happened 99 Years Ago in the Tulsa Race Massacre." June 19, www.pbs.org/newshour/nation/what-happenbed-99-years-ago-in-the-tulsa-race-massacre.

Fritsch, Jane. 1992. "Riots in Los Angeles: The Mayor; Los Angeles Mayor Criticizes Chief for Slow Action on Riot." *New York Times*, May 4. Gale in Context: Biography, https://smcproxy1.saintmarys.edu:3248/apps/doc/A174872062/BIC?u=nd_stmarys&sid=BIC&xid=910ce146. Accessed 29 June 2020.

———. 1992b. "Riots in Los Angeles: The Police Chief; As Los Angeles Storm Swirls, Chief of Police Is Oddly Quiet." *New York Times*, May 2. Gale in Context: Biography, https://smcproxy1.saintmarys.edu:3248/apps/doc/A174871948/BIC?u=nd_stmarys&sid=BIC&xid=ed8b89f0. Accessed 29 June 2020.

Gay, Roxane. 2020. "Remember, No One Is Coming to Save Us." *New York Times*, May 30, www.nytimes.com/2020/05/30/opinion-sunday-trump-george-floyd-coronavirus.html.

Goleman, Daniel. 1992. "Riots in Los Angeles: What to Say; The Harsh Lessons Faced By Children." *New York Times*, May 3. Gale in Context: Biography, https://smcproxy1.saintmarys.edu:3248/apps/doc/A174872905/BIC?u=nd_stmarys&sid=BIC&xid=4e9383a8. Accessed 29 June 2020.

Grant, Shawn. 2020. "Doc Rivers: 'It's Amazing Why We Keep Loving This Country, And This Country Does Not Love Us Back." *The Source*, August 26, www.thesource.com/2020/08/26/doc-rivers-its-amazing-why-we-keep-loving-this-country-and-this-country-does-not-love-us-back/.

Geddes, Jennifer L. 2009. "Religious Rhetoric in Response to Atrocity." In *The Religious in Responses to Mass Atrocity: Interdisciplinary Perspectives*, edited by Thomas Brudholm and Thomas Cushman, 21–37. Cambridge: Cambridge UP.

Islam, Hafsa. 2020. "My Family's Restaurant Caught Fire in the Minneapolis Protests. Let It Burn." *Washington Post*, May 31, www.washingtonpost.com/opinions/2020/05/31/my-familys-restaurant-caught-fire-protests-let-it-burn-oppressive-systems-with-it/.

Janson, Donald. 1968a. "7 Die as Fires and Looting Spread in Chicago Rioting." *New York Times*, April 6, 1, 23.

———. 1968b. "5,000 Troops Are Flown to Chicago for Riot Duty." *New York Times*, April 6, 1, 63.

———. 1968c. "Illinois City is Calmer." *New York Times*, April 8, 1, 30.

Jaycox, Michael P. 2016. "The Civic Virtues of Social Anger: A Critically Reconstructed Normative Ethic for Public Life," *Journal for the Society of Christian Ethics* 36, vol. 1: 123–43.

Joerstad, Mari. 2018. "Sing Us The Songs of Zion: Land, Culture, and Resistance in Psalm 137, 12 Years A Slave, and Cedar Man," *Horizons in Biblical Theology* 40, vol. 1: 1–16.

Johnson, Thomas A. 1968. "Scattered Violence Occurs in Harlem and Brooklyn." *New York Times*, April 5, 1, 26.

Jones, Kimberly. 2020. "How Can We Win." www.youtube.com/watch?v=sb9_qGOa9Go.

Kendi, Ibram X. 2019. *How to Be an Antiracist*. One World.

Leonnig, Carol D., Aaron C. Davis, Dan Lamothe, et al. 2021. "Capitol Breach Prompts Urgent Questions about Security Failures." *Washington Post*, January 7, www.washingtonpost.com/politics/capitol-breach-security-failures/2021/01/06/e1e09b80-5061-11eb-b96e-0e54447b23a1_story.html.

Lowery, Wesley. 2014. "Police Use Tear Gas on Crowd in Ferguson, Mo., Protesting Teen's Death." *Washington Post*, August 12, www.washingtonpost.com/news/post-nation/wp/2014/08/12/police-use-tear-gas-on-crowd/.

Marshall, Kendrick. 2020. "Tulsa Race Massacre. For Years, It Was Called a Riot. Not Anymore. Here's How It Changed." *Tulsa World*, July 7, https://tulsaworld.com/news/local/racemassacre/tulsa-race-massacre-for-years-it-was-called-a-riot-not-anymore-heres-how-it/article_47d28f77-2a7e-5b79-bf5f-bdfc4d6f976f.html.

Martin, Douglas. 2008. "Thomas A. Johnson, Pioneering Black Journalist, Dies at 79." *New York Times*, June 5, www.nytimes.com/2008/06/15/nyregion/05johnson.html.

Massingale, Bryan. 2003. "Anger and Human Transcendence: A Response to 'A Rahnerian Reading of Black Rage.'" *Philosophy & Theology* 15, vol. 1: 217–28.

McCaulley, Esau. 2020. "What the Bible Has to Say About Black Anger." *The New York Times*, June 14, www.nytimes.com/2020/06/14/opinion/george-floyd-psalms-bible-html.

McFadden, Robert D. 2011. "Tom Wicker, Times Journalist, Dies at 85." *The New York Times*, November 25, www.nytimes.com/2011/11/26/us/tom-wicker-journalist-and-author-dies-at-85.html.

Middleton, Waltrina N. 2020. "For My Cousin, Murdered at Mother Emanuel: Lament, Not Forgiveness." *The Christian Century* 137, vol. 15: 26–29.

"Military Control Is Ended at Tulsa / Civil Law Restored, One Negro Agitator under Arrest, Three Others Sought / Plot by Negro Society? / Wealthy Men of Race Say Hotheads Were Busy Hours Before the First Clash." 1921. *New York Times*, June 4, 1. www.obits.mlive.com/obituaries/kalamazoo/obituary.aspx?n=don-janson&pid=123731320.

Molina, Alejandra. 2020. "Black Lives Matter Co-Founder Denounces Pat Robertson for Saying the Movement Is 'Anti-God.'" *Religion News Service*, September 12, https://religionnews.com/2020/09/12/black-lives-matter-co-founder-denounces-pat-robertson-for-saying-the-movement-is-anti-god/.

Ozick, Cynthia. 1998. "The Symposium." In *The Sunflower: On the Possibility and Limits of Forgiveness* by Simon Wiesenthal, with a symposium edited by Harry James Cargas and Bonny V. Fetterman, 213–19. New York: Schocken Books.

Pear, Robert. 1992. "Riots in Los Angeles: Challenger; Nation Needs Healing, Clinton Says." *New York Times*, May 4. Gale in Context: Biography, https://smcproxy1.saintmarys.edu:3248/apps/doc/A174872088/BIC?u=nd_stmarys&sid=BIC&xid=b1d3aadb. Accessed 29 June 2020.

Perez, Evan. 2021. "Man in 'Camp Auschwitz' Sweatshirt during Capitol Riot Arrested, Law Enforcement Official Says." CNN, January 13, www.cnn.com/2021/01/13/politics/camp-auschwitz-shirt-capitol-arrested/index.html.

Peters, Carmichael. 2003. "A Rahnerian Reading of Black Rage." *Philosophy & Theology* 15, vol. 1: 191–215.

Reinhold, Robert. 1992 "Riots in Los Angeles: The Blue Line; Surprised, Police React Slowly as Violence Spreads." *New York Times*, May 1. Gale in Context: Biography, https://smcproxy1.saintmarys.edu:3248/apps/doc/A174871866/BIC?u=nd_stmarys&sid=BIC&xid=a939cd76. Accessed 29 June 2020.

Stowe, David W. 2016. *Song of Exile: The Enduring Mystery of Psalm 137*. Oxford.

Thomas, R. Eric. 2020. "It Does Not Matter If You Are Good." *Elle*, May 29, www.elle.com/culture/career-politics/a32712287/cnn-omar-jimenez-arrest-response/.

www.thetrumparchive.com, January 6, 2021, 6:01:04 PM EST.

Tschaepe, Mark. 2016. "Addressing Microagressions and Epistemic Injustice: Flourishing from the Work of Audre Lorde," *Essays in the Philosophy of Humanism* 24, vol. 1: 87–101.

"Tulsa in Remorse to Rebuild Homes; Dead Now Put at 30—Citizens . . . Voice Shame Over Riots That Razed Negro Quarter. Blame Police and Sheriff." 1921. *New York Times*, June 2, 1–2.

Van Gelder, Laurence. 1968. "Dismay in Nation: Negroes Urge Others to Carry on Spirit of Nonviolence." *New York Times*, April 5, 1.

Washington Post Staff. 2021. "How Pro-Trump Insurrectionists Broke into the U.S. Capitol." *Washington Post*, January 6, www.washingtonpost.com/politics/interactive/2021/video-timeline-capitol-breach/?no_nav=true&tid=a_classic-iphone. www.washingtonspectator.org/about/

Wicker, Tom. 1968. "Thousands Leave Washington as Bands of Negroes Loot Stores." *New York Times,* April 6, 23.

"Widespread Disorders." 1968. *New York Times*, April 5, 26.

Chapter 14

Rethinking "God-breathed" in the Age of #BLM

A Womanist Reading of 2 Tim 3:10–17

Angela N. Parker

¹⁰ Now you have observed my teaching, my conduct, my aim in life, my faith, my patience, my love, my steadfastness, ¹¹ my persecutions, and my suffering the things that happened to me in Antioch, Iconium, and Lystra. What persecutions I endured! Yet the Lord rescued me from all of them. ¹² Indeed, all who want to live a godly life in Christ Jesus will be persecuted. ¹³ But wicked people and impostors will go from bad to worse, deceiving others and being deceived. ¹⁴ But as for you, continue in what you have learned and firmly believed, knowing from whom you learned it, ¹⁵ and how from childhood you have known the sacred writings that are able to instruct you for salvation through faith in Christ Jesus. ¹⁵ All scripture is inspired by God and is useful for teaching, for reproof, for correction, and for training in righteousness, ¹⁷ so that everyone who belongs to God may be proficient, equipped for every good work. (2 Tim 3:10–17, NRSV)[1]

I remember, as a graduate student in my New Testament PhD program, reading William H. Myers's (1991) essay entitled "The Hermeneutical Dilemma of the African American Biblical Student" and experiencing difficulty understanding his argumentation. In his work, Myers argues that a Eurocentric worldview and approach serve as the hidden and subtle ideology lying underneath the ways that the history of interpretation unfolds. While arguing that understanding African American experiences and communities in relationship to biblical canon would release the Eurocentric stronghold over the hermeneutical dilemma, Myers obliquely references hermeneutical motifs such as authorial intent, inspiration, inerrancy, and propositional revelation as also being related to Eurocentric worldviews. While Myers specifically argues African American studies face a hermeneutical dilemma because of our Eurocentric training, I argue that we also face an inspiration and authority dilemma as well.

As a seminary student reading Myers, I confess that I had difficulty understanding his argumentation because questions of authority of Scripture and the meaning of hermeneutics were new to me. I imagined that everyone read the Bible as "God-breathed" and, therefore, inerrant and infallible. Truthfully, it took many years for me to even understand that I could critically read the biblical text as a woman because, in my own upbringing, my gender prohibited me from "teaching or usurping authority" over men, according to the King James Version of 1 Timothy 2:12.

Similar to my own upbringing, there are students in my seminary classroom who embrace an uncritical view of the biblical text and who exude wholehearted faith in the "infallible and inerrant truth of the Bible," as "the authoritative word of God." These students usually come from conservative evangelical backgrounds with a variety of identities. These students can be white, Black, brown, etc. and share fundamentalist impact from their own communities. Many such students have come to seminary after having attended a fundamentalist college where there were no women professors (white, Black, or brown). These students may also have already served in ministerial roles and are seeking a professor who rubber stamps what they think they already know about the biblical text.

In another context, I identify white supremacist authoritarianism within biblical interpretation as a guiding factor behind issues of inerrancy and infallibility (Parker 2021). While not wanting to discuss inerrancy extensively, I define the term "inerrant" as simply meaning "free from error" and the way that many evangelical and mainline Protestants employ the term as a way to describe the "trustworthiness" of the biblical text as God's word (ibid.). The related concept of "infallibility" is the characteristic of being incapable of failing to accomplish a predetermined purpose. The Protestant Reformers broke with the Catholic Church by stating that only the biblical text is infallible, whereas Catholic doctrine teaches that the teaching of the church under the authority of the pope, its earthly head, is infallible as well (ibid.). Accordingly, inerrancy, infallibility, and authority have connections to human authority in the beginnings of our understandings of these concepts. The problem with these terms is that they are often connected to the issue of *theopneustos,* or "God-breathed," as traditional commentators interpret 2 Timothy.

In my tenure as a professor, I have often witnessed African American students upholding an unshakeable faith in biblical infallibility that often requires them to suppress their own Black identity in support of white idealized understandings of the biblical text. Therefore, this essay interrogates and ponders the idea of *theopneustos* as God-breathed and what that may mean for Black identity and the ways life experiences and sufferings may relate to the idea of God-breathed Scripture. Essentially, connecting *theopneustos* not just to divine authority but also to human authority may, with nuance, unpack ideas relating to justice in contemporary society and in relationship to pressing issues such as the #BLM movement in the US.

This essay unfolds as follows. First, I provide background on 2 Timothy. Second, I discuss the concept of authority. Third, I provide a background of 2 Timothy, specifically engaging with the work of Clarice J. Martin's entry "1–2 Timothy, Titus" in *True to Our Native Land* (2007) and "The Haustafeln (Household Codes) In African American Biblical Interpretation: 'Free Slaves' and 'Subordinate Women'" (1991). Finally, I engage the issue of *theopneustos* as I rethink Paul's "heroic" experiences contrasted with womanist heroic experiences, Paul's sufferings contrasted with womanist sufferings, and how engagement with experiences and sufferings provide a complex and nuanced understanding of *theopneustos* as "God–breathed" and authoritative for creative interpretation of Scripture.

THE 2 TIMOTHY CONTEXT

Second Timothy is one of the "Pastoral Letters" that include 1 Timothy and Titus. These two other letters share similar language with 2 Timothy. Such comparable language includes the issues of teaching (*didaskalia*), godliness (*eusebia*), and relating to God in a godly manner (*eusebos*). These pastoral letters contain words and highlight doctrinal teaching that do not appear in authentic Pauline literature. Further, 2 Timothy differs from 1 Timothy and Titus in a number of ways because of the assumption that the author is in prison and facing imminent death. Specifically, 2 Timothy reads as a last will and testament, while engaging extant Jewish sources instead of the Hebrew Bible alone. In 2 Tim. 3:8, the author seemingly engages the apocryphal story of Moses known to us through the Cairo Genizah-copy of the *Damascus Document* as opposed to the Exodus narrative in the Septuagint.

Although 2 Timothy claims to be a letter composed by the apostle Paul (while imprisoned and awaiting execution), not all scholars believe that Pauline authorship is authentic. Indications that Timothy is a "third generation" Christian in 1:5, combined with an emphasis on "right teaching," leads to the conclusion that the letter is responding to communal conditions of the believing community after Paul's lifetime.[2] The letter primarily addresses proper doctrine and church leadership.

While Pauline authorship is declared in the opening salutations, it seems highly unlikely that the historical Paul is writing 2 Timothy. Since this letter is probably arising from a "Pauline" school that culminated sometime between the beginning and middle of the first century (100–150 CE), 2 Timothy falls under the category of pseudepigrapha. As a pseudepigraphon, the letter attributes authorship to Paul although someone(s) else actually composed it. In present day parlance, we often think of such practices as plagiarism; however, writing in someone else's name was a common practice among ancient writers. Such attribution was intended to give the unknown author(s) and their writing authority and influence. In this case, Paul's name is attributed to the writing to give *apostolic* authority and influence. Similar to 1 Timothy, most scholars date the Pastorals late because of the internal evidence of organizational issues, creedal statements, and actions as the guardians of the "faith." For the purposes of this essay, I am dating this letter to the Domitian persecution in the 90s CE, with a "look back" to the Neronian persecution of 67 CE when Paul purportedly was martyred under Nero. Moreover, throughout the essay, I sometimes refer to the author of this epistle as Paul, though I doubt he authored it.

BREATHING NEW AUTHORITY

As a New Testament professor, I often encounter students who come into the seminary classroom with this phrase set in their heads: "The Bible Says it, I believe it, that settles it" (Sarfati 2004). Thinking through Myers's (1991) work in *Stony the Road We Trod*, similar to his understanding of the hermeneutical dilemma of the African American student and the connection to a Eurocentric worldview, I specifically teach and engage the authority dilemma that students encounter when they enter seminary as also related to a Eurocentric worldview. Students must develop an authority standpoint that expands beyond "the Bible says it, I believe it, that settles it." Since the Bible, as the "Word of God," is their ultimate authority, they tend to dismiss questioning what they read in an English translation. One of my jobs as a professor is to expand every student's understanding of authority and authority's relationship to the biblical text that is set in the context of the biblical text and not in the context of a Eurocentric worldview alone. Understanding the Roman imperial context becomes important to expand a student's view of authority.

The English word "authority" descends from the Latin word *auctoritas*. In Roman imperial society, *auctoritas* is distinct from the word *imperium*. Imperium (from which we derive "imperial") connotes the idea of rights held by government officials. In contrast, *auctoritas* allows for the interpretation of and elaboration upon the wisdom of those who came before. As Hebrew Bible/Old Testament scholar William Brown (2007) notes, *auctoritas* is more creative. While precedent matters when it comes to *auctoritas*, what matters more is having conversations with what comes before *and* after. Therefore, the idea of authority actually stems from movement between interpretation and contextualization. In many ecclesial settings, I still experience pastors and ministers interpreting texts without deep and thought-provoking contextualization.[3] As a biblical scholar I understand the importance of contextualization as a part of interpretation; however, many students (and even preaching pastors today) do not recognize contextualization as part of interpretation. How would our faith communities be transformed if we fully embraced an idea of biblical authority that lives and breathes in such a movement between contextualization and interpretation? How would our faith communities transform society if we embraced the need for an abiding sense of connection to what has happened in the past while having continued conversation with our present and imagining what future transformation could entail?

Furthering the authority conversation, Katie Cannon (2007) shows how African American professors depart from the "normative" (read "white male") assumptions in our various guilds to bring a radical critique to inherited Eurocentric traditions and kerygmatic assertions that minimize Black people's actualization of our God-given authenticity. In performing a womanist reading of 2 Timothy, I engage Cannon's idea of departing from the normative ways of reading biblical texts by maximizing the authority within one's own identity to actualize the individual reader's ability to exert our God-given, inspired breath—our authority. Part of my job as professor is to develop a creative understanding of biblical authority propelled by and enabled by a God who continues to breathe in and through the interpreter today. Such a creative understanding allows students to imagine readings of Scripture that foster a healthy society in which all participants are able to make distinctive and valuable contributions and therefore *BREATHE!*

WOMANISM AND 2 TIMOTHY

As I ponder 2 Timothy, I will engage Clarice Martin's womanist understanding of the Deutero-Pauline literature.

Clarice Martin (2007) understands at least three broad factors when considering a continuum of possibilities that gave rise to the historical situations of the pastoral epistles. First, Martin argues that the Deutero-Pauline communities may be understood as dissident communities faced with the potentially threatening intrusions of the ideologies and retributive power of Rome. The Pauline recipients were keenly aware of their tenuous relationship with imperial authorities. Thus, the Deutero-Pauline writers exhort their recipients to embrace the ideals of good citizenship, conformity to prevailing social norms, and accommodation with government and worldly authorities for the sake of peace for the church (see 1 Tim 2:1–2, Titus 3:1).

Second, Martin (2007) argues that the Deutero-Pauline communities may have faced teachings and resistance from individuals and groups who were responsible for fomenting internal divisiveness within their faith communities. Therefore, the recipients were encouraged to remember and to imitate the example and disposition of Paul—their faith model par excellence—in their quest for steadfastness and perseverance in faith and ministry. The communities may have developed a fiery resolve to exhibit unfaltering moral virtue, holiness, and wisdom that would counter vituperative opponents (1 Tim 1:3–7, 6:3–6; 2 Tim 2:1–26).

Finally, Martin (2007) highlights evidence that Christian traditionalists within the faith communities feared an erosion of prevailing social mores that required Christian women and enslaved believers (both male and female) to continue to conform unqualifiedly to their roles as "low–status subordinates" in the assemblies that met within Greco-Roman households (*oikos*) (Martin 2007, 412). Since such prevailing social mores were a foundation block of Roman ideology and society, the authors of the Deutero-Pauline letters issue stern warnings against what might be termed "egalitarian excess" (ibid.). For these Christian traditionalists, the communities must rigidly conform to paternal power (*patria potestas*) that upholds rule of the paterfamilias (the father/husband/slave master—as the ultimate authority) (ibid.). Therefore, any deviance that potentially challenged or subverted those traditional protocols would be viewed as "egalitarian excess." A libertine or liberationist eschatological ethic wherein free Christian women and enslaved persons (males and females) viewed themselves as fully freed from these customary social constraints and mores likely had its roots in the more egalitarian vision of the pre-Pauline formula in Galatians 2:28: "there is no longer free or slave, there is no longer male and female; for all of you are one in Christ Jesus" (Martin 2007).

As she outlines African American biblical hermeneutics, Martin states that African Americans found resonance with at least four broad themes or motifs in the Pastoral letters: (1) the generational transmittal of the Christian faith (as signaled in the textual reference to Timothy's grandmother Lois and mother, Eunice); (2) the suggestion of qualities for church leaders; (3) the more contentious instruction for navigating the terrain of gender politics relative to women's leadership, agency, and service with the church; and (4) the Pauline model of fidelity and perseverance in faith portrayed in 2 Timothy (2007, 412). As I engage Cannon and Martin's work, I focus on the generational transmittal of Christian faith from mother to child within a womanist leadership framework while engaging the idea of the women's experiences, sufferings, *and* authority within and beyond the context of 2 Timothy 3:10–17.

Finally, Martin (2007) states that one hallmark of African American biblical hermeneutics (practices of interpretation) through the centuries is its culturally nuanced agreement with the rallying cry of sixteenth-and seventeenth-century reformers: the church is a dynamic institution, created to be the ever-reforming embodiment of the pilgrim people of God in a changing world (*ecclesia reformata semper reformanda*—the church reformed and ever to be reformed) (410). The project and enterprise of African American biblical hermeneutics has in every age fired the engines of profound change in both church and society (ibid.). As I read 2 Timothy 3:10–17, I engage authority in a dialectical and dynamic way for a reforming church today.

A WOMANIST READING OF 2 TIMOTHY 3:10–17

In between the opening (1:1–2) and the closing (4:19–22) of the letter, the author repeats that Timothy must "rekindle the gift of God" without shame (1:3–10). Simultaneously, the author encourages Timothy (and others of the community) to be mindful of the traditions that were passed down to them. All is stated in the author's context of his own imminent death.

After the salutation, the author discusses Lois and Eunice. Likely written with a similar chronological frame, probably during the reign of emperor Domitian in Asia Minor 90–110 CE, the letter appears to be what some scholars describe as a "third generation" correspondence (Martin 2007, 412). The first generation of Jesus's follower's include Timothy's grandmother Lois, while the second generation would be his mother, Eunice. Timothy, standing as a sterling representative of the third generation, appears to pass on the precious faith legacy of his ancestor(s). Since the author mentions these early followers of Jesus (i.e., grandmother and mother), the writer seems to suggest a passing of generational time (1:3–3). Exhortations that discuss courage and self-control of church leaders continue in 1:6–2:13. Official leaders are advised to "pass down" what they have learned from others (i.e., the "faith"). In 2:14–3:9, the writer also warns official leaders to avoid various heresies, corruptions, and passions while showing effectiveness in passing down sound doctrines (again *didaskalia*). By the time we get to 3:10, readers have learned that the epistle includes further exhortation that leaders must continue in the faith and teaching, specifically related to the idea of "God-breathed" Scripture.

Rethinking Pauline "Heroic" Experiences

¹⁰ Now you have observed (*parakolouthesas*) my teaching (*didaskalia*), my conduct, my aim in life, my faith (*pistei*), my patience, my love, my steadfastness.

Scholars note that 2 Timothy 3 contains the following enthymeme: (1) a man of God should do good works; (2) Scripture equips one for good works; and (3) therefore, study Scripture in order to be approved (Witherington 2006).[4] However, how does a varied understanding of experience interact with the way that interpreters such as Witherington engage the author's experience? Specifically, what does it look like to reimagine the author of 2 Timothy's appeal to Paul's experiences before the author appeals to Scripture or sacred writings? Further, interpreters of 2 Timothy such as Witherington point to Paul as a hero or the paradigmatic example of what a Christian leader is to be. On the other hand, feminist scholars Melanie Johnson-DeBaufre and Laura S. Nasrrallah (2011) argue for moving beyond the heroic Paul that contemporary preachers such as John MacArthur espouse. Specifically, Johnson-DeBaufre and Nasrallah point out how MacArthur preached a sermon that highlights the heroic traveling missionary who serves as example for contemporary Christians (usually masculine) to compete for territory both in jobs and in their neighborhoods (Johnson-DeBaufre and Nasrallah 2011). Scholars continue this worship of Paul that even impacts contemporary preaching today. Hero worship of Paul connects Paul's experience with the idea of *theopneustos* (God–breathed) in Scripture (see Witherington 2006). However, my question becomes "Is there enough room for other heroes and experiences that can engage within an interpretation of 2 Timothy that does not focus solely on the Pauline figure?" I wonder what it looks like to imagine other people, specifically womanist heroes, in this 2 Timothy narrative? As the church reforms and develops two thousand years after Pauline literature, what does it look like to think of African American and womanist heroes of the faith after Paul? Can a womanist interpretation of 2 Timothy accomplish a slightly different interpretation beyond the heroic worship of Paul—as we imagine a *mother* invoking language similar to 2 Timothy to her *daughter* in ministry?

Comparing and Contrasting Pauline "Heroic" Experiences with Womanist Experiences

One framework that allows me to rethink experience with *theopneustos* is the work of Black feminist and womanist writers. The first work is a volume edited by Toni C. King and Alease Ferguson entitled *Black Womanist Leadership Tracing the Motherline*. The second work is by Cheryl Townsend

Gilkes, entitled *If It Wasn't For the Women*. Both works interact with the ideas of womanist motherhood and leadership within Black communities but from a diverse viewpoints.

Womanist writers Toni C. King and Alease Ferguson coined the term *allomothers* as those other women who help to mother and develop the character of youth in their communities (King and Ferguson 2011, ix). Allomothers are women within cultural communities that transmit certain gender-specific cultural insider knowledge that could not be recognized or understood in the context of current paradigms of leadership and authority (King and Ferguson 2011, ix). In my reading, since Paul writes to Timothy as a son, I argue that rethinking experience with *theopneustos* allows a reimagination for allomothers to impart similar information to daughters in ministry. What culturally specific support must women in ministry receive today? How can we rethink experiences of sexism in ministry that the author has not even engaged for Timothy? The epistle writer advises Timothy to not allow community members to disregard his youth. I argue that rethinking the role of experience means that allomothers must tell daughters to not allow community members to disregard and disrespect their gender in ministry.

Allomothers may, in fact, tell their daughters in ministry not only to "observe," but to follow after my teachings and experiences. The verb *parakoloutheo* is an important one, meaning more than just "follow" or "take note of" (Witherington 2006, 358). In the 2 Timothy text, the Greek word *parakoloutheo* normally translates to "observe" but it has a deeper meaning. In Stoic circles it referred to the close relationship of the disciple and master wherein the disciple not only learns from, but also imitates the example of, the master (Epictetus 1.7.33; 2.24.19, 2009). Particularly, the author advises Timothy not to allow others in ministry to "label" him as a youth without any experience. Similarly, in Black parlance, womanist scholars such as Cheryl Townsend Gilkes argue that Black women should not allow the "labeling" from others to be used against Black women (Gilkes 2001, 161–80). As Gilkes describes, labeling is the moral placement of Black women in such a way that devalues and stigmatizes the goods, services, political efficacy, social honor, and respect of Black women. Similar to the work of King and Ferguson and the language of allomothers, Gilkes describes a "lifting as we climb" metaphor that portrays Black women as leaders for other Black women (Gilkes 2001, 174–76). Townsend Gilkes, contra King and Ferguson, does identify how the "matriarch" label was detrimental to some Black women since the idea of matriarchy was yoked to the idea of an emasculating Sapphire figure (Gilkes 2001, 176–78). Nonetheless, Gilkes is similar to King and Ferguson when she identifies that Black churchwomen are hierarchical and authoritarian in their own right, even as they are willing to "mother" others toward developing effective political participation and leadership (Gilkes 2001, 206). In my understanding, the experiences of labeling, coupled with the language of observing, share similarities with the Greek text of 2 Timothy and Black parlance regarding allomothers and womanist mothering.

Rethinking Pauline Suffering with Suffering in the Context of #BLM

> [11] my persecutions, and my suffering the things that happened to me in Antioch, Iconium, and Lystra. What persecutions I endured! Yet the Lord rescued me from all of them.

In verse 11, the author moves to language of *tois diogmois, tois pathemasin,* which connote persecutions and sufferings. However, what would a blended Jewish and Greek audience hear in the writer's language? It seems that the writer's language highlights issues of imperial persecutions that he experienced as a result of living for Christ. Historians note that the Neronian persecution began 67 CE (Eusebius of Caesarea 2.25.7, 2019) and legend, according to Gaius of Rome, also quoted by Eusebius, purported that Paul was beheaded as a Roman citizen at the third milepost on the Ostian Way, at a spot called Aquae Salviae, in the year 67. Early Jesus followers would have known and adhered to Pauline hero worship. Early Jesus followers would easily adhere to the idea that Paul led an admirable and influential life and then suffered imperial persecution by Nero, even though 2 Timothy may have been written by a Deutero-Pauline writer during imperial persecution under Domitian in the 90s CE.

The nature of imperial persecution stems from sufferings. Specifically, the writer uses the phrase *tois pathēmasin*. In other writing such as Romans 8:17, authentic Paul uses the verb *sympaschomen,* which is a cognate for the noun *pascha* (i.e., which could either mean the formal Passover meal or Jesus as the sacrifice, as Paul uses in 1 Cor 5:7). Instead of *pascha*, the Deutero-Pauline writer uses *tois pathēmasin,* just as authentic Paul used it in Romans 7:5. In his Romans commentary, Robert Jewett notes that this word would be known to the original Roman auditors as suffering related to the Roman Empire (Jewett 2007). One would also connect this suffering to that which Jesus suffered at the hands of the Roman Empire on the cross. So even as Jesus suffered, Paul also suffered similar imperial sufferings and persecutions as well.

Is there a way to think through Roman imperial persecution that may be similar to imperial persecution suffered in the present context of the United States of America? Attention to contemporary sociologists' work may help.

According to Julian Go of Boston University, during the #BLM protest in Ferguson, Missouri, police forces used tear gas canisters, MRAPs (light armored vehicles), and short-barreled 5.56 mm rifles based on the military M4 carbine (Go 2020). Go argues that #BLM related incidents attest to the militarization of American policing. That is, civilian police draw from imperial-military ideas and pattern themselves around the ideas that minoritized communities are to be treated as natives to be colonized in their own countries, similar to the Jewish presence in the Roman Empire (ibid.). Legend stated that Paul was under military escort and imprisonment during the last years of his life. The American police system is modeling itself after the military and their imperial tactics as identified in other countries. However, these tactics are used against #BLM activists who reside in and are citizens of the United States of America. Similar persecutions and sufferings occur in today's day and age. The final question, though, becomes, how do these sufferings and persecutions dynamically interact and reform a church that is beholden to the authority and inspiration of God-breathed Scripture?

Theopneustos as "God–Breathed" and "God–Inspired" Scripture

The issue of *theopneustos* as God-breathed or God-inspired is not a new area of study for biblical scholars. As early as 1980, H. Wayne House argues that the problem posed in the translation of *theopneustos* is whether it is a passive verbal form or an active verbal form (House 1980). If passive, the word emphasizes that Scripture's source is the breath of God. Scripture, therefore, originates in and comes from God. If the word has an active meaning, the emphasis is that the Scripture is filled with the breath of God, that is, it is inspiring. House (1980) lands on the idea that Scripture is passive and thus, emphasizes Scripture's source as the breath of God.

Craig Keener (2020) argues that an understanding of "God-breathed" must be in the context of relationship, tradition, and community of faith. The idea that every Scripture is God-breathed hinges on the four *pros*–clauses ("for" teaching, rebuking, correcting, and training) that come together to the one *hina* clause "so (in order) that the servant of God may be thoroughly equipped for every good work" (3:17). Keener argues that the writer gives the ultimate purpose of Scripture's inspiration. While Keener argues that Scripture has a divinely intended purpose for salvation, it also appears that the author likens Paul's experiences and sufferings as a "lead up" to Scripture's purpose for training the ultimate "person of God" (*anthrōpos tou theou*). Keener and others argue that the four prepositional clauses may be said to form two groups, the first two dealing with doctrine (orthodoxy) and the second with behavior (orthopraxy).

Building upon Keener and others, however, I would argue that while training up the person of God accordingly, this text connects their experiences and suffering to the God-breathed nature of Scripture. I argue that there is almost a "play" between God's breath and humanity's breath so that the person of God may be well-equipped for every kind of good work. Andrew Wilson (2015) argues that Scripture and jazz music share something in common. God uses Paul, Isaiah, and Peter as instruments of God to create God's musical breath. However, I take Wilson (2015) further, to argue that the experiences and sufferings serve as a part of the breath that God uses when God "plays" persons of God such as Paul, Peter, and even contemporary womanist heroes of faith and leadership.

While I agree with both Keener and House, there is still movement and play on what Scripture and its interpretation and engagement with humanity means. As I have highlighted experiences and sufferings as the author's lead up to understanding Scripture as *theopneustos,* it seems to me that attention to how the interpreters dynamically interact with God's breath is highly important. Specifically, how can we understand and interpret the experiences and sufferings of womanist mothers and the experiences and sufferings of the #BLM movement to help us understand the concept of "God-breathed?"

In literature outside of the New Testament, "God-breathed" occurs in reference to the *Sibylline Oracles* (cf. *Sibylline Oracles* 1918, 5:308, 406). Greek words with the - *tos* ending tend to be passive rather than active, so even in outside literature, a better understanding may be that "every Scripture is inspired." However, what is exactly meant by that is still up to debate. God breathed life and meaning and truth into them all (see similarly Num 24:2; Hos 9:7; cf. Josephus 2007, *Ag. Ap.* 1.37–39; 2 Pet 1:21) but there is no explanation on how that works. This is where the human actors, their experiences, and their sufferings come into play. Does the Spirit lift the mind of the writer to see, understand, and write in such a manner that it is almost mechanical dictation? While I certainly do not believe that mechanical dictation occurs within the mind of the writer, I do believe that the creative breath of God intermingles with the creative living souls of the writers to bring about creative understandings of Scripture. I think that attention to experiences, sufferings, and persecutions in each person's life help in the continued interpretation and hermeneutic surrounding Scripture. Similar to the creation narratives of Genesis that state how God breathed into *ha-'adam* ("the human one," Gen 1) and they became a living soul, I argue that there is a dynamic and dialectic relationship between God's breath and humanity's breath, experiences, and sufferings.

In a previous writing, I argue that the reasons why evangelicals and many mainline Protestants highly regard the doctrines of inerrancy and infallibility stem mainly from the Protestant Reformation's interpretation of 2 Timothy

3:16–17: "All scripture is *inspired by God* (*theopneustos*) and is useful for teaching, for reproof, for correction, and for training in righteousness, so that everyone who belongs to God may be proficient, equipped for every good work," NRSV, emphasis mine (Parker 2021). However, what that entails is people in authority and with access to the most power are the ones who determine the "proper," "orthodox," and "only" right interpretation of Scripture. The arbiters of power within biblical interpretation point to inerrancy and infallibility under the guise of objectivity that does not take into account lived experiences.

In this chapter, I interpret and engage the idea of "God–breathed" in relation to the words "I can't breathe," uttered by both Eric Garner and George Floyd in their final moments. These words have been taken up as a slogan of the #BLM movement. What does it look like to think of authority and *theopneustos* from the underside? From the point of view of those who find themselves at the receiving end of imperial machinations against Black and brown bodies? My own loose translation of 2 Timothy 3:16–17 is as follows:

> All Scripture is God-breathed and advantageous toward teaching, toward rebuke, toward correcting faults, toward instruction in justice, so that the person of God may be capable of finishing all good works.

The writer of 2 Timothy suggests that God's breath in the biblical text is advantageous toward a desired end. I translate the Greek preposition *pros* as "toward" to stress the continued movement to which God's breath compels humanity. And I specifically use the term "justice" as opposed to "righteousness" to prod readers toward an idea of faith-based social justice that is inherent even in our ideas of individual righteousness and salvation. The underlying theme of this essay is that our faith communities cannot fully breathe because of the tainted views of authority that we have imbibed in many of our church traditions.

The Protestant church's main understanding of Scripture is that it is God-breathed and originates from God. So the emphasis is that Scripture partakes of the quality of the creative breath of God, and Scripture is profitable. However, this essay argues that the creative breath of God intermingles with our own breath in the ways that we contemporary readers, specifically contemporary womanist readers of Scripture, must rethink experiences, rethink sufferings, and rethink *theopneustos* as contemporary readers and interpreters understand and interrogate issues of authority.

CONCLUSION

As I have pondered 2 Timothy 3:10–17, I have rethought and reimagined the issues of authority, experiences, sufferings, and persecutions all in relationship to the term *theopneustos* as God-breathed and God-inspired. In this text, I have argued that we have to rethink experiences and sufferings particularly from a womanist point of view in order to create a more nuanced understanding of God-breathed that is not specifically related to "orthodox" meanings of Scripture alone. Accordingly, some concluding thoughts and paths forward are in order.

First, Black womanist leaders ask particular questions regarding trauma, racism, classism, and sexism in the personal and social histories of Black women and how, in light of these experiences and oppressions, they transmit leadership skills to their daughters in society and, specifically for me, in ministry (King and Ferguson 2011). In these questions, Black womanist leaders have to exorcize the trauma of racism, classism, and sexism. When we read 2 Timothy uncritically we may find that the letter, while alluding to Lois and Eunice, does not possess an understanding of the gendered ways that racism (remember, Timothy is half Greek and half Jewish), classism, and sexism affect how women read and engage 2 Timothy. Allomothers must remind daughters of the racism, classism, and sexism they may experience even as they train to be leaders in congregations that may not want to accept their leadership.

Secondly, womanist mothers and allomothers can begin to think of the 2 Timothy example, coupled with their own experience, as a starting point to their own examples of leadership. Just as the author reminded Timothy of his aim, faith, patience, etc., womanist mothers and allomothers can perform similar tasks for their own daughters in ministry. These examples serve as access points to stories that show mentorship and leadership training to womanist daughters.

Third, just as the writer of 2 Timothy served as a guide and a leader, womanist allomothers do the same even when they are not the direct biological mothers of the womanist daughter. The author served as a mentor and example to Timothy even when he was not Timothy's biological father. However, it would behoove me not to advise acting like Paul as a father without observing that his behavior toward Timothy did have negative consequences. Specifically, womanist writers such as Mitzi Smith (2019) highlight the issue of respectability politics that the Paul of Acts of the Apostles engaged in forcing Timothy to become circumcised. Womanist allomothers would do well to mentor and encourage daughters without falling into the respectability politics that occurs in many Black churches.

Fourth, in the area of theological education, womanist scholars must be at the forefront of guiding students through the authority dilemma that stems from a surface understanding of authority. How can expanded views of God-breathed and authority help the African American seminary student become adept at preaching the biblical texts without succumbing to a superficial white authorized reading of sacred Scripture? In this way, the solution to the authority dilemma must be a combination of contextual research and the interdisciplinary workings of various critical theories that uphold African American identity. Further, as womanist scholars teaching in seminary contexts, I argue that many of us must continue to wrestle white supremacist authority from Eurocentric and white-identified readings of Scripture that do not question Pauline authority and also blindly accept both authentic Paul and Deutero-Pauline use of respectability politics.

Perhaps these small steps may be the ways that authority and God-breathed understanding can converse with liberation for more groups of people who read the biblical text as sacred and authoritative. Let us continue to rethink what "God-breathed" means in our varied and complex identities.

NOTES

1. All Scripture quotations are from the New Revised Standard Version unless I state otherwise.

2. The idea of "right teaching" comes from the use of *didaskalia* in 2:2, 2:15.

3. Anecdotally, this past summer I attended church services with extended family. Since I am the biblical scholar in my family, relatives often ask me what I think of a sermon. I often regale my family members with contextualization of biblical texts that they do not hear in their ecclesial lives.

4. Any enthymeme is a rhetorical argument used in oratorical practices that are described as "the body of proof" according to Aristotle's *Rhetoric* 1, 1.3,11. As a trained rhetor, Paul uses rhetoric in his argumentation. See also Aristotle's *Rhetoric* II.XX.1.

WORKS CITED

Bate, H. N. and M. A. England, trans. 1918. *The Sibylline Oracles*. Books III-V. Society for Promoting Christian Knowledge. London, UK: Macmillan

Brown, William P. 2007. *Engaging Biblical Authority: Perspectives on the Bible as Scripture*. Louisville: Westminster John Knox.

Cannon, Katie Geneva. 1985. "The Emergence of Black Feminist Consciousness." *Feminist Interpretation of The Bible*, edited by Letty M. Russell, 30–40. Philadelphia: Westminster.

———. 2007. "The Biblical Mainstay of Liberation." *Engaging Biblical Authority*, edited by William P. Brown, 18–26. Louisville: Westminster John Knox.

Epictetus. Translated by George Long. 2009. *The Enchiridion, or Handbook: With a Selection from the Discourses of Epictetus*. Auckland: Floating.

Eusebius of Caesarea. 2019. *The History of the Church: A New Translation*. Berkeley: University of California Press.

Ferguson, S. Alease, and Toni C. King. 2011. *Black Womanist Leadership Tracing the Motherline*. Albany: State University of New York Press.

Go, Julian. 2020. "The Imperial Origins of American Policing: Militarization and Imperial Feedback in the Early 20th Century." *The American Journal of Sociology* 125.5: 1193–1254. https://doi.org/10.1086/708464.

House, H. Wayne. 1980. "Biblical Inspiration in 2 Timothy 3:16." *The Bibliotheca Sacra* 137, vol. 545: 54–63.

Jewett, Robert. 2007. Roy David Kotansky, and Eldon Jay. Epp. *Romans: a Commentary*. Minneapolis: Fortress.

Johnson-DeBaufre, Melanie, and Laura Nasrallah. 2011. "Beyond the Heroic Paul: Toward a Feminist and Decolonizing Approach to the Letters of Paul." *The Colonized Apostle: Paul in Postcolonial Eyes*, edited by Christopher D. Stanley, 161–73. Minneapolis: Fortress.

Josephus, Flavius. 2007. *Flavius Josephus, Translation and Commentary. Vol. 10, Against Apion*. Translated by John M. G. Barclay. Leiden: Brill.

Keener, Craig S. 2020. "GREEK VERSUS JEWISH CONCEPTIONS OF INSPIRATION AND 2 TIMOTHY 3:16." *Journal of the Evangelical Theological Society* 63, vol. 2: 217–31.

Martin, Clarice J. 1991. "The Haustafeln (Household Codes) In African American Biblical Interpretation: 'Free Slaves' and 'Subordinate Women.'" *Stony the Road We Trod: African American Biblical Interpretation*, edited by Cain Hope Felder, 206–31. Minneapolis: Fortress.

———. 2007. "1–2 Timothy, Titus." *True to Our Native Land: an African American New Testament Commentary*, edited by Brian K. Blount, et al., 409–36. Minneapolis: Fortress.

Myers, William H. 1991. "The Hermeneutical Dilemma of the African American Biblical Student." *Stony the Road We Trod: African American Biblical Interpretation*, edited by Cain Hope Felder, 40–56. Minneapolis: Fortress.

Nullens, Patrick. 2013. "Theologia Caritatis and the Moral Authority of Scripture: Approaching 2 Timothy 3:16–17 with a Hermeneutic of Love." *European Journal of Theology* 22, vol. 1: 38–49.

Parker, Angela N. 2021. *If God Still Breathes, Why Can't I: Black Lives Matter and Biblical Authority*. Grand Rapids, MI: Eerdmans.

Oden, Thomas C. 1989. *First and Second Timothy and Titus*. Louisville: John Knox.

Sarfati, Jonathan, 2004. *Refuting Compromise*. Green Forest, AR: Master Books.

Smith, Mitzi J. 2019. "Paul, Timothy, and the Respectability Politics of Race: A Womanist Inter(con)textual Reading of Acts 16:1–5." *Religions* 10, vol. 3: 190. https://doi.org/10.3390/rel10030190.

Townsend Gilkes, Cheryl. 2001. *If It Wasn't For the Women.* Maryknoll, New York: Orbis Books.

Turner, Sonya M. 2011. "Mother's Transformative Medicine: An Inoculation against Intergenerational Stagnancy." *Black Womanist Leadership: Tracing the Motherline*, edited by Toni C. King et al., 179–92. Albany: State University of New York Press.

Wilson, Andrew. 2015. "That's the Spirit!: What Scripture and Jazz Music Have in Common." *Christianity Today* 59, vol. 1: 28.

Witherington, Ben, III. 2006. *A Socio–Rhetorical Commentary on Titus, 1–2 Timothy and 1–3 John*. Downers Grove: InterVarsity.

Chapter 15

Leah and Dinah in the Face of Abuse

What Do I Tell My Daughter?

Kamilah Hall Sharp

Tarana Burke (2017) found the #MeToo movement to bring awareness to and encourage support of Black and Brown girl survivors of sexual abuse. When celebrity white women began to use the #MeToo hashtag and emerged with their stories of abuse, the Black girls for whom the movement was created were once again silenced and ignored. Although Black girls and women in the United States are victims of sexual assault at a higher rate compared to girls and women of other races, their abuse is often ignored or receives little attention (Planty et al. 2013). While many sexual assault incidents go unnoticed or unreported, sometimes they reach the headlines (Harris 2020; Larimer 2015). In these moments, one finds that Black girls are assaulted in places where they should be safe (Zheng 2020). It is disturbingly clear that the bodies of Black girls and women are not valued and are thus perpetually in positions of peril. Since the kidnapping and enslavement of African people brought to the Americas, the bodies of Black people, particularly women and girls, have been at risk of and subjected to violence. Thus, Black women have understood that their bodies are under constant scrutiny and danger regardless of space, and Black mothers must address it. My passion for a mother's voice in this matter emerged in a discussion at Daughters of the African Atlantic Fund Consultation of African and African Diasporan Women in Religion and Theology in Bahia, Brazil, in July 2018.

My family consists of wise Black women, determined men, and resilient children known to use the power of their voices for more than three generations. Our family has more young girls than young boys, and the girls are womanish. Practical theologian, Melva Sampson (2012) created the social media hashtag #raisingwomanishgirls. This hashtag has become a descriptor of embodied and empowering parenting. Raising womanish girls requires constantly holding in tension wanting our daughters to be critical thinkers who ask questions, which outsiders may consider wanting to know "too much for your own good" (Walker 1983). In #raisingwomanishgirls, we resist the culturally traditional maternal response of, "What did you just say?," to affirm our daughters' curiosities. We *should* expect womanish girls experiencing and witnessing the world around us to ask questions.

As the mother of a pre-teen womanish daughter, it is often exhausting to answer her seemingly incessant questions, ranging from the mundane to the more magnificent complexities of life. For example, on the anniversary of the assassination of the Reverend Dr. Martin Luther King Jr., over dinner that night, my daughter asked me, "Why do we say Jesus was crucified and Dr. Martin Luther King was assassinated?" The intellect and insight from which she raised this theological and political question affirmed that even though she has yet reached a double-digits age, my young daughter is attentive, contemplative, and will raise her voice for answers. Moreover, she has a rightful expectation that I respond to her with an answer as forthright and as engaging as her inquiry.

Critical inquiries like these are plentiful, so I must constantly stay prepared. Though I jokingly added #justbeingAnaya when I answered one of her questions, the reality is that my daughter is genuinely her authentic womanish self when learning about the world around her through her queries. As a result, her questions can quickly turn into deep conversations. I am committed to answering her questions as honestly as possible—even when difficult. Understanding that my daughter's Black girl body is a potential site of danger in this country, the challenge is navigating conversations to keep her informed and safe while not living in debilitating fear of negative possibilities.

Now that she can read well and is the daughter of a preacher, she is becoming more familiar with biblical texts, even those that I find problematic. I have had conversations with her about women's agency over our bodies, but I am aware that she will eventually identify women's loss of agency in the biblical text. What then am I to say about violence against women? Particularly since, as womanist biblical scholar Renita Weems (1995) notes, "[v]iolence against women in the Bible is virtually always cast in sexual terms," I wonder about my answers and our conversations when she asks about sexual violations such as the rape of Dinah in Genesis 34. As an emerging Hebrew Bible scholar, preacher, and womanist mother of a womanish girl "reading her way through the struggle" and engaging these "texts of terror," the lingering question is "What do I tell my daughter?" (Weems 1991; Trible 1984).

While I self-identify as a womanist and engage in womanist biblical interpretation that is concerned about all people, as the mother of a young Black girl, I am particularly concerned about Black girls. This essay uses a womanist maternal thought hermeneutic to read Genesis 34, which seeks to ascertain what happened to Dinah and Leah and how to engage honest conversations with girls about the implications. My approach as a womanist is to raise contextual questions, interrogate the text, and identify issues within the text that support the survival and wholeness of all people. By reading the biblical text from the perspective of a Black woman living in the margins, I seek silenced persons and give them a voice. With that voice, I relate issues in the biblical text to the lived experiences of Black daughters and mothers. Motherhood is an extension of my womanist praxis as a site of resistance and struggle (Abdullah 2012).

Womanist Hebrew Bible scholar Stephanie Buckhanon Crowder (2016) defines womanist maternal thought as an approach to understanding what it means to be Black, a woman, and a mother. A womanist maternal thought hermeneutic interrogates the biblical text with the quadruocentric attention to gender, race, class, and language and their intersectional impact in Black mothers' lives (Martin 1990). Attending to questions and concerns as an interpreter, I seek to develop strategies that help secure the safety of my daughter, and children globally.

GENESIS 34

Genesis 34 begins with Dinah going out to visit other women when she is seized and assaulted by Shechem. He then has his father arrange for him to marry Dinah. However, her brothers, angered by what happened to their sister, trick the Hivite men to become circumcised as part of the wedding agreement. While the Hivite males are healing, the brothers kill them and plunder the city. This is not a passage I have heard preached in church, yet biblical scholars offer a variety of interpretations. What *really* happened between Shechem and Dinah when he saw her out in the land? Scholars broadly interpret this encounter by focusing on the actions of Simeon and Levi and not addressing what happened to Dinah, not viewing it as rape (Bechtel 1994; Lipka 2006), suggesting it was consensual (Brueggemann 1982), or placing the blame on Dinah for what happened (Gunkel and Biddle 1997). Regardless, there are womanist and feminist scholars that name the assault of Dinah as rape (Russaw 2018; Scholz 2000; Schulte 2017).

Dinah, the daughter of Jacob's first wife Leah, sets out to visit other women in the area. Her going out is also the only time in which Dinah does something by herself, an act that has been viewed as inappropriate (Schroeder

2007). The imposition upon her agency is notable as Dinah is only identified by her name throughout the passage in relation to her parents or brothers. Leah is only mentioned here at the beginning of the passage. After the first verse, every time Dinah is mentioned, something is happening *to* her or the narrator is speaking *about* her. This is an example of passively minimizing Dinah's voice, body, and experience. As such, this is where a #MeToo movement gives voice to women like Dinah who were hushed by failing to mention their names and hearing their stories.

In verse two, when Shechem sees Dinah, he *lqḥ*, *škb* and *'nh*—which I translate as "he seized her," "he laid her," and "he raped her." There is consensus in scholarship on defining the first two actions, but not the third verb (Van Wolde 2002; Bader 2006; Scholz 2000). In the Hebrew Bible, what is translated and interpreted as rape varies (Claassens 2016). The term *'nh* in 2 Samuel 13, which narrates the attack on Tamar, is translated as rape (NIV) and interpreted as rape (Peters 2021; Claassens 2016). In Judges 19 and 20, *'nh* and *yd'* are also translated and interpreted as rape of the Levite's secondary wife (NRSV; Smith 2017). While *'nh* has variant usages, some scholars insist that it does not translate as "to rape." Bader (2006) notes the term is used thirteen times in the Hebrew Bible to delineate sexual intercourse by consensual sex, rape, and socioreligious infractions. However, when other violent actions are used in conjunction with this word, it escalates the implicit violence, and it is often interpreted as rape. As noted, this controversial word is also used in the rape narratives of the Levite's secondary wife and of Tamar (Jdgs 19; 2 Sam 13). In each of these stories, a young woman is taken without her consent, sexually assaulted, and is determined to have been raped.

Clearly, what contemporary culture views as rape differs from biblical culture, and I do not want to critique the passage based solely on twenty-first-century standards. For instance, while rape of a woman or girl in biblical culture was regarded as a crime against the male person, his property, or pride, rape of a girl or woman in contemporary culture assigns victimization to the female and not the male. However, I contend that one cannot overlook the violence happening to this young girl or woman, given it is in the biblical text, or brush it off as the way things were done during that time. Residual attitudes about how to regard violence against girls and women today remain. However, for me, to not address this assault is not an option, as I would be derelict in my commitments to advocate for marginalized people, whether in biblical texts or in my lived experiences. Thus, the biblical text that deals with women and sexual violence must be named and addressed to disrupt normalizing rape culture.

Definitions of rape have varied over time and disciplines, as have the laws addressing rape (Scholz 2000; Keefe 1993; and Rape, Abuse & Incest National Network 2016). While modern rape laws focus on the victim's loss, ancient and biblical laws such as Deuteronomy 22:28 focused on the financial loss to the male relative of the woman raped, as he was considered the victim (Schulte 2017). Hebrew Bible scholar Kimberly Russaw (2018) posits that Dinah did not have control over her body, her father did, and she could not have consented. Additionally, Hebrew Bible scholar Cheryl Anderson (2004) contends Dinah's consent is moot under Deuteronomic Law because the injury would be against the father and not the daughter. In the biblical text the concern about rape was always the shame and violation of the property of the husband or father. Anderson (2004) further points out that not only do the Deuteronomic Law and biblical codes not recognize rape as a crime against the female, neither do they give any consideration to the female experience in the case of rape. Further, the burden of proof of rape was placed on the violated girl or woman. Deuteronomy 22:23–27 dictates that if a young woman is attacked and does not cry for help, she should be stoned to death. Though modern laws do not call for young women to be stoned, the girl's experience is not always considered; blaming the victim and repeated victimization through the courts are arguably comparable to stoning. Like the women who lived under Deuteronomic Laws, contemporary women are shackled with the burden of proof and insufficient change fails to ensure that rapists are held accountable (Sanchez 2021).

Kimberlé Crenshaw, critical race theorist and attorney, notes that the historical view over time is that rape victims had to resist their assailants, or their claims of rape were rejected. If there was no struggle, it was interpreted that the woman consented to the intercourse, assuming "a true rape victim would do everything possible to protect her honor even to the point of death" (Crenshaw 1991). Then when the issue of rape intersects with race, class, and sexuality, it becomes even more complicated. For example, in the history of the United States, sexual assaults of Black women were not considered rape because initially, Black women were considered property and therefore unrapeable (Smith 2018). When Black women were enslaved, it was viewed as the right of a slaveholder to demand sex from her (Slatton 2020).

For the trajectory of my analysis of this text of terror, I conclude rape to be the experience of sexual penetration without consent. This terrible truth is what I have explained to my daughter is to be named as rape. Though this definition may not be what biblical writers had in mind, it is what I want my daughter to understand to be rape. In examining the passage and considering the three verbs given together to describe Shechem's actions, I interpret this encounter as a violent assault; Shechem raped Dinah. Even though it may not fit the biblical category of rape since the reader is not given what Dinah's response or actions were during this assault, this amounts to rape. Choosing the term "rape" to translate is within the bounds of the Hebrew language (Gravett 2016). I argue that it is of vital importance to name this encounter as rape, especially for Black girls and women who are told that sexual assaults on their bodies do not amount to rape. Regardless of the survivor's response, including what they did or did not do, where they were, what they said to resist, or wore that could be interpreted as seductive or otherwise inappropriate, it is rape.

Throughout this harrowing ordeal, readers do not "hear" Dinah speak. From the time she leaves her home to visit women in verse 1, is seized and raped by Shechem in verse 2, until her brother takes her from his home in verse 26, Dinah does not speak. The narrator has silenced her—not unlike contemporary attitudes and the judicial system which both implicitly and explicitly demand silencing rape survivors by shaming, requiring arbitrary proof that a rape occurred, and the unyielding process of gathering such proof through rape kits and other victims testimonies. Though she is introduced as the daughter of Leah, the narrator makes no record of Leah's words of lament or comfort. Esther Fuchs (1989) argues a maternal role model is created in biblical narratives that promote the interest of the male child rather than of the female child. It is noticeable that mothers in the Hebrew Bible intervene on behalf of sons but not their daughters, as when Sarah has Hagar sent away for the benefit of her son Isaac (Gen.21:9–10), Bathsheba makes sure Solomon is crowned king (1 Kgs 2:13–22), and Rebekah schemes against Esau for her favorite son Isaac (Gen 27:5–17).

However, in both Dinah and Tamar's rape in 2 Samuel 1:17, it is the brothers—who share the same mother with each young girl—who take action against the assailant. Could the brothers' response be because of their mother's wishes (Bronner 2004)? This question and others surrounding the absence of the mother's voice from the story become warranted due to the depth of the silence in the text. Hence, the silencing of women and girls to meet a particular agenda is problematic in the biblical text and our current cultural, theological, and hermeneutical contexts. While the narrator does not allow Dinah or Leah to speak, we can extract something from this silence by delving into the women's lives apart from this rape story.

Leah was the older daughter of Laban and is described as *rkwt* in Hebrew, which can be defined as "weak" or "tender," and as *astheneis* in the Septuagint (the LXX), which can also be translated as "weak." She is constantly presented as less desirable and valuable than her sister Rachel. In Genesis 29:30, Jacob loved Rachel more than Leah, and because she is unloved, God opens her womb. When Jacob is afraid that Esau will kill him, he puts Leah and her children in front of Rachel and Joseph, showing no regard for their lives, nor interest in protecting them (Gen 33:1–2). Leah bears six sons for Jacob before she gives birth to Dinah. After the birth of each son, his name and its meaning are stated, but not so with Dinah. Although Dinah is the only female character in the Bible whose birth is mentioned, there is no celebration for her birth and no etymological information given about her name (Fuchs 1989). While the birth of sons in this patriarchal society was coveted and even necessary for the survival of women, is that yet the only reason for Leah's reaction to the birth of her daughter? Could it be because, as one who was once a daughter and now a mother and wife, she knew far too well the difficulties for a young girl of navigating the world around her? Perhaps just as she had no control over her body as a young girl, whom her father gave to Jacob (a man who did not love her as much as he did her sister, if at all), she feared the fate of her daughter in a world that did not value her personhood, body, or feelings. Could it be that while Leah, who has been cast in the image of a weak woman that is not as beautiful as Rachel and inferior to her, is named here, her words about the abuse of her daughter are not viewed as worth adding to the story?

Leah is characterized as weak and primarily passive, although this may not align with her true self. Black women are also consistently presented in stereotypical images that are not authentic and true, for example, as jezebels, mammies, etc. Though the images are not necessarily considered passive, the long-held stereotypes such as harlot, matriarch, and *strong Black woman* all come at a heavy cost to the lives of Black women (Walker-Barnes 2014). These stereotypes are the basis for which the narratives of Black women as un-rapeable were created, which prevented the words of the Black women from being heard and/or believed. These false narratives have caused Black women to suffer and/or be silenced—a narrative intimately familiar in Dinah's story, as she is one who endured assault but is not allowed to speak of her own experience.

Before being raped, Dinah is introduced as the daughter of Leah in verse 1 and is described as the daughter of Jacob after her rape in verse 5. In the rapes of Tamar and the Levite's secondary wife, the mothers are not mentioned, and there is no action taken by the fathers in these passages either. This is important since Deuteronomic law clearly cites the crime of rape as a violation against the father. The narrator explains that Dinah is going out to visit the other women in the area. Russaw (2018) asserts that based upon her being called a *n'rh,* or young woman, Dinah was likely going out alone to perform some supportive family function like gathering water as she went out to visit the other women. A girl should be able to safely retrieve water; however, the narrative indicates that a young girl had no safe place in that culture. Young girls in an ancient culture are much like young girls in our culture, who find they are not safe at home, school, or even church. Where they are unsuspectedly vulnerable to sexual assault, young girls today are not safe.

A BLACK GIRL'S REALITY

The harsh reality for young Black girls and women is that they are [disproportionately] raped by those outside their race, by those of their race and within their community. When Tarana Burke sat across from a thirteen-year-old girl and listened to her disclose the details of the sexual abuse she experienced at the hands of her mother's boyfriend, while she could not form the words at that time in her mind, she thought, "me too." Burke, the thirteen-year-old girl, and too many other Black girls continue to be assaulted by relatives, family friends, and other people they know (Smith 2017). When the girl disclosed this assault, Burke quickly ended the conversation by referring the child to a colleague for help. She immediately felt anguish and guilt for not continuing to listen to the girl and not offering her support. Recognizing that silencing harms a survivor of assault, Burke created the *Me Too Movement* to increase awareness and to help amplify the voices of survivors of sexual assault who have been silenced by fear, family, or facing public scrutiny.

Black girls and women who are sexually assaulted are less likely to report their assaults and thus more likely to be re-assaulted (Slatton 2020). Though Black survivors of sexual assault may be silenced when the perpetrator is Black or of another race, underlying reasoning for the silencing may differ. A significant reason that girls do not want to report sexual assault is because of the fear of not being believed. In the case of intra-racial assaults, victims weigh disclosing their assaults with harming the reputation of "a good Black man." For example, Anita Hill and Desiree Washington were both seen as race traitors for disclosing their assaults and harassment (Slatton 2020). When sexual assault claims were made against R. Kelly and Bill Cosby, there continued to be widespread support of these men, while the survivors of their assaults were shunned (Leung and Williams 2019). While it is difficult enough to not be believed by those outside your community, whose ideas of you have been shaped by white supremacy and a history of debasing Black women, it is much more difficult when members of your community do not believe you. Often the disbelief of people from the same community also comes from internalized white supremacy and the history of debasing Black women.

One must ask why the words of young Black girls and women were disbelieved when charges were alleged against R. Kelly, even with video footage? Why were the girls considered responsible for what happened? The young girls were dismissed because they were "being fast"; it is a common assumption that Black girls are sexually advanced and that Black women are promiscuous (Davis 2018). The trope that Black women are "whores" remains in the psyche of this country. Unfortunately, this ideology applies to Black bodies with female genitalia regardless of age. In the biblical story, the narrator chooses the term *n'rh* to describe Dinah, which can obscure the age of the girls who are quite young, though it is often translated as "young woman." Thus, young girls are not seen as young. And when they are assaulted, they are held responsible for the assault. This perspective aligns with early rabbis, who blamed Dinah for her assault because she left home alone (Neusner 1985). The assailant's violations were not the focus, only the actions of the girl were scrutinized.

After her rape, Dinah's father, Jacob, is informed of what has happened to her but does not act to defend or vindicate her. He simply waits for his sons to return. Who told Jacob about Dinah's rape? Could Leah have been the one to let him know that his daughter had been assaulted? How did Leah respond to the news of her daughter's assault? Would the response to hearing of her rape have been any different if the assailant was Israelite rather than Hivite? Was Dinah questioned or blamed by her parents for what was done to her? There are so many questions that can be raised about the rape of Dinah. Similarly, survivors of rape often find themselves facing countless questions after their assault. Sometimes these can facilitate processing their trauma, giving voice to their experience, but unfortunately, at other times, these questions can silence them.

Dinah's rape is an ancient story that coincides with the current reality of many young girls. As a "collective we," we live and participate in a rape culture where we have become desensitized to sexual assaults, particularly against girls and women (hooks 2000). When a man can say, "Grab them by the p—y" and "You can do anything" and still be elected president of the United States, we are reminded that girls and women are not safe (Frenthold 2015). Black girls and women are even more vulnerable to these attacks. The disregard for their lives and lack of protection experienced in such attacks are evidenced in the accounts of Cyntoia Brown, Gabrielle Union, and Simone Biles of their sexual assaults (Brown-Long 2019; Union 2017; Holcombe 2019). Unfortunately, the danger for Black girls and women is not limited to the United States; it is a global problem (Planty 2013). Mothers who face this harsh reality may be alarmed but must become informed and consider ways to prepare their daughters for places and spaces that are not safe. For these reasons, as a mother reading the rape of Dinah in Genesis 34, preparing to have a conversation with my daughter about this horrifying passage included in the Bible that we hold as sacred text, I must tell her something to help fortify her.

LESSONS TO A BLACK DAUGHTER

Considering the prevalence of sexual abuse in our culture, sexual assault of Dinah in the biblical text, and the silence and oppression surrounding both, I know that I cannot have a surface conversation about these issues. It is important to equip my daughter and other girls to confront sexual abuse head-on. First, I will tell my daughter to have courage. What does it truly mean to have courage, a familiar yet almost flippantly used term that is sometimes ambiguous as an embodied mediated action? Many of the ideas about courage come from stories we hear or read. Models of courage often come from those we see. For some contemporary readers, there seems to be little, if any, courage displayed by Leah or Dinah in the text. Nevertheless, I believe there is still something to be learned about courage from this story. "Courage is self-affirmation 'in-spite-of,' that is, in-spite-of that which tends to prevent the self from affirming itself" (Tillich 2000). Like me, Sampson raises the question, "What does it mean for Black girls and women to embody that which is self-affirming despite the dangers they face each day and the narratives that claim their lives have no value?"

How do I talk about this with my daughter? I will tell my daughter that she must have an embodied courage—a womanish way of being in the world that recognizes the dangers and acknowledges the fear that emerges as a result, and in spite of this, stands for what is right. An embodied courage allows the use of emotion to fuel the steps taken to survive and thrive. Still, embodied courage is not always well received coming from girls and women, particularly in patriarchal cultures. So she must be aware there is a cost for exercising embodied courage. In order to achieve an embodied courage, one should be informed, communal, and willing to act and to love one's self *regardless* (Walker 1983).

Then, to empower my daughter's embodied courage, I must continue to define what the Bible is and what it is not. The Bible is something we take seriously and can look to for insight, inspiration, and to know and understand God. However, the Bible is not God. Further, the words of God are in the Bible; but all of the words in the Bible are not the words of God. Though she has read and heard some empowering and guiding passages, many others are troubling and violent and cannot be ignored. However difficult the stories are, she must read these stories for herself and not depend on anyone else to be the sole interpreter of the meanings a text holds for her—not even me. Engaging these biblical stories for herself will require wrestling, and wrestling with the text does not mean you affirm texts that do not affirm you (Gafney 2017). Thus, I must continue to affirm her womanish ways and tell her to continue to ask her questions, even when she questions the Bible.

Like so many others, I was taught not to question the Bible and not to question God. I do not want her to have that type of limitation on her experience with the Bible. Historically, women have been socialized not to question or critically engage the biblical text. This often prevents them from questioning the Bible and questioning anyone or anything they perceive as having authority over their lives to their detriment. Black girls and women must know they can and should question people, systems, and even biblical texts that do not affirm them, which oppresses them or prevents them from flourishing.

Thus, I must provide the space for my daughter to ask questions freely and perhaps even prompt her to ask others, such as: Where is God in this passage? Where are the girls and women in the passage? Why do some avoid calling it rape? Why do some interpretations place the blame on Dinah? What makes this sacred? Where do I see myself affirmed? Questions such as these or others from Black girls and women can help them discern what is life-giving and affirming from what is oppressive and abusive in the biblical text and their lived experience. Asking questions is a tool of informing, understanding, surviving, and creating. By questioning, hopefully, she can become more informed and begin to understand the issues surrounding the rape of Dinah and how it connects to the very real lived experiences of girls and women around us. Further, questioning fosters active listening and clear speaking, both essential to surviving and creating a purposeful life.

Next, I will teach my daughter that embodied courage has a communal aspect. Sociologist Aurora Figueroa and researcher Katherine Hurtado (2016) rightly argue that Africana women need to conspire to reject sexual violence against women and help eliminate their marginalization and oppression. They called for women to conspire together through their Afrodiasporic Feminist Conspiracy, a place of solidarity with women from different backgrounds and communities, and formulated ways for them to act. I will teach my daughter that we are part of a conspiracy in which Black women and girls support one another and work together to eliminate violence and oppression that prevents the safety and flourishing of all women in jeopardy. While one can assume that Dinah received some support from Leah or other women, it is unclear. I imagine that Leah and the women of the community lamented with her and comforted her. However, our support of other girls and women must be clear. I assert a life-giving conspiracy such as this amongst Black women is embodying courage necessary to protect girls and women throughout the world.

Embodied courage requires one to actively listen to others' voices as a communal act of being informed. I teach my daughter that when someone shares their experiences with her to listen, especially in cases of sexual abuse. For a girl to share her experience of sexual abuse is difficult and we must have the courage to listen to her pain to actively support her. There may be discomfort and pain in hearing about a person you care about being harmed, but it does not compare to that which the person sharing may be experiencing. Also, as part of the conspiracy to support each other, listen, believe Black girls, and let them know that you believe them. Survivors of abuse do not want or need to be blamed for their assault as some have blamed Dinah. Survivors want to know that they are heard and believed (Gagnon et al. 2018). Thus, we must listen and believe one another to keep women and girls from being silenced.

Neither Dinah nor Leah speaks in the entire passage. Their voices are muted. While it is possible that in an assault such as this one, the victim and her mother could be silent, it is also likely they had something to say, but their words were left out of the record. The reader can read about the traumatic experience but will not hear it through Dinah's voice. In discussing this passage with my daughter or other young girls and women, I must inform them that silence in the face of abuse is not the way forward (Smith et al. 2019). Given the lack of details on Leah's response, I emphasize that the Bible does not always illustrate models of action for us. There are some passages like this one when there are situations presented and we must choose how we will respond in a just, loving, life-affirming, and life-giving way. Thus, I must embody the model of speaking.

It is essential to name and talk about abuse that happens, tell the stories when they are ours to tell and support others in narrating their own stories. Even though Black girls are questioned and are more often not believed, tell what happened, even if the perpetrator is someone we love—and who is supposed to love us. Telling the story is a way of asserting your agency and protecting yourself and others from further abuse. Whether in a biblical text or a lived experience, speaking the truth about violence and injustice is a part of embodying the courage necessary to protect bodies and lives that are in danger, which may or may not be your own. Black girls and women must be encouraged to speak up as much as possible to ensure that our stories are heard and that our presence is felt to create the changes we want. Therefore, we are compelled to speak up and #SayHerName.

Lastly, Black girls must be urged to love their whole selves, *regardless*. Genesis 34 does not clearly indicate that Dinah or Leah did not love themselves, however, elsewhere in Leah's story, it is clear Jacob loved Rachel more than Leah and she was not his first choice (Gen 29:30). What is it like for a person to continue to try to gain the love of a person who loves someone else? Can she love herself? Dinah was born after Leah had six sons and there is no explanation for her name or celebration of her birth as had been for the sons. After she is raped, given to her rapist for marriage, taken back home by her brothers, what is to become of Dinah? Did she have to continue to deal with the stigma of what happened to her? A contemporary example of this is the horrible experiences of the Nigerian girls who were abducted and impregnated by Boko Haram after they escaped captivity; however, they did not escape the shame of rape-induced pregnancies and the life-long reminder of their harrowing ordeal (Quist-Arcton 2017). The only information given is she is included as one of the descendants who went to Egypt. Yet despite all she had been through, was she able to love herself? What would self-love look like for her? I contend it is essential for Black girls to love their whole selves despite the world's perception and their lived experiences. This act of self-love is a revolutionary act of resistance that enables them to embody courage and continue to create a liberated life shaped by self-love. Further, while it is unclear whether Dinah ever saw self-love modeled by her mother, Black girls must see self-love modeled through their mothers or women in the community.

CONCLUSION

I will tell my daughter that Shechem raped Dinah and several people participated in silencing her. My daughter must know that we cannot participate in her silencing or the silencing of anyone who suffers abuse. Thus, she must embody courage and interrogate the text of the Bible and the world before her to resist that which does not affirm her life and to work to create a world that does. This embodied courage will require her to support Black girls and women, believe them, and stand with them, and to love her whole self, *regardless*. In doing so, #MeToo can be realized as a movement of sexual assault awareness and survival.

WORKS CITED

Abdullah, Melina. 2012. "Womanist Mothering: Loving and Raising the Revolution." *The Western Journal of Black Studies* 36, vol. 1: 57–67.

Anderson, Cheryl B. 2004. *Women, Ideology, and Violence: Critical Theory and the Construction of Gender in the Book of the Covenant and the Deuteronomic Law.* 394 vols. New York: T and T Clark.

Bader, Mary Anna. 2006. *Sexual Violation in the Hebrew Bible: A Multi-methodological Study of Genesis 34 and 2 Samuel* 13, vol. 87. New York: Peter Lang.

Bechtel, Lyn M. 1994. "What If Dinah Is Not Raped? (Genesis 34)." *Journal for the Study of the Old Testament* 19, vol. 63: 19–36.

Bronner, Leila L. 2004. *Stories of Biblical Mothers: Maternal Power in the Hebrew Bible.* Dallas: University Press of America.

Brown-Long, Cyntoia. 2019. *Free Cyntoia: My Search for Redemption in the American Prison System.* New York: Simon and Schuster.

Brueggemann, Walter. 1982. *Genesis*. Atlanta: John Knox.

Burke, Tarana. 2017. "#MeToo was Started for Black and Brown Women and Girls. They're Still Being Ignored: Women of Color Experience the Highest Rates of Sexual Violence, But They Are Not at the Center of the Current Discussion About Sexual Harassment." *Washington Post.* https://www.washingtonpost.com/news/post-nation/wp/2017/11/09/the-waitress-who-works-in-the-diner-needs-to-know-that-the-issue-of-sexual-harassment-is-about-her-too/

Claassens, L. Juliana. 2016. "Trauma and Recovery: A New Hermeneutical Framework for the Rape of Tamar (2 Samuel 13)." *Bible Through the Lens of Trauma,* edited by Christopher G., Boase, Elizabeth Frechette, 177–92. Atlanta: Society of Biblical Literature.

Crenshaw, Kimberlé. 1991. "Mapping the Margins: Intersectionality, Identity Politics, and Violence against Women of Color." *Stanford Law Review* 43.6: 1241–99.

Crowder, Stephanie R. Buckhanon. 2016. *When Momma Speaks: The Bible and Motherhood from a Womanist Perspective.* Louisville: Westminster John Knox.

Davis, Patricia. 2018. "They're Just Trying to Keep a Black Man Down: The (not so) Curious Case of R. Kelly." *Feminist Media Studies* 18, vol. 3: 494–97.

Frenthold, David A. 2015. "Trump Recorded Having Extremely Lewd Conversation About Women in 2005." *Washington Post*, October 8. https://www.washingtonpost.com/politics/trump-recorded-having-extremely-lewd-conversation-about-women-in-2005/2016/10/07/3b9ce776-8cb4-11e6-bf8a-3d26847eeed4_story.html?utm_term=.db3a4254fb94.

Figueroa, Aurora Vergara, and Katherine Arboleda Hurtado. 2016. "Afrodiasporic Feminist Conspiracy: Motivations and Paths Forward from the First International Seminar." *Meridians* 14, vol. 2: 118–29.

Fuchs, Esther. 1989. "The Literary Characterization of Mothers and Sexual Politics in the Hebrew Bible." *Semeia* 46: 151–66.

Gafney, Wilda. 2017. *Womanist Midrash: A Reintroduction to the Women of the Torah and the Throne.* Louisville: Westminster John Knox.

Gagnon, Kerry L., Naomi Wright, Tejaswinhi Srinivas, and Anne P. DePrince. 2018. "Survivors' Advice to Service Providers: How to Best Serve Survivors of Sexual Assault." *Journal of Aggression, Maltreatment & Trauma* 27, vol. 10: 1125–44.

Gravett, Sandie. 2016. "Reading 'Rape' in the Hebrew Bible: A Consideration of Language." *Journal for the Study of the Old Testament* 28, vol. 3: 279–99.

Gunkel, Hermann, and Mark Biddle. 1997. *Genesis.* Macon: Mercer University Press.

Hall Sharp, Kamilah. 2018. "Leah and Dinah in the Face of Abuse." Presentation at Daughters of the African Atlantic Fund Consultation of African and African Diasporan Women in Religion and Theology. Bahia, Brazil.

Harris, Elizabeth A. 2020. "'Surviving R. Kelly' Recap: The Year Everything Changed." *New York Times,* January 14. https://www.nytimes.com/2020/01/04/arts/television/surviving-r-kelly-2.html.

Holcombe, Madeline. 2019. *CNN.* August 8. https://www.cnn.com/2019/08/08/us/simone-biles-usa-gymnastics-one-job/index.html.

Keefe, Alice A. 1993. "Rapes of Women, Wars of Men." *Semeia* 61: 79–97.

Larimer, Sarah. 2015. "Ex-cop on Trial for Rape of 13 Women 'Used Power to Prey' on Victims, Prosecutor Says: Former Oklahoma City Police Officer

Daniel Holtzclaw is Charged with 36 Counts of Rape, Sexual Battery, and Other Charges." *Washington Post,* December 11. Accessed on May 5, 2021. https://www.washingtonpost.com/news/morning-mix/wp/2015/12/08/ex-cop-on-trial-for-rape-used-power-to-prey-on-women-prosecutor-says/.

Leung, Rebecca, and Robert Williams. 2019. "#MeToo and Intersectionality: An Examination of the #MeToo Movement Through the R. Kelly Scandal." *The Journal of Communication Inquiry* 43, vol. 4: 349–71.

Lipka, Hilary. 2006. *Sexual Transgression in the Hebrew Bible.* Vol. 7. Sheffield: Sheffield Phoenix.

Martin, Clarice J. 1990 "Womanist Interpretations of the New Testament: The Quest for Holistic and Inclusive Translation and Interpretation." *Journal of Feminist Studies in Religion* 6, vol. 2: 41–61.

Neusner, Jacob. 1985. *Genesis Rabbah: The Judaic Commentary to the Book of Genesis; A New American Translation; Volume III: Parashiyyot Sixty-Eight through One Hundred on Genesis 28: 10 to 50: 26.* Atlanta: Scholars.

Peters, Kurtis. 2021. "Together in Guilt: David, Jonadab, and the Rape of Tamar." *Journal for the Study of the Old Testament* 45, vol. 3: 309–19.

Planty, Michael Langton, et al. 2013. *Female Victims of Sexual Violence, 1994–2010.* US Department of Justice, Office of Justice Programs, Bureau of Justice Statistics. https://bjs.ojp.gov/content/pub/pdf/fvsv9410.pdf

Quist-Arcton, Ofeibea. 2017. "The Lament of the Boko Haram 'Brides.'" National Public Radio, August 17. https://www.npr.org/sections/goatsandsoda/2017/08/27/545912049/the-lament-of-the-boko-haram-brides.

Rape, Abuse & Incest National Network (RAINN). 2016. "Sex Crimes and Penalties." https://rainn.org/about-sexual-assault.

Russaw, Kimberly D. 2018. *Daughters in the Hebrew Bible.* Lanham, MD: Rowman & Littlefield.

Sampson, Melva. 2012. www.facebook.com/melvasampson.

———. 2012. "I'm Exhausted But I Do Want to Be Well: Raising Womanish Girls, The Performance of Mothering and Wading in Murky Waters." *The Feminist Wire,* October 30. http://www.thefeministwire.com/2012/10/im-exhausted-but-i-do-want-to-be-well-raising-womanish-girls-the-performance-of-mothering-and-wading-in-murky-waters/.

Sanchez, Ray, Sonia Moghe, Kristina Sueglia. 2021. "Bill Cosby Is a Free Man after Pennsylvania Supreme Court Overturns Sex Assault Conviction." June 30. https://www.cnn.com/2021/06/30/us/bill-cosby-to-be-released/index.html.

Scholz, Susanne. 2000. *Rape Plots: A Feminist Cultural Study of Genesis 34.* New York: Canterbury: P. Lang.

Schroeder, Joy A. 2007. *Dinah's Lament: The Biblical Legacy of Sexual Violence in Christian Interpretation.* Minneapolis: Fortress.

Schulte, Leah Rediger. 2017. *The Absence of God in Biblical Rape Narratives.* Minneapolis: Fortress.

Slatton, Brittany C. and April L. Richard. 2020. "Black Women's Experiences of Sexual Assault and Disclosure: Insights from the Margins." *Sociology Compass* 14, vol. 6: 1–12.

Smith, Dianne, Loyce Caruthers, and Shaunda Fowler. 2019. *Womanish Black Girls: Women Resisting the Contradictions of Silence and Voice*. Gorham, ME: Myers Education.

Smith, Mitzi J. 2017. "Dis-membering, Sexual Violence, and Confinement: A Womanist Intersectional Reading of the Story of the Levite's Wife (Judges 19)." *Insights from African American Interpretation*. Minneapolis: Fortress.

———. 2018. *Womanist Sass and Talk Back: Social (In)justice, Intersectionality, and Biblical Interpretation*. Eugene, OR: Cascade.

Tillich, Paul. 2000. *The Courage to Be*. New Haven: Yale University Press.

Trible, Phyllis. 1984. *Texts of Terror: Literary-Feminist Readings of Biblical Narratives*. Philadelphia: Fortress.

Union, Gabrielle. 2017. *We're Going to Need More Wine: Stories that are Funny, Complicated, and True*. New York: HarperCollins.

Van Wolde, Ellen. 2002. "Does 'Inná Denote Rape? A Semantic Analysis of a Controversial Word." *Vetus Testamentum* 52, vol. 4: 528–44.

Walker, Alice. 1983. *In Search of Our Mothers' Garden: Womanist Prose*. San Diego: Harcourt Brace.

Walker-Barnes, Chanequa. 2014. *Too Heavy a Yoke: Black Women and the Burden of Strength*. Eugene, OR: Cascade.

Weems, Renita J. 1991. "Reading Her Way Through the Struggle: African American Women and the Bible." *Stony the Road We Trod: African American Biblical Interpretation*, edited by Cain Hope Felder, 57–78. Minneapolis: Fortress.

———. 1995. *Battered Love: Marriage, Sex, and Violence in the Hebrew Prophets*. Minneapolis: Fortress.

Zheng, Lili. 2020. "One Year Later, Family of Atatiana Jefferson Waits for Justice." In *NBCDFW*. October 9. https://www.nbcdfw.com/news/local/one-year-later-family-of-atatiana-jefferson-waits-for-justice/2458229/.

Chapter 16

Antichrist and Anti-Black
1 John and "Black Lives Matter"

Dennis R. Edwards

"Do not be astonished, brothers and sisters, that the world hates you" (1 John 3:13).

During a conversation with one of my great aunts, I was struck afresh by her resilience and tenacious faith under the oppression of American racism and patriarchy. Our conversation was prompted by the release of the movie, *The Help*, which centered southern white women's experiences with their African American maids in the early 1960s. My great aunt, who was pushing ninety years old, had no desire to see the movie and offered a rhetorical question: "Don't you know all the females in your family did domestic work for white people?" My great aunt, her older sister (my grandmother), and my mother became part of the Great Migration when they left South Carolina and headed north sometime in the 1930s. They became cooks and maids for white people and, despite their marginalization, profoundly impacted their families, neighbors, and in some cases their churches, relying upon their faith in Jesus Christ, as well as their hard-earned wisdom. These women—and so many other Black people like them—demonstrate how Black lives, despite the oppression and marginalization caused by whiteness, not only matter but are exemplars of faith that "conquers the world" (1 John 5:4).

The brief writing known as 1 John supports the notion that Black lives matter, even though some professing Christians balk at the #BLM movement. The letter offers insights into the development of Christian division, which is the result of multiple factors. Doctrinal convictions are typically offered as the main reason for ecclesial separation, as if those convictions are distinct from cultural values. However, theological understandings and cultural codes of behavior are intertwined. For example, racism, sexism, and classism are built into some theological perspectives, exposing divisions within American Christianity (Douglas, 2011; Jones, 2020; Tisby, 2019). Exploring 1 John's message of perseverance informs our appreciation of how Black life has meant perseverance in the face of evil. After addressing some contextual issues, I proceed to explain how 1 John presents the recipients' "blackness," which I understand to symbolize resistance to oppression, resilience in light of trauma, and faith (Fields 2001; Wimbush 2000). I also highlight how "whiteness" is a dehumanizing power and relates to 1 John's concept of anti-christ characterized by hatred (e.g., 3:15; 4:20). Finally, I demonstrate how 1 John supports the notion that Black lives matter because the letter celebrates the love, faith, and tenacity of a marginalized community, which is analogous to Black lives in our contemporary society.

CONTEXTUAL MATTERS

First John does not bear the stereotypical marks of an ancient letter (e.g., there is no superscript and no closing salutations) and does not claim to be written by anyone named John. For convenience, however, I will refer to the anonymous author at times as John and call the work a letter because of its traditional designation as one of the so-called Johannine Epistles. Internal evidence from the letter suggests that the first readers were a faithful community estranged from the broader society and most notably from secessionists, those who were presumably sisters and brothers of the faithful at some previous time. While the original audience may not have been plagued by organized, imperial persecution, "That the Johannine community would be detested by non-believers who encountered it, we may well suspect" (Brown 1979, 64–65). Juliet Lieu comments on the community's perseverance while under oppressive forces, and connects 1 John 2:12–17 to the expectation for justice found in various prophetic and apocalyptic writings: "It is easy to see how such expectations, with their graphic imagery, could give hope and meaning to groups who felt themselves alienated and powerless in society, and whose conviction of the supreme power of God and of their place in God's purposes seemed to have little realization in the present" (Lieu 2008, 90). First John's audience is given the same sort of eschatological hope found in writings addressed to, or originating from oppressed people, such as Zech 14:1–21and Rev 2:1–7.

As most commentators point out, 1 John has often been read as an anti-Gnostic or anti-Docetic polemic. Gnosticism is complex and "its precise meaning in any given case is often hard to discern" (King 2003, 5). It has generally been considered as a thought and practice of various groups claiming *gnosis*—an esoteric knowledge—and was eventually deemed heresy by Christianity. Docetism (from the Greek verb, *dokeō*, "I seem" or "I appear"), a component of Gnosticism, espouses the notion that Jesus did not have a flesh-and-blood body, but only appeared to be human (King 2003, 208–13). Several passages in 1 John might suggest that Docetism is in view, such as:

> We declare to you what was from the beginning, what we have heard, what we have seen with our eyes, what we have looked at and touched with our hands, concerning the word of life (1:1).... Who is the liar but the one who denies that Jesus is the Christ? This is the antichrist, the one who denies the Father and the Son" (2:22).... By this you know the Spirit of God: every spirit that confesses that Jesus Christ has come in the flesh is from God, and every spirit that does not confess Jesus is not from God. And this is the spirit of the antichrist, of which you have heard that it is coming; and now it is already in the world (4:2–3).

John's purpose in writing might not have been to address the heretical notion that Jesus Christ merely appeared in human form while on earth. Raymond E. Brown represents scholars who do not "interpret the Johannine secessionists through a knowledge of later heresies" (1979, 113). Rather than stressing the fleshiness of Jesus, 1 John focuses upon the significance of Jesus's presence in the world and in the life of his followers. This is to say that John's primary emphasis is on what Jesus taught, how he lived, how and why he died, and how he continues to guide true believers. The physical appearance of Jesus is a mystery because neither the Johannine Epistles, the Gospels, nor any other canonical NT writing offers descriptions of what Jesus looked like. This is not to suggest that physical features are inconsequential and have no significance in the world, but that when it comes to Jesus, the NT writers sought to place emphasis on something other than Jesus's physical features. Therefore, 1 John's focus on Jesus "coming in the flesh" (e.g., 4:2–3) is more about the Lord's mission and ministry than it is about fleshly existence in general. The writer's Christological emphasis is on personhood—the Lord's humanity—which transcends physical appearance while upholding the dignity of all human beings. John's *en sarki* ("in the flesh") assertion is a shorthand meant to signify the fullness of Jesus's incarnation, not merely the fact of his physical nature (Minear 1970, 299; Brown 1982, 505). "Whatever else 'in the flesh' may denote, it must denote a mode of existence shared with the other sons [sic] of God, a mode which enables the Triune God to participate fully in fellowship with and in the community of confessors, a fellowship which can be defined as eternal life" (Minear 1970, 300). Because true believers are "born of God" (2:29–3:2) and possess God's "seed" (3:9) they participate in Jesus Christ's humanity (4:4).

The brief pastoral communication that is 1 John seeks to encourage the faithful by reinforcing love's supremacy, thereby strengthening communal bonds, while simultaneously denouncing the beliefs and actions of the secessionists, without naming particular individuals (Brown 1979, 103–44). Although John is capable of calling out individual opponents (e.g., Diotrophes in 3 John 9), the author's point in 1 John is that the antagonists are antichrist (2:18; 4:1–3) and communicate as such because they: walk in darkness (1:6); lie (1:6; 2:4); say, "we have no sin" (1:8); do not obey the Lord's commandments (2:4); hate brothers and sisters while claiming to be in the light (2:9; 4:11–24); love the world's system (2:15–17); deceive themselves (1:8) as well as others (2:26); are lawless (3:4); deny that Jesus Christ has come in the flesh (4:3); are idolaters (5:21). First John urges followers of Jesus Christ to love one another according to the Lord's great commandment (2:10; 4:7–5:3), to recognize the reality of Jesus's presence in the world (e.g., 4:1–6; 5:6–12), to refuse to be duped by the antichrist (2:18–21; 4:2–3), and to overcome (2:13–14; 4:4; 5:4–5) because they are victors rather than perpetual victims.

THE "BLACKNESS" OF 1 JOHN'S FIRST READERS

Although 1 John addresses and focuses upon those who remain steadfast in their faith, much scholarly attention has been devoted to identifying those who left the community (see most any exegetical commentary, such as Streett 2011; Schuchard 2012, 14–17). Some formerly within the Johannine community apparently had professed faith in Jesus Christ but demonstrated beliefs and behaviors that betrayed them as antichrist (2:18, 22; 4:3). Neither the secessionists nor the remnant are named, prompting Judith Lieu to refer to the original recipients of 1 John as "equally shadowy" as the unknown author (Lieu 1991, 12). Ironically, those shadowy followers of Jesus are living "in the light" because of their love for one another (2:10). I refer to the recipients of 1 John as Black because blackness is "a symbol abounding in meaning and force" (Fields 2001, 13; cf. Wimbush 2000), not merely indicating skin color, but depicting a vulnerable population's faith, resistance, and resilience in the face of oppression. Some theologians, like James Cone, describe God as Black because of God's solidarity with the oppressed: "The blackness of God means that God has made the oppressed condition God's own condition. This is the essence of the biblical revelation. By electing Israelite slaves as the people of God and by becoming the Oppressed One in Jesus Christ, the human race is made to understand that God is known where human beings experience humiliation and suffering" (Cone, 2010). Scholars who identify Christ as Black, refer to social condition if not always to biological characteristics.

> Although Jesus' ethnicity and dark-skinned complexion are certainly important aspects of Christ's blackness, to call Christ black points to more than simply ancestry or biological characteristics. Throughout black religious history, black people have believed that Christ identified with the black struggle against the tyrannies of a white racist society. To call Christ black affirms this identification. (Douglas and Burkett 2011, 410)

Black theology affirms God's solidarity with the marginalized, a theme found repeatedly throughout the Bible (e.g., Douglas 1994; Cone 1997; Mofokeng, 1983). Blackness not only identifies the Divine as Black, but also helps to define the correlative reality of vulnerable people regardless of their geographic location or even the historical era in which they lived. This is to say that blackness links oppressed people throughout time, as demonstrated, for example, in African American identification with Israelites enslaved within Ancient Egypt.

Whiteness, which is not primarily or necessarily about skin color, but about power, marginalizes those not designated white, creating and maintaining a hierarchy where European heritage is assumed to be intellectually, physiologically, morally, and spiritually superior, necessitating an apparent mandate to subdue and rule over nonwhites. "Racism is based on the concept of whiteness—a powerful fiction enforced by power and violence. Whiteness is a constantly shifting boundary separating those who are entitled to have certain privileges from those whose exploitation and vulnerability to violence is justified by their not being white" (Kivel 2002, 17; Bush 2004, 15–18). Consequently, whiteness distorts any ideal picture of what Christian faith entails. It is like how Kelly Brown Douglas chronicles the way "platonized Christianity" aligns itself with power (2005, 132). But some African American Christians reinterpreted the Christian faith, dispensing with an enslaving god in favor of the liberating God of Exodus. Vincent L. Wimbush elaborates on the value and significance of having the African American experience serve as the starting point for studying the Bible: "Almost from the beginning of their engagement with it, African Americans interpreted the Bible differently from those who introduced them to it" (2009, 17). That different approach to the Bible "reflects and draws unto itself and engages and problematizes a certain complex order of existence associated with marginality, liminality, exile, pain, trauma" (ibid.). Black Christian faith, therefore, resembles the faith of the first readers of 1 John because their faith was also refined by the heat of oppression. Consequently, the way in which 1 John affirms how these early Jesus-followers matter to God and should matter to the world supports our contemporary assertions that Black lives matter.

Scholars often focus on alleged theological differences between the faithful remnant and those who left the community, but there is something else at stake. The recipients of 1 John were not merely at ideological loggerheads with the secessionists; they were hated by them, according to 3:11–17:

> For this is the message you have heard from the beginning, that we should love one another. We must not be like Cain who was from the evil one and murdered his brother. And why did he murder him? Because his own deeds were evil and his brother's righteous. Do not be astonished, brothers and sisters, that the world hates you. We know that we have passed from death to life because we love one another. Whoever does not love abides in death. All who hate a brother or sister are murderers, and you know that murderers do not have eternal life abiding in them. We know love by this, that he laid down his life for us—and we ought to lay down our lives for one another. How does God's love abide in anyone who has the world's goods and sees a brother or sister in need and yet refuses help?

Brown comments that in the above passage, the author of 1 John "unmasks the motivating force behind them [i.e., the secessionists] as the other great player in the apocalyptic drama of evil, the devil" (1982, 429). The Christian community, to borrow from Dr. Martin Luther King, Jr., must find the strength to love despite the hatred that hovers over them (Slater 2007, 499–500). And that hatred sometimes emerges from within the community. Those like Cain operate within the sphere called kosmos (3:13), which is 1 John's term for all that opposes God (2:15, 16, 17; 3;1; 4:3; 5:19) and includes those who seceded. Cain is the archetypal sinner, empowered by the devil, and represents how hatred of the faithful is rooted in opposition to God. We must not miss the irony that those who have at some time professed Christian faith eventually betray by their confessions as well as their actions that they are aligned with the world, the devil's domain (5:19), and not with Christ. Similarly, Black people—often especially women—have long dealt with the reality of having hatred directed toward them, often most vehemently from those who claim to have faith in Christ (Douglas 2011, 146).

According to 3:11–17, social tensions are evident within the Johannine community. We ought not minimize the social dimension of the conflict by placing alleged Christological controversies at the center of our reading of John's letters (Johnson 2010, 497). In our time, whiteness has often sought to mute the voices of marginalized people by highlighting alleged doctrinal differences at the expense of examining and evaluating societal sins caused by whiteness. This is to say that white Christians have had the power to dismiss Black Christians' arguments concerning race, power, and privilege, especially whenever we articulate a theological perspective that is different from that of the dominant culture. Therefore, highlighting theological formulations while minimizing social conflict, serves as an attempt to camouflage racism.

WHITENESS AS RELATED TO ANTICHRIST

The tensions within 1 John's audience may have occurred for social reasons rather than theological ones. According to 3:11–17, discussed above, the antichrist faction behaves like the world and not like siblings in the faith. The world, in its opposition to God and God's people, is consonant with the broader society, i.e., the Roman Empire. Referring to 1 John's author as "elder," Kenneth L. Waters asserts that "The elder equates the apostate and schismatic spirit with the attitude of the empire (world) toward the Johannine church. It is hate without differentiation. Schismatics and apostates actually become the face of the empire" (2017, 550). Waters describes a situation not unlike that of the contemporary USA where white supremacists typically claim an indistinguishable allegiance to both Jesus Christ and to the nation, marginalizing people who ostensibly share the same Christian faith. Opponents of the Johannine community's faithful remnant are "antichrist" (4:3), "of the world" (4:5) and hate those who remain (3:13). As is often the case in NT writings, neither the author's nor the community's opponents are named or described with such specificity that later readers could readily identify them. Paul's letter to the Galatians, for example, does not name the ones who have excised the apostle and "bewitched" the faithful (Gal 3:1). Presumably the original readers knew all the necessary details about their opponents, but such is not the case for contemporary readers, so we practice mirror reading of the NT in an attempt to construct a profile of unnamed opponents. Since John does not give precise descriptions or names of the rivals, we are driven to conclude that who the antagonists are is less important than how they act. Such is the case when analyzing white supremacy. People generally prefer to focus on overtly racist people and not on unjust systems. For example, police brutality, especially against people of color, typically gets attributed to so-called "bad apples" within police forces rather than to a system that needs to be overhauled or even dismantled. In evangelical circles, the tendency is to individualize spiritual concepts such as faith, sin, and salvation, thereby failing to acknowledge the corporate and systemic dimensions of evil (Emerson and Smith 2000; Douglas 2011). Some Christians, therefore, prefer to scrutinize whether or not particular actions on the part of individuals or institutions should be labeled racist instead of exploring how various societal policies intersect, overlap, and conspire to oppress. Some white people resist a systemic analysis of whiteness and racism because, "Thinking about whiteness as a system of privilege is a huge source of anxiety for individuals who consider themselves white" (Garner 2007, 5). Robert Jones adds, "For whiteness is the mortar holding together the fortress of white supremacy, and if it crumbles, those walls will inevitably collapse. Because of its binding importance, the idea of whiteness has been, and remains today, vigilantly defended" (2020, 22–23). If we reckon only with individual acts of prejudice, to which all people are susceptible, we fail to expose and denounce the systemic evil associated with whiteness. The indictment of whiteness as antichrist involves more than focusing upon particular individuals but addresses, as 1 John does, the systemic and pervasive spiritual evil behind the behavior of individuals. That evil is called antichrist.

Black lives, as 1 John suggests, share in the humanity of Jesus, the one who has come in the flesh (4:2; 2 John 7). We identify whiteness as antichrist (2:18; 4:3) in that it fails to recognize Jesus's humanity and through hate (3:11–17), ignores the presence of Jesus in others. Whiteness is not as much about skin color as it is about the power to create and maintain a social hierarchy. In that regard, whiteness can be seen as a form of Gnosticism, a heretical notion often refuted by appeals to 1 John. Although 1 John may not have been written to address the impending threat of Docetism vis-à-vis Gnosticism, the document played a role in later attempts to refute Gnosticism, such as Against Heresies by Irenaeus, the second-century bishop of Lyons. J. Kameron Carter, in his chapter, "Prelude on Christology and Race: Irenaeus as Anti-Gnostic Intellectual," connects ancient Gnosticism to the neo-Gnosticism of whiteness with a focus on the writings of Irenaeus (Carter 2008, 11–36). Carter praises Irenaeus as one who "thinks within a theological imagination suited to diagnosing how modern racial discourse generally and how whiteness in particular functions" (ibid., 23). Gnosticism was more than a theological notion; it had anthropological implications because the Gnostics' denial of the physical nature of Jesus created a stratified view of humanity. Irenaeus was not addressing the modern construct of race, but he was confronting a form of what Denise K. Buell calls "ethnic reasoning" (Buell 2005, 2). Ethnic reasoning refers to a persuasive strategy used by early Christians "to legitimize various forms of Christianness as the universal, most authentic manifestation of humanity" (ibid.). Carter, applying Buell's insights, observes Gnosticism's hierarchical view of humanity in light of Irenaeus's writings, and connects ancient Gnosticism to the way whiteness functions to stratify humanity. Carter's analysis of Irenaeus allows us to see that confessing Jesus Christ's earthly existence declares the inherent equality of humanity: Jesus coming *en sarki* means that he shares in our humanity and, as the atoning sacrifice for the sins of the entire world and not just for elites (2:2), Jesus affirms the equality of all humans.

In following Carter's analysis, we are drawn to conclude that whiteness is akin to Gnosticism in its creation of a spiritual elite who deny the humanness of others. Whiteness creates an image of Jesus that denies the Lord's actual existence, serves to marginalize and oppress others, and reinforces hierarchies. By affirming and emphasizing the physical presence of Jesus, 1 John also validates the personhood of all who, like Jesus, have had their humanity questioned, devalued, and even demonized. When it comes to Black people, Christians of European descent viewed us as evil—as savage, inferior, and destined for servitude. Jesus, therefore, was Black, particularly in the sense of bearing societal shame due to his relative lack of worldly status. Yet the dishonor Jesus faced is not confined to his earthly passion. It dishonors the Lord whenever he is depicted or described in ways that attempt to erase his marginalized Jewish identity. Ironically, whiteness has denied the coming of Jesus *en sarki* by creating physical images of the historical Jesus that could never accurately represent him, such as depictions of a man possessing long blond hair and blue eyes. Casting Jesus in the mold of the oppressor is a denial that Jesus has come in the flesh, and such denial comes from the spirit of the antichrist (4:3). People mesmerized by whiteness, raising a white Jesus as their vanguard, exercised violence, coercion, and deception to exploit physical difference as a means to gain power and prominence. Whiteness imagined it could determine the fate of Black people's souls, even debating whether or not we could be saved (Tisby 2019, 50; Bowens 2020, 37). Even if 1 John was not initially written to refute Gnosticism, the letter's affirmation of Jesus Christ's humanity and his solidarity with the marginalized, counters the neo-Gnosticism of whiteness.

BLACK LIVES MATTER AND 1 JOHN

Remaining or abiding is what characterizes the faithful sisters and brothers within the Johannine community (2:19). The Greek verb *menō* ("remain" or "abide") is one of John's favorite words and occurs twenty-four times in the brief letter (see several uses in the Gospel of John, e.g., 15:4, 5, 6, 7, 9, 10, 16). The locus of abiding is inverted around the faithful: they remain in what God provides, and what God provides remains in them. The children of God remain in the light (2:10), in the Son (e.g., 2:24, 27, 28), and in love (e.g., 4:15) while God's word (2:14), the message about Jesus (2:24), God's anointing (2:27), God's seed (3:9), God's love (3:17), God's spirit (4:13), and God's self (4:16) abides in them. Abiding epitomizes true believers while the ones possessed by the antichrist spirit depart. Accompanying the notion of abiding in 1 John is another description of the faithful that testifies to and affirms much of the African American experience. Those who abide conquer or overcome (*nikaō* in 2:13, 14; 4:4; 5:4). African Americans have overcome the manifold threats to our existence perpetrated by whiteness. While there is no need to chronicle specific acts of violence visited upon African Americans, a fitting pastoral summary comes through Carlyle Fielding Stewart III: "It is no accident, then, that after centuries of murders, atrocities, floggings, lynchings, rebuke, discrimination, oppression, alienation, exploitation, degradation, and human devaluation, we are still alive" (1997, 1–2). "We have come over a way that with tears has been watered/ We have come treading our path through the blood of the slaughtered": those lines are part of James Weldon Johnson's poetic portrait of the African American experience of overcoming.

True followers of Jesus "walk as he walked" (2:6) and have conquered the evil one (2:13, 14). The evil one, although unnamed, is the historic adversary (Satan) of God's people. The evil one's influence is not limited to instigating personal transgressions but includes animating unjust oppressive systems (see Eph 2:2). In 1 John 3:12, while the evil one is behind Cain's murderous act, Cain serves as one example of the devil's manifold works which are vanquished through the Son of God's life, death, and resurrection (3:8). The faithful children of God, who await the returning Jesus and who will be like him (3:2), have conquered the antichrists (4:4). All who participate in Christ, being born of God, conquer the world (5:4), a feat accomplished through faith (5:5). Although they have been victimized by antichrist forces, the faithful followers of Jesus are victorious over the devil's attacks. The same can be said of Black people who through faith resisted evil and stand as victors alongside Jesus Christ.

CONCLUSION

An African American retired federal judge gave the eulogy at my great aunt's homegoing service, held at the Washington, DC, church she had attended for nearly seventy years. My great aunt was one of the first people to hold the judge when he was a newborn, since she was best friends with the judge's mother. The eulogist focused on how my great aunt's faith in the Lord Jesus Christ was evident in multifaceted ways. I could not help but to marvel at the ironic juxtaposition of my great aunt's life in Washington, DC, and that of well-known faith leaders who clamor to get the ear of presidents but whose quest for power and influence counteract their claims of devotion to Jesus Christ. In the nation's capital, not far from the White House, the US Capitol, and all the monuments, we were celebrating a woman whose faith and fortitude in many ways surpassed that of those who occupied the hallowed halls of the US government buildings. The Bible consistently affirms that Black lives—like that of my great aunt—matter, are valued by God, and typically represent Jesus Christ in the world more accurately and effectively than the lives of apparently powerful and influential people.

First John provides an example of how blackness, while symbolizing marginalization and oppression, also testifies of faithfulness and victory. Throughout much of Christian history, whites demonized blackness

(Wimbush 1991, 84). But 1 John demonstrates that God empowers humans who have been designated Black because of their worldly status to be victorious over the forces of evil. While ultimate victory over evil is realized in the eschaton—the end of time as we know it—faith propels us to appropriate eschatological hope in the present. Eschatological hope means resisting the oppressive power of whiteness and affirming the resilience of blackness.

WORKS CITED

Bowens, Lisa M. 2020. *African American Readings of Paul: Reception, Resistance, and Transformation*. Grand Rapids, MI: Eerdmans.

Brown, Raymond E. 1979. *The Community of the Beloved Disciple*. New York: Paulist.

———. 1982. *The Epistles of John. AB 30*. Garden City, NY: Doubleday.

Bush, Melanie E. L. 2004. *Breaking the Code of Good Intentions: Everyday Forms of Whiteness*. Lanham, MD: Rowman & Littlefield.

Buell, Denise Kimber. 2005. *Why This New Race: Ethnic Reasoning in Early Christianity*. New York: Columbia University Press.

Carter, J. Kameron. 2008. *Race: A Theological Account*. Oxford; New York: Oxford University Press.

Cone, James H. 1997. *God of the Oppressed*. Revised edition. Maryknoll, NY: Orbis.

———. 2010. *A Black Theology of Liberation*. Fortieth anniversary edition. Maryknoll, NY: Orbis.

Douglas, Kelly Brown. 1994. *The Black Christ*. Maryknoll, NY: Orbis.

Douglas, Kelly Brown, and Delbert Burkett. 2011. "The Black Christ." *The Blackwell Companion to Jesus. Blackwell Companions to Religion*, edited by Delbert Burkett, 410–26. Malden, MA: Wiley-Blackwell.

Emerson, Michael O., and Christian Smith. 2000. *Divided by Faith: Evangelical Religion and the Problem of Race in America*. Oxford; New York: Oxford University Press.

Fields, Bruce L. 2001. *Introducing Black Theology: 3 Crucial Questions for the Evangelical Church*. Grand Rapids: Baker Academic.

Garner, Steve. 2007. *Whiteness: An Introduction*. London; New York: Routledge.

Johnson, Luke Timothy. 2010. *The Writings of the New Testament: An Interpretation*. Third Edition. Minneapolis: Fortress.

Jones, Robert P. 2020. *White Too Long: The Legacy of White Supremacy in American Christianity*. New York: Simon & Schuster.

King, Karen L. 2003. *What Is Gnosticism?* Cambridge, MA: Belknap Press.

Kivel, Paul. 2002. *Uprooting Racism: How White People Can Work for Racial Justice*. Rev. ed. Gabriola Island, BC: New Society Publishers.

Lieu, Judith. 1991. *The Theology of the Johannine Epistles*. Cambridge/New York: Cambridge University Press.

———. 2008. *I, II & III John: A Commentary*. NTL. Louisville: Westminster John Knox.

Minear, Paul S. 1970. "The Idea of Incarnation in First John." *Interpretation* 24.3: 291–302.

Mofokeng, Takatso Alfred. 1983. *The Crucified among the Crossbearers: Towards a Black Christology*. Kampen: Uitgeversmaatschappij J.H. Kok.

Schuchard, Bruce G. 2012. 1–3 John. Concordia Commentary. Saint Louis: Concordia.

Slater, Thomas B. 2007. "1–3 John." *True to Our Native Land: An African American New Testament Commentary*, edited by Brian K. Blount, Cain Hope Felder, Clarice J. Martin, and Emerson B. Powery, 496–517. Minneapolis: Fortress Press.

Stewart, Carlyle Fielding. 1997. *Soul Survivors: An African American Spirituality*. 1st ed. Louisville: Westminster John Knox.

Streett, Daniel R. 2011. *They Went out from Us: The Identity of the Opponents in First John*. Beihefte Zur Zeitschrift Für Die Neutestamentliche Wissenschaft Und Die Kunde Der Älteren Kirche, Bd. 177. Berlin; New York: De Gruyter.

Tisby, Jemar. 2019. *The Color of Compromise: The Truth about the American Church's Complicity in Racism*. Grand Rapids: Zondervan.

Waters, Kenneth L. 2017. "Empire and the Johannine Epistles." *Review and Expositor* 114, vol. 4: 542–57.

Wimbush, Vincent L. 1991. "The Bible and African Americans: An Outline of an Interpretative History." In *Stony the Road We Trod: African American Biblical Interpretation*, edited by Cain Hope Felder, 81–97. Minneapolis: Fortress.

———. 2000. "Introduction: Reading Darkness, Reading Scriptures." *African Americans and the Bible: Sacred Texts and Social Textures*, edited by Vincent L. Wimbush, 1–48. New York; London: Continuum.

PART V

Responses

Chapter 17

John's Apocalypse and African American Interpretation

Thomas B. Slater

In *Stony the Road We Trod*, Thomas Hoyt, Jr., wrote an insightful and instructive essay on African American biblical interpretation (1991). In that essay, Hoyt makes several salient points. First, he argues that the authority of scripture for African American Christians is established in "the story." African Americans found their story in the biblical story, first in the book of Exodus and also in the Gospels. Like the biblical writers, persons of African descent communicate more frequently through narratives. Hoyt argued, "Biblical interpreters could profit from a more intense exploration of the relationship of oral forms to textual forms. Such an approach to the text would . . . explore the meaning of the text for those who are on the margins" (1991, 25).[1]

Secondly, Hoyt discussed the need to employ images and imagination in biblical interpretation. Biblical writings use images to convey their messages to their readers. He states that scholars should then use their imagination as a means to convey to their modern readers the meaning behind the messages in Scripture. "Scripture is more than a body of abstract thought and generalizations. It is usually very concrete, especially in the narrative parts" (Hoyt 1991, 34). He adds that the imagery and symbols within Scripture cannot be "grasped with only the intellect but also with the imagination" (ibid., 34–39). Hoyt correctly understood that the meaning of Scripture is found where the reader connects the biblical story with her own story, a process which involves the imagination.

Hoyt saw African American biblical scholarship doing something which has been desperately needed in biblical studies: *reconnecting knowledge about the faith with actually having faith.* A major failure of biblical studies in ATS seminaries is the assumption that learning naturally leads to commitment.

That is not always the case. While philosophy can create a strong rational commitment, the pull of religion is stronger because it involves an existential commitment that defies reason. Such a commitment cannot be comprehended by reason alone. It requires faith and faith is best transmitted in story. That is why Plato's *Timaeus* is a creation story and not a philosophical treatise. Therefore, "the story" should have meaning in the congregation and also in the academy, a fact which too many academicians have not acknowledged or have not perceived. This study will demonstrate how subsequent African American commentators have done what Hoyt advocated three decades ago.

African American biblical interpretation has maintained a close connection to the African American Church because it does not have the luxury of being abstract or irrelevant. The reality of white racism in American society has created intellectual and existential urgency with the African American community. For this reason, African American scholars tend to be more contextual and less esoteric and/or speculative. Many African American biblical scholars have employed cultural studies, also known as social-scientific studies, as a means to relate the biblical story with their contemporary context. In this way, they follow the example of Howard Thurman in *Jesus and the Disinherited*, who argued that because Jesus was socially marginalized he would identify more with the Black American community than any other community in America.

When one examines the work of African American writers on John's Apocalypse, one finds much of what Hoyt advocated three decades ago. This study will examine the work of Brian Blount and Shanell Smith as representative scholars in order to see how Hoyt's perspective has developed in the past three decades. In 2000, Brian Blount began a series of writings on Revelation as a response to a regional politico-religious crisis. He sees the book serving as a model for Christian witnessing during a time of repression. This is a rather positive reading of the Apocalypse and it displays the influence of Black liberation theology on Blount. On the other hand, Shanell Smith, writing after 2010, has a more negative reading of the Apocalypse; her reading shows the influence of feminist and womanist perspectives. Both writers interpret the Apocalypse from their social locations and involve social-scientific research methods.

BRIAN BLOUNT AND THE INFLUENCE OF BLACK LIBERATION THEOLOGY

Blount published three significant works on Revelation between 2000 and 2009. In the first essay, entitled "Reading Revelation Today: Witness as Active Resistance," Blount (2000) argued that Revelation is resistance literature.[2] He followed with *Can I Get a Witness: Reading Revelation through African American Culture* (2005) and his major commentary on Revelation in the New Testament Library (2009). Blount intentionally chooses a cultural studies approach as his primary method of interpretation. "The cultural studies interpreter doesn't merely sit on the sidelines and record the struggle; she participates in it" (Blount 2005, 11). He continues that cultural studies turns the reader into a change agent: "This is precisely the effort I will want to make with regard to an African American reading of John's Apocalypse" (ibid., 12).

Blount argues that in Revelation, *martys* should not be translated "martyr" but "witness," someone who has faithfully borne a testimony before Roman authorities regardless of the possible consequences, just as Christ himself bore witness (ibid., 46–49). The imperative of an unwavering witness is central to Blount's thesis: "Revelation craves witness as engaged, resistant, transformative activism that is willing to sacrifice everything" (ibid., 38). This type of witness may be understood as sedition when done before Roman officials demanding fealty to the Emperor. Christians must be willing to make the sacrifice then and now. Blount sees this same type of steadfast witness in the civil rights movement of the 1950s and 1960s. He calls this correlation between John's subculture and his own as reading "from below," where the once silenced voices take center stage (ibid., 14–21, 41–45).

In his *Revelation* commentary, Blount expands his argument considerably. He describes Revelation as a mean book, but it is not mean-spirited. By this, he means that God's people are never encouraged to meet violence with violence. While Christ may be described in military terms, his method of victory is not his weapons but his witness. It is through his nonviolent, faithful witness that Christ becomes "the behavioral faith model for the believers in John's Asia Minor. . . . It is in the understanding of that lordship claim and the nonviolent testimony to it that one comprehends the meaning and purpose of John's work" (Blount 2009, 5).

For Blount (2009), the social setting of Roman Asia is one where politics and religion have become inseparable in the imperial cult. Religious piety and patriotism have become viewed as one and the same social demand. He does not perceive an empire-wide persecution of Christians, but only sporadic maltreatment that targeted specific individuals who confessed being Christ-believers when they either refused to affirm their loyalty to Rome or would not recant their religious affiliation (ibid., 11).

Blount (2009) envisions a Christology in which the Lamb never stops being a Lamb and the Lamb never stops being a lion. Vulnerability and conquest belong together in the book's narrative. He argues that when readers saw the Lamb they heard the footsteps of the lion. The conqueror and the conquered coexist in the same person. The weak Lamb, then, does not subvert the powerful lion; the Lamb's weakness, its slaughter, is precisely the way the lion works out its power. "The lion *sLambs* God's opposition" (ibid., 117; emphasis in the text). Blount continues that slaughter was not the goal, but "an active ministry of resistance that would witness to the singular lordship of Jesus Christ" (ibid., 118). As Jesus's death led to his empowerment, so too the slaughter of Asian Christians would eventually lead to "eternal life in a new heaven and new earth" where the lordship of Christ would be displayed in its entirety (ibid.).

Blount reflects the influence of Black liberation theology. He sees the Apocalypse responding to a regional repression of first century Christians in the Roman province of Asia. He describes the book as resistance literature and sees the image of the slain Lamb as the prime example of this. While Blount is sensitive to inclusive language and how some feminists and/or womanists read the Apocalypse, he is not nearly as critical of the book as Shanell Smith, to whom we now turn.

SHANELL T. SMITH: A POSTCOLONIAL WOMANIST READING OF REVELATION

Womanism is a distinctive approach which takes into account the struggles of African American women due to their ethnicity, gender, and class. Thus, womanists take to task scholars of all communities and both genders who are insensitive to the interrelated problems of racism, sexism, and classism. This approach stands in contrast to feminism, which primarily addresses gender inequality, on the one hand, while, on the other, continuing to employ racist language (e.g., using "black" as a pejorative term), a particularly telling criticism of persons very sensitive about the use of language.

Smith published her dissertation in 2014 under the title *The Woman Babylon and the Marks of Empire: Reading Revelation with a Postcolonial Womanist Hermeneutic of Ambiveilance* (2014). Smith brings together postcolonial hermeneutics developed from African American liberation theology and a womanist critique (while paying tribute to Clarice Martin along the way). "To the best of my knowledge these two approaches have only been employed individually in Revelation scholarship and never in tandem" (Smith 2014, 9). One of Smith's aims is to "draw attention to John's own imperialistic and patriarchal ideology, thereby challenging the general African American notion that John stands fully over and against empire" (ibid., 20–21).

Smith creates a new term to designate her work, namely "ambi*veil*ance." She developed this term by combining W. E. B. DuBois's concept of "the veil" and Homi Bhabha's theory of colonial ambivalence. She argues that the veil suggests a covering that hinders African Americans from seeing and being their true selves. This is particularly acute for African American women who generally see themselves either through white American cultural criteria or through the perspective of African American men. Moreover, she argues that veiling does not occur only in the Church but also in the academy (ibid., 11). Smith writes that "[a]t times, in a negotiation with my environment, I have consciously masked my true self, keeping my inner thoughts, goals, and dreams unspoken, in order to remain in solidarity with the oppressed, and to thwart any possibility of being labeled as an 'uppity' black woman, one who does not truly understand 'the struggle'" (ibid., 172). She further states (correctly) that she is not alone: it is a means of survival and also a means of protecting one's place at the table of American elitism (ibid.).

Ambi*veil*ence is similar to Otto's concept of the holy in that it is simultaneously attractive and repulsive. For Smith, this means that the woman Babylon creates a tension in the Apocalypse "in her dual representation as both colonizer and colonized" (ibid., 12). Ambi*veil*ance means that women of color in Europe and North America often participate in the finer things of the Empire, but they also associate with women who are victims of the Empire, producing an inner tension which is not easily absolved.

Smith argues that the Apocalypse presented John as an itinerant prophet, not the Apostle, who was a Palestinian Jew well acquainted with the Hebrew Bible. He exhorted the seven congregations in Asia to stand against Roman imperialism, the imperial cult, and Roman social norms. John's Apocalypse responds to a regional, sporadic repression of Asian Christians and John sees the potential for the regional repression to spread throughout the entire empire. She sees John arguing on two fronts: (1) with Roman Asian society in general and (2) with Asian Christians who had become more accommodating to the larger society. Christians must respond to Roman imperialism through their witness to Christ Jesus (ibid., 105–24).

Smith looks specifically at the woman Babylon in the final chapter. She examines the metaphors of woman and city, focusing on the destruction of the woman/city and its implications for violence upon women. She concludes that the metaphorical figure of the woman Babylon at once combines an exploited brothel slave and an empress/imperial city. John has abused her body until she is destroyed. As such, the woman Babylon is a participant in imperial power and also its victim. This imagery is both attractive and repulsive; it is ambi*veil*ent (ibid., 125–74).

This reading has personal meaning for Smith from which she does not run away: "Reading the woman Babylon's text includes a reading of myself and the pain and trauma associated with my existence, and I sympathize with her" (ibid., 166). She notes the physical abuse and the killing of the woman, which mirror the mistreatment of enslaved Black American and the negative connotations of her name that remain to this day and remind her of the racism which continues to survive in American society. On the other hand, as a person of privilege, Smith also resonates with the woman's association with and participation in the Empire. It is difficult for Smith "to ignore the texts that further perpetuate slave ideology and embrace—albeit with adaptation—the texts that give me hope, when it comes to the 'text' of the woman Babylon" (ibid., 166–67). Smith has painted a picture of an abused woman who cannot be ignored easily. She raises questions from her social location that others from other social perspectives might not have seen, but they are no less relevant.

Our discussions of our two representative voices end here. Let us turn now to some concluding remarks.

CONCLUDING REMARKS

Blount and Smith both display the type of exegetical research and results that Hoyt proposed three decades ago. In fact, Hoyt was merely putting into scholarly parlance what African Americans have been doing for some time. It is what Thurman did in *Jesus and the Disinherited*, what Kenneth Waters did in *Afrocentric Sermons*, what Clarice Martin (2005) did in "Polishing the Unclouded Mirror: A Womanist Reading of Revelation 18:13," what Renita Weems did in *Just a Sister Away*, what Obery Hendricks did in *The Politics of Jesus*, and it is what Andrew Lincoln said I did in his review of my *Ephesians* commentary (Slater 2012; Lincoln 2014).

Again, Hoyt stressed the importance of aligning the biblical story with the African American story and also the need for the study of the role of imagery and the use of imagination in biblical interpretation. Blount does this. His work reflects his social location as one who came to adulthood during the height of the civil rights movement and Black liberation theology. He employs cultural studies in order to connect the biblical narrative with his own context, arguing that John's Apocalypse was essentially resistance literature. He sees the Lamb/lion imagery as central to the story and employs his imagination to express his findings: "The lion *sLambs* God's opposition."

Smith also emphasizes the story, but she does so as a womanist influenced by liberation theology. Smith agrees with Blount on the social context and the need for faithful witnessing. However, her postcolonial womanist perspective leads to a different reading of the Apocalypse by means of her method of ambi*veil*ence. Herein is exegetical imagination at its best. Smith also criticizes the book's patriarchal and imperialistic language. She compares the woman Babylon and the plight of enslaved Black women. Moreover, she identifies with the woman Babylon who is both conqueror and conquered, one who has access to circles of influence but is limited due to her gender and ethnicity. Thus, she participates in the process, but she is still an object and not a subject in it.

Blount and Smith provide two outstanding examples of African American biblical interpretation since Hoyt. They do not assume one universal meaning that fits all persons and all places. They provide readings which are informed by who they are (just as all interpreters do). By so doing, they help to raise the consciousness of us all and help persons from other communities to see things that they might have missed. We are indebted to them, and all men and women like them from all ethnic, gender, and religious perspectives who realize that their voice must be heard and do not shy away because they may sing in a smaller choir or even a choir of one.

NOTES

1. This article is dedicated to the memory of Thomas Hoyt, one of my heroes as an aspiring New Testament academician. Hoyt's point is noteworthy. Something is not necessarily true, accurate, or more meaningful because someone wrote it on paper nor is something untrue, inaccurate, or insignificant because it is transmitted orally, e.g., *Roots*.

2. *Cf.* Callahan 1999 and Slater 2009, which is an update of my 2003 Jackson Lecture, Ministers' Week, Perkins School of Theology, Southern Methodist University.

WORKS CITED

Callahan, Allen Dwight. 1999. "Apocalypse as Critique of Political Economy: Some Notes on Revelation 18." *Horizons in Biblical Theology* 21: 46–65.

Darden, Lynne St. Claire. 2015. *Scripturalizing Revelation. An African American Postcolonial Reading of Empire*. Semeia 80. Atlanta: Society of Biblical Literature.

Felder, Cain Hope, editor. 1991. *Stony the Road We Trod: African American Biblical Interpretation*. Minneapolis: Fortress.

Hoyt, Thomas, Jr. 1991. "Interpreting Biblical Scholarship for the Black Church Tradition." *Stony the Road We Trod: African American Biblical Interpretation*, edited by Cain H. Felder, 17–39. Minneapolis: Fortress.

Lincoln, Andrew. 2014. "Review of T. B. Slater. Ephesians. Smyth & Helwys series (Macon, GA: Smyth & Helwys, 2012)." *Catholic Biblical Quarterly* 76: 379–80.

Martin, Clarice. 2005. "Polishing the Unclouded Mirror: A Womanist Reading of Revelation 18:13." *From Every People and Nation: The Book of Revelation in Intercultural Perspective*, edited by D. Rhoads. Minneapolis: Fortress.

Slater, Thomas. 2009. "Context, Christology and Civil Disobedience." *Review & Expositor* 106: 51–56.

Smith, Shanell T. 2014. *The Woman Babylon and the Marks of Empire: Reading Revelation with a Postcolonial Womanist Hermeneutic of Ambiveilence*. Emerging Scholars series. Minneapolis: Fortress.

Weems, Renita J. 1988. *Just a Sister Away: A Womanist View of Women's Relationships in the Bible*. Philadelphia: Innisfree.

Chapter 18

Race Still Matters

Mapping the Afterlives of Stony the Road We Trod

Clarice J. Martin

> Working with those rules, the text, if it is to take improvisation and audience participation into account, cannot be the authority—it should be *the map*. It should make way for the reader (audience) to participate in the tale.... If my work is to be functional to the group (to the village, as it were) then it must bear witness and identify dangers as well as possible havens from danger; it must identify that which is useful from the past and that which ought to be discarded; it must make it possible to prepare for the present and live it out; and it must do that by not avoiding problems and contradictions but by examining them.
>
> —Toni Morrison ("The Writer Before the Page" 2019, 267; italics added)

Cartographers have never confined their centuries-old craft to the perfunctory tasks of charting river routes, migration trails, or fine-tuning the geographical boundary markers of towns, cities, nation states, and empires. Map making has served a host of systemic and institutional interests: providing visual documentation of imperialist conquests and expansionism, and artfully documenting the unending and wide-ranging sociocultural and economic interests, clashes, and claims of governments, religions, and geopolitical entities. Contemporary cartographical studies confirm what we have always known: the art and science of cartography have always been epistemologically situated, with existential implications of profound consequence relative to issues of identity, power, and more (Kent and Vujakovic 2018).

Toni Morrison, one of the preeminent standard-bearers of great world literature, invites readers to view the project of writing literature as akin to "mapping" and "Map making." Map classifications markers vary widely, depending on the chronological period and interests of the map designers. Some maps and atlases illumine the internal character and structures of selected countries, others document the dissolution and dispersal of peasant farmers, the entrenchment of theocracies. Maps may foreground historical movements and moments, or they may render discrete communities and peoples as invisible—consigned to the subaltern and liminal dust heap on the human canvas of persons worthy of note. Functionally, Morrison argues, effective writing necessarily functions like the "map" that provides history, guidance, clarity, imaginative—if not visual "breadcrumbs"—for readers who move through the narrative story or tale. But for Morrison, language, rife with explicit indicators, signifiers, or perhaps mystifying masks, must coax readers beyond an intellectually disengaged surveillance of words and ideas as mere "data," to compel reader participation. Ideally, the language world of the text must necessarily bear witness to, and seek to rout, death-dealing dangers, while theorizing and authorizing resistance strategies that promote human agency, liberation, and life (Morrison 2019, 264). Making visible life's problems and contradictions remains theoretically and pragmatically central to her project.

The compelling essays in this remarkable anthology of and sequel to *Stony the Road We Trod* bear the unmistakable hallmarks of a gripping and ever-evolving cultural history of Black peoples in the African Diaspora within the twenty-first century. Every essayist reminds us that "Race Still Matters" in this historical moment. Like contemporary cartographers, they interweave new narrative maps with pertinent historical constructions and reconstructions from an ancient—but still consequential—past. But they also deftly heighten and magnify the interface between their particular sociocultural histories and the present world we live in. We see this in some essayists' creative hermeneutical revisioning and enlivening of traditionalist interpretations of Hebrew Bible and Christian Testament traditions, and we see this in essays that foreground explicit dangers (and, in Morrison's words, "possible havens from dangers") to Black women, men, and children. Yet readers can still trace, in many of the crisp and lucid essays, the golden thread that interweaves, tracks, and documents the dynamic, creative, and life-giving impulses of a durable and robust Africana philosophy of existence. From moving, enlightening, and seasoned historical reminisces honoring some of the pioneering African American biblical interpreters of the twentieth century (essays by Brian Blount, William Myers), to radically and imaginatively enlarged reassessments of Christological traditions in the Gospels (Mitzi Smith provides an erudite, commanding, rigorously detailed, and persuasive case for Jesus as a *doulos* or "slave," while Allen Callahan's bold declaration of Jesus as a "Thug" demands a hearing—and Powery's eloquent case for placing human bondage at the center of the Christian story crystallizes the historical-theoretical issues with expert analysis of the data), the essays markedly "de-sentimentalize" and nuance our understanding of the social history of the Jesus movement. Moreover, these essays "reimagine" the significance of these data for an America deeply committed to perpetuating its centuries-old legacy of anti-Blackness and white supremacy.

"Bitter the chastening rod." When James Weldon Johnson penned those painfully visceral words in the poem, "Lift Ev'ry Voice and Sing" in 1899, at the dawn of the twentieth century, persons who lived through that period would have been thoroughly familiar with the torturous material instruments and life-robbing practices used to "chasten" and control the enslaved: long, thick, wooden or metal "chastening rods" and similar instruments used in floggings, whips, stocks, nooses, and more. Slave codes, laws, and religion were all pressed into service to maintain and reinforce white hegemony. As several essayists in this volume document in their analytical reflections, racialized violence against Black bodies continues unabated in our present cultural moment and national life. Essayists Marcus Shields, Wil Gafney, Stacy Davis, and Kamilah Hall Sharp bear witness to state-sanctioned violence against Black peoples, decrying the historically entrenched legal, social, and systemic constructions that sheathe and fuel the machinery of rape, assault, and death. Bolstered by the assurance of majority citizen silence and acquiescence to the evil—racial violence continues, deemed to be "business as usual."

Mapping and Map making, for Morrison, invites writers and readers to assume a perennially sustained and engaged analytical posture, where both interlocutors interrogate and extend the rich matrices of the possible interpretations of histories, texts, and narratives beyond essentialist and facile universalist worldviews. Morrison decries such reductionism: "The writer's responsibility (whatever her or his time) is to change the world—improve his/her own time. Or, less ambitious, to help make sense of it. Simply in order to discover that it does make sense. Not *one* sense. What is the point of 2 billion people making *one* sense" (Morrison, 270). Morrison insists, like the essayists in this volume, that we all participate in the project, enlarging and reconstructing the existential landscape so that life in the present can be fully lived. Contemporary readers are invited to join the struggle, to glean from these essays collaborative, activist strategies to eradicate the death-dealing tide of violence that roils daily against Black and Brown bodies, to counter the hegemonic practices of dominance and violence normatively fueled by white supremacy in America. The essayists who helpfully deconstruct the vision and work of persons in the Black Lives Matters Movement are emblematic of the kind of activism of which Morrison speaks. The preceding essays some thirty years later have bequeathed to us illimitable and inestimable counter-cultural markers and map(s) to join the struggle to enact justice grounded in legal, social, and public policy practices in our time.

WORKS CITED

Kent, Alexander, and Peter Vujakovic, editors. 2018. *The Routledge Handbook of Mapping and Cartography.* New York: Routledge.

Morrison, Toni. 2019. *The Source of Self-Regard. Selected Essays, Speeches, and Meditations.* New York: Alfred A. Knopf.

Chapter 19

"To Think Better Than We Have Been Trained"

Thirty Years Later

Renita J. Weems

Because whiteness lies at the center of biblical studies, the accepted way of doing biblical scholarship is one that engages white questions, white concerns. The system forces scholars of color, especially those who receive their doctoral trainings in the western educational system, to be familiar with white scholarship. In the United States, a doctoral student has to pass a comprehensive or qualifying exam after taking their coursework, and in many schools the materials for the comprehensive exams are a huge stack of books written by white scholars. To be a biblical scholar is to be white. Biblical scholarship training is a whitewashing machine.

—Ekaputra Tupmahu 2020

This question for a cultural nationalism or cultural sovereignty inadvertently keeps us captured in the formational energies of white self-sufficient masculinity. . . . Theological education in the West was born in white hegemony and homogeneity, and it continues to baptize homogeneity, making it holy and right and efficient when it is none of these things.

—Willie Jennings 2020

It has taken decades (centuries, more likely) for the field of biblical studies to evolve enough for it to be able to look at its own racist history. More nonwhite scholars had to arrive on the doorsteps of the field refusing to assimilate into scholarly mimicry, insisting upon bringing their race, gender, sexuality, class, and social location questions with them as legitimate objects of inquiry. There is no denying that the field warded off for as long as it could questions about modern-day application by locking texts' meaning(s) into the past and insisting that the only way to unlock that meaning was to get behind the text and listen to the voice of the ancient writer with every linguistic, historical, and methodological tool at one's disposal. The field has undergone seismic changes since the publication of STR in 1991. For one thing, the methodology we trained in, historical-critical method, already showing signs of wear and tear in 1991, was under assault by the rise of cultural and interdisciplinary studies which challenged historical criticism's core beliefs about universality and objectivity, and that meaning must be extracted by going to the text. There remain many interpreters who continue to cling to historical approaches, but it is safe to say that some of the most exciting work in the field is influenced by and draws on interdisciplinary perspectives to explain the Bible's enduring impact in and upon culture, movements, institutions, and public discourse. Other facts that contribute to changes taking place in the field are the demographic shifts within the field since 1991 (the influx of women and racial-ethnic minorities), professional changes (the shrinking number of teaching positions), and the powerful inertia embedded in the biblical studies field that lends itself to "the stubborn invisibility of whiteness" (Tupamahu, 2020) that clouds the field. Despite sleek graduate school web pages touting programs that offer "broad coverage of many areas," "flexible programs," and "benefits from one of the most diverse faculties and student bodies in American doctoral education," graduate schools in religion haven't managed to shake their missional past, which has been to assimilate students around a (white male) universalizing authorial norm and to equip them with a tool box of stratagems that would leave untouched what Willie Jennings (2020) calls the white/Eurocentric, imperialist "formational energies" of the field. To be sure, all educational systems count on a certain amount of assimilation in order to sustain their traditions. But let's face it, biblical studies is at its core a racialized enterprise that was founded to unite a bloody, war-torn, fragmented Europe around the vision of itself as a colonial superpower, *Europa Pax*.[1] It has always been the task of the scholar of color to resist being naïve about the epistemologies embedded in her discipline and resist becoming complicit in reproducing those epistemologies in her research. How exactly does one do that? It helps by heeding the call of black feminist poet/novelist Toni Bambara (1939–1995) to "think better than you have been trained."[2] I will say more about this later in the essay.

Scholars of color in biblical studies[3] and religious studies[4] have written their fair share about the challenges of being trained in white academic spaces. They have passed along stories of interactions with professors, classmates, and in classroom settings where questions about Africa, Black women, slavery, and the Black church were discouraged or ignored, and Black students were left to conclude that if they wanted to succeed in their studies it would be better to avoid raising such topics. William Myers' (1991) essay in STR, "The Hermeneutical Dilemma of the African American Student," offers a very illuminating discussion about the roadblocks African American students face in biblical studies courses in the form of lectures, assignments, and examinations that focus on Eurocentric figures and interests, and not to mention a methodology that safeguards itself from the questions flesh-and-blood readers trying to live up to the Bible's vision have about how to apply the Bible to their real-life social, political, and economic realities. Williams Myers captured the alienation Black students enrolled in biblical studies classes felt at that time, alienation from an approach that showed no interest in their context and a curricular environment that seemed only to reemphasize the point.

> In a rather insidious way, this approach creates a dilemma for the African American biblical student. Since the literature is dominated by a Eurocentric approach, the lectures, assignments, and examinations in the discipline of biblical studies tend to prepare the African American student to answer more Eurocentric-oriented questions and concerns. (Myers 1991, 41)

Jennings (2020), writing thirty years after Myers, confirms that theological studies in general have changed, but not as much as it ought to accommodate a diverse student population answering the roll and the diverse make-up of faculty calling the roll in theological classrooms. This brings me to the main point of my reflection on the thirty years since the publication of STR. The biblical field has evolved enough to accommodate research not only on its difficult past but also on the role the Bible plays in undergirding whiteness. When referring to critical normative biases within the field, scholars today are less likely to talk about Eurocentricism and more likely to talk about whiteness, white privilege, and the white gaze. We have the field of ethnic studies, with "White studies" as a subdiscipline in that field,[5] to thank for providing a framework for understanding whiteness as a historically and socially constructed racial category, one defined by privilege and power, and upheld by structures that produce white privilege and perpetuate systemic racism. Contributors to STR represent the first critical mass of Black biblical scholars, most of us trained in the field in the seventies and eighties,[6] when the historical-critical field was beginning to show cracks but was still the hegemonic norm.[7] We were part of a generation that pursued doctorates not just as a result of the Black power, civil rights, student protests, and Black and white feminist movements of the seventies, but because of them. We brought race, culture, gender (and with many, our faith traditions) with us into the field. The alienation and hostility we felt in the predominant white spaces we inhabited prevented us sometimes from asking the questions in graduate seminars that mattered to us.[8] We had to finish our programs and take our spaces as new scholars in the field before we could embark on the long, hard journey of retooling, refashioning, "learning, unlearning, and relearning" what we needed to know—which is what Toni Cade Bambara had in mind when she talked about "thinking better than you have been trained." Teaching yourself what you weren't taught, what others tried to prevent you from learning, what you need to know to find answers to do your work. Katie Cannon spoke often about doing the work our souls had to have. STR provided many of us our first opportunity to go beyond our training as graduate students— drawing on the discussions in literary criticism, Black studies, Black feminist studies, white feminist studies, Black theology, and so on.[9] We were able to lay the ground for what, for many of us, would become our life's work which, is to "recover, enlarge, and proclaim" the tradition of Black biblical interpretation.[10]

We entered graduate school right about the time the old paradigm known as the historical-critical study of the Bible was beginning to show signs of serious fraying. The West as a world power was experiencing a series of destabilizing blows culturally, politically, socially, demographically, and intellectually, which resulted, among other things, in an influx of new voices into the academy, new faces around the table, new sets of questions into the discourse. We enrolled in graduate programs not just as a result of the civil rights movement, the student protests and women's movement—not to mention the political assassinations of the decade before—but because of them. We arrived on the scene bringing our full selves with us, which included not only our race, gender, sexuality, or class, but also our kinspeople and their genius, blasting open our disciplines' borders by insisting upon bringing to the center cultures and epistemologies previously confined to the margins.

We were bringing fresh perspectives to the field, challenging conventional Eurocentric scholarship, highlighting the African presence in biblical texts, and laying the groundwork for emerging Afrocentric and womanist approaches to biblical interpretation. We were able to do that because by the 80s, the field itself had experienced some fracturing and eventual fragmentation—requiring a range of interdisciplinary skills for understanding human subjectivity and interactions—which served to break the theoretical and practical hold of the traditional, positivistic, historical method of interpretation.

Cultural studies, with its arsenal of interdisciplinary perspectives and theories, was still in its infancy when STR was published in 1991. We concurred with cultural critics that neutral, value-free, objective research was nonexistent and that questions modern readers have about the Bible cannot be sidelined, but it would take more voices and more publications in the field for us to arrive where we are today, when one can write, as Ekaputra Tupamahu has, that the field is guilty of whitewashing scholars of color, and the bottom does not fall out.

As we enter the third decade of the twenty-first century, it is encouraging to witness newer voices and new approaches continuing to puncture holes into the old historical paradigm. It is especially refreshing to be able to have a choice of a number of anthologies published since STR by succeeding generations of Black biblical scholars, male and female, pursuing new research about the Bible's impact upon culture[11] and how its reception in culture has informed, shaped, and impacted Black life, Black politics, Black media representation, Black institution building, and Black public intellectualism. Studies of the reception of the Bible are now a fixed part of the field, thanks to influence of scholarly movements like cultural studies, interdisciplinary studies, critical race theory, and the like. These fields of analyses encourage scholars to reflect upon the significance of their work with respect to the material conditions of real flesh-and-blood people's lives. After all, there is a relationship between what people believe and how they live their lives, and the Bible has in the past, and continues, to play a role in not only shaping individual beliefs but more importantly shaping social movements, political gambits, and institutional practices.

Change was afoot even in the 1970s and 1980s, when many of us were in graduate school, and it is wonderful to see the fruit of that change resulting in expanded discourses in the field, a profusion of subdisciplines, a diverse range of disciplinary methods, demands for new and more program units in SBL, and publications that extend beyond the walls of the academy to engage everyday readers in thinking about how modern debates distort the message of the Bible or how the Bible, despite claims by overzealous factions, is not helpful in adequately addressing and resolving pressing issues of the day.[12] Approaches that were referred to as alternative or experimental or trendy criticisms when I was a student—feminist, womanist, African American, Asian, Latinx, queer/trans, post-colonial, minority criticism, liberation criticism, and so forth—have decades later staked out their spaces and become permanent residents in a field that decades earlier teetered on decline due to its obsessive insularity.

I wish to close by pointing to other factors, external to the field, that demand the field be self-reflexive and transparent about its biases, its assumptions, its whiteness, and its history of proving useful to powers intent upon colonizing populations. The extraordinarily painful events of recent years remind the world that the US, like all empires, is a land of contradictions. The US is in the midst of a deep, painful, and necessary reckoning over its desperate efforts to preserve a white status quo, as witnessed in the repeated fatal police shootings of Black and brown people, the increase in violence against women, the virulent criticism directed at Black women by the media, the systematic efforts around the country to erect barriers to voting, the disproportionate harm COVID has caused in minority communities, and the willingness the country showed to elect to its highest office a raging demagogue and would-be dictator who encouraged hate groups and domestic terrorism, who schemed to overturn legitimate election results, who attacked the press and civil servants, who blatantly profited from his public office, and who repeatedly lied to the public for his own selfish purposes. Finally, the rise of far-right political movements in many other Western democracies and the rise of Black Lives Matter and Say Her Name solidarity protests in these other countries make clear that the US is not alone, and that racial profiling of Black and brown people is widespread, even in countries often held up as models of democratic governance by the international community. All of these—theoretical, cultural, political, and global forces—combine to make it possible for scholars of color today to talk openly about the stubborn and violent whiteness of their academic training and the subtle pressure exerted on them by the guild, the institutions where they work, and even within the classroom to de-politicize the classroom, to avoid talk about race, sexuality, gender, class, power, and authority, to keep silent about one's commitments as a professor, to read the Bible through the eyes of the powerful, the winners, the white gaze. But books like *Bitter the Chastening Rod* prove that there is no going back. We cannot unknow what we now know about police killings of Black women and men, the rise of white supremacy, etc. There is no return to a precritical period of reflecting on the discipline, the Bible, and its use in the hands of extremists. We have the responsibility to think and teach better than we have been trained. Even with thicker, more nuanced, and theoretically more sophisticated methodological tools at our disposal, we cannot avoid the need to be self-reflexive about our location and our training, because while the Bible may be neutral, and has no meaning beyond itself, readers and the act of reading itself are not so innocent.

NOTES

1. See Wei Hsien Wan (2018, 219–29).
2. Toni Cade Bambara (1980).
3. New Testament scholar Cain Hope Felder (1943–2019), who served as the chief editor of the *Stony The Road* book project and whose own research focused on the presence of Black people in Old and New Testaments, described in his first book *Troubling Biblical Waters: Race, Class and Family* what led to his interest in focusing on ancient Afro-Asiatic historiography: "I began to realize that my own theological training and graduate studies had treated most of ancient Africa as

peripheral or insignificant. I also recognized that aspects of European historiography and archeology have been tainted by a self-serving, racialist hermeneutic that sought not objective truth but careful, 'scientific' ways of reinforcing the superiority and normative character of Western culture (i.e., white people) as the *sole arbitrator* of the biblical tradition."

4. Writing in an early memoir about his experiences as a graduate student in theology, James Cone (1982, 76), the progenitor of Biblical Theology as a field of academic study, wrote, "The academic structure of white seminary and university curriculums requires that black students reject their heritage or at least regard it as intellectually marginal. When black students study the Bible and church history, almost nothing is said about black people's heritage that would suggest that they have anything to contribute intellectually in those areas."

5. For a helpful discussion about the origins of whiteness as a field of study, see Amy Sueyoshi (2013).

6. The two oldest contributors were John W. Waters (1965–2018) and David T. Shannon (1934–2008), who graduated from Boston University in the 1960s with PhDs in Old Testament Studies. A third contributor was Charles Copher, one of the first Blacks to receive a PhD in Old Testament (Boston University, 1947). Copher (1913–2003) taught Old Testament at ITC from 1948–1978. Copher lectured on a wide range of topics. By the time STR was published, Copher was long retired from ITC. One of his essays was included in the volume in honor of his work.

7. See Fernando Segovia (1995).

8. See my essay written in tribute to womanist colleague Katie Cannon, foremother of womanist Christian social ethics: Renita J. Weems (forthcoming). There I write about Katie's dream of becoming the first Black woman biblical scholar and enrolling in Union Seminary in NY in 1974 as a student in the Old Testament department. But she would have to abandon that dream when, after enduring racist, sexist, elitist treatment by professors, she was dismissed from the program by her advisor under the excuse that she had failed to prove to the department that she was a serious enough student. She would eventually regroup, apply to the Ethics PhD program, graduate as the first Black woman with a PhD from Union and the first Black woman with a doctorate in ethics, and from there become the founding scholar of a field that would come to be known as womanist studies in religion.

9. The truth is that biblical studies has always been a rather porous field, meaning it has never really generated any unique methods and is best understood as a field that has always utilized methods from different disciplines in order to answer different questions about the Bible.

10. See Renita J. Weems (1991, 57–70) which served as a prescient start to helping me clear a space in my research and in the discipline for what would come to be known as womanist biblical interpretation with its emphasis on centering Black women's experiences in their role as interpreters, readers, and producers of knowledge when it comes to the interpretation of the Bible and its application in Black women's liberation activism. See my forthcoming essay, "Writing Black Women Into View: A Beginning."

11. See, e.g., Wimbush 2001; Blount 2007; Page 2010; Smith 2015; Byron and Lovelace 2016; and Bailey, Liew and Segovia 2021.

12. There are others, but fine examples I wish to name are: Gafney, 2017; Hendricks 2021; Mitzi Smith, 2018; Angela Parker, 2021.

WORKS CITED

Bailey, Randall, Benny Tat-Siong Liew and Ferdinand Segovia. 2021. *They Were All Together in One Place?: Toward Minority Biblical Criticism.* Atlanta: Society of Biblical Literature.

Bambara, Toni Cade. 1980. "What I Think I'm Doing Anyway." In *The Writer on Her Work,* ed. Janet Sternberg, 79. New York: Norton.

Blount, Brian, et al., editors. 2007. *True to Our Native Land: An African American New Testament Commentary.* Minneapolis. Fortress.

Byron, Gay L., and Vanessa Lovelace, eds. 2016. *Womanist Interpretations of the Bible: Expanding the Discourse.* Atlanta: Society of Biblical Literature.

Cone, James. 1982. *My Soul Looks Back.* Maryknoll, NY: Orbis.

Felder, Cain Hope. 1989. *Troubling Biblical Waters: Race, Class and Family.* Maryknoll, NY: Orbis.

Gafney, Wil. 2017. "A Reflection on the Black Lives Matter Movement and Its Impact on My Scholarship." *Journal of Biblical Literature* 136: 204–207

Hendricks, Obery. 2021. *Christians Against Christianity: How Right-Wing Evangelicals Are Destroying Our Nation and Our Faith.* Boston: Beacon.

Jennings, Willie. 2020. *After Whiteness: An Education in Belonging.* Grand Rapids, MI: Eerdmans.

Myers, William. 1991. "The Hermeneutical Dilemma of the African American Student." *Stony the Road We Trod. African American Biblical Interpretation*, edited by Cain Hope Felder, 40–55. Minneapolis: Fortress.

Page, Hugh R., Jr. et al., eds. 2010. *The Africana Bible: Reading Israel's Scriptures from Africa and the African Diaspora.* Minneapolis: Fortress.

Parker, Angela. 2021. *If God Still Breathes, Why Can't I?: Black Lives Matter and Biblical Authority.* Grand Rapids, MI: Eerdmans.

Segovia, Fernando. 1995. *Reading from this Place, Vol. 1: Social Location and Biblical Interpretation in the United States.* Philadelphia: Fortress.

Smith, Mitzi J. 2018. *Womanist Sass and Talk Back: Social (In)Justice, Intersectionality, and Biblical Interpretation.* Eugene, OR: Cascade.

Smith, Mitzi J., ed. 2015. *I Found God in Me: A Womanist Biblical Hermeneutics Reader.* Eugene, OR: Cascade.

Sueyoshi, Amy. 2013. "Making Whites from the Dark Side: Teaching Whiteness Studies at San Francisco State University." *The History Teacher* 46. 3: 373–96.

Tupamahu, Ekaputra. 2020. "The Stubborn Invisibility of Whiteness in Biblical Scholarshp." Political Theological Network. November 12. https://politicaltheology.com/the-stubborn-invisibility-of-whiteness-in-biblical-scholarship/.

Wan, Wei Hsien. 2018. "Re-examining the Master's Tools: Considerations on Biblical Studies Race Problem." *Ethnicity, Race, Religion: Identities and Ideologies in Early Jewish and Christian Texts, and in Modern Biblical Interpretation*, edited by Katherine M. Hockey and David G. Horrell, 219–29. London: T&T Clark.

Weems, Renita. 1991. "Reading *Her Way* Through the Struggle: African American Women and the Bible." *Stony the Road We Trod. African American Biblical Interpretation*, edited by Cain Hope Felder, 57–79. Minneapolis: Fortress.

———. Forthcoming. "Struggling Through Injury To Do The Work Our Souls Must Have: Katie Cannon and the Bible." *Walking Through the Valleys: Womanist Explorations in Justice, Leadership, Embodied*, edited by Emilie Townes, Stacey Floyd-Thomas, Alise P. Gise-Johnson, and Angela D. Sims.

———. Forthcoming. "Writing Black Women Into View: A Beginning." *How Do You Read It?: A Womanist Methodologies Reader*, edited by Valerie Bridgeman and Stephanie Crowder. Lanham, MD: Lexington Press.

Wimbush, Vincent, editor. 2001. *African Americans and the Bible: Sacred Texts and Social Structures*. New York: Continuum.

Appendix

(These lists were compiled by Ericka Dunbar in consultation with a number of scholars in the field. The figures—104 scholars with terminal degrees, 11 students in PhD programs—are of August, 2021.)

AFRICANA BIBLICAL SCHOLARS WITH EARNED TERMINAL DEGREES IN HEBREW BIBLE/ OLD TESTAMENT AND NEW TESTAMENT

Amen, Richetta (NT, Graduate Theological Union, 2016)
Akoko, Dorothy (HB/OT, Chicago Theological Seminary, 2012)
Anderson, Cheryl (HB/OT, Vanderbilt, 2000)
Aymer, Albert (NT, Drew, 1936–2021)
Aymer, Birchfield (NT, Boston; deceased, 1944–2018)
Aymer, Margaret (NT, Union, 2004)
Bailey, Randall (HB/OT, Emory, 1997)
Bailey, Wilma (HB/OT, Vanderbilt, 1995)
Bass, Debra Moody (HB/OT, Drew, 2002)
Bennett, Harold (HB/OT, Vanderbilt)
Bennett, Robert (HB/NELC, Harvard, 1974)
Blount, Brian K. (NT, Emory, 1992)
Bowens, Lisa (NT, Princeton, 2013)
Braxton, Brad R. (NT, Emory, 1999)
Bridgeman, Valerie (HB/OT, Baylor, 2002)
Brown, Michael Joseph (NT, University of Chicago, 1998)
Burgh, Theodore W. (HB/OT, University of Arizona, 2000)
Burton, Keith (NT, Northwestern, 1994)
Byron, Gay L. (NT, Union, 1999)
Callahan, Allen Dwight (NT, Harvard, 1992)
Callender, Dexter (HB/OT, Yale)

Carson, Cottrell R. (NT, Union, 1999)
Charles, Ronald (NT, Univ of Toronto, 2014)
Copher, Charles (HB/OT, Boston, 1947; deceased, 1913–2003)
Crowder, Stephanie Buckhanon (NT, Vanderbilt, 2000)
Darden, Lynne S. (NT, Drew, 2011; deceased, 1955–2017)
Davidson, Steed (HB/OT, Union, 2005)
Davis, Stacy (HB/OT, Notre Dame, 2003)
Dickerson, Febbie (NT, Vanderbilt, 2017)
Dube, Musa (NT, Vanderbilt, 1997)
Dunbar, Ericka Shawndricka (HB/OT, Drew, 2020)
Edwards, Dennis R. (NT, Catholic University of America, 2003)
Felder, Cain Hope (NT, Columbia University 1982; deceased, 1943–2019)
Franklin, Naomi (HB/OT, Duke, 1990)
Fentress-Williams, Judy (HB/OT, Yale, 1999)
Gafney, Wil (HB/OT Duke Divinity, 2005)
Galloway, Lincoln (NT, Emory University, 2001)
George, Larry (NT, Vanderbilt, 1997)
Greaux, Eric (NT, Duke, 2003)
Green, Bridgett (NT, Vanderbilt, 2021)
Green, Ruben H. (HB/OT, Vanderbilt, 1934–2008)
Greene, John (HB/OT, Boston, 1980; deceased, 1944–2021)
Grizzle, Trevor (NT, Southwestern Baptist, 1984)
Hartsfield, Wallace Jr. (HB/OT, Emory, 2013)
Hendricks, Obery (NT, Princeton, 1995)
Hopkins, Jamal-Dominique (NT, University of Manchester, 2006)
Hoyt, Thomas Jr. (NT, Duke, 1975; deceased, 1941–2013)
Jacobs, Mignon (HB/OT, Claremont, 1998)
Jerkins, Marcus (NT, Baylor)
Johnson, Vivian (HB/OT, Harvard, 2005)
Johnson, Willa Mathis (HB/OT Vanderbilt, 1999)
Junior, Nyasha (HB/OT, Princeton, 2008)
Kaalund, Jennifer (NT, Drew, 2015)
Kebaneilwe, Mmapula Diane (HB/OT, Univ of Murdoch, 2012)
Kemp, Joel (HB/OT, Boston College 2017)
Lettsome, Raquel S. (NT, Princeton, 2005)
Lewis, Lloyd (NT, Yale, 1985)
Lovelace, Vanessa (HB/OT, Chicago Theological Seminary, 2012)
Marbury, Carl H. (NT, Harvard)
Marbury, Herbert (HB/OT, Vanderbilt, 2003)
Martin, Clarice (NT, Duke, 1985)
Mbuvi, Amanda (HB/OT, Duke, 2008)
McCaulley, Esau (NT, University of St. Andrews, 2017)

McClenney, Madeline (HB/OT, Duke, 2001)
Mbuwayesango, Dora (HB/OT, Emory, 1998)
Myers, William H. (NT, University of Pittsburgh, 1991)
Nave, Guy (NT, Yale, 2000)
Ngwa, Kenneth (HB/OT, Princeton, 2005)
Niang, Aliou (NT, Texas Christian University, 2003)
Page, Hugh R., Jr. (Near Eastern Languages and Civilizations, Harvard, 1990)
Parker, Angela N. (NT, Chicago Theological Seminary, 2015)
Peters, Melvin K. H. (HB/OT, University of Toronto, 1975)
Powery, Emerson (NT, Duke, 1999)
Redding, Ann Holmes (NT, Union, 1999)
Reed, Justin (HB/OT, Princeton, 2020)
Reid, Stephen Breck (HB/OT, Emory, 1981)
Rewolinski, Edward (NT, Harvard, 1978)
Ross, Jerome (HB/OT, Pittsburgh, 1997)
Russaw, Kimberly (HB/OT, Vanderbilt, 2016)
Sadler, Rodney (HB/OT, Duke, 2001)
Sanders, Boykin (NT, Harvard, 1975)
Sechrest, Love (NT, Duke, 2006)
Scott, Thomas (NT, Harvard, 1979)
Shannon, David (HB/OT, Pittsburgh; deceased, 1934–2008)
Slater, Thomas B. (NT, University of London, 1996)
Smith, Abraham (NT, Vanderbilt, 1989)
Smith, Mitzi J. (NT, Harvard, 2006)
Smith, Shanell T. (NT, Drew, 2012)
Smith, Shively (NT, Emory, 2015)
Smith, Terry Ann (HB/OT, Drew, 2011)
Spencer-Miller, Althea (NT, Claremont, 2014)
St. Clair, Raquel (NT, Princeton, 2015)
Stubbs, Monya (NT, Vanderbilt, 2005)
Tinsley, Annie (NT/HB, University of Birmingham, UK, 2010)
Venable-Ridley, C. Michelle (NT, Temple University, 1995)
Waters, John (HB/OT, Boston, 1970)
Waters, Kenneth (NT, Fuller, 1999)
Weems, Renita J. (OT/HB, Princeton, 1989)
Williams, Demetrius K. (NT, Harvard, 1997)
Williams, Jeremy L. (NT, Harvard, 2021)
Williams, Marvin Suber (NT, Vanderbilt)
Wimbush, Vincent L. (NT, Harvard, 1983)
Wright, Edwina (HB/OT, Harvard, 1996; deceased 1946–2007)
Yorke, Gosnell (NT, McGill, 1987)

STUDENTS IN PHD PROGRAMS IN BIBLICAL STUDIES

Day, Quonekuia (HB/OT, London School of Theology, Northwood, England)
Johnson, Nicholas (NT, Drew)
Khumalo, Minenhle (HB/OT, Drew)
Knight, NaShieka (HB/OT, Brite)
Norton, Yolanda (HB/OT, Vanderbilt)
Okang, Janet (NT, Drew)
Sharp, Kamilah Hall (HB/OT, Brite)
Shields, Marcus (NT, University of Edinburgh)
Thomas, Eric (NT, Drew)
Williams, Christopher (NT, Boston College)

Editors and Contributors

EDITORS

Ericka S. Dunbar Hill, PhD, is visiting professor of Hebrew Bible at Payne Theological Seminary, Wilberforce, OH. She holds a PhD in Hebrew Bible (biblical studies) from Drew University.

Angela N. Parker, PhD, is assistant professor of New Testament and Greek at Mercer University's McAfee School of Theology, Atlanta, GA. She has written many articles and essays and is the author of *If God Still Breathes, Why Can't I? Black Lives Matter and Biblical Authority* (2021). Dr. Parker is ordained with the Missionary Baptist Association.

Mitzi J. Smith, PhD, is the J. Davison Philips professor of New Testament at Columbia Theological Seminary, Decatur, GA. She is coeditor of *Minoritized Women Reading Race and Ethnicity* (2020) and *Interrogating the Matthean Great Commission* (2014); coauthor of *Toward Decentering the New Testament: A Reintroduction* (2018); author of *Womanist Sass and Talk. Social (In)Justice, Intersectionality and Biblical Interpretation* (2018), and *Insights from African American Interpretation* (2017); and editor of *I Found God in Me: A Womanist Biblical Hermeneutics Reader* (2015). She is working on a womanist reading of First Corinthians and a womanist reading of the Lucan Jesus.

CONTRIBUTORS

Brian K. Blount, PhD, is president and professor of New Testament in the Walter W. Moore and Charles E.S. Kraemer Presidential Chairs at Union Presbyterian Seminary. He is the general editor of *True to Our Native Land. An African American Commentary on the New Testament* (2007). Blount is the author of numerous publications including the following books: *Cultural*

Interpretation: Reorienting New Testament Criticism (1995); *Go Preach! Mark's Kingdom Message and the Black Church Today* (1998); *Then the Whisper Put on Flesh: New Testament Ethics in an African American Context* (2001); *Can I Get a Witness? Reading Revelation Through an African American* Lens (2005); *Revelation. A Commentary in the New Testament Library Series* (2009); and *Invasion of the Dead. Preaching Resurrection* (2014).

Theodore W. Burgh, PhD, whose artwork appears on the cover of BTCR, is a Professor in the Department of Philosophy and Religion at the University of North Carolina Wilmington. He completed his graduate studies at the University of Arizona. Dr. Burgh's areas of expertise, focus, and interest are the Archaeology of the Ancient Near East in general and Israel in particular, anthropology, Israelite religion, religions of the ancient Near East, and archaeomusicology. He has been excavating in Jordan and Sicily since 1996. Dr. Burgh has also written on numerous topics in Hebrew Bible/Old Testament including but not limited to music, transcriptions, translations, religion, and various artifacts and their connections to life during the Iron Age or biblical period.

Allen Dwight Callahan, PhD, is an independent scholar, workshop facilitator, and consultant. He has taught biblical languages and literatures at the Harvard Divinity School, and has served as associate chaplain at Brown University and as theologian in residence at Metropolitan Baptist Church in Washington, DC. He is the author of *The Talking Book: African Americans and the Bible* (2006) and *A Love Supreme: A History of Johannine Tradition* (2005), as well as many scholarly articles, and has appeared as an expert commentator in documentaries aired on PBS, the History Channel, and the Discovery Channel.

Ronald Charles, PhD, is associate professor associate professor, Department for the Study of Religion, University of Toronto. A Haitian-Canadian, he did his PhD in Religious Studies at the University of Toronto (Department for the Study of Religion). Charles is the author of *Paul and the Politics of Diaspora* (2014), *Traductions Bibliques Créoles et Préjugés Linguistiques* (2015), and *The Silencing of Slaves in early Jewish and Christian Writings* (2020). His research and teaching interests are the interdisciplinary study of ancient Christian literature, Mediterranean identity and race in antiquity, slaves in the Greek and Roman world, classical reception, and method and theory in the academic study of Religion.

Stacy Davis, PhD, is professor and chair of religious studies and theology at Saint Mary's College, Notre Dame, IN. She teaches courses on religious conversion, Jewish and Christian interpretation of the Hebrew Bible, Torah, and prophets. Her recent publications include *Haggai and Malachi* for the Wisdom Commentary Series (2015), and essays in *Womanist Biblical Interpretation: Expanding the Discourse* (2017), the *Oxford Handbook of the Minor Prophets* (2021), *The Cambridge Companion to the Hebrew Bible and Ethics* (2020), and *The New Jerome Biblical Commentary* (forthcoming).

Dennis R. Edwards, PhD, is associate professor of New Testament at North Park Theological Seminary. He is the author of several essays and articles, as well as 1 Peter in *The Story of God* Bible Commentary series (2017); *Might from the Margins: The Gospel's Power to Turn the Tables on Injustice* (2020) and *What is the Bible and How Do We Understand It?* (2019). Dr. Edwards also has served in pastoral ministry for three decades.

Wil Gafney, PhD, is the Right Rev. Samuel B. Hulsey professor of Hebrew Bible at Brite Divinity School, Fort Worth, TX. She is the author of *Womanist Midrash: A Reintroduction to Women of the Torah and of the Throne* (2017), a commentary on Nahum, Habakkuk, and Zephaniah in the *Wisdom* series (2017); *Daughters of Miriam: Women Prophets in Ancient Israel* (2008); and co-editor of *The Peoples' Bible* and *The Peoples' Companion to the Bible* (2008). She is the author of a *Women's Lectionary for the Whole Church* and translator of its biblical selections (2021). Gafney is an Episcopal priest canonically resident in the Diocese of Pennsylvania and licensed in the Diocese of North Texas.

Clarice J. Martin, PhD, holds the Jean Picker chair of Philosophy and Religion at Colgate University. She is the first African-American woman to earn a PhD (Princeton Theological Seminary) in New Testament. Martin is an associate editor of *True to Our Native Land: An African American Commentary on the New Testament* (2007) and the author of many seminal journal articles and essays, including the following: "The Eyes Have it: Slaves in the Communities of Christ-Believers," Christian Origins, Vol. 1, A People's History of Christianity, eds. Richard A. Horsley and Denis R. Janz, 221–39 (2005); "Womanist Interpretations of the New Testament: The Quest for Holistic and Inclusive Translation and Interpretation" (1990; reprinted 2001); "Somebody Done Hoodoo'd the Hoodoo Man: Language, Power, Resistance, and the Effective History of Pauline Texts in American Slavery," Slavery in Text and Interpretation, Semeia 83–4 (2000): 203–33; and "Womanist Biblical Interpretation," Dictionary of Biblical Interpretation. Vol. 2 (1999): 655–58.

William H. Myers, PhD, is professor of New Testament and Black church studies at Ashland Theological Seminary. He is author of "The Hermeneutical Dilemma of the African-American Biblical Student," *Stony the Road We Trod: African American Biblical Interpretation* (1991); *The Irresistible Urge to Preach: A Collection of African American Call Stories* (1992; reprinted 2015); "No Risks, No Rewards: Acts 8:26–40," *The Journal of Religious*

Thought, Vol. 49, No. 1 (1992); *God's Yes Was Louder than My No: Rethinking the African American Call to Ministry* (1994; reprinted 2015); and numerous other essays and articles. Myers served as Pastor of New Mount Zion Baptist Church in Cleveland, Ohio, for over fifteen years before recently retiring. He is also the founder of the McCreary Center for African American Religious Studies in Cleveland.

Hugh R. Page, Jr., PhD, is professor of theology and Africana studies; and vice president and associate provost at the University of Notre Dame. His PhD is in Near Eastern Languages and Civilizations from Harvard University. His research interests include early Hebrew poetry; Africana biblical interpretation; the role of mysticism and esotericism in Anglican and Africana spiritualities; and the Blues aesthetic. He is author of *Israel's Poetry of Resistance: Africana Perspectives on Early Hebrew Verse* (2013); general editor of *The Africana Bible: Reading Israel's Scriptures from Africa and the African Diaspora* (2010); and one of the co-editors for both the *Fortress Commentary on the Old Testament and Apocrypha* (2014) and Esotericism in African American Religious Experience: "There is a Mystery" (2015).

Emerson B. Powery, PhD, is a professor of biblical studies and assistant dean for the School of the Arts, Culture, and Society at Messiah University, Mechanicsburg, PA. He is coauthor of *The Genesis of Liberation: Biblical Interpretation in the Antebellum Narratives of the Enslaved* (2016) and one of the associate editors for *True to Our Native Land: An African American Commentary on the New Testament* (2007).

Marcus W. Shields is a doctoral candidate at the University of Edinburgh. He is currently a doctoral candidate at the University of Edinburgh in Scotland completing his Doctor of Philosophy (PhD) in New Testament and Christian origins. His research interests focus on the political action of slave bodies in "non-liberative spaces" in the Roman Empire.

Kamilah Hall Sharp is a PhD candidate in Hebrew Bible at Brite Divinity School and co-pastor of The Gathering, A Womanist Church in Dallas. She is a coauthor of *The Gathering, A Womanist Church: Origins, Stories, Sermons, and Litanies* (Wipf & Stock, 2020).

Thomas B. Slater, PhD, served as professor of New Testament Language and Literature at McAfee for thirteen years before being named professor emeritus at the occasion of his retirement. Dr. Slater has written two books and edited a third: *Christ and Community* (Bloomsbury T&T Clark); a commentary on the book of Ephesians in the Smyth & Helwys Commentary Series (2012); *Afrocentric Interpretations of Jesus and the Gospel Tradition* (2015), and *Revelation as Civil Disobedience: Witnesses Not Warriors in John's Apocalypse* (2019). An ordained elder in full connection in the Georgia North Region of the Christian Methodist Episcopal Church, Dr. Slater has pastored five congregations in Arkansas, Virginia, and Georgia and been an associate pastor in four other congregations.

Renita J. Weems, PhD, is an independent Hebrew Bible scholar, public theologian, and sought-after preacher who lives in Nashville, TN. She has taught at Vanderbilt Divinity School and Spellman College and served as an administrator at American Baptist College. Dr. Weems is the first black female to receive a PhD in Hebrew Bible (Princeton Theological Seminary). She has authored many essays and a number of books, including *Just a Sister Away* (1991), *Listening for God: A Minister's Journey Through Silence and Doubt* (2000), *Showing Mary: How Women Can Share Prayers, Wisdom and Blessings from God* (2002), *I Asked for Intimacy* (1993), and *Battered Love: Marriage, Sex, and Violence in the Hebrew Prophets* (1995).

Jeremy L. Williams, PhD is assistant professor of New Testament at Brite Divinity School in Fort Worth, TX. His Harvard University PhD dissertation is entitled "Making Criminals: The Rhetoric of Criminality in Acts of the Apostles." He received his M.Div. from Yale University and his undergraduate degree from Vanderbilt University. He is an ordained elder and has served as a lead pastor in the Christian Methodist Episcopal Church.

www.ingramcontent.com/pod-product-compliance
Lightning Source LLC
Chambersburg PA
CBHW020111010526
44115CB00008B/781